Argentina Betrayed

PENNSYLVANIA STUDIES IN HUMAN RIGHTS

Bert B. Lockwood, Series Editor

A complete list of books in the series
is available from the publisher.

ARGENTINA BETRAYED

Memory, Mourning,
and Accountability

Antonius C. G. M. Robben

PENN

UNIVERSITY OF PENNSYLVANIA PRESS

PHILADELPHIA

Published by
University of Pennsylvania Press
Philadelphia, Pennsylvania 19104-4112
www.upenn.edu/pennpress

Printed in the United States of America on acid-free paper
1 3 5 7 9 10 8 6 4 2

Library of Congress Cataloging-in-Publication Data

Names: Robben, Antonius C. G. M., author.
Title: Argentina betrayed : memory, mourning, and accountability / Antonius C. G. M.
   Robben.
Other titles: Pennsylvania studies in human rights.
Description: 1st edition. | Philadelphia ; University of Pennsylvania Press, [2018] | Series:
   Pennsylvania studies in human rights | Includes bibliographical references and index.
Identifiers: LCCN 2017046030 | ISBN 9780812250053 (hardcover : alk. paper)
Subjects: LCSH: State-sponsored terrorism—Argentina—Social aspects. | Political
   violence—Argentina—Social aspects. | Trust—Political aspects—Argentina. | Trust—Social
   aspects—Argentina. | Memory—Political aspects—Argentina. | Transitional justice—
   Argentina. | Argentina—Social conditions—1983-
Classification: LCC HV6433.A7 R63 2018 | DDC 982.06/4—dc23
LC record available at https://lccn.loc.gov/2017046030

CONTENTS

ABBREVIATIONS

AAA — Alianza Anticomunista Argentina (Argentine Anti-Communist Alliance)

APDH — Asamblea Permanente por los Derechos Humanos (Permanent Assembly for Human Rights)

CADHU — Comisión Argentina de Derechos Humanos (Argentine Human Rights Commission)

CELS — Centro de Estudios Legales y Sociales (Center for Legal and Social Studies)

CGT — Confederación General de Trabajo (General Labor Confederation)

CIDH — Comisión Interamericana de Derechos Humanos (Inter-American Commission on Human Rights)

CONADEP — Comisión Nacional sobre la Desaparición de Personas (National Commission on the Disappeared)

COSOFAM — Comisión de Solidaridad con Familiares de Presos y Desaparecidos (Solidarity Commission with Relatives of Prisoners and Disappeared)

EAAF — Equipo Argentino de Antropología Forense (Argentine Forensic Anthropology Team)

ERP — Ejército Revolucionario del Pueblo (People's Revolutionary Army)

ESMA — Escuela Superior de Mecánica de la Armada (Navy Mechanics School)

FAMUS — Familiares y Amigos de los Muertos por la Subversión (Relatives and Friends of the Victims of Subversion)

HIJOS — Hijos por la Identidad y la Justicia, contra el Olvido y el Silencio (Children for Identity and Justice, against Oblivion and Silence)

IACHR — Inter-American Commission on Human Rights

JG — Juventud Guevarista (Guevarist Youth)

NN — Nomen Nescio (No Name)

OAS	Organization of American States
PCR	Partido Comunista Revolucionario (Revolutionary Communist Party)
PRT	Partido Revolucionario de los Trabajadores (Revolutionary Workers Party)
UCR	Unión Cívica Radical (Radical Civic Union)
UES	Unión de Estudiantes Secundarios (Union of High School Students)

Argentina Betrayed

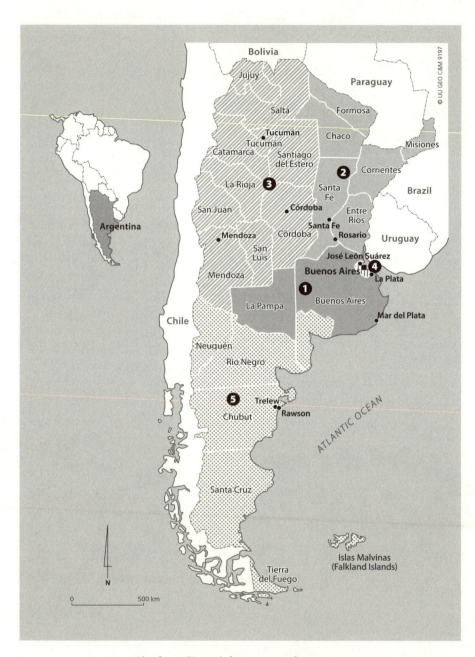

The five military defense zones of Argentina

INTRODUCTION

Trust and Betrayal

The arrival at a teeming Plaza de Mayo of the five-hundred-yard-long banner displaying the youthful images of thousands of disappeared Argentines was heralded by a band of drummers and a group of dancers who had been steadily making their way through the crowd-lined Avenida de Mayo that connects Argentina's congress building with the presidential palace. The disappeared who had been persecuted and assassinated by the military regime were about to make their glorious entry into the heart of Buenos Aires on this Day of Memory in March 2010. The dancers and drummers stepped aside upon reaching the Plaza de Mayo. This gesture allowed the banner to take center stage in the historic square and honor the disappeared and their relatives. They walked as one because the political lives and deaths of the disappeared were entwined with the protests of the relatives at the Plaza de Mayo, where Argentina's independence had been proclaimed in May 1810 and where presidents and dictators had won and lost the support of popular crowds. The banner symbolized the continued influence of the disappeared on Argentine society and the enduring care of their relatives for nearly four decades.

My sentiment was bittersweet as I recalled standing at the same Avenida de Mayo on 10 December 1983 to watch President Raúl Alfonsín make his way to the Plaza de Mayo in an open limousine. The expectant smile on his face made a lasting impression on me. Alfonsín had just been inaugurated in Congress after having won the October elections on a call for truth and justice and the promise that the disappearances would soon be clarified. Now, twenty-seven years later, this hope had mostly evaporated, lost in the illusion of time, but at least the disappeared and their relatives had gotten the nation's attention, and many perpetrators were in prison for crimes against humanity committed during the dictatorship that had ruled Argentina between 1976 and 1983.

The Argentine armed forces had taken control on 24 March 1976 on the pretext of eliminating the guerrilla insurgency, jump-starting the economy, and laying the foundation for a lasting democracy. Tens of thousands of enforced disappearances, hundreds of thousands of anguished relatives, and a traumatized society were the price. How have Argentines been struggling with the human, social, and symbolic losses inflicted by the military regime? In particular, how have trust and betrayal shaped and reshaped the long-term consequences of the state's repressive violence and Argentina's sociocultural traumas since the fall of the dictatorship in 1983? Finally, how did the unending confrontations between conflicting social groups and a multifaceted state influence the memory, mourning, and accountability of Argentina's many losses?

Trust is essential to state and society. Trust makes social interaction and political institutions possible, whereas betrayal may lead to social and political disintegration. I believe that these two analytical concepts are of considerable explanatory value for understanding how traumatized societies struggle with the unresolved legacies of a repressive past. As far as the concepts of state and society are concerned, they refer to heterogeneous, layered, and multifaceted sociocultural constructions in which trust and betrayal are manifested in multiple differentiated ways. They do not constitute autonomous, homogeneous wholes because society is replete with social strife among conflicting individuals, groups, and interests, while state organs, such as local and national administrations, the parliament, the judiciary, and the armed forces, may be at odds with one another and be engaged in corruption and clientelism behind a façade of stately formality.

Authoritarian, repressive regimes undermine the trust embedded in society and extended to state agents and institutions by creating an uncertain environment in which the state can strike unawares. Suspicion and mistrust can penetrate all levels of state and society because trusting relations are besieged by the ever-present threat of betrayal. This book focuses on the dynamics of trust and betrayal to explain how, between 1983 and 2016, Argentina dealt with the sequels of its violent past in key areas of national contestation. Trust and betrayal have been important modalities of social and political relations in Argentina, not only during the dictatorship but also during its aftermath when democracy returned to the country. National governments, the armed forces, former guerrilla organizations, associations of searching relatives, and human rights organizations have harbored considerable mutual mistrust and have each, in their own way, been suspicious of internal betrayal. Successive presidents have periodically changed course regarding their handling of national commemorations, criminal accountability, and reconciliation policies. They contributed to a general feeling of precariousness among Argentine citizens about an untrustworthy state. Furthermore, the changing narratives and testimonies about political violence and military repression by the opposed historical protagonists and the gradual disclosure of past truths and falsehoods have fed a mutual mistrust in a divided civil society that has hindered the mourning of Argentina's multiple losses. Argentina has therefore remained a traumatized society that continues in open conflict over its past because of the ongoing dynamics of trust and betrayal—dynamics that are, in fact, implicating increasingly more social sectors as complicit with the dictatorial regime. The framing of Argentina's disappearances in terms of genocide is the latest manifestation of this mistrust. Genocide is, after all, the ultimate betrayal, the worst violation of trust among human beings and social groups.

On 24 March 2010, Estela de Carlotto and Nora de Cortiñas, as the most prominent representatives of the Grandmothers of the Plaza de Mayo and the Mothers of the Plaza de Mayo Founding Line, were leading the presentation of the banner of the disappeared. I may have met Nora de Cortiñas for the first time in Buenos Aires in April 1978, one year after her son Gustavo had disappeared. On that day, I was walking across the Plaza de Mayo when suddenly three or four women approached me and told me in desperation that their children had been taken, they did not know where. Nora de Cortiñas could very well have been among these women, who were quickly pushed away from me by a policeman and two civilians. She had become one of the movement's new leaders after its founder, Azucena Villaflor de De Vicenti, had been abducted and disappeared. Eight persons had been dragged away during a gathering at the Santa Cruz Church on 8 December 1977. Azucena and four others were taken two days later. In another repressive move, the dictatorship forbade the Thursday afternoon demonstrations of the mothers at the Plaza de Mayo, as they were fearful they might jeopardize the upcoming World Cup soccer tournament of June 1978.[1] Only the most fearless mothers, among them Nora de Cortiñas, maintained their presence at the square by approaching passersby like me who might be foreign journalists who could spread the word abroad about their protests.

In 1990, I had three in-depth interviews with Nora de Cortiñas. She told me about the long days spent searching for her son and the profound sense of betrayal when she discovered in 1982 that Gustavo Niño—the young man who had frequented the weekly gatherings at the Santa Cruz Church in search of his abducted brother—turned out to be undercover Navy Lieutenant Alfredo Astiz. Astiz was a free man in 1990 thanks to an amnesty intended to bring social peace to Argentina by ending the prosecution of perpetrators. Nora strongly opposed the amnesty law: "reconciliation with the assassins, the torturers, and those who disappear people is impossible. There are prisons for them. . . . I don't want to forgive them" (interview on 16 November 1990). Nora never changed her mind throughout her life-long activism.

The National Day of Memory for Truth and Justice, popularly known as the Day of Memory, was created by Congress in 2002 to remember the disappeared and commemorate the coup d'état of 24 March 1976. The human rights movement took advantage of the national holiday to remind Argentine society that the accountability of perpetrators and collaborators had been cut short by the amnesties and pardons of the late 1980s. Yet, Argentine history is full of unexpected turns, and by 2006 a new cycle of trials against the Argentine military and police had begun. Years of street protests and the persistence of human rights lawyers had paid off. The Day of Memory demonstrated that the disappeared had not been abandoned. Although the national holiday was intended as a nonpartisan commemoration, public presence and oratorical prominence at the Plaza de Mayo in Buenos Aires became an annual political contest.

The Day of Memory in 2010 began officially at 11:30 A.M. with a speech by President Cristina Fernández de Kirchner at the former Navy Mechanics School (ESMA), where one of Argentina's largest secret detention centers had been housed. She emphasized that the recovery of the identity of babies kidnapped during the dictatorship was "a victory over oblivion and death," and she rejected the suggestion by some politicians to stop prosecuting the perpetrators: "Nobody judges the past, but rather concrete crimes committed by concrete men."[2] She was not giving her speech in the Casa Rosada, the presidential palace at the Plaza de Mayo, as if to distance herself from the discord among the human rights organizations and political groups marching toward the square.

The day's program had been hotly debated among the sixty participating organizations that refused to share the podium erected at the square's center because of their different stance toward the reigning Peronist government. The compromise, hammered out after long negotiations, was eventually broken when state officials intervened at the last moment and started the music festival two hours earlier than planned, thus allowing opposition groups less time to air their disapproval of the government. The pro-government Mothers of the Plaza de Mayo Association, led by Hebe de Bonafini, was present for President Cristina de Kirchner's speech at 11:30 A.M., and at 5:00 P.M. opened the music festival to celebrate an artistic culture that the dictatorship had been unable to destroy. The Mothers of the Plaza de Mayo Founding Line, headed by Nora de Cortiñas, carried the large banner representing the disappeared to the nation's symbolic center at 2:00 P.M. and departed before the rival Mothers Association stepped on stage. The Grandmothers of the Plaza de Mayo joined Argentina's president at the ESMA and accompanied both organizations of mothers at the Plaza de Mayo. Finally, dozens of leftist groups with names such as Revolutionary Peronism, Tupac Amaru, and Neighborhoods on Their Feet entered the square around 4:00 P.M. and read a critical message to the Kirchner government, which was drowned out by the loud music coming from the podium.

The next day I met Nora de Cortiñas at her office. Decades had passed since I had first met her. Now eighty years old, she was still trying to determine what had happened to her son Gustavo and was tirelessly taking to the streets to demand the prosecution of the assassins. She commented that the Plaza de Mayo had been divided between pro-Kirchner and anti-Kirchner groups or, as the opposition newspaper *Clarín* wrote, between "orthodox Kirchnerists, reluctant Kirchnerists, and furious Kirchnerists versus Marxism-Leninism, Trotskyists, Maoists, picketers, and anarchists. K vs. anti-K. Two marches, two events, and two different worldviews."[3] Nora lamented the censorship of antigovernment forces and the festive atmosphere of the day's closing event: "We have nothing to celebrate on the 24th of March. It is a day to remember, to denounce, to reflect, and to continue accusing the project of the civil-military sector" (interview on 25 March 2010). The commemoration at the Plaza de Mayo in 2010 showed that what united the mothers and grandmothers, namely the emotional attachment to the disappeared and the demand for the accountability of the executioners, at the same time divided them when they quarreled over how to express this attachment in public and give shape to their ambiguous entanglement with the Argentine state.

In my previous book, I demonstrated how the complex interplay of political violence and sociocultural trauma affected several social domains of Argentine society between 1945 and 1990 (Robben 2005a). The betrayal and mistrust that had pervaded the military dictatorship influenced Argentine society in the decades thereafter. The armed forces continued to betray the Argentine people by refusing to open the books on the disappeared, thus condemning relatives to an interminable search for kidnapped babies and the skeletal remains of their abducted loved ones. These two conflicting groups were mistrustful of Argentina's successive governments that followed an unpredictable path between accountability and pacification. Before entering into a conceptual discussion of trust and betrayal, I will provide a short history of the political violence in twentieth-century Argentina until the fall of the military regime in 1983 as a prelude to this book's analysis of its aftermath.[4]

A Concise History of Political Violence in Argentina

Argentina has been weighed down by political violence since the Spanish viceroy was deposed during the May Revolution of 1810, and a successful war of independence was fought against Spain. This anticolonial war evolved into a period of intermittent civil wars between regional warlords and the central government in Buenos Aires. In the same period, the young republic embarked on a territorial conquest of Patagonia and the destruction of its native population. Charles Darwin, who traveled extensively in Argentina between 1832 and 1834, noted the connection between economy and genocide. "This war of extermination, although carried on with the most shocking barbarity, will certainly produce great benefits; it will at once throw open four or 500 miles in length of fine country for the produce of cattle" (Darwin 1988:172).

The civil wars ended in 1852, and the Argentine state was consolidated in the decade of its so-called National Organization. The constitution was written, Congress was installed, and the economy expanded thanks to increasing agricultural exports and foreign investments. Argentina attracted many immigrants from Europe between 1865 and 1880, including refugees from the Paris Commune who began organizing the rapidly growing working class and in 1872 founded a chapter of the First International.

In search of new grazing lands, cattle ranchers clashed with the native inhabitants at a frontier where trade, theft, intermarriage, and kidnapping occurred at the same time (Duncan Baretta and Markoff 1978; Jones 1993).

Peace treaties were as easily made as broken. In 1878, the Argentine government decided to make the Río Negro its southernmost natural line of defense against Indian raids. An expeditionary force of six thousand soldiers, equipped with horses and Remington rifles, advanced in five divisions across the vast pampas, killing and enslaving native warriors and families (Punzi 1979; Viñas 1982). More expeditions followed, and in April 1883 President Roca congratulated General Villegas on his final victory: "Beyond that enchanting blue lake at whose margins the Argentine bayonets pitch their tents, at the same sites where in the near future towns will arise, there are no more indians, daring tribes or terrible chiefs left to terrorize cattle herders and prevent the cultivation of land" (Walther 1980:547).

Argentina was booming by the late nineteenth century. Nearly two million immigrants arrived between 1900 and 1908, escaping poverty in Europe but finding only more exploitation in an overpopulated Buenos Aires (Lynch 1993; Rock 1987). The harsh repression of strikes and street protests during the first decades of the twentieth century culminated in the Tragic Week (la Semana Trágica) of January 1919, when members of the army and police killed thirty-four workers (Díaz Araujo 1988). Authoritarianism reigned in Argentina after the country's first military coup d'état in 1930. An era of political corruption and economic decline began, known as the Infamous Decade, in which political opponents were subjected to waterboarding and the electric prod was added to the arsenal of torture instruments (Unamuno 1988).

The repressive political climate ended in 1945 when the populist leader Juan Domingo Perón came to power with the support of the Argentine working class. He started an emancipatory movement that freed exploited workers "from the fear of losing their job, to look upon the foreman as an equal, to feel protected by the union representative, and not to hear constantly the bark of misery" (Luna 1973:320). Tensions with the Catholic Church arose in 1950 when Perón stated that Peronism's ideology of social justice embodied the essence of the Christian faith. His growing authoritarianism provoked failed military rebellions in 1951 and 1952, and the stepped-up state repression of political opponents created much bad blood. In fact, Argentina's first documented disappearances occurred in December 1946 when the police shuttled five political detainees among different police stations in La Plata and denied having them in custody (Lamas 1956:47–53). The street protests against Perón gained momentum in 1952, and military conspiracies were brewing. The turmoil reached its climax in 1955. The presidential palace at the Plaza de Mayo was bombed in June 1955 by the rebellious Navy, causing hundreds of civilian deaths (Portugheis 2015). The uprising failed, but the anti-Peronist opposition only grew in strength until a successful coup d'état on 16 September 1955 forced Perón to flee the country.

The military junta immediately proscribed the Peronist Party, and even forbade mentioning the names *Perón* and *Evita* in public. In addition, many worker benefits were revoked to raise the productivity of Argentina's industry. The overwhelmingly Peronist working class considered these measures to be acts of revenge and supported a resistance movement against the dictatorship that came to inspire the political violence of the 1970s. More than two hundred Peronist groups, with around ten thousand members in Buenos Aires alone, sabotaged the country's economy. There were strikes, street protests, fire bombings, and armed operations (James 1988:77–80).

On 9 June 1956, Peronist officers staged a rebellion that was beaten down brutally, leaving thirty-four dead. Hundreds of Peronists were arrested. Ernesto Jauretche, who would join the Peronist guerrilla organization Montoneros in the early 1970s, recalled how deeply he was affected by his mother's detention. "The first time they took my mother, they also disappeared her. For one month, we searched for her everywhere but they told us: 'She's not here, she's not here.' We searched for her at military bases, everywhere. Executions were taking place and we didn't have any news about my mother, we didn't know where she was. The history of the disappearances is indeed very old" (interview on 6 April 1991).

The Peronist resistance movement petered out in the late 1950s. The military had handed over power to the civilian government of Arturo Frondizi in 1958, and the labor unions avoided open confrontations with the state. Nevertheless, a rural guerrilla insurgency, inspired by the Cuban Revolution of 1959, sprang up in Tucumán Province. The small group soon fell apart, however, because of internal disagreements and offensive police operations. Insurgents again attempted revolution in June 1963. Argentine guerrillas trained in Cuba entered Argentina to create a liberated zone in the province of Salta, but they failed because they lacked support from the rural population and an urban working class that was organized in noncombative labor unions. Union leaders had developed close ties with the political establishment and had cultivated clientelistic relations with the rank and file through pension funds, medical care, and jobs for loyal members (James 1988:130–142). Some even supported the coup d'état of 28

June 1966 by retired General Onganía because President Frondizi's successor, Arturo Illia, wanted to improve the internal union democracy and eradicate the rampant clientelism.

The pact between union leaders and military rulers was broken when the junta decided in August 1966 to impose the forced mediation of labor conflicts and abolish the right to strike. Working-class resistance grew and coalesced with the rebellious spirit of a younger generation inspired by the Cuban Revolution. In 1969, massive street demonstrations of workers and students erupted in industrial cities such as Córdoba and Rosario. The middle classes sympathized with the antigovernment protests but did not approve of the armed violence (Carassai 2014). Small guerrilla groups misinterpreted this solidarity as the coming of a revolution, and benefited from the crowd mobilizations to recruit members.

The military dictatorship failed to control the increasing number of antigovernment street protests that demanded the return of Perón, who had been living in exile since 1955. The junta decided to hold national elections in March 1973 but excluded Perón from the ballot. The Peronist Party won the elections, and its candidate, Héctor Cámpora, assumed power on 25 May 1973. His presidential pardon of nearly four hundred incarcerated political prisoners became a watershed in the Argentine military's thinking about counterinsurgency warfare and convinced them that total annihilation was the only correct response to a future resurgence of armed violence. Only weeks before the pardon Navy Captain Horacio Mayorga had warned against "the presence of a violent left that can sink us into a killing process, and if the dead are ours it will then be the law of the jungle" (Potash 1996:503).

Perón returned to Argentine soil on 20 June 1973 during a violent confrontation at Ezeiza Airport between revolutionary Peronists with roots in the guerrilla insurgency and orthodox Peronists backed by the traditional Peronist labor unions. Many Argentines believed that the country's political violence would end once Perón became president of Argentina on 12 October 1973. Indeed, the Peronist guerrilla organizations demobilized their combatants, but the Marxist People's Revolutionary Army (ERP) continued to attack the armed forces, convinced that the revolutionary process begun in 1969 was maturing into victory. The violence increased further when the internecine fighting between left-wing and right-wing Peronists heated up again; it escalated further after Perón's death in July 1974, when his widow Isabel Martínez de Perón became Argentina's new president. The Montoneros began fighting it out with right-wing death squads that operated out of the Ministry of Social Welfare with the support of several labor unions and some military officers. The guerrilla insurgency was financed by ransom payments for kidnapped businessmen, and it acquired weapons and medical supplies by attacking military bases and police stations.

The Peronist and Marxist guerrilla insurgency consisted of around five thousand combatants in 1974–1975. The death squads numbered around one thousand operatives. Right-wing assassinations between May 1973 and March 1976 have been estimated at 1,165, while 480 assassinations were attributed to the guerrilla organizations (Moyano 1995). Isolated from a popular hinterland that became disenchanted with the political violence, the revolutionary movement would now face a revengeful militarized state.

The Argentine armed forces decided that the time had come for the state to enforce its constitutional monopoly on violence, and in February 1975 they entered into offensive operations against a rural insurgency of the People's Revolutionary Army in Tucumán Province. On 6 October 1975, the Peronist government gave the armed forces the mandate "to execute the military and security operations necessary to annihilate the actions of the subversive elements throughout the country's territory" (PEN 1975). On 24 March 1976, the military deposed President Isabel Martínez de Perón, an ominous decision that was supported at first by broad layers of the middle class that wanted the political violence to end (Carassai 2014:171–177). The coup was only in part undertaken to combat the insurgency. The military had already received extensive freedom of operation in October 1975, while the guerrilla organizations were on the defensive by late 1975. The dictatorship's greater objectives were to eradicate Argentina's heterogeneous revolutionary movement, restore the economy, and transform Argentine society through a Process of National Reorganization (Proceso de Reorganización Nacional) that would establish a lasting democracy and protect the so-called Argentine way of life and its Western Christian culture (Robben 2005a:171–189).

The combined police, gendarmerie, and armed forces were mobilized in an asymmetrical conflict characterized by disproportionate state violence against a dwindling guerrilla insurgency and an amorphous political opposition movement. The most succinct summary of the mode of operation was provided by Vice-Admiral Luis María Mendía, who told officers shortly before the military coup: "Thus, we shall act with civilian clothing, in quick

operations, intense interrogations, practices of torture and physical elimination by means of operations in aircrafts from which, during the flight,
the living and narcotized bodies of the victims will be thrown into the air,
thus giving them 'a Christian death'" (Feierstein 2006:152).

Tens of thousands of captives were held in hundreds of secret detention
centers. An unknown number were released within days or weeks once it
was determined that they did not pose a threat to Argentine society and
culture. Whereas the toll from guerrilla attacks on police and military
between 1960 and 1989 has been established at 508 dead (Díaz Bessone
2001), the precise number of assassinated-disappeared remains unknown.
A truth commission concluded in 1984 that 8,960 persons were missing
permanently (CONADEP 1984:479, 1986:447). In 2015, the Peronist government documented the assassination and enforced disappearance of
8,631 persons, while 783 cases were still under investigation (Secretaría de
Derechos Humanos 2015).[5] The human rights movement, however, consid-
ers these figures misleading because many abductions were never reported.
It claims that thirty thousand Argentines were disappeared.

When in August 2016 Argentine President Mauricio Macri was asked
about the number of disappeared, he responded, "I'm not going to enter
into this debate. I have no idea whether there were nine or thirty thousand."[6] Estela de Carlotto of the Grandmothers of the Plaza de Mayo
accused the president of trying to discredit the human rights organizations
as liars and of changing the discussion about state terrorism to one about
numbers.[7] Jorge Auat, the public prosecutor for crimes against humanity,
also disagreed with President Macri, saying that not the number but the
immensity of the crime was at stake, because "it is clear that life is no longer
the same after the crimes of the dictatorship, and that is why these are
crimes against humanity."[8] The slogan of the Day of Memory in March
2017 was therefore appropriately "They are 30,000."[9] The heated public
debate about the number of disappeared, taking place thirty-three years
after the military fell from power, demonstrates that the impact of the disappearances on Argentine society continues to be deep, and that the mutual
mistrust within the divided society and with the government is an enduring
legacy of the authoritarian state's betrayal of its citizens.

The disappearances paralyzed many Argentines politically during the
dictatorship. The military repression was not just intended to break the
revolutionary movement but also served to undermine the Argentine people's trust in order to prevent them from organizing an effective resistance.

The military was therefore taken aback when a group of mothers began a weekly protest at the Plaza de Mayo that quickly drew national and international attention. Growing human rights demonstrations, the junta's poor economic policies, and the defeat in the Falklands/Malvinas War against a victorious United Kingdom ushered in the fall of the regime. A transitional military government assumed power in June 1982, and free general elections were held in October 1983. Raúl Alfonsín won overwhelmingly, and he became president of Argentina on 10 December 1983. He inherited a country that was anxious about the fate of the disappeared and bewildered by the military repression that had profoundly damaged people's trust in the Argentine state, each other, and themselves.

Trust and Betrayal

How is trust created among people? The child psychologist Erik Erikson has sought the answer in early human development: "The infant's first social achievement . . . is his willingness to let the mother out of sight without undue anxiety or rage, because she has become an inner certainty as well as an outer predictability" (Erikson 1963:247). This basic trust or "parental faith" (250) is tested in games of peekaboo, when the mother covers her eyes and then reappears with a smile without producing any anxiety or rage in the baby. The mother has become a loving, trusted caretaker and the baby a trustworthy person who has mastered the fear of separation. However, the peekaboo game also harbors a subtle menace of betrayal that, when enacted unpredictably by an untrustworthy parent, may harm the cultivation of basic trust (Erikson 1963:248).[10] According to Erikson (248) and Robert Laing (1960:40), basic mistrust or ontological insecurity is then created that may lead to a weak trusting relation between parent and child, an unstable identity, and difficulty forming trusting bonds in adulthood. Violence, exploitation, and incest are, unfortunately, all-too-common violations within the home that disturb the human development of children. Selective neglect may also be caused by extreme poverty, as was shown in a groundbreaking ethnographic study of maternal attachment and infant death in a starving shantytown in Northeast Brazil (Scheper-Hughes 1992, 2014).

The mutual trust of parents and children is not based on an obligation or a contract, even though it might be cultivated in those terms, but arises in a nurturing, loving relationship that continues to be reproduced among family members after childhood.[11] Family members know that they can rely on one another and may express this trust in sensorial ways, as is shown in the following example of an Argentine mother and her adolescent son who were blindfolded and forcibly separated during a repressive operation by the Argentine police.

On 15 April 1976, five men disguised with wigs and false beards shot their way into the house of Floreal Avellaneda, who was being sought out for forbidden union activities. He escaped through a window and survived the dictatorship in hiding. The assailants decided to abduct his wife and their fourteen-year-old son instead. In her account from 1985, Iris Etelvina Pereyra de Avellaneda recalled how she and her son Floreal Edgardo were beaten and then taken out into the street.

> I was holding him by the hand. At a certain moment they indi-cated that we had to lean against the top of a car. That was the last time I saw my son, looking at me while they were putting a blindfold on my eyes and a hood as well. I can still sense its filthy smell. We had our hands free and instinctively I searched for those of my son but I didn't find them. I then raised my voice asking for him, and the police commissioner answered unwillingly: "I'll bring him right now." And, in fact, they put us together in the same vehicle. They put us in the back seat. My son squeezed my right hand as if to give me courage. We remained silent. (*El Diario del Juicio* 1985, 2:2)

After having been tortured at the police station of Villa Martelli to dis-close the whereabouts of Floreal Avellaneda, mother and son were sepa-rated. A torturer told her that she was going to be executed, and he granted her three final wishes. "I asked him about my son," she recalled nine years later during her court testimony, "and he answered that I shouldn't ask anymore because 'Your son, we already tore him to pieces'" (*El Diario del Juicio* 1985, 2:3). She was released in July 1978, and heard that her son's body had washed ashore on the coast of Uruguay in mid-May 1976. The autopsy report stated that his death had been the result of impalement (Almirón 1999:194; Feitlowitz 1998:208).

The sensorial expressions of trust by mother and son attenuated the anxiety about their forced separation and served to affirm the parental safety guaranteed by their trusting relationship. Trust caused abducted mothers to try to protect their children against the repressive state at great personal cost. María Elisa Hachmann de Lande endured forty-eight hours of torture to conceal her son's whereabouts. "At that time they thought that it would be easier to force the mother to say something, no? Or say where they were. But if I gave life to my son, would I then bring him death?" (interview on 13 April 1990). Luis José Bondone, who had been abducted together with his two adult sons, became alarmed when a torturer told him that they would now break one of his sons, just as they had already broken his other son: "It didn't come to my mind that they were young athletes, far better capable of resisting than me. Is it the sentiment of protection that all parents have inside which makes us think that our children are always vulnerable or more vulnerable than us, their parents?" (Bondone 1985:19). In addition to the traumatizing violence against a person's life, the attack on the parent's provision of safety can be traumatizing in and of itself (Charuvastra and Cloitre 2008:309). Torturers tried to exploit the inability of captive family members to protect one another. They harmed the basic trust of these victims by attacking their faith in the certainty of parental protection nurtured during childhood, as Jacobo Timerman (1981:148) observed during his time in captivity: "The entire affective world, constructed over the years with utmost difficulty, collapses with a kick in the father's genitals, a smack on the mother's face, an obscene insult to the sister, or the sexual violation of a daughter. Suddenly an entire culture based on familial love, devotion, the capacity for mutual sacrifice collapses." The torture of family members by placing one physically on top of the other or in each other's presence was particularly damaging because they experienced the reality that ultimately, in extreme situations, they could not expect any mutual protection from external threats. Children are especially vulnerable because their basic trust has not yet been sufficiently strengthened by the development of social trust outside the home. This precariousness is revealed in the case of thirteen-year-old Pablo Miguez, who was tortured in the presence of his helpless mother, Violeta, according to one eyewitness: "And when Pablito returns, he says: 'They tortured me,' and he was hurting all over, then the mother—who was a very strong woman of great human quality and moral strength—explained that they had tortured Pablito in front of her, and all this because Violeta had apparently not given them the title deed of her house" (El Diario del Juicio 1985, 14:319).[12]

Trust and security seem natural allies when children are young or under direct threat, but they can become opposites when the lives of parents and children grow apart. Some Argentine parents chose to be supportive of their children when they joined a guerrilla organization, instead of persuading them to flee abroad to safety. "I knew that it was best not to argue with the children when they took such a decision. What I most wanted was that they wouldn't lose their trust in me. One way or the other I was always at their side, and I thought that the worst I could do was to leave them unprotected, that they would feel abandoned by their mother. Society was already hostile enough to them" (Herrera 1987:182). Matilde Herrera struggled to accept her children's political choices. She tried to maintain the routines of a normal household and continued with the weekly family dinners, but she had mental flashes of her children's uncertain lives and felt as if she was drowning in her emotions. "I became more anxious with each day that passed. I began to cry everywhere: in buses, on the street. I used dark sunglasses and repeatedly felt that tears were running down my face. I was afraid to draw attention" (Herrera 1987:183). Within one year, Matilde Herrera's daughter Valeria, her sons Martín and José, her daughters-in-law María Cristina and Electra, and a grandchild born in captivity had all disappeared.

Other mothers chose safety over trust but equally struggled with the impossible choice. Elsa Sánchez de Oesterheld cut off all contact with her husband and four daughters when they went into hiding for belonging to the Montoneros. By doing this, she hoped to protect them from detection, but the loss of communication also prevented her from helping them survive. The five family members disappeared nonetheless (Robben 2005a:261–262). Their death continued to haunt her. "It is not death as such, but how they died. Because the fact of knowing the humiliation, torture, and horror our disappeared endured before dying makes me think that an execution, for example, would have been much more humane. . . . Death doesn't make me anxious because I know that my daughters, my husband, were at peace once they died. What worries me, what torments me, what makes me crazy is what happened before their death" (interview on 15 April 1991). Elsa's inability to protect her children, and to be at their side when they died, troubled her in her restless sleep, year after year.

Trust, love, and longing became key motivating forces behind the steadfast search by parents and relatives for the disappeared (including their ossified remains in anonymous graves), as well as for the protests, commemorations, and demands for truth and justice. Publicly, the moral legitimacy of protecting one's children made the presence of the mothers at the

Plaza de Mayo obvious, and therefore so hard for the Argentine military to handle. On a personal level, the disappearances made the mothers feel that they had let their children down by having failed to protect them. Feelings of survivor's guilt, of having been responsible for the abduction, of being an unworthy mother, and maybe even of having betrayed the relationship of love and trust—however unfounded these emotions may be—made the mothers determined to find their children, even if they were dead (Robben 2000b:82). Trust was for mothers a wellspring of energy and emotion that could still move them to tears and provoke anger decades later when recalling their children's disappearance. This spiritedness roused them to political action because parental trust extends beyond the home into different social domains. Fathers were generally less involved in the search, for reasons I explained in my previous book (Robben 2005a:305–306). The most relevant reason for this discussion of trust was given by Matilde Herrera, who emphasized the emotional bond between mother and child forged during delivery: "I'm just someone who has lost in a brutal way the entire product of her insides. I think that a man can understand that, but I don't know if all men are able to feel it" (Gabetta 1983:57).

Can basic trust—an attachment nurtured in the home—be applied to other realms of civil society and used as a concept to analyze state repression? Eisenstadt and Roniger (1984:31–41) have argued that the basic trust developed in early childhood is extended later in life to other interpersonal relationships that are pursued because of people's emotional yearning for the original trust. This expansion into the world diminishes the basic trust between parents and children as competing spheres of social interaction come into play, precisely what happened to Matilde Herrera and Elsa Sánchez de Oesterheld when their children decided to join the guerrilla movement. Anthony Giddens also situates basic trust at the foundation of society. It instills an ontological security that allows people to interact with strangers in an unpredictable social and political environment. Basic trust provides "a sort of *emotional inoculation* against existential anxieties. . . . a defensive carapace or *protective cocoon* which all normal individuals carry around with them as the means whereby they are able to get on with the affairs of day-to-day life" (Giddens 1991:39–40; emphasis in original). Of course, the caveat must be made that this protective cocoon is not spun in an unsafe home. Homegrown social mistrust carries into the outside world because "as people enter public life they bring with them their intimate experiences of trust and mistrust, and the lessons about their social world thus produced" (Ystanes 2016:38).

Trust and trustworthiness are thus not limited to the basic trust nurtured during early childhood. Trust is continuously shaped and reshaped through complex interactions beyond the home in civil society and with the multifaceted state.[13] In this book, I will use the term *social trust* for interpersonal and group relations in society, including the home, and *political trust* for interactions with state agents and state institutions because people's trust in the state is tied to their experience with its officials and authorities (Levi and Stoker 2000:495). But how does trust work itself out in social and political practice? Social scientists agree that trust is a social glue that binds people and societies together and that social relations corrode when mistrust takes over.[14] They accept trust as a given of social reality, and concentrate their research on its functional properties and consequences. But what, ultimately, is the nature of trust?[15]

Marcel Mauss and Georg Simmel asked this fundamental question at the beginning of the twentieth century. They argued that trust contains "some part of oneself" (Mauss 1990:12) or "some additional affective, even mystical, 'faith' of man in man" (Simmel 1950:318) that maintains social relations despite the many uncertainties involved. Mauss (12) observed that trust emerges in the act of giving: "to make a gift of something to someone is to make a present of some part of oneself . . . [and therefore] one must give back to another person what is really part and parcel of his nature and substance." Trust cannot be reduced to the interacting individuals or the gifts themselves because trust exists but for the grace of the relationship. Mauss (13) could not imagine a society of purely contractual, conflicting, or repressive relations because a society without bonds of trust would be at war with itself. Simmel shared this understanding: "without the general trust people have in each other, society itself would disintegrate" (Möllering 2006:2). In fact, we know that trust can even survive under the most extreme circumstances, such as concentration camps and forced labor camps (Todorov 1996). Also, Argentina remained a functioning society during and after the dictatorship because certain social realms and relations were not affected as much by betrayal and mistrust as others.

Mauss and Simmel did not explain precisely what they meant by the faith of trust. I will turn to Mauss further below, but as far as Simmel is concerned, I follow the lead of Guido Möllering. Möllering (2006:109–111) has argued in the spirit of Simmel that trust involves the suspension of the doubt that relations may go awry. People make a leap of faith when they trust others on the basis of limited knowledge and reasonable expectations, and thus they take the accompanying uncertainties and vulnerabilities for granted. This bracketing of doubt and uncertainty is understandable under the routine conditions of everyday life in a stable home or society, but betrayal is always just around the corner in the form of domestic violence and political conflict as well as war, revolution, or authoritarian rule, as becomes immediately clear in the case of Argentina.

In March 1976, the Argentine armed forces assumed control of the country. According to Lieutenant-General Videla, the malfunctioning state and the discordant society had to be thoroughly reorganized, "through order, work, the full observance of ethical and moral principles, justice, the complete realization of man, and through the respect of his rights and dignity" (Verbitsky 1988:148). Instead, the military rulers violated people's rights and multiple trusting relations by ordering illegal operations. The enforced disappearances betrayed the state's trustworthiness as the guardian of the nation's well-being, and attacked the trusting relationships among family members. Searching relatives were met with denial, and the trust of the disappeared in their fellow human beings became severely damaged when they were tortured by their interrogators and betrayed by their broken comrades. Some survivors remained forever mistrustful of society and the state because they could not accommodate their traumatic experiences into an everyday world of trust. However, to supporters of the military regime, the authoritarian state proved trustworthy by defending the constitution against a violent insurgency at the price of temporarily suspending people's rights for the common good.

Betrayal can damage relationships. People are disappointed when their expectations are not met or when they are cheated or lied to. Psychologists consider betrayal to be commonplace in social relationships but add that this does not prevent people from entering into new relations, because humans have a fundamental need for companionship (Jones, Couch, and Scott 1997). In fact, trust implies that one accepts the possibility of betrayal. Furthermore, people may also maintain troubled relationships that include betrayals because they have hopes for improvement or are trapped in dependency. Betrayal, suspicion, mistrust, and manipulation are present in human relations because social conflicts and power struggles exist in the heart of society and the state. Anthropologists have shown the existence of mistrust in social and political relations in many cultures.[16] They define betrayal as the violation of trust or the breaking of a secret. Of course, keeping a secret may imply both trust and betrayal because these terms are ambiguous. They may carry different moral values for people with opposing interests. For example, Argentine commanders who met with searching relatives face-to-face pretended to be truthful and trustworthy when they denied their involvement in the enforced disappearances because they were unwilling to break the secret of concealed operations and state terrorism.

The stakes were so high in dictatorial Argentina that mistrusting relations between officers and civilians were maintained even with awareness of the ongoing betrayal. Commanders kept up the appearance of compassion, while searching parents sustained a friendly demeanor in the hope that their military relatives and acquaintances might help them. Behind these outward niceties, the commanders mistrusted the parents for having failed to raise their children to become patriotic citizens and for lying about their political activism. The searching parents, in turn, did not trust the officers, and suspected them of hiding the truth about the disappearances. Trust and betrayal were thus complementary constituents of social and political relations in dictatorial Argentina and persisted in areas of national contestation after the junta fell from power. This permanent tension between trust and betrayal added a processual mutability to those relations or, in the formulation of Kelly and Thiranagama (2010:17): "The fear of betrayal is at the productive core of social and political interaction." Trust is then no longer the bracketing of betrayal or the suspension of doubt that a relationship may go awry, as has been argued by Simmel and Möllering, but rather becomes defined through betrayal. This recognition leads to mistrusting relations because there is always the doubt that relations may be disappointed. It is this ongoing conscious awareness of uncertainty that drives the dynamics of trust and betrayal.

What makes betrayal the violation of trust? Simmel and Möllering did not ask this question, but Marcel Mauss provides an important lead with his understanding of gift-giving.[17] If reciprocity means "that one must give back to another person what is really part and parcel of his nature and substance . . . some part of his spiritual essence, of his soul" (Mauss 1990:12), then betrayal is the appropriation of that part. Mauss implies here that the gift, whether understood culturally as a part of the spirit, the soul, or the person's constitution, is taken and not returned. What is at stake here, in my opinion, is not something that belongs to the donor but the relationship between the two persons. Betrayal is not about taking something owned by another, as in the case of theft; betrayal appropriates the relationship forged through social trust. In more general terms, betrayal imperils a relationship's reciprocal potential and the future social exchanges that maintain the relationship. Betrayal can therefore end a relationship when the deceit is discovered, but the relationship may also remain open when the betrayed person is unaware of the betrayal or because he or she still has hopes of reaping some benefit, as was explained earlier in the case of personal meetings between Argentine commanders and searching relatives.

Torture is one of the most extreme forms of betrayal because torturers enter the social constitution of people by appropriating and then inserting themselves in the attachment relation that originated the victims' basic trust. Torturers dissolve the inner certainty and outer predictability of security that was nurtured between parent and child, and use pain to create a perverse relationship of absolute dependency in its stead. Torture victims are known to call out in vain for their mother or father, feeling abandoned by their last emotional anchor in life, and then surrender to the torturer in utter helplessness. Torturers turn their victims into extensions of themselves through violence and subjugation, as in the case of one Argentine guard who treated a captive as his pet. "He would make him wag his tail, bark like a dog, lick his boots. It was impressive how well he did it, he imitated a dog as if he really were one, because if he didn't satisfy the guard, he would carry on beating him. . . . Later he would change and make him be a cat" (CONADEP 1986:72).

The effects of torture may extend to society. Jean Améry (1980:40), who had been tortured by the SS during World War II, had this to say about this humiliating disintegration of social trust: "Whoever has succumbed to torture can no longer feel at home in the world. The shame of destruction cannot be erased. Trust in the world, which already collapsed in part at the first blow, but in the end, under torture, fully, will not be regained." The harm done by torture may make survivors experience a lasting anxiety in the presence of other human beings, and even of close family members, as has also been observed among children abused by parents, siblings, or relatives. Betrayal is thus not limited to interpersonal relations but can extend to society as a whole when a repressive regime creates a culture of fear or commits political betrayal through an untrustworthy state.

Betrayal is the apostasy of trust. This abandonment of the bracketing of doubt in social and political relations, and the heedfulness to uncertainty, creates increased social distance and adversity. For example, the division of the Mothers of the Plaza de Mayo in April 1986 into two organizations, each with its own human rights agendas and street protests, was experienced by both as betrayal—a betrayal of the bond forged during the collective search for their children and the defiant demonstrations at the Plaza de Mayo, a bond of unconditional trust that had withstood even the disappearance and torture of several mothers.[18]

Betrayal carries substantial emotional costs. "Regardless of the specific type of betrayal, all forms of betrayal result in loss; loss of trust; loss of a relationship or friendship; loss of a sense of security and predictability, loss of time, energy, and effort devoted to that relationship or friendship; loss of integrity; and loss of self-esteem" (Kowalski 2009:174). These losses need to be mourned, and the more so when the betrayal affects people in their most intimate relationships and attachments. The mourning of such betrayal was complicated in Argentina by the knowledge that the bereaved relatives were being betrayed knowingly about the true fate of the disappeared and that this betrayal continued for decades on end.

The term *betrayal* carries negative moral connotations, but what was betrayal for the victims, survivors, and critics of the Argentine dictatorship created legitimacy and trust among its advocates and beneficiaries for serving higher national interests that superseded the suffering of individual citizens. This greater good justified in their eyes the distribution of false information to searching relatives, the complicity of the judiciary, and the repressive infrastructure that affected many Argentines. These dynamics of trust and betrayal were most prominent during the years of military rule, but remained operative during democracy.

Methodology

"To articulate the past historically does not mean to recognize it 'the way it really was' (Ranke)," wrote Walter Benjamin in 1940 during his exile from Nazi Germany in Paris: "It means to seize hold of a memory as it flashes up at a moment of danger" (Benjamin 1999:247). I have tried to capture such memories of the past in Argentina whenever they arose during public and political confrontations about the dictatorship's long aftermath. My research was conducted in Buenos Aires during my principal fieldwork period between April 1989 and July 1991 and during periodic visits in the decades thereafter. In addition, I have followed events in Argentina daily by reading the national newspapers *Clarín*, *La Nación*, and *Página/12*, and kept a log book to track emergent issues of contention and conflict.

My fieldwork comprised several research methods. Participant observation was conducted at commemorations, political rallies, protest marches, human rights demonstrations, and criminal trials. I also witnessed the exhumation of a mass grave and the excavation of a former torture center and attended the reburial of exhumed disappeared persons. I attended public presentations by retired army commanders and religious masses said in honor of officers killed by the guerrilla insurgency. Literature research was carried out in public and private libraries, and archives were consulted to obtain court records, legal documents, clandestine publications, and secret battle orders. I conducted more than one hundred in-depth interviews that elicited life histories and combined open questions with topic lists. The interviewees were mostly historical protagonists of the armed forces, guerrilla organizations, the human rights movement, and the Catholic Church who had occupied leading positions during the dictatorship.[19] Most interviewees were thus public figures, and I have therefore used their real names in this book. Also, prosecutors, lawyers, social and political scientists, forensic anthropologists, journalists, and activists working on behalf of either the military or the human rights movement were approached. Most interviews were tape-recorded and transcribed. I discouraged off-the-record remarks and took them seriously only when they could be verified by other interviewees.

Through my years of residence in Buenos Aires, I have had many informal conversations with the doormen at my apartment building, the newspaper vendors at the street kiosk, grocers, booksellers, and a string of storekeepers. They were not actively involved in any activity or organization related to my research, and neither were most of my Argentine friends, but we did discuss the dictatorship and current political events as they unfolded. These conversation partners were not representative of Argentine society, but our casual exchanges, if only for a few minutes but also during long conversations that ended in the wee hours of the morning, were nevertheless important to give me a sense of the different opinions circulating in Argentine society.

The question of reliability cannot be avoided in a book about trust and betrayal. The large number of interviewees made cross-checking among kindred spirits quite easy and allowed me to delineate their shared arguments and viewpoints. Significant differences occurred between conflicting groups, however, because each tried to persuade me of their side of the story and the morality of their conduct. These partial, partisan truths were conflicting discourses among people who occupied other positions of power and had different judicial statuses. I was very conscious of the fact that a former disappeared revolutionary, a retired general, and a mother searching for her son spoke in different registers because they were not equal interlocutors. Certain information could of course be confirmed or dismissed via contemporary documents, court records, and testimonies, but of greater value for my research were their discourse and points of view. The events described in my concise history of political violence in Argentina can be understood only within the discourse of my interviewees. I have therefore made the conflicting accounts and interpretations central to my analysis because their juxtaposition defines the areas of national contestation that organize this study. I will have much more to say about my interviews in the book's conclusion, but let me say here that at times I sensed a certain suspicion toward me. My affinity with the human rights movement and abhorrence of the systematic torture and enforced disappearances were evident to everyone, but my willingness to speak with all parties involved—including sworn enemies whose lives were connected by an enforced disappearance—raised some eyebrows about my intentions and sympathies.

The areas of national contestation that are this book's subject matter were identified through a grounded theory methodology. I used the inductive approach common in ethnographic research (Bernard 2006:492; Charmaz and Mitchell 2008). General themes and analytical categories emerged from close readings of field notes, transcribed interviews, and written texts. These diverse sources also provided the quotes, illustrations, and exemplars that give an empirical content to the book's main themes. The comparison of data within the emergent themes, their interpretation with different theoretical concepts, and the search for plausible connections among themes in the wider Argentine historical context helped me delineate the key areas of national contestation in Argentina. These areas related to the most disputed sequels of the dictatorship, such as the historical reconstruction of the political violence and the accountability of perpetrators. This method may seem rather intuitive, but the hermeneutic spiraling among emergent themes and the larger research universe—interpreting the part from the whole and vice versa rather than tacking back and forth between part and whole—served to advance my knowledge of the issues at stake (Hoy 1978).

This process yielded eight areas of national contestation that make up the eight empirical chapters of this book. The selection of topics was made easier by the writing of several comparative articles about Chile and Argentina (Robben 2010a, 2010b, 2014, 2015). The contrasts and similarities between the two post-authoritarian countries sharpened my understanding of how the two military states influenced the transition from dictatorship to democracy in other ways.

In line with the grounded theory approach (Charmaz 2006; Glaser and Strauss 1967), my examination of the ethnographic data within each area of contestation generated a theoretical concept that provides each chapter with its analytical focus. These concepts made it possible to compare fundamental disagreements among social groups and analyze their conflicts within the context of Argentine political history. Thus I present in each chapter's introduction my conceptual approach to the ensuing ethnographic analysis.

A comparison of the eight areas of national contestation yielded finally the dynamics of trust and betrayal that tie them together, and helped to fine-tune the analysis. This demarcation of areas is necessary because post-authoritarian Argentine society is not paralyzed by betrayal and mistrust. Most people lead their lives, go to work, come home, and maintain friendships and family ties in a functioning society. My grounded conceptual framework guides my analysis to those areas of national contestation that manifest Argentina's ongoing struggle with the legacies of its repressive dictatorship. This framework has been designed specifically for the Argentine context. Some of its key concepts will not apply elsewhere but others very well may, such as the dynamics of trust and betrayal. I believe therefore that this approach can be of use to the study of other societies that have awakened from repression, war, and political violence.

Argentina's Areas of National Contestation

This book examines the sequels of Argentina's brutal military repression from the perspective of trust and betrayal through an analysis of the conflicting discourses, practices, and courses of action in eight areas of national contestation. Chapter 1 explains the interplay of political violence and sociocultural traumas between 1945 and 1983 that resulted in the complicated aftermath analyzed in later chapters. Sociocultural trauma is the struggle to mourn and understand indelible violent events and massive human losses, together with the reliving of troubling memories in the present and fears about renewed outbreaks of violence in the future. Extended periods of state repression and certain intrusive violent events caused sociocultural traumas in Argentina that incited more political violence with still more traumatizing consequences. These violence-trauma-violence dynamics occurred on four interrelated levels of social complexity, namely the public, political, domestic, and mental domains. The dynamics became manifested in violent crowd contests, armed confrontations between the Argentine military and revolutionary insurgents, families touched by the repression, and the selves and subjectivities of captives harmed by prolonged torture and disappearance. The betrayal of basic, social, and political trust through torture, disappearance, armed conflict, and the repression of public protest percolated through the four social domains and has affected Argentina up to the present.

Chapter 2 describes four historical periods of Argentine memory politics whose most important discursive frames were dirty war, the two-demons theory, state terrorism, and genocide. The Argentine military regime had done its utmost to erase the traces of repression. Memory politics was practiced with each disappearance, cremated body, and death flight. Chapter 2 demonstrates how the spirals of violence and trauma ensured a collective memory composed of parts of the conflicting social memories of human rights organizations and military interest groups, in competition with an Argentine state that tried to impose various national narratives. The conflicting social memories were generated in conjunction as contesting parties denounced each other's rendition as a betrayal of the past for ignoring the histories of political violence experienced by the adversarial groups. These conflicting social memories were set in different discursive frames, which provided internal coherence and interpretational direction to the partisan social memories, commemorative practices, and material representations.

Testimonies represent people's personal experiences much more closely than the social memories discussed in Chapter 2. Chapter 3 focuses on the trustworthiness of witnesses of military repression and the credibility of testimonies whose truth came in several guises. Mistrust toward the testimonies of adversarial groups characterizes this area of contestation. Accusations of betrayal against other witnesses, which implied the deliberate infliction of legal, political, and emotional harm with false testimonies, were less common. Denunciations of abduction, torture, and disappearance were presented to human rights organizations and international fact-finding missions during the dictatorship. They were consistently dismissed by the military for being false and politically motivated. Testimonial narratives, known in Latin America as *testimonios*, were published during the regime's latter years to evoke empathy for the victims of persecution. After the arrival of democracy in December 1983, these testimonios were succeeded by depositions to a truth commission created to find information about the disappeared and document the military state's repressive structure. The most compelling denunciations were incorporated in the 1985 trial against nine junta commanders. Witnesses for the prosecution faced hostile lawyers who disputed their trustworthiness and accused them of collusion. The amnesties and pardons of the late 1980s made these different forms of testimony obsolete, and testimonial chronicles appeared that sought to record the past with close attention to everyday life, emotion, agency, and subjectivity.

Chapter 4 addresses the betrayal of searching relatives and the Argentine people by state agents during and after the dictatorship. It delineates a range of discursive strategies from secrecy and silence to denial, justification, and partial confession. The trustworthiness of perpetrator testimonies was doubted because of the constitutional guarantee against self-incrimination, but the appeal to the right of silence was often regarded as a sign of guilt and a betrayal of the victims. The Argentine armed forces remained silent during the dictatorship about the structure of military repression, and dismissed critical international reports as a coordinated campaign against Argentina. The overwhelming evidence from witness testimonies, exhumations, and written documentation gathered in the first years of democracy caused a change from silence to denial. High-ranking officers and their lawyers brought to mind the tragedies of war, the legitimate self-defense against the guerrilla insurgency, and the imminent danger to nation and Christian culture. Eventually, a few officers admitted to their participation in state terrorism, but at the cost of intimidation and physical assault by former comrades who wanted them to maintain the pact of silence and withhold their secret knowledge from the Argentine people.

The military pursued their sovereign control over Argentina through necropower and territoriality. *Necropower* refers to the capacity to decide over life and death. Territoriality implies the dominion over the country and its inhabitants. Chapter 5 examines how the armed forces and police took control of Argentina's sovereignty through the disappearance and assassination of sovereign bodies and their burial in anonymous graves throughout the country's territory. The military believed that the future of the country was at stake when the political violence increased after Perón's death in July 1974. Determined to secure Argentina's sovereignty by monopolizing state power, they staged a coup d'état in March 1976, closed the country's democratic institutions, and began abducting and assassinating guerrilla insurgents and political opponents. They also betrayed people's political trust by concealing and destroying the bodies of the assassinated captives. The final destination of these disappeared is at the center of an area of national contestation. The relatives of the disappeared united on the basis of social trust into a protest movement that challenged the authoritarian state and ushered in a democracy that reclaimed national sovereignty and restored the rule of law. Exhumations became a means to reclaim political, territorial, and corporeal sovereignty from the military during democracy.

Chapter 6 analyzes the principal types of accountability that have constituted a dynamic area of contestation in Argentina. It shows how justice became an increasingly heterogeneous process as the decades passed, and the state came to be regarded as unreliable. A trustworthy state protects its citizens and holds offenders accountable, irrespective of their social position. Maintenance of the rule of law is particularly important when a country is in the midst of a political transformation and people's political trust in the state has yet to be earned. In December 1983 President Alfonsín created a truth commission (CONADEP) to examine the massive disappearances during the dictatorship and to determine the authoritarian state's responsibility. He also brought the military juntas to trial. Five junta commanders were convicted in December 1985, and hundreds of officers were indicted. Growing disgruntlement in military ranks about the trials, together with the government's desire to reconcile Argentine society, resulted in sweeping amnesty laws and presidential pardons in the late 1980s that seriously damaged people's political trust in the multifaceted state. Frustrated about this impunity, children of the disappeared brought popular justice to the doorstep of amnestied torturers through public shaming. The admission by an army commander that the Argentine military had a standard operating procedure for kidnapped babies led in 1998 to the renewed arrest of many officers. Shifting political forces, and especially pressure from the human rights movement, achieved the derogation of amnesties and pardons by the Supreme Court in the mid-2000s. It was the start of many human rights trials. The detained officers felt betrayed by an untrustworthy state that had retracted the impunity laws and by their former commanders who refused to assume responsibility for the repressive structure. More than two thousand defendants were indicted between 2006 and 2016.

The resumption of the trials in 2006 occurred in the midst of a discursive shift from state terrorism and crimes against humanity to genocide. The representation of Argentina's military repression as genocide has made the process of justice more complex. State terrorism by military forces against insurgents and political opponents, however horrible the abuses may have been, contains a repressive logic that is missing from the indiscriminate extermination of people. Chapter 7 demonstrates that genocide remains a contested discursive frame in Argentina that revolves around the question whether disappeared captives were assassinated for who they were or for what they did. The proponents believe that only the historically laden term *genocide* is commensurate with the loss, betrayal, and sociocultural trauma inflicted during the dictatorship. The genocide discourse has resulted in a call to accountability for a growing number of civilians. After members of the armed forces and police were prosecuted by the thousands, judges, journalists, and businessmen have been accused of complicity with the dictatorship. Ultimately, Argentine society as a whole is considered collectively responsible. The consequence is a spreading of social and political mistrust through Argentine society.

Argentina has been mourning the consequences of authoritarian rule and massive disappearances for nearly forty years, while at the same time trying to build a working democracy and establish the rule of law. How to attend to the losses of political violence and the sociocultural traumas has been an issue of frequent contestation in Argentine society. Generally regarded as separate processes occupying separate time frames, mourning is often understood as accepting painful losses, whereas recovery implies building a new future on the ruins of the past. Instead, Chapter 8 argues that relegating the dead to the past is a betrayal of basic and social trust. They deserve to be actively remembered, according to the bereaved, and to leave their mark on Argentina. National mourning is conceptualized in Chapter 8 as a dual process that involves a politics of oscillation in which conflicting social groups and the multifaceted state try to impose their desired combination of loss- and recovery-oriented measures on society.

National mourning also includes perpetrators who are forced to face the havoc they wrought and therefore try to influence the reconstitution of society and how it deals with the traumatic past. Loss orientation has become manifested in exhumations, trials, memorials, and commemorations. Recovery orientation has involved economic and symbolic reparations, amnesties and pardons, and initiatives of national reconciliation. Loss orientation was dominant between 1983 and 1990, but the oscillatory dynamics of the dual process of national mourning leaned increasingly toward recovery orientation and became the prevailing mode of coping between 1990 and 1998 through amnesties, pardons, and reparative measures. The renewed prosecution of Argentine perpetrators in 1998, and then again in 2006, increased the attention to loss orientation. By 2016, numerous human rights trials and sites of memory combined loss- and recovery-oriented coping through a comprehensive dual process of national mourning.

In the concluding chapter, I will argue that trust in Argentina is not the suspension of doubt that a social relation may go awry but that trust is conditioned by the suspicion of betrayal. The awareness that people may have hidden motives and ulterior interests resulted in mistrusting relationships between adversarial groups and the multifaceted state. These dynamics of trust and betrayal also influenced my rapport with the research participants, whether these were mothers of the disappeared, former military and guerrilla commanders, or bishops and politicians. The varying degrees of trust and mistrust in these relations were reflections of the ambiguous relations in Argentine society itself, as became clear on the Day of Memory in 2010. Mothers who had defied the dictatorship with unusual courage out of love and trust for their abducted children and continued their protests despite the disappearance of their fellow protesters were three decades later mistrustful of each other's political projects and the public remembrance of their greatest loss, as if time was corroding a social trust forged under years of hardship and borne out of their most intimate but violated bond.

CHAPTER 1

Trauma

On 16 June 1955, shortly after midday, twenty-six bombers from naval aviation were circling above an overcast Buenos Aires poised for attack. The sky finally cleared at 12:40 P.M., and the airplanes began bombing the Plaza de Mayo in a rebellion against President Juan Domingo Perón, causing great havoc. The presidential palace sustained a direct hit that killed twelve people. Perón remained unscathed because he had taken refuge in the Ministry of War. Civilians died from the shattered glass that fell from the Treasury building, and a bus filled with schoolchildren fleeing home was hit. Meanwhile, trucks carrying Peronist workers were arriving. They wanted to come to Perón's aid, as they had done on 17 October 1945, when their leader had been detained by the military government. They asked for weapons to assist the army in repelling the three hundred marines advancing from the harbor. Soon, four Sherman tanks arrived to attack the rebel troops from the rear. Further bombardments took place at 1:10 P.M. and 3:30 P.M. Some naval planes were shot down by anti-aircraft fire and fighter planes manned by loyalist Air Force pilots, but most rebel bombers escaped to Uruguay. The naval uprising failed that day, leaving 309 dead and more than 2,000 wounded, many of them civilians. One eyewitness described the scene the day after: "We saw a bus with dead children and their heads crushed against the roof. At the square, there were dolls thrown on the pavement, abandoned by young girls who had run away, terrified by the bombardment" (Cháves 2005:119; Comisión de Afirmación 1985:46; Portugheis 2015).

In his radio address at 6:00 P.M., Perón told the Peronist workers to return home and leave the fighting to loyalist government troops. But the desire for revenge was too great. The metropolitan curia at the Plaza de Mayo went up in flames that night, because the Catholic authorities had supported the opposition movement against Perón since 1952, and seventeen churches were ransacked or set on fire while police and firemen stood by passively. In a reconciliatory gesture, Perón dealt out only mild sanctions against the rebels, but the political opposition continued unabated. The Catholic Church hierarchy kept up its pressure, a new coup was in the making, and the crowds of both Peronists and anti-Peronists filled the streets of Buenos Aires. Perón made an about face. At a major Peronist rally, he announced that the time of retaliation had arrived: "The watchword for every *peronista*, whether alone or within an organization, is to answer a violent act with another violent act. And whenever one of us falls, five of them will fall" (Torre and Riz 1993:262). Because of this ominous threat, and the Peronist union central's intention to form an armed militia, the Army and Navy rose again in rebellion on 18 September 1955. Perón fled to the Paraguayan embassy, and left the country on 3 October (Potash 1980:200–202; Torre and Riz 1993:262–263). General Lonardi became Argentina's president but was ousted in January 1956 by military hard-liner General Aramburu.

The bombardment of the Plaza de Mayo became the first sociocultural trauma of the Peronist movement. Weapons of war had attacked a Peronist crowd. A state apparatus had betrayed its constitutional mission to protect the Argentine people, had violated their political trust in the state, and in so doing had revealed the vulnerability of street mobilizations. Crowds, according to Canetti (1966), produce feelings of equality and gregariousness that relieve participants temporarily of the residues of resentment left by economic exploitation and social inequality. Perón had addressed these grievances in his speeches and had improved Argentina's labor conditions with his policies. The Peronist rallies dignified his following and transformed the unorganized popular masses into an invincible, disciplined crowd, according to Perón (1985b:325). The aerial assault was therefore a traumatizing attack on the most public manifestation of Peronist identity and against the trust forged at the Plaza de Mayo as Peronists sang the Peronist march and cheered for Perón. Ultimately, the bombing damaged the infinite unity and mutual attachment experienced by people in a crowd as well as the belief in the force of mass association.

The bombardment of 1955 embroiled Argentina in a spiral of violence that did not escalate by itself. The notion that violence begets violence is thoroughly ingrained in Western thought and can be found as much in Greek tragedies like the *Oresteia* by Aeschylus as in the work of contemporary scholars such as Girard (1992), Kalyvas (2006), Minow (2002), Feldman (1991), Taussig (1987), and Van Creveld (1991). The spiral of violence is believed to be fueled by a tit-for-tat dynamic of hatred and revenge. In Argentina, at least, the mounting violence was mediated by repeated socio-cultural traumas. Outbursts of political violence produced sociocultural traumas and then became the products of the sociocultural traumas they produced. Political violence did not simply lead to more violence, but violence begot trauma, and trauma led to more violence. Through the decades, these dynamics generated an overdetermined whole with escalating degrees of violence and accumulative trauma that were noticeable at multiple levels of society and that turned trust and betrayal into the scales of people's political lives and everyday preoccupations.

This chapter explains the violence-trauma-violence dynamics in Argentina between 1955 and 1983 through their manifestation in street crowds, politicomilitary organizations, families, and the self. These four levels of social complexity correspond respectively to the public, political, domestic, and mental domains. Each level has unique practices, meanings, and social relations that are controlled by the complementary modalities of trust and betrayal. Their historical coexistence created interlinkages whose consequences spilled over from one level to another. For example, abductions took place in the political domain among armed organizations, affected the lives of the searching relatives in the domestic domain, and harmed tortured persons in the mental domain. Argentina was neither hit suddenly by an outbreak of crowd protests, revolutionary insurgency, or state repression nor traumatized by one bombardment or massacre, but their accumulation across four social domains resulted in a violent and traumatized society. Violence and trauma percolated through the interconnected yet distinct levels of social complexity, touching many citizens directly and the Argentine people as a whole indirectly because of the nationwide turmoil. The multiple manifestations of political violence and sociocultural trauma reinforced one another over time through continued betrayal, and they corroded people's trusting relations. The multilevel mistrust did not dissipate when democracy returned but continued to influence Argentine society because of several enduring sociocultural traumas.

The Multiple Meanings of Trauma

Violence can become traumatic when major injuries, losses, and threats to life and limb provoke horror, terror, or helplessness (Green 1990; Weathers and Keane 2007). Such psychic trauma comprises three aspects: the violent event, the victim's subjective perception, and the psychological response to the event. Life-threatening events, the death of loved ones, and hurting other human beings can all lead to psychic trauma (Green 1990).[1] Charuvastra and Cloitre (2008) have argued that not only fear but also insecurity can be traumatizing. The attack on people's social attachments may leave them so vulnerable and unprotected that they can become traumatized, as was clear in Argentina when family members were helpless during an abduction in the home. Jennifer Freyd and her collaborators have stretched the meaning of psychic trauma even further by arguing that fear and betrayal are different dimensions of trauma. Abused children may develop a betrayal trauma because the sexual violence inflicted by a parent violates the trusting relation (Freyd 1996; Bernstein and Freyd 2014; Gobin and Freyd 2014).[2] I agree that betrayal can be emotionally very damaging, but I share Richard McNally's concern about the risk of conceptual creep by spreading the concept of psychic trauma so thin that it applies to any experience of stress, pain, loss, and suffering (McNally 2010). What I take from this discussion is that psychic trauma involves intrapsychic and interpersonal processes, that betrayal can exacerbate emotional harm, and that the traumatizing violation of attachment relationships can become manifest on different levels of social complexity and not exclusively on the mental level.

People have the resilience to recover from traumatic experiences—without forgetting them—because they succeed in integrating them into their interpretation of the world. Such was the case with captured Argentine insurgents who regarded torture as inevitable in a class war and a necessary sacrifice for the revolution. A minority of victims develop posttraumatic stress disorder (PTSD) years or decades after the precipitating event. "Salient features are memories of the traumatic event or their avoidance, a negative mood, aggression, sleeping difficulties, reckless behavior, and hypervigilance" (Pillen 2016:97). Such psychic rupture reverses people's ontological security in a topsy-turvy world that is incommensurate with everyday life in a society where trust and trustworthiness in human relations are taken for granted (Herman 1997; Robben 2000b; Saporta and van der Kolk 1992). For example, Gampel (2000) has shown that traumatized Holocaust survivors cannot reconcile and psychically integrate the everyday background of safety with the background of traumatic camp experiences, and therefore try to keep these disparate realities apart.

An awareness of the devastating social dimensions of traumatizing violence paved the way for the term *social trauma*. A social trauma is not a psychic trauma writ large but describes the process of traumatization on the group level, even when many members do not suffer from psychic trauma or have not experienced the violence in person. "Whether or not it manifests in individual disorders, the deterioration of social interaction is in and of itself a serious social disturbance, an erosion of our collective capacity to work and love, to assert our unique identity, to tell our personal and communal story in the history of peoples" (Martín-Baró 1994:115). A social trauma is not the sum of individual suffering but refers to ruptured social bonds and destroyed collectivities. "It is possible to describe social dislocations and catastrophes as social traumas if they massively disrupt organized social life" (Smelser 2004:37). Just as psychic trauma has been called a wound to the mind, metaphorically speaking, so social trauma is an injury "to the basic tissues of social life that damages the bonds attaching people together and impairs the prevailing sense of communality," according to Kai Erikson's (1976:154) influential study of an Appalachian mining community hit by a deadly wave of water-saturated slag. This social trauma was caused by the disaster and the disassembled neighborhood ties after homeless survivors were dispersed over different trailer parks. Erikson (1995:198) speaks of "a loss of confidence in the surrounding tissue of family and community, in the structures of human government, in the larger logics by which humankind lives." Social trauma may impair a community's functioning by damaging social and political trust, but it may also incite social protest and political action, as will be shown in this chapter.

Social trauma is not an inevitable reaction to massive violence, and we must be careful not to equate social trauma with social suffering. Societies and social groups have shown a remarkable resilience under adverse circumstances and have found ways to reconstruct what was lost and broken through posttraumatic growth. Sometimes, however, they become defenseless when coping strategies fail. As I have explained elsewhere (Robben 2005a:346–349), repeated excessive violence may eventually prevent traumatized groups from functioning. A case in point is the Argentine guerrilla insurgency that was relentlessly pursued by the armed forces. After recovering from one blow after another, replacing fallen combatants and shoring up the chain of command, the guerrilla movement finally succumbed. The political ideals, the secret meetings and safe houses, the camaraderie and friendship, and the ideological faith in a final victory—all collapsed through attrition, capture, and betrayal. Likewise, assaulted societies are periodically reminded of past atrocities that are incommensurable with post-catastrophe times, as Friedlander (1993:48–58) has argued about the Holocaust. In post-authoritarian Argentina, shattering experiences resurfaced when mass graves were opened, former captives gave testimony in court, searching grandmothers found kidnapped grandchildren, and the military openly denied the disappearances. Such evocations of traumatic experiences were ways of struggling with the meaning of past atrocities.

Violence may also entail cultural traumas that manifest the inability to make sense of the onslaught. "Cultural trauma," observes Alexander (2012:6), "occurs when members of a collectivity feel they have been subjected to a horrendous event that leaves indelible marks upon their group consciousness, marking their memories forever and changing their future identity in fundamental and irrevocable ways." Cultural trauma involves a cultural disorientation because meanings and explanations that have been taken for granted have become obsolete. In the same vein, Sztompka (2000:449) defines cultural trauma as "the culturally defined and interpreted shock to the cultural tissue of society," and he delineates a traumatizing sequence that begins with a major upheaval, continues with unsatisfactory interpretations of the catastrophe, and leads to social and cultural disruption.

Social trauma and cultural trauma can be distinguished analytically but may also overlap in empirical reality. I will therefore employ *sociocultural trauma* as a generic term unless specific issues of cultural meaning or social disruption need to be addressed.[3] Sociocultural trauma in Argentina stems from prolonged difficulties of mourning mass deaths and cumulative shattering events. Disturbing memories are relived in the present, and there is a persistent fear about repression or death. The traumatic past becomes indelible when people or groups cannot reconcile themselves with their losses and fail to integrate them into a shared narrative. Unexpected revelations and the appearance of new material evidence are disturbing because they cannot be accommodated in acceptable explanations. When satisfactory interpretations cannot be formulated, the traumatic past intrudes on the present, influences the future, and is relived in multidirectional social memories that attribute contested meanings to past experiences. In short, society is traumatized, not in a medical or pathological sense but as a result of complex historical and sociopolitical processes.[4]

I am aware of existing critiques that address the use of the term *trauma* in relation to state violence and human rights violations.[5] Trauma has become a moral construct that is generally associated with victims, not perpetrators. "As a result, the clinically describable trauma experienced by individuals who are immoral, or whose behavior should not be empathized with, is neglected in both scholarly and popular accounts of trauma. Indeed, perpetrators are considered potentially traumatized only when they can be viewed also as victims, such as child soldiers and individuals who commit crimes under duress" (Mohamed 2015:1167). However, like power, trauma is a double-edged concept that helps elucidate the complex relation between perpetrators and victims but does not imply their moral equivalence. The fact that power is a key dimension of both domination and resistance, exercised differently by rulers and ruled, does not disqualify the concept. The additional critique by Kleinman (1999) and Fassin and Rechtman (2009) that the concept of trauma tends to medicalize a sociopolitical condition can be avoided by always analyzing sociocultural trauma together with the political violence that preceded it, as I am doing in this chapter. Our human compassion for the tortured and subjugated should not make us blind to understanding dictators and perpetrators—to seeing them not as unilineal evildoers but as people with human contradictions and vulnerabilities, including psychic traumas. The same applies to sociocultural traumas, which is this book's main interest. The armed forces and the guerrilla insurgency traumatized one another, and state terrorism traumatized Argentine society, but I do not regard them as morally interchangeable. Ignoring some sociocultural traumas because they affect unsavory groups and organizations would hamper our analysis. Argentina's predicament in the last four decades can only be understood when all pertinent protagonists, organizations, and state institutions are included in one comprehensive analysis of the complex multilevel dynamics of political violence and sociocultural trauma.

In December 1983, Argentina was a traumatized society. This qualification does not mean that Argentina was a malfunctioning society but that the country was beset with several sociocultural traumas that influenced its memories of the past, its dealings in the present, and its plans and courses of action in the future. Without implying in any way a moral equivalence of the Argentine military and police, guerrillas and political activists, disappeared persons and searching relatives, they were all affected by the overdetermined whole of violence and trauma that came into being in 1955.

Street Crowds, State Repression, and Social Foment

Street crowds became the groundswell of Argentine political life after the rise of Juan Domingo Perón to national prominence on 17 October 1945. On that day, workers formed "an enormous and silent, almost subterranean, force" that converged on the Plaza de Mayo in Buenos Aires to demand Perón's release from internment after being ousted from the military government (Luna 1973:284). Crowds had been assembling on Argentina's streets and squares since the mid-nineteenth century, but they only took center stage in Argentine politics through their periodic mobilization under Peron's tutelage. Crowd mobilizations became the preferred form of political protest and legitimation in Argentina (Robben 2005a:5–10; Torre 1995). Peronist crowds were the acme of the unchained popular masses, and Perón (1985a:37) believed that only a strong leader could control their impulsive nature. They expressed the popular resentment of social, political, and economic wrongs and celebrated the dignity, social gains, and political rights of workers as full citizens of the republic. These class-conscious crowds were the seedbed of future armed resistance and revolutionary insurgency.

The success of crowd gatherings as a means of Peronist protest and legitimation forced the middle class to contest public space in like fashion when worries about Perón's increasing authoritarianism surfaced. A growing opposition in the armed forces had already resulted in two military rebellions. In addition, the suspicion that the Peronist movement was trying to take the place of Argentina's Catholic youth, labor, and charity organizations caused a falling-out with the Catholic Church. The first crowd contest erupted in Córdoba in September 1954. A march of ten thousand Peronist high school students was upstaged by a Catholic rally that attracted eighty thousand people. In the following months, more than a dozen large Catholic demonstrations were organized in Buenos Aires that clashed frequently with Peronist supporters. Perón added fuel to the fire by declaring in May 1955 the official separation of church and state. Rumors surfaced about a coup d'état, and the loyal Peronist union central CGT (Confederación General de Trabajo) began to organize its rank and file to support Perón (Robben 2005a:16–19). The mobilization failed to deter the forces of rebellion. The seat of government was attacked on the ground and from the air on 16 June 1955, as described in this chapter's introduction. The threat of more violence three months later persuaded Perón to leave the country.

The bombardment of the Plaza de Mayo on 16 June 1955 became part of the Peronist identity as a sociocultural trauma: horror and terror about the attack, an overall fear of crowd mobilization, a strong distrust of the armed forces, and an inability to come to grips with the dead. The armed forces had turned their weapons against the people they were mandated to protect. The betrayal exacerbated the sociocultural trauma of the assaulted crowd. This betrayal was not so much interpersonal but political because people's trust in the state was violated. The Peronist rank and file felt orphaned by Peron's exile. It relived its demise at the Plaza de Mayo in oral narratives and was afraid to gather in crowds. In the following years, small groups tried to retake the streets of Argentina by shouting Perón's name, painting slogans, and staging silent protest marches, but the large masses of before failed to materialize because most Peronists had retreated in fear from the public domain.

The bombardment of the Plaza de Mayo in June 1955 might have shaken the social trust of crowds and betrayed people's political trust in the state, but their belief in the Peronist cause was unbroken. A broad resistance movement emerged as the effects of the traumatic events percolated through Argentine society. Groups of militant workers organized strikes, sabotaged factories, derailed trains, and set grain deposits on fire. In June 1956, Generals Valle and Tanco rose against the military government. Their rebellion was quelled at the cost of thirty-four dead. Not the execution of General Valle, however, but the massacre of eight workers in José León Suárez on 10 June 1956 became a sociocultural trauma for the Peronist movement.

Late in the evening of 9 June 1956, a group of men were listening to a boxing match at a home on the outskirts of Buenos Aires when the police burst in. Only the proprietor and two visitors were vaguely connected to the rebels, but all were taken to a police station. On 10 June at 4:45 A.M., the order was given to execute the detainees. Three men were released, and the remaining fourteen were driven to the garbage dump of José León Suárez. The 1957 rendition of this event by Rodolfo Walsh spoke to the imagination of Peronists who were experiencing the humiliation, disenfranchisement, and loss of worker rights inflicted by the military government. "They make the persons under arrest walk by the edge of the vacant lot," narrated Walsh (1988:94). "The guards push them with the barrel of their guns. The pick-up truck enters the street and lights their backs with the headlamps. The moment has arrived." One man fell on his knees and pleaded for his life, and then the first shot rang out. Three men fled under the cover of darkness, while three others survived by playing dead. The remaining eight were assassinated. "In the glare of the headlights where the acrid smoke of the gun powder boils, a few moans float over the bodies stretched out in the garbage dump. A new crackling of gun shots seems to finish them off" (99).

This shocking event was relived in the account by Rodolfo Walsh, passed to second-generation Peronists, and commemorated with pipe bombs and impromptu street protests every tenth of June. The José León Suárez Massacre, as the execution was known, became a sociocultural trauma because of the utter defenselessness of ordinary Peronists who were betrayed by a hostile state and were assassinated at a garbage dump, discarded like human waste. Every Peronist was now believed to be fair game. Perón called for revenge. "We must make them feel the terror themselves. This will be achieved through a campaign of intimidation that comprises all actions against persons, families, and their belongings. The more violent and intense the intimidation campaign will be, the more certain and faster will be its effects" (Perón 1973:395). The Peronist resistance resumed its acts of sabotage and furtive displays of public protest. In November 1956, Perón ordered the start of guerrilla operations. "The more violent we are, the better: terror can only be beaten by greater terror" (Cooke 1973 1:35). Several commando groups were formed, but armed operations never got off the ground or were detected by police informers. The Peronist resistance petered out in the late 1950s due to increased state repression and lack of support among the Peronist rank and file.

The electoral proscription of the Peronist party was lifted in 1965, but its return to Congress was short-lived because the military grabbed power in June 1966. The dissolution of political parties, the obligatory arbitration of labor conflicts, and the prohibition of strikes and street demonstrations stirred the political cauldron. The overall discontent galvanized during a two-day insurrection of students and workers in Córdoba in May 1969. The sociocultural trauma of the June 1955 bombardment had been overcome. The protesters came prepared with metal bars, slingshots, small firearms, and ball bearings to fight the mounted police. They descended in a pincer movement on the fortified city center and forced the police to retreat. Hundreds of barricades were erected that sealed off two student neighborhoods, and snipers from a small communist organization kept the police at bay. Police and army finally occupied Córdoba after waging a pitched battle. The number of deaths was estimated to be between sixteen and sixty (Robben 2005a:49–51).

The Cordobazo, as the grassroots insurrection became known, increased people's trust in the power of organization, mobilization, and mass protest. This mastery of the sociocultural trauma, and the awareness of the dictatorship's repressive capabilities, made protest crowds engage in a tug-of-war with the security forces. Street demonstrations continued to be repressed with disproportionate force in the following years, but none of them caused a sociocultural trauma. People's yearning to express their resentment against the military government in the presence of tens of thousands of protesters was stronger than the fear of death.

Revolutionary War and Counterinsurgency

The urban insurrections of the late 1960s shifted the political initiative from the Peronist working class to a new generation inspired by the Cuban Revolution. Marxist and Peronist guerrilla organizations emerged that interpreted the massive street protests of 1969 as portents of revolution. For the Argentine military, the upcoming decade of guerrilla insurgency was marked by one single assassination. On 29 May 1970, former President Pedro Aramburu was abducted by two young Peronist guerrillas. He had been a ringleader of the September 1955 coup against Perón and the architect of the ensuing state repression (Gillespie 1982:96–97). He was charged by a revolutionary tribunal of Montoneros for the 1955 bombardment of the Plaza de Mayo, the 1956 executions at José León Suárez, and the disappearance of Evita's embalmed body in 1957 (Firmenich and Arrostito 1974:25). For young Peronists, Aramburu's execution meant an end to the impunity of Argentina's political leaders and demonstrated that the military were not invincible. Many young Peronists joined the guerrilla insurgency, encouraged by the groundswell of crowd protests and urban insurrections. They identified with the injustices suffered by the Peronist movement and had internalized its sociocultural traumas. Furthermore, they experienced the humiliations themselves when they were imprisoned and tortured. New violent events were added to old ones, and previous shattering experiences were given new meanings that cascaded into sociocultural traumas.

The frequency of armed operations rose steeply after 1969, only to decline in 1972 because of an effective counterinsurgency campaign (Moyano 1995:27–28). By mid-1972, many seasoned guerrillas were held in a maximum security prison in Rawson, a small Patagonian town 1500 kilometers south of Buenos Aires. On 15 August 1972, two hundred inmates took control of the facility in a massive escape attempt. The six highest ranking commanders were the first to arrive at the airport and waited for nineteen comrades to join them in a plane hijacked earlier by four guerrillas. The commanders decided to depart for Chile when the group did not show up. The nineteen guerrillas surrendered at the airport on the condition of safe conduct, and were taken to the Trelew naval airbase. There, they were interrogated and mistreated. One week later, on 22 August at 3:30 A.M., the prisoners were taken from their cells and shot. Sixteen prisoners were dead and three were wounded (Eloy Martínez 1997; Robben 2005a:119–125). Alberto Camps, one of the three survivors, later reported that Navy Lieutenant Bravo had said: "Now they will see what anti-guerrilla terror means" (Urondo 1988:108).

The assassinations became known as the Trelew Massacre, echoing the José León Suárez Massacre, and proved once more that state agents could not be trusted. The two massacres were mentioned in one breath, recontextualizing one with the other and reinforcing the sociocultural trauma of both. The 1956 and 1972 executions foreshadowed future massacres and moved guerrillas, as well as the military, to exact revenge. The chant "Soon they're going to see / Soon they're going to see / When we avenge the Trelew killings" (Gillespie 1982:166) was not an idle threat at Montonero demonstrations. Rear-Admirals Berisso and Quijada were assassinated in 1972 and 1973. The Navy, in turn, hunted down the three survivors of the Trelew Massacre. All three had been disappeared by 1982.

The crowd pressure was so great between 1969 and 1972, the guerrilla operations so menacing, and the national disenchantment with General Lanusse's regime so widespread, that free elections were held. The Peronists won an overwhelming victory. One of the first deeds of President-elect Cámpora on 25 May 1973, the day of his inauguration, was to decree the amnesty of almost four hundred political prisoners, among whom were Aramburu's abductors (San Martino de Dromi 1988 2:33–39). The military were shocked. The guerrillas had been given due process, had been convicted by the Federal Penal Chamber, and were now released to restart their revolution. The indignation at the general amnesty fused with the military's shock at Aramburu's execution and the reprisal killings for the Trelew Massacre. Military officers feared for their lives and the safety of their families. They were determined to annihilate the revolutionary left if the political violence erupted again.

Perón returned from exile on 20 June 1973. The expectant crowd at Ezeiza Airport numbered more than one million people, but the celebration turned into tragedy because of tensions between the two wings of the Peronist movement. The right wing was formed by the Peronist party and the Peronist labor unions that had weathered decades of repression and had maintained close ties with Perón. They were nationalists and orthodox Peronists. The left wing consisted mostly of young, second-generation Peronists and was organized in the Peronist Youth and the Montoneros. They had socialist sympathies and called themselves revolutionary Peronists. Their street protests and guerrilla operations in the early 1970s had done much to topple the dictatorship. The orthodox and revolutionary wings each felt entitled to determine Argentina's future, and crowd mobilizations were a key means to demonstrate their strength and obtain political influence. The Peronist left exalted Perón the Revolutionary who had spoken of national liberation and Argentine socialism, while the Peronist right adhered to Perón the Justicialist who had brought dignity and social justice to the working class. The welcoming of Perón at the airport was to be a contest of forces, one that prevented Perón from landing at Ezeiza and resulted in thirteen dead and many wounded (Robben 2005a:68–70; Verbitsky 1986).

My concern here is neither with any possible psychic traumas nor with the panic of the crowd but with the betrayal within the Peronist movement. The numerically superior left wing had been attacked by a better organized and armed right wing. The second-generation Peronists had sacrificed themselves to enforce the aging leader's return and were now prevented from uniting with him at the welcome reception (Robben 2005a:64–72). Peronists had turned on Peronists. The social trust among comrades in arms forged during the Peronist resistance in the late 1950s and in the fight against the dictatorship in the early 1970s had evaporated. A deadly feud developed within the Peronist movement that was saturated with mistrust and treachery.

Perón failed to appease Argentina when he replaced Cámpora as president in October 1973. Ultranationalist death squads like the Argentine Anti-Communist Alliance (AAA) appeared, and the Marxist guerrillas believed that they were accelerating the revolutionary process begun in

1969 with attacks on military bases. On 1 May 1974, a Labor Day crowd of only 70,000–100,000 people gathered at the Plaza de Mayo because the Ezeiza tragedy had made many Argentines afraid of being caught in the factional fighting. Perón's relation with the Peronist Youth and Montonero leaders had deteriorated steadily since late 1973.

Perón had strengthened his ties with the orthodox wing and sidelined leftist Peronist politicians. Perón appeared on the balcony of the presidential palace at 5:00 P.M. The public announcer called for one minute of silence in memory of Evita Perón and all deceased Peronists. As the quiet descended over the Plaza de Mayo, the Montoneros began a roll call of their dead, and during Perón's speech criticized him out loud for the right-wing Peronists in his government. Perón was furious. He emphasized that the labor unions were the backbone of the Peronist movement, and humiliated the left-wing Peronists by calling them immature. They felt betrayed by the person whose return from exile had been exacted with their blood. Tens of thousands of revolutionary Peronists vacated the Plaza de Mayo in the first Peronist crowd defection in Argentine history. The defectors not only turned their backs on Perón but also left thousands of loyalists behind. Alcira Argumedo remained loyal to Perón and stayed put. She still has one image burned in her memory from that day: "a very dark-skinned kid, very much from the rural heartland, who tears himself away. He had a large sign that said MONTONEROS. He tears himself away and says, 'Sons of bitches, traitors, traitors!' Mind you, arriving with that column, and he pulls out. I saw several of such cases, several of such reactions" (interview on 9 April 1991). Marriages ended at the Plaza de Mayo as one partner abandoned a loyalist spouse in a state of shock, and friendships forged during years of struggle and imprisonment ruptured that afternoon (Robben 2005a:75–77).

Perón died two months later, on 1 July 1974. His wife, María Estela Martínez de Perón, succeeded him as Argentina's president but lacked any authority. The political violence increased. The Marxist ERP (People's Revolutionary Army) continued with its armed operations, and the factional fighting between revolutionary and orthodox Peronists escalated. Right-wing death squads were active, and the Montoneros decided in September 1974 to go underground and wage an urban guerrilla war. Armed violence was replacing crowd mobilization as a manifestation of political power.

The armed forces in 1975 received an extensive mandate to destroy the guerrilla insurgency. The sociocultural trauma of the numerous assassinations of military officers and the blanket amnesty of imprisoned guerrillas in 1973 could now be overcome. By late 1975, the revolutionary insurgency had been crippled. The military decision to take charge of the country on 24 March 1976 was therefore not an attempt to wage a more effective counterinsurgency war but to restructure Argentina. The guerrilla insurgency was an excuse to gain a free hand to remake Argentine society and culture through the Process of National Reorganization.

Cultural War, State Terrorism, and the Dismantlement of Political Subjectivity

The Argentine armed forces waged their cultural war on three fronts: the public front of crowds, the politicomilitary front of revolutionary movements, and the mental front of the self. They adapted the three fundamental Clausewitzian objectives of classical warfare to counterinsurgency warfare and state terrorism, which followed one another when the definition of *enemy* expanded from guerrilla combatants to political opponents. These objectives were gaining control of territory, destroying enemy forces, and breaking the enemy's will (Clausewitz 1984:90).

The Argentine people were placed under a curfew on the day of the coup d'état; public gatherings and street protests were outlawed; and the armed forces, gendarmerie, and police took physical control over the country. Next, the state's security apparatus was mobilized to combat the remaining guerrilla insurgency and the heterogeneous political opposition. Using medical metaphors, military commanders referred to revolutionaries as a cancer of society and a gangrene of the mind that had infected Argentina. As Susan Sontag (1990:83) has observed: "To describe a phenomenon as a cancer is an incitement to violence. The use of cancer in political discourse encourages fatalism and justifies 'severe' measures." Precisely in this way, Admiral Guzzetti said in August 1976: "When the social body of the country has been contaminated by a disease that corrodes its entrails, it forms antibodies. These antibodies cannot be considered in the same way as the microbes. As the government controls and destroys the guerrilla, the action of the antibody will disappear, as is already happening. It is only a natural reaction to a sick body" (Schell 1979:193). Finally, the enemy's will to fight had to be broken, and this battle had to be won on the terrain of the human psyche with its ideological convictions and political agency (General Vilas in D'Andrea Mohr 1999:53; Villegas 1976:25, 1987:12). This conquest implied eliminating Argentine revolutionaries physically or occupying the mental space of the survivors by destroying their political agency. The existence of this third front explains why thousands of tortured disappeared were released after days or weeks, and why around two hundred captured guerrillas went through the Navy's rehabilitation program. The violence and trauma at the personal level, however, were not restricted to the people's psyche but extended into their social trust and political subjectivity.

Abductions were generally carried out at night. Typically, an assault team dressed as civilians would ring the doorbell or force its way into the targeted house. Captives were searched, hooded, beaten, briefly interrogated, and then driven to a secret detention center. After registration, they were subjected to a depersonalization procedure. Captives were given a number, forced to undress, and tied to an iron bed frame. They became nonpersons. Blindfolding made the disoriented inmates completely dependent on their captors and made them vulnerable to unpredictable humiliations, beatings, and sexual assaults (Robben 2005a:223–228).

The first torture session might serve to gather information about the identity and whereabouts of comrades in the same guerrilla unit, labor union, or front organization, but just as often captives were tortured for hours on end in silence. Depersonalization evolved into dehumanization by calling captives rats or animals, sometimes even forcing them to bark like a dog or cry like a cat. Torture was regarded by the military as a continuation of the armed struggle into the minds, bodies, and selves of the captives. Short of assassination, traumatization was considered the most effective means to eliminate the enemy and complete the victory on the ground into the political subjectivity of the vanquished. Situated at the intersection of self, emotion, and power, political subjectivity was dismantled through traumatization (Luhrmann 2006:356; Robben 2005a:211–212).

The trajectory of abduction, torture, and disappearance was intended to create social mistrust against other human beings and political mistrust against associations that might threaten the state. "Prolonged captivity also produces profound alterations in the victim's identity. All the psychological structures of the self—the image of the body, the internalized images of others, and the values and ideals that lend a person a sense of coherence and purpose—have been invaded and systematically broken down" (Herman 1997:93). In other words, the captive's future social and political engagement was to become crippled through psychic trauma and mistrust. As

Montonero Juan Gasparini was told after spending one year at the secret detention center of the Navy Mechanics School (ESMA): "with what has happened to you and with what you've seen, you're not going to get involved in any odd adventure anymore" (Gasparini 1986:142). Gasparini's harrowing experience was meant to leave a lasting imprint on his self and subjectivity before sending him into exile.

An estimated four thousand disappeared persons passed through the ESMA secret detention and torture center. Most were assassinated for posing a possible threat to Argentine society. Captives considered harmless were released, while those recoverable for Argentina were placed in a rehabilitation program intended to overcome their shattering experiences through resocialization and a step-by-step reincorporation into society. Gasparini was among a group of around two hundred captured Montoneros who passed through the ESMA rehabilitation program, while an unknown number of captives survived a similar program at the Campo de Mayo army base (Davis 2013:3).

Testimonies about the ESMA program indicate that the resocialization of participants—who had first been depersonalized, dehumanized, and traumatized—began with a removal of the hoods. They were given clothing and moved to larger cells. Captives who responded well to these privileges were given small tasks, such as taking photographs of new captives or translating foreign newspaper articles. Positive responses included a demonstrable emotional indifference to the torture of fellow inmates as proof that the desocialization had been successful. Later, when their self-confidence increased, captives were unshackled. They were given better food and could use the bathroom facilities. They might even be allowed to spend a night at home and return to the ESMA in the morning. An estimated 70 percent of the ESMA participants in the rehabilitation program were eventually set free. The final decision was made after several psychological assessments confirmed that the revolutionary subjectivity had been dismantled and the resocialization into the regime's worldview had been successful (Robben 2005a:250–255).

The military success of the rehabilitation program was questionable from the beginning. In October 1979, within a year of their release from the ESMA, three ex-disappeared gave a highly publicized presentation at the National Assembly of the French parliament. Perhaps they had not been resocialized after all because of their strong ideological convictions. They described the organization of the ESMA, the torture practices, assassinations, and the Navy's undercover operations in Europe. Dozens of officers were identified and denounced by name or nickname (Martí, Milia, and Solarz 1995). Two other former ESMA captives gave their public testimony in Madrid in February 1982 (Daleo and Castillo 1982). The fall of the military dictatorship in 1983 opened the door to more testimonies of ESMA survivors: in the press, at the truth commission, and at the trial against the junta commanders (Actis et al. 2001; CONADEP 1986; Gasparini 1988). This activism demonstrates that the dismantlement of the political subjectivity and the inculcation of the regime's worldview had failed, but I doubt if these ex-disappeared fully regained their social and political trust after years of torture and captivity.

Elsewhere, I gave several reasons for keeping thousands of disappeared persons in captivity for extended periods and then assassinating them anyway (Robben 2005a:255–256). The reason most relevant for this book is that the confinement of captives with a dismantled political subjectivity was considered a sign of victory. Traumatization and desocialization revealed that the will to fight and the social and political trust needed for practicing politics had been broken. Captives with severe psychic trauma, who were completely apathetic, were assassinated (*El Diario del Juicio* 1985 14:303). The same fate befell those who defiantly maintained a high morale, despite years of torture and humiliation, as happened to the Montonera Norma Arrostito, who had participated in the abduction of former President Aramburu in 1970 (Martí et al. 1995:52).

Traumatic experiences caused by other human beings have the highest chance of leading to PTSD; rape is the most damaging traumatic experience among men and women (Charuvastra and Cloitre 2008:303–304). The infliction of pain by fellow human beings attacks the sociality and trust of the captives by betraying the attachment relationship that makes them social beings. It undermines their ontological security and disrupts the dynamics of social interaction. Améry argued that the body conceals a self built on trust that ruptures together with the body. "The boundaries of my body are also the boundaries of my self. My skin surface shields me against the external world. If I am to have trust, I must feel on it only what I *want* to feel. At the first blow, however, this trust in the world breaks down" (Améry 1980:28; emphasis in original). The traumatization of disappeared insurgents and political opponents by the Argentine armed forces was a calculated strategy on the mental front of the cultural war. The minds, selves, social trust, and political subjectivities of captives were shattered and transformed by the torture practices. What the Argentine military failed to anticipate was the reaction of the relatives of the disappeared.

The state terrorism was so brutal that the already dwindling revolutionary insurgency became out-traumatized through war crimes and crimes against humanity. The ERP leadership admitted defeat in April 1977 and retreated into exile. The Montoneros held on for a few more years but went asunder in 1979. An internal status report concluded that 95 percent of the disappeared Montoneros had been caught through betrayal because abducted comrades had been mentally broken (Gasparini 1988:146). Calveiro (1998:130) and Longoni (2007:44) have argued that the emphasis on treason and betrayal by the defeated Montoneros served to explain away the defeat, to stigmatize the survivors of disappearance as collaborators, and to avoid a questioning of the organization's poor leadership. Worse still, relatives of the disappeared have accused former disappeared and ex-prisoners of having survived by betraying their disappeared loved ones (Longoni 2007:11; Park 2014:45). Yet, irrespective of the number of collaborating captives involved and the extent of the betrayal, mistrust arose in the guerrilla organizations, as former Montonero Ernesto Jauretche explained: "Everything produced an impressive demoralization in the heart of the organization. One couldn't walk in the street. Nobody knew where it was safe because also your own comrades were informers" (interview on 20 April 1991).

Mistrust was precisely what the Argentine military intended to achieve among the insurgents, according to an Argentine counterinsurgency manual from 1967: "The first victory is achieved by instilling fear in the adversary. Thus, one task of the forces of order consists of instilling such fear among the guerrillas. Fear leads to distrust, and distrust leads to uncertainty" (Masi 1967:80). Referring to the enforced disappearances, General Virgilio Górriz told me: "[The guerrillas] carry out an operation, and lose two or three men. They end the operation. They leave and they don't know afterwards whether the others are dead, have been taken prisoner, or something like that. Terror then turns against them. If one of them stays alive, then it is likely that they [the captors] will make him talk. So, this other man who holds all strings in his neighborhood sees himself obliged to leave, has to go abroad, or something like that" (interview on 20 December 1989).

The disintegration of the guerrilla command structures, the instruction to commit suicide with a cyanide capsule when caught, the lack of safe houses, the betrayal by broken collaborating comrades, and the disillusion about a revolution believed to be a historical certainty, caused a complex sociocultural trauma from which the revolutionary insurgency did not recover. Demoralized and defeated, the surviving guerrillas fled abroad or went into internal exile. The heterogeneous political opposition also disintegrated, not by counterinsurgency warfare or anti-terrorism, as the military labeled their operations, but by state terrorism and crimes against humanity.

Family Disruption and Collective Protests

The nefarious state terrorism left deep scars on Argentine society and the relatives searching for their disappeared loved ones. The house raids violated the homes where care between parents and children had been nurtured. These disturbing intrusions by an omnipotent state carried a high symbolic burden through its forced transgression of the deep-seated cultural opposition between public and domestic space. The violation of safety experienced in the home undermined the mutual trust of family members. People's inner, parental, and symbolic protective shields were shattered by the abductions in the home, which in turn jumbled multiple cultural oppositions of inner and outer into an uncanny whole (Robben 2000b). Relatives might suffer from an acute psychic trauma when witnessing a violent abduction, and there were some who were troubled by severe depression or PTSD afterward, but all were affected by the ensuing social and cultural traumas (Kordon, Edelman, Lagos, et al. 1988). The social trauma was caused by the disruption of families and their stigmatization and social isolation in society. The disappearances altered family life, its daily routines and rituals, its joys and intimate feelings. The cultural trauma affected some more than others. Families who were politically conscious knew the price of militant activism and might have personally experienced state repression during earlier dictatorships, but other families found the abductions incomprehensible and relived them endlessly in memory.

Initially, many relatives did not take any public action, afraid that doing so might bring harm to their missing children or endanger other family members. Raquel Marizcurrena remembered her family's reaction: "After my son and his wife disappeared, I never again heard from any of my seven sisters or my brother. They all avoided us. It has been seventeen years since I last saw them. They were terrified that the same thing would happen to them" (Arditti 1999:83). Some families became divided or even remained passive, as in the case of military families, but most united behind the search (Kordon, Edelman, and Lagos 1988:45; see also Agger and Jensen 1996:120). The disappearances also damaged Argentine society because of a prevailing mistrust. The junta painted the picture of a war against shadowy terrorists who concealed bombs in schools and nurseries. Anyone was suspect, even members of the Church and the armed forces. Social isolation and mistrust damaged people's self-confidence and self-worth, as Arendt (1975:474–477) demonstrated in her study of repressive states.

The abductions attacked the relations of trust, safety, protection, and love of family members. Parents felt guilty about having been unable to protect their children, of whom almost two-thirds were abducted at home (CONADEP 1986:11; Secretaría de Derechos Humanos 2015:1560). Parents' feelings of helplessness during military raids translated into feeling that they had failed their abducted children and betrayed their basic trust. Feelings of guilt and impotence were further reinforced when parents realized that the disappeared were dead and that they had been unable to comfort them in their final hour. Irma Morresi grasped the full extent of this sentiment only when her mother died: "when I was watching over my mother, I could close her eyes. That I had not been there at that moment [for my son Norberto], you see. That one can embrace him, even at the end, but to be there personally at the moment of death of a son, a father, anyone . . . With my mother, I was left with a peace. . . . I say: 'Oh, why didn't this happen to me with my son?' At the moment when I closed my mother's eyes, I swear to you, I was thinking of my son. I had this inside of me" (Panizo 2012:243).

After a period of anxiety and terror, the parental love, basic trust, and misplaced feelings of guilt energized the emotional reserves to search year after year for the disappeared children. Parents who had been unable to protect their pregnant daughters from abduction were driven by feelings of love, trust, and protection in their search for missing grandchildren. If the disappeared family member had not been taken from the home, then the searching relatives would visit the place of abduction to gather as much evidence as possible. It was general knowledge that the authorities detained suspected guerrilla combatants and political activists, so parents visited prisons and military bases. The submission of a writ of habeas corpus was also common, and proved to be equally fruitless. Having exhausted institutional and legal means, informal channels were used through the Church and armed forces. Relatives endured all sorts of insults, intimidations, humiliations, and extortion schemes during their search.

Searching relatives were not only betrayed by state agents, priests, and bishops, as I will show in Chapters 4 and 5; they were betrayed as well by the guerrilla commanders who had sacrificed their sons and daughters to the revolution at a time when the chances of victory were doubtful. This betrayal began on 6 September 1974 when the Peronist Montoneros decided to return to the armed struggle, and the ERP founded a standing revolutionary army with a hierarchical command structure and troops in olive green uniforms (Gillespie 1982:164; M. Santucho 1988:41).[6] Tens of thousands of noncombatant cadres and political sympathizers were left unprotected when the guerrilla combatants moved underground. The Montoneros were Latin America's richest guerrilla organization, with more than US$100 million in its war chest, but it refused to distribute funds that would allow collaborators and sympathizers to retreat to safety (Fernández Meijide 2013:144; Gasparini 1990:65). Sixteen years after this fatal decision, Alcira Argumedo is still filled with indignation: "It's a murderous decision because they knew very well that they were condemning these people . . . because these were people of the neighborhood, these were people who couldn't move, who had their children, who were workers, who had no means at all. They were giving them away to the repression" (interview on 9 April 1991). María Adela de Antokoletz, a founding member of the Mothers of the Plaza de Mayo, accused the guerrilla commanders of arrogance, of "believing that they were the owners of truth" (interview on 9 November 1990). But there are also parents who refuse to cast blame on the commanders. Lila Orfanó and her husband were disappeared for ten days in 1976. Their two sons were also abducted in 1976 and remain missing, but Lila does not hold the Montonero leadership responsible: "My sons were politically active [in the Montoneros] because they were convinced about what they were doing. Nobody led them by the nose, you see? They were not cattle. They were thinkers. For this I do not blame them, but I blame them for being very rash because they were not going to achieve anything with guns. . . . They would first have to raise the political consciousness of the people" (interview on 12 November 1990).

The coup d'état of 24 March 1976 did not make the guerrilla commanders pause and rethink their strategy. ERP commander Mario Santucho expected a popular uprising and that same morning he wrote the inflammatory editorial "Argentines, to arms," in which he anticipated that "a river of blood will separate the military from the Argentine people" (Seoane 1991:297). Instead, the Argentine military attacked with full force, and the most important guerrilla commanders decided to leave the country, but Santucho was killed in a fire fight on 19 July 1976, the day he was scheduled to fly to Cuba. Montonero commander Mario Firmenich made a successful escape in September 1976, but, despite the disappearance of thousands of comrades, he still ordered a suicidal counteroffensive in 1979. Before the operation got under way, naval officer Jorge Perren told Graciela Daleo, who was being held captive at the Navy Mechanics School: "We know that they're going to return. They're going to return in the middle of the year, and we're going to be waiting for them with a butterfly net" (interview on 24 October 1990). About 140 guerrillas were captured, of whom only 16 survived (Robben 2005a:163).

Aside from some informal contacts, the Mothers and Grandmothers of the Plaza de Mayo were reluctant to cooperate with human rights organizations in Argentina and Europe that maintained links to the guerrilla organizations. The exiled commanders were mistrusted for betraying their rank and file and for pursuing political objectives instead of finding their disappeared cadres and combatants. Relatives preferred a collective search among themselves, because the state, its agents, the guerrilla commanders, and even relatives and friends could not be trusted. Individual suffering transformed into political protest, and this joint action helped searching relatives cope with their personal anguish. The dictatorship was caught off guard by the mothers' protests because they inverted the military intrusion and traumatization of the domestic domain by exercising in public their maternal right to know the whereabouts of their children (Robben 2005a:304–306).[7]

The counterinsurgency war and state terrorism did not leave the military untouched. Aside from losing hundreds of men, the armed forces traumatized themselves by the crimes against humanity they committed. The decentralized repression had undermined the hierarchical command structure by giving hundreds of small task groups a great liberty of action with little oversight (Fernández 1983:23; Reato 2012:38–41, 145–148; Robben 2005a:192–198). Officers and NCOs carried out operations for which they were ill trained, and low-ranking officers betrayed the most fundamental rights of fellow citizens, in the course of which they damaged their personal integrity and military ethics. The ambivalent emotions about defeating the insurgency and dismantling the revolutionary movement, while smearing the uniform with atrocities, led a subterfuge life even after the fall of the dictatorship. I use the term *sociocultural trauma* here not to equate the troops morally with the guerrilla combatants and the political opponents but to emphasize that the regime's repressive structure and violent agency influenced the military discourse, the troops, and their actions and decisions after the dictatorship fell from power. The denial of the disappearances, the military rebellions, and the refusal to reveal the whereabouts of kidnapped babies can be better understood when analyzed in terms of a sociocultural trauma than as a rational strategy.

The self-inflicted sociocultural trauma was reinforced in June 1982 through a humiliating defeat on the Falkland/Malvinas Islands by British troops. Argentina had invaded the islands to add force to its historical claim to the archipelago and to divert people's attention from the growing labor unrest and human rights protests in Argentina. The shameful return to Argentina devastated the defeated troops. Instead of welcoming servicemen in a parade through Buenos Aires and commemorating the dead comrades left behind on the windswept South Atlantic islands, the veterans of war entered the country furtively. The military defeat and the dishonorable arrival in Argentina created lasting wounds on the armed forces, whose political and emotional sequels deserve to be qualified as traumatic (Lorenz 1999). One officer summed up this situation as follows: "They ordered us to fight against the subversion, saying that we were defending society against the enemy. . . . We were not prepared for that type of fight and they made us do things that we never dreamed of as military men. They said it was for our families. . . . Immediately upon our return [from the Falkland/ Malvinas Islands], they treated us as criminals, they hid us as if we were lepers. . . . The trials ended up crushing us. We didn't speak of anything else in the barracks. The generals didn't defend us; they didn't even take notice of our requests for reforms" (Captain Breide Obeid cited in Grecco and González 1988:224–225).

The conviction of five junta commanders in 1985 and the indictment of many officers caused much resentment and political mistrust against the state. Lower-ranking officers felt betrayed by their commanders who had failed to provide a legal foundation to the repression and refused to declare in court that they had ordered their troops to torture and disappear captives. The psychiatrist Jonathan Shay (1995:195) discovered in his treatment of Vietnam veterans the political danger of traumatized soldiers: "Unhealed combat trauma diminishes democratic participation and can become a

threat to democratic political institutions. Severe psychological injury origi-
nates in violation of trust and destroys the capacity for trust. When mistrust
spreads widely and deeply, democratic civic discourse becomes impossible."
Argentina proved him right.

In 1987, six military bases rose in rebellion against the ongoing trials.
President Alfonsín defused the tense civil-military relations by passing legislation that declared most officers immune from prosecution for acting under
due obedience. The general amnesty appeased the military, but their continued denial of any involvement in the disappearances came back to haunt
them. Massive traumatic experiences cannot be silenced indefinitely because
their multilevel consequences cannot be erased. The public denial by superior
officers, implying that their debasing practices had never taken place, was
intolerable to lower-ranking personnel. Traumatized people, whether victims
or perpetrators, need the world to accept the reality of their experiences in
order to integrate them into individual consciousness and collective memory
(Robben 1996). Denial relegates those experiences to the realm of fantasy.
Some officers suffered from PTSD and were convicted for deeds they knew
were true, and society felt betrayed by a military that had been granted
amnesty in the late 1980s but refused to reciprocate by providing information
regarding the disappearances and the kidnapped babies.

Conclusion

The belief that violence breeds violence is as common as the assumption
that societies need to repress the memory of massive violence for a prolonged period before they can confront and mourn the past. Social scientists have derived this understanding from psychoanalysis and Holocaust
studies. Inspired by the psychoanalytic notion of deferred action or belatedness, this dissociation is considered necessary to protect society against disturbing recollections that might ignite old tensions and endanger the
recovery process (Brett 1993; Freud 1968b:12–18; LaCapra 1996; Laplanche
and Pontalis 1973:111–114). These ideas have guided analyses of Holocaust
memory. "The traumatic event is repressed or denied and registers only
belatedly (nachträglich) after the passage of a period of latency. This effect
of belatedness has of course been a manifest aspect of the Holocaust"
(LaCapra 1998:9). Numerous scholars have demonstrated how the Holocaust was "silenced" after World War II in Europe, the United States, and

Israel.[8] This response to massive death has been common in many other societies with traumatizing pasts, but such deferred action did not occur in Argentina, South Africa, and several Balkan countries.

Psychic trauma and personal memory are intricately related in the contradictory representation of shattering events because the many overwhelming impressions of a traumatic experience can never be encoded fully in memory (McNally 2003:190; Schacter 2001:174). The obstruction to either total recall or total erasure, along with the unending search for meaning, makes psychic traumas undigestible and personal memories obsessive. Persistent problems in coping with psychic trauma may for a small number of people develop into PTSD.

Psychoanalytic theory has developed two explanatory models about posttraumatic reactions. One model explains the recurrent recreation of disturbing events in nightmares and psychoses as compulsive attempts to become familiar with intrusive experiences. This heightened awareness serves to cope with the unknowable and erect anew the protective inner barrier ruptured by the traumatizing assault. The other model clarifies the progressive withdrawal from painful memories into an emotionally restricted private world that suppresses the most intense traumatic experiences. The first model emphasizes selective remembering, while the second underlines selective forgetting (Brett 1993:67; Freud 1968b; Herman 1997:37–50). Both responses help to create universes of meaning that may give people a sense of mastery, orient them to the future instead of the past, and allow them to function better by giving their experiences a place in life.

The psychodynamic duality of selective forgetting and selective remembering also helps to understand the reliving of massive violent events on higher levels of social complexity. "Like psychological ambivalence, its manifestation at the sociocultural level sets the stage for the frequently observed tendency for generation after generation to engage in compulsive examining and reexamining, bringing up new aspects of the trauma, reinterpreting, reevaluating, and battling over symbolic significance" (Smelser 2004:54). On the one hand, recurrent re-experiences serve groups in their search for meaning, precisely because they have selective recollections of the violent events. On the other hand, deliberately shutting out the most inexplicable or undesirable memories makes the traumatic event more manageable. The major difference between psychic trauma and sociocultural trauma is that different groups have different social memories that mutually constitute one another through repeated contestation.

Argentina's sociocultural traumas were not silenced, disavowed, or repressed when the dictatorship ended but were remembered, relived, and narrated. Adversarial groups became enmeshed in each other's memory politics and hindered one another in overcoming their traumas. People could not mourn the losses and integrate their traumatic experiences in a collective understanding when others denied that those experiences had taken place. The violence-trauma-violence dynamics produced very divergent social memories. Antagonistic groups situated these memories in conflicting discursive frames that perpetuated rather than surmounted the sociocultural traumas.

In the decades after 1983, recurrent traumatic memories kept intruding on Argentine society that sustained the social and political mistrust that had arisen during the dictatorship. Relatives continued to search for their disappeared children and grandchildren, ex-disappeared tried to recover from their torture and captivity, unexpected testimonies were given, and new material evidence appeared. Furthermore, traumatized perpetrators had to deal with their mental specters, and the military were trying to redefine their place in Argentine society after losing a conventional war in the South Atlantic and being tried for crimes against humanity committed during the counterinsurgency war and the state terrorism. These returning intrusions from an unelaborated past, the emotional responses they elicited, and the political debates and public protests they provoked, beckoned for meaning as a deeply divided nation was unable to construct a national narrative about its violent past, and in effect remained a traumatized society for decades after the fall of the military regime in 1983.

CHAPTER 2

Memory

Since the return to democracy in December 1983, a month with hopes for the future and anxiety about the fallout of the years past, Argentina has been struggling with the memory of the dictatorship as remembrance fell by the wayside of time. Memories differ from remembrances. Remembrances are personal evocations, while memories are reflective recollections of the past, as French philosopher Paul Ricoeur (2006:39) observes, that mint certain remembrances as genuine whereby "the recognized past tends to pass itself off as a perceived past." The distinction between remembrances and memories is not a parting of waters because remembrances continue to alter memories, and memories can evoke neglected remembrances. If they are so variable, then what makes people trust or mistrust each other's remembrances and memories?

The previous chapter explained that traumatic experiences are so overwhelming that they can never be registered in full and that trauma and the unknowable are therefore created together. People may doubt the remembrances of others, and even their own, because of the bewildering experiences from which they originated. Remembrances will be discussed in the next chapter about testimonies. This chapter examines the trustworthiness of social and collective memories. Social memory applies to a specific group, whereas collective memory refers to a heterogeneous composite of parts of social memories. This collective memory is influenced by a multifaceted state that tries to create a dominant national memory. Memory is an important area of contestation in Argentine society in which state organs and adversarial groups dispute each other's rendition of the traumatic past.

Maurice Halbwachs, who had a great influence on anthropology's understanding of collective memory, rejected "the idea that the past is in itself preserved within individual memories," because the "individual calls

recollections to mind by relying on the frameworks of social memory"
(Halbwachs 1992:173, 182). In a critique of Halbwachs, Ricoeur (2006:95)
argues that memory as individual recollection and social recognition cannot
be reduced to one another because they constitute each other reciprocally.
Ricoeur distinguishes therefore between individual, social, and collective
memory. He attributes different memories "to oneself, to one's close relations, and to others" (132) and poses the rhetorical question: "Does there
not exist an intermediate level of reference between the poles of individual
memory and collective memory, where concrete exchanges operate between
the living memory of individual persons and the public memory of the
communities to which we belong?" (131). These concrete exchanges consist
for Ricoeur of narratives, representations, and memorializations.[1]

Memory has been such a complex area of national contestation in
Argentina that no single particular theoretical approach can explain the
convoluted memory construction during the country's turbulent history.
The first two decades after the fall of the military regime were characterized
by a competitive memory construction based on mutual mistrust. The
twenty-first century has been marked by a transnational memory construction influenced by cosmopolitan discourses of human rights and the legacy
of major historical events. My conceptualization of memory in Argentina
has been inspired, aside from Ricoeur, by the works of Bakhtin, Foucault,
Rothberg, Levy and Sznaider, and Irwin-Zarecka.[2]

Bakhtin's (1981) analysis of the dialogic qualities of language and literature, next to their unifying tendencies, has helped me understand that polemic
discourse is as much a constitutive quality of social memories as is their struggle for hegemony. This rivalry is not only verbal but also manifested in
material and ritual contests, such as memorials and countermemorials and
commemorations and countercommemorations. Foucault has added the
nuance that social memories are not autonomous constructs competing for
supremacy in the public sphere but are mutually constitutive within collective
memory. Collective memory is not a succession of hegemonic social memories, in which one social memory is replaced in whole by another, but "an
unstable assemblage of faults, fissures, and heterogeneous layers that threaten
the fragile inheritor from within or from underneath" (Foucault 1977:146).

Argentine scholars have analyzed Argentina's social and collective memories principally as contentious constructions. Vezzetti (2003) has described
how partisan narratives changed during critical historical events. Cerruti
(2001:24) has depicted the development of collective memory as "Waves

and levels that certainly will continue to evolve and grow, with moments of silence and forgetting, and moments in which everything seems to converge towards the past." She regards the fight for truth and justice by human rights organizations as the engine of this memory process. Finally, Guber (1996) has interpreted the competing representations of Argentine history as dynamic layers of memory. New layers are added and old ones may resurface during historical cataclysms.

Memory contestation about a violent, traumatizing past influences whether people trust each other's social memories. The social memory of a group of people believed to distort a passionately felt truth will not be trusted because this memory leads to a contrary historical narration that can have undesirable political consequences. The definition of Argentina's political violence in the 1970s as a civil war, a revolution, state terrorism, or a defense of sovereignty influences whether to prosecute, pardon, or praise the belligerents. Social memory in Argentina thus became the measure of trust and betrayal for human rights organizations, military interest groups, former guerrilla organizations, and state organs such as the armed forces and the national government.

Argentina's competitive memory construction became increasingly replaced after 2005 by international discourses of victimhood and human rights, and an interest in the Holocaust and global terrorism as historical tragedies comparable to Argentina's recent past. Social memories were no longer shaped through an action-reaction process of social memories and counter-memories but became influenced by transnational memories. Furthermore, Levy and Sznaider (2006:2–6) have demonstrated how the Holocaust became expressed in cosmopolitan memory cultures of human rights as a universal symbol of evil and was then appropriated and transformed into specific national contexts, such as the Atlantic slave trade and the Rwandan genocide. Levy and Sznaider's notion of cosmopolitan memories dovetails with Rothberg's work on multidirectional memories that emerge in "a malleable discursive space in which groups do not simply articulate established positions but actually come into being through their dialogical interactions with others; both the subjects and spaces of the public are open to continual reconstruction" (Rothberg 2009:5). Argentina illustrates this clearly by the contrast between the human rights movement that began to mirror the disappearances into the Holocaust, and military support groups that emphasized the similarities between Argentina's guerrilla insurgency and the global terrorism that followed 11 September 2001.

   A final source of inspiration has been the work of Irwin-Zarecka (1994), who helped me understand how social memories are organized in discursive frames that steer people's understanding of past events and make each frame coherent through a particular interpretational vantage point. She shows how discursive frames interpret memories at certain historical periods because of political struggles among actors and groups vying for dominance: "questions about framing direct our attention to the powers inherent in public articulation of collective memory to influence the private makings of sense" (Irwin-Zarecka 1994:4). Discursive frames transform certain personal remembrances that resonate with those of like-minded others into social memories, whereas other remembrances stay private but may become relevant in the future, in another political context. Discursive frames bestow trustworthiness on social memories by providing plausible interpretations of experiences through meaningful narratives and logical reasoning.

   The collective memories of Argentina's past were constructed out of selective parts of conflicting social memories in terms of dominant discursive frames—at first through the polemical struggles between a multifaceted state and adversarial social groups and later through the adoption of transnational discourses. For example, members of the Argentine military generally agreed that the dictatorship had been waging a just war against a revolutionary insurgency. The political ideology of the guerrilla organizations and the attacks on military bases convinced them of the just war frame as a credible interpretation of the political violence and a justification for the extensive repression. This understanding of the past was shared by only a minority of Argentines because most Argentines distrusted the military's rendition. They found the state terrorism frame used by the human rights organizations more convincing and their social memories more trustworthy. State terrorism then became the dominant discursive frame for a period of time.

   This chapter analyzes memory as an area of national contestation through four dynamic oppositions: denial and disclosure (1983–1987), rebellion and defense (1987–1995), confession and reckoning (1995–2005), and accountability and revision (2005–2016). Each opposition developed new, conflicting social memories that added to previous ones, thus further enhancing the polyphonic complexity of Argentine collective memory. Certain social memories were more prominent in the construction of Argentina's collective memory than others. The choice was guided by discursive frames that identified parts of certain social memories as more faithful while dismissing others as inessential or purely for internal circulation, only to be overlaid at a later time by new discursive frames and other selections of social memories believed to yield a more truthful and politically effective collective memory. In other words, these interpretive or discursive frames privileged particular social memories over others, competed for trust-worthiness, and betrayed other social memories by refusing to acknowledge them as genuine. To complicate matters further, contesting parties began to draw in the 2000s upon cosmopolitan and multidirectional memories to buttress their conflicting narratives. Dirty war was the initial interpretation by military and guerrillas of the political violence during the dictatorship and became replaced by the terms *two-demons theory* or *two terrorisms* after the fall of the military regime in 1983. This frame ultimately failed to con-vince the Argentine people, who mainly heard testimonies about military abuses. State terrorism became the dominant frame in the late 1980s, whereas genocide has become increasingly important since the mid-2000s.

Denial and Disclosure

The transitional military government did its best to influence Argentina's collective memory about the dictatorship during the months leading up to the October 1983 presidential elections. In April 1983, an official document was released that formulated the principal reasons for the military repres-sion: "The Argentine Republic suffered since the mid-60s from a terrorist aggression that, with the use of violence, tried to achieve a political project destined to subvert the moral and ethical values shared by an immense majority of Argentines" (Junta Militar 1983:1). The government tried to impress four points on the Argentine people. One, the military response had been a legitimate anti-revolutionary war against a guerrilla insurgency supported by Cuba and the Soviet Union. This war had been won at the cost of hundreds of patriotic officers, soldiers, and policemen. Two, the junta had put Argentina on the right track. It halted the political disintegra-tion, stimulated the economy, and ended corruption and nepotism. Three, the war was not a conventional war between uniformed troops but a coun-terinsurgency war that demanded unconventional methods. Operations were carried out with a constitutional mandate and within the margins of the law. Torture and disappearance were not officially sanctioned but were the inevitabilities of irregular warfare. Four, the armed forces were an inextricable part of Argentine society, had stood at the birth of the nation, and were the only stable state institution since the days of independence.

The transitional government was trying to create a national narrative, which they hoped would be accepted by the Argentine people. This historical rendition only increased people's mistrust of the military because the portrayal was blatantly untrue. There was indeed political violence in the mid-1960s, but the document failed to mention that the military coup of 1966 had contributed significantly to its emergence. The 1976 authoritarian regime had gone one step further: it had staged a coup on the pretense that the nation's existence was in peril while the guerrilla insurgency was in decline. Furthermore, corruption, nepotism, and abuse of power had not been curbed but soared during the dictatorship.

The military master narrative was set in the discursive frame of dirty war, a term that assumed that international war conventions were broken out of tactical necessity. Outside Argentina, the term *dirty war* has become synonymous with the torture, disappearance, and assassination of tens of thousands of civilians by the military regime, but its etymology reveals a serpentine trajectory. The term *dirty war* (*sucia guerra* [sic]) first appeared in the 7 March 1974 issue of the ultranationalist magazine *Cabildo* to describe the Marxist guerrilla insurgency (Curutchet 1974). The term was adopted in August 1974 by the Peronist left to denounce the death squads of the Peronist right. "Comrades, there's no longer any sense in beating about the bush. We cannot simply continue to call repression what is in fact a war. A dirty war (*guerra sucia*) against the people" (Galimberti 1974:2). The term's meaning shifted again after the March 1976 coup d'état when the Montoneros accused the armed forces of war crimes. "This is a dirty war, like all wars waged by reactionary armies. It is not just dirty because it uses the people's sons to fight against their brothers and their interests, but because it doesn't even respect the war conventions. The enemy assassinates the wounded, tortures and executes prisoners, and turns its brutality against the relatives of the people's combatants" (*Evita Montonera* 1976, 12:32).

The term *dirty war* was soon used by the Argentine military to describe the unconventional methods deployed by both belligerents. "This is a dirty war, a war of attrition, dark and sly, which one wins with resolve and calculation, and principally with the help of the people supporting the cause being defended" (Vilas 1976:9). Dirty war had become a self-referential discursive frame that interpreted the armed violence as a just war fought with indiscriminate means against so-called subversives who threatened the Argentine national being and its Western, Christian culture. It was a cultural war, as I have argued elsewhere (Robben 2005a:172), waged to determine Argentina's future and way of life. The term *dirty war* was thus embedded in two Manichaean worldviews in which all means were allowed. General Díaz Bessone told me in 1989, "We haven't violated the law of God. For me, this is a just war because we weren't the ones who attacked" (interview on 24 July 1989). The guerrilla insurgency also believed itself to be waging a just war, namely against a praetorian military that protected an exploitative ruling class: "against that violence by the exploiting class, the masses put up their own war, the just war of popular resistance" (*El Combatiente* 1976, 219:8).

The dirty war frame failed to convince the human rights movement. Most Argentines supported the view of the human rights movement—in part because of its moral high ground and in part because of the testimonies of torture victims in the press—that the term *dirty war* was inaccurate because a war implied a military confrontation between two hostile armies representing sovereign states (Frontalini and Caiati 1984). Instead, the Argentine military had usurped state power and used state terror against a defenseless Argentine population and a guerrilla insurgency that had been nearly defeated in December 1975. The moral antagonism and conflicting social memories of the military and the human rights movement solidified their internal trust by "maintaining social bonds and claiming authority, for mobilizing action and legitimating it" (Irwin-Zarecka 1994:67). Profound disagreements over the morality and politics of the dirty war articulated concomitant memories, and this public contest was fought in the news media to persuade the Argentine people of their truth. The uncertain fate of the disappeared proved to be the litmus test of credibility.

The military junta had declared in April 1983 that "those who appear on the lists of disappeared and are not living in exile or in hiding are considered dead in legal and administrative terms, even when now the cause and occasion of the unexpected death or the place of burial cannot yet be determined" (Junta Militar 1983:13). The military were greatly mistrusted, and the opinion in May 1983 of Argentine Nobel Peace Prize laureate and ex-disappeared Rodolfo Pérez Esquivel carried more weight: "there are still people alive in concentration camps, and if there is only one person alive then he or she must be freed alive" (*Somos* 1983, 346:16). I will analyze the military's discourse about the disappearances in Chapter 4, but here it is clear that conflicting memory constructions and the suspicion of betrayal shared in these years a discursive arena centered on the continued denial by the military that systematic disappearances had taken place, and the sustained efforts by human rights organizations to disclose them.

In December 1983, newly elected President Raúl Alfonsín installed the National Commission on the Disappeared (CONADEP). Although the CONADEP has become known as one of the world's first truth commissions (Hayner 2001:14), this label fails to convey its full mission. The CONADEP bore a closer resemblance to the fact-finding missions that visited Argentina during the dictatorship because the commission was created to find the disappeared that were still in the military's hands, at least according to Pérez Esquivel. On the evening of 20 September 1984, the CONADEP presented its report to the Argentine government, accompanied by seventy thousand people united under the slogan "punishment for the guilty." A summary of the report, entitled "Never Again" ("Nunca Más"), became available at newsstands around the country. It sold 110,000 copies within one month and more than half a million copies worldwide by 2007 (Moreno Ocampo 1999:682; Crenzel 2008:131). This was the first systematic description of military repression widely available to the Argentine people, and it added an authoritative, official narrative to the conflicting voices of the armed forces and the human rights movement.

The CONADEP report did not pronounce all disappeared dead but did mention "that many of them are dead and that their bodies have been scattered or destroyed as part of a planned policy of making them disappear" (CONADEP 1986:233). This conclusion was psychologically devastating and politically unacceptable to many searching relatives. The meaning of a disappeared person as someone alive yet missing had changed into someone dead yet unaccounted for. Unlike in the case of the Holocaust, where the absence of forensic proof for millions of exterminated camp inmates was explained by the Nazi logic of genocide and the existence of gas chambers and crematoria, the Argentine military regime lacked such open genocidal ideology and visible infrastructure of mass murder. It had always denied having the disappeared in captivity and thus, paradoxically, nurtured a hope that was hard to abandon. In fact, Hebe de Bonafini of the Mothers of the Plaza de Mayo stated in December 1984: "Yes, we are certain that there are disappeared persons alive. There are many very desperate mothers who receive very concrete facts about their children but who don't undertake anything because they feel abandoned by the government" (*Madres* 1984, 1(1):2). In June 1985, truth commission member Magdalena Ruiz Guiñazu testified in court that "unfortunately we have found nobody alive, not even in hospitals. We went to the Borda [psychiatric hospital] with relatives, examining patient by patient to see if we could find anyone" (*El Diario del Juicio* 1985, 7:156). However, CONADEP's presumption of death failed to undo the military's denial of the disappearances, and this corroded the political trust in the Argentine state.

The CONADEP report became portrayed in the media as voicing the government's so-called two-demons theory (la teoría de los dos demonios) by stating in the prologue: "The armed forces responded to the terrorists' crimes with a terrorism far worse than the one they were combating" (CONADEP 1986:1). President Raúl Alfonsín had rejected the term *dirty war* and emphasized that the Argentine military and guerrilla insurgents had been two evils; two armed gangs or two terrorisms that had both been responsible for the escalating violence. This discursive frame was undergirded by two decrees that ordered the prosecution of seven guerrilla commanders and nine junta leaders (San Martino de Dromi 1988, 2:547–549). Argentina's decade of political violence thus became reduced to the confrontation of two armed enemies.

The major flaw in the two-demons theory is not just that it suggests a symmetrical armed conflict between two opposed forces, whereas it was a disproportionate attack by state forces on a crumbling guerrilla insurgency, but that it ignores the crucial contribution of the heterogeneous political opposition to the revolutionary climate of the 1970s and the dictatorship's assault on a political opposition movement that ranged from labor unions and student unions to grassroots organizations and agrarian leagues. The armed violence deserves instead to be interpreted as only one of several political practices during a complex period of Argentine history. The insurgency would not have emerged, or at least not have grown to such proportions, without class-conscious groups that organized labor strikes, rallied street demonstrations, and mobilized a grassroots resistance. These symbiotic practices ceased once the guerrilla organizations became militarized and tried to feed on the political opposition movement for its combatants. The larger political support dried up and the logic of armed contest took over when the Argentine military began to equate political opponents with guerrilla combatants. According to the abducted physician Norberto Liwski, one officer "told me they knew I was not involved with terrorism or the guerrillas, but that they were going to torture me because I opposed the regime, because: 'I hadn't understood that in Argentina there was no room for any opposition to the Process of National Reorganization'" (CONADEP 1986:21–22). The Alfonsín government's two-demons theory failed to emphasize that the armed conflict was asymmetrical, that the military response was excessive, and that a heterogeneous opposition movement had contributed to a revolutionary atmosphere that was receptive to political violence.

After the members of the Supreme Council of the Armed Forces failed to carry out the presidential decree by refusing to prosecute their peers, the nine junta commanders who had ruled Argentina between 1976 and 1982 were tried in a civilian court. The trial of April–December 1985 was the state's second comprehensive attempt to influence Argentina's collective memory. Its reconstruction did not replace but added to the memory forged by the CONADEP report (Osiel 2000). The proceedings were published in the weekly magazine *El Diario del Juicio*, which sold millions of copies. Months of painful testimonies by survivors of secret detention centers, mothers searching for their disappeared children, and grandmothers trying to recover their grandchildren, contrasted with the curt answers and lapses of memory by the military officers. The hearings were public but President Alfonsín decided that television broadcasts would be mute and restricted to three minutes a day to avoid turning the trial into a spectacle (Feld 2002:26, 38). Fear of the military was probably the real reason. The image of the nine junta commanders sitting in the accused stand and the soundless sobs of the witnesses gave the trial an unreal quality that mirrored the ambiguous status of the disappeared (neither dead nor alive) and the truth commission's contradictory conclusion (all disappeared are dead but there is little forensic evidence).

The sentencing of the once omnipotent military commanders had a tremendous impact on a collective memory saturated with heart-wrenching testimonial accounts and the CONADEP report. The systematic questioning by judges, lawyers, and public defenders about the precise place and circumstance of abduction, torture, and rape convinced many people. The court's authority temporarily suspended the memory contestation between the military and the human rights organizations (González Bombal 1995:210–214). Collective memory was now under the sway of the judges. The conviction of Lieutenant-General Videla, Admiral Massera, and three other junta commanders in December 1985 for organizing "secretly a criminal mode of combating terrorism" (Cámara Nacional 1987, 1:266) and the thirty-year sentence of Montonero commander Firmenich in May 1987 confirmed the government's two-demons theory.

Former guerrilla insurgents criticized the two-demons theory. Some spoke of a civil war harking back to the nineteenth century, while others compared Argentina's political violence to the anti-imperialist struggles in Vietnam and Nicaragua. Both rejected a moral equation of troops and insurgents because the revolutionary violence of the 1970s was regarded as a justified response to the exploitation of Argentine society (Cazes Camarero 1986). These discursive frames failed to catch on because of the public prestige of the human rights movement that also rejected the two-demons theory frame but preferred the term *state terrorism* as a reaction to the military's denial of systematic disappearances (Frontalini and Caiati 1984). The dynamics of denial and disclosure between 1983 and 1987 placed the two parties in an adversarial opposition, whereas the former guerrillas became sidelined in the public debate. The human rights movement and the military were thus locked in conflicting recollections, in which the first disregarded the role of the guerrilla insurgency and the second downplayed the systematic abuse of noncombatant political opponents. The military could not accept the accusations at the cost of self-incrimination, while the human rights movement, of course, could not accept the denials. These dialogical dynamics marked a shift toward state terrorism as the discursive frame of the human rights movement and would become the dominant interpretational frame after 1987 when the government withdrew from the public debate to embark on a politics of forgetting and pacification.

The 1984 CONADEP report, the 1985 verdict, and years of survivor testimonies yielded so much incriminating evidence that a response became inevitable. The military reacted with three discursive strategies that resembled the typical responses of most repressive regimes: "the classic discourse of official denial, the conversion of a defensive position into an attack on the critic, and the partial acknowledgment of criticism" (Cohen 2001:102).

First, the military reiterated that Argentina had been in a state of war. Whereas they had used dirty war as their discursive frame between 1976 and 1983, in 1984 they shifted to terms also used during the dictatorship, such as *anti-revolutionary war* and the *fight against subversion*. The armed forces had the constitutional right and obligation to defend its sovereignty, they argued. The Argentine military criticized the two-demons theory and spoke of a fight between good and evil. They drew comparisons with the

Allied bombardments of Dresden and Hiroshima to justify the use of unconventional means to achieve victory and spoke of having fought a decisive battle in the Cold War between capitalist and communist ideologies. These incipient transnational references would take another twenty years to mature into a sustained multidirectional memory discourse. Second, the denial of systematic disappearances had been discredited by the truth commission and the trial of the junta commanders. In the face of growing material proof, the military cast doubt on the quality of the evidence, the forensic methodology, the credibility of the testimonies, the political ideology of the eyewitnesses, and the circumstances under which the disappearances had taken place. The third discursive strategy consisted of portraying the military as victims of political persecution and regarding the convicted military commanders as martyrs.

Notwithstanding these three discursive strategies, high-ranking military officers were at a loss about how to respond to the prosecution of officers accused of crimes against humanity. Officers who had participated in counterinsurgency and intelligence operations were becoming disgruntled about their commanders' passiveness in defending them. They were determined to escape prosecution and make Argentine society put the past to rest.

Between 1983 and 1987, the dynamics of denial and disclosure organized the diverse social memories of the Argentine state, military interest groups, ex-guerrillas, survivors of disappearance, former political prisoners, searching relatives, and members of human rights groups into three conflicting discursive frames that yielded a continuous flow of new revelations about past abuses and an equally persistent succession of disavowals. Denials and disclosures developed through dialogical interaction, as Bakhtin (1981) and Foucault (1977) have theorized, and were set in opposite discursive frames (Irwin-Zarecka 1994). The juxtaposition of the state's two-demons theory, the military's anti-revolutionary war, and the frame of state terrorism proposed by the human rights movement was eventually decided in favor of the latter because of the convincing survivor testimonies.

Rebellion and Defense

The conviction of five junta commanders in December 1985 paved the way for more prosecutions. However, growing disgruntlement in military ranks and Alfonsín's desire to reconcile Argentine society led Congress to pass a

Full Stop Law (Ley de Punto Final) on 23 December 1986. The law imposed a sixty-day statute of limitations on new indictments, but hundreds of complaints were filed nevertheless. In protest, six army bases rose in mutiny in April 1987.

The Plaza de Mayo was packed to capacity as people feared another coup d'état. President Alfonsín boarded a helicopter near the presidential palace to confront rebel leader Lieutenant-Colonel Aldo Rico personally. Rico assured him that they were not after a fall of the government but only wanted a national reconciliation and a political solution to the trials. Alfonsín confided to Rico that he was about to submit new legislation to Congress, and Rico agreed to surrender (Grecco and González 1988; López 1988:74–82; Norden 1996:128–130; Waisbord 1991).

On 4 June 1987, the government proposed the Due Obedience Law (Ley de Obediencia Debida), which filled many people with disgust and caused the human rights movement to accuse Alfonsín of betraying his electoral promise of truth and justice. The amnesty law distinguished three levels of commission. The higher the rank, the greater the responsibility. Most accusations against officers were thus declared unfounded because they had carried out orders given by higher-ranking officers. Only theft, rape, and the kidnapping of babies remained punishable.

Now free from prosecution, retired military officers continued to contest the state's two-demons theory. Books appeared about the guerrilla insurgency and the gestation of a revolutionary war in Argentina (Díaz Bessone 1988; FAMUS 1988; Méndez 1988). Amnestied generals wrote op-ed pieces in conservative newspapers to emphasize that the Argentine armed forces had been at war, and religious services were held to honor fallen comrades. The solidarity organization FAMUS, or Relatives and Friends of the Victims of Subversion, held commemorations at the Plaza de Mayo. Also, an initiative was undertaken in 1989 to erect a memorial "to defend the memory of those Argentine and foreign heroes and martyrs immolated in the unending holocaust by the servants of Marxist subversive ambitions" (Cambareri 1990:28). These efforts openly antagonized and entrenched the human rights movement and made searching relatives and human rights activists only more determined to proclaim their social memories in public.

President Alfonsín's successor, Carlos Saúl Menem, completed the reconciliation policies by pardoning 277 indicted guerrillas, policemen, and rebel officers in October 1989. The release in December 1990 of the

convicted Montonero commander Firmenich and the incarcerated junta
members Videla, Viola, Agosti, Massera, and Lambruschini was regarded
by President Menem as a final effort in pursuit of national pacification and
an end to the two-demons theory on which the original indictments had
been founded. Former President Alfonsín regarded the pardons as willful
forgetting: "One cannot decree the amnesia of an entire society because
every time anyone tried to sweep the past under the carpet, the past
returned with a vengeance."[3]

Deeply shaken by the presidential pardons and without much power of
public mobilization for what most Argentines considered a closed
chapter—as indicated by the poor attendance at annual commemorations of
the coup d'état between 1989 and 1995—the human rights movement feared
that the collective memory of the dictatorship would slowly dissolve (Lorenz
2002). The human rights movement survived these lean years of memory
politics through the continued exhumation of mass graves by forensic
anthropologists, the weekly protests of the Mothers of the Plaza de Mayo,
and the successful search for kidnapped children by the Grandmothers of the
Plaza de Mayo. Meanwhile, lawyers examined international law for ways to
hold the Argentine military accountable. Furthermore, whereas memorialization had been rejected in the mid-1980s as a symbolic acceptance of death
and a closure of the human rights protests, by 1990 numerous initiatives were
taken to create permanent reminders of state terrorism. Memorialization
consisted of preserving memory sites, raising memorials, and documenting
survivor testimonies. A few memorials had been erected since 1983, but the
number of memorial plaques, street names, monuments, monoliths, and
murals increased rapidly after 1990 and especially in the years leading up to
the twentieth anniversary of the military coup in 1996 (Díaz 2002). Yet, these
efforts also created mistrust between human rights organizations. The two
separate organizations of the Mothers of the Plaza de Mayo, which had split
in 1986, were at odds over the memorialization. The Mothers of the Plaza de
Mayo Founding Line supported the memorials, but the Mothers of the Plaza
de Mayo Association was against it, favoring street politics instead (Robben
2000a). Nevertheless, both organizations continued to share the same discursive frame of state terrorism to understand the military regime, and both
maintained their weekly presence at the Plaza de Mayo.

State terrorism (*terrorismo de estado*) was already a preferred term
among Argentines living in exile during the dictatorship. They distinguished the political violence inflicted by nonstate insurgents from the

illegitimate violence employed by the state (Duhalde 1983:19). The term *state terrorism* did not become dominant in Argentine public discourse after the fall of the military dictatorship in 1983 because of the government's two-demons theory. The military's persistent denial of torture and disappearances continued after the amnesty laws of 1986 and 1987 and motivated survivors to accumulate further proof of state terrorism. Numerous accounts appeared in magazines, books, and the media that affirmed the testimonies given during the 1985 trial against the junta commanders.[4]

The dynamics of rebellion and defense between 1987 and 1995 demonstrated the political fluctuations of Argentina's collective memory construction and the divergence among the participants. Every group had its own truth and public agenda. Officers on active duty had accomplished a judicial closure of the past with a successful rebellion, while veteran officers of the dictatorship continued to divulge their social memory about Argentina's anti-revolutionary war, denying any wrongdoing. Former guerrillas returning from exile had kept a low profile, and a number of ex-disappeared had joined the human rights movement. The human rights movement had been forced to relinquish the demand for accountability, and concentrated now on memorializing the past and turning state terrorism into the dominant discursive frame. Finally, the Argentine state pursued the pacification of Argentine society and withdrew from active memory politics. These diverse interests were to clash in the next decade.

Confession and Reckoning

The confession of Navy Captain Francisco Scilingo in March 1995 that he had thrown sedated captives from a plane stirred popular resentment that had been smoldering in Argentine society about the continued impunity of perpetrators. The pardoned junta members reaffirmed their denial of any wrongdoing immediately, but the active-duty commanders of the three armed forces and the police admitted in April 1995 that their institutions had been responsible for human rights violations. Army Commander General Balza declared that the political violence had begun with the guerrilla operations in 1973, and that the "Army, educated and trained for classical warfare, did not know how to confront this demented terrorism with the law," adding that "almost all of us are guilty of the confrontation among Argentines by act or omission, by absence or excess, by consent or by

advice."[5] This official pronouncement created a public split between two
social memories among the military. A group of seventy retired generals,
many of them active during the dictatorship, issued a declaration defending
the repression. They reiterated that the guerrillas had started the political
violence by assassinating General Aramburu in 1970, attacking police stations, and kidnapping businessmen to finance the insurgency. The military
had acted in a lawful manner by sentencing captured guerrillas in federal
court, only to see them released by the amnesty of 25 May 1973. The escalating violence and political chaos in 1974 and 1975 could have been halted only
by a coup d'état.[6] General Balza's admission broke the military pact of denial
but was nevertheless received with ambivalence by the human rights movement. Balza had acknowledged the torture and disappearances in veiled terms
but had used the state's two-demons theory to explain the violence.

The military admission of guilt encouraged former guerrillas to speak
out publicly as well. A few had written about the insurgency during the late
1980s (Cazes Camarero 1989; Gasparini 1988; Mattini 1990; J. Santucho
1988), and some had found their way into grassroots organizations and
the human rights movement, while many were living private lives. They
confirmed that many comrades had been subjected to the state's repressive
practices but emphasized that the armed insurgency was their own free
choice. They had been revolutionaries first, and torture victims second
(Anguita and Caparrós 1997, 1998a; Diana 1997; Jauretche 1997; Perdía
1997). The participation in the public debate by former guerrilla commanders upset many relatives of the disappeared. They blamed the commanders
for the death of their loved ones and accused them of hypocrisy by accepting the amnesties and pardons that had benefited them and the military
while not coming forward to help clarify the disappearances by providing
the names of missing combatants and the circumstances under which they
had disappeared.

The admissions of guilt by Scilingo and Balza made Congress accept an
initiative in February 1998 to derogate the amnesty legislation and pass a
law to erect a monument to the victims of state terrorism. The veterans
responded immediately. The first of three in memoriam books was published in 1998; it contained short biographies of the victims of Argentine
terrorism between 1960 and 1989 "to pay a well-deserved homage to those
who sacrificed their lives in defense of Argentine society in a fight that
culminated during the disastrous decade of the seventies" (Díaz Bessone
2001:9). The books list 508 casualties of the armed and security forces and

174 civilians assassinated by the revolutionary insurgency. In conjunction, a commemorative plaque was revealed at the officers' club on 29 May 1998 with the inscription "Memory and Truth" and a list of eighty-one club members who had been assassinated. The publications, documentaries, and public commemorations by the retired military served mainly to close ranks because the general public was hardly included (Acuña 2000; AUNAR 1999; Gassino and Bonifacino 2001). What these veterans had not anticipated was that the greatest threat would come from Army Commander Balza, who wanted to distance himself from his former superiors. Balza declared in June 1998 that the Argentine military had used a standard operating procedure to separate children from their abducted parents and give them to military families. The pardoned Lieutenant-General Videla was arrested on 9 June on kidnapping charges, and many other officers were to follow.[7]

The embattled veterans felt betrayed by General Balza and abandoned by the armed forces, which refused to provide legal counsel. Unexpected support came from a young generation of civilians that used new media to present a revisionist history of the 1970s. In 2000, the web-based group Argentines for Complete Memory (Argentinos por la Memoria Completa) emerged in support of the incarcerated military: "we try to mobilize those people who do not have a partial or hemiplegic memory . . . and show together that the memory of our society will not be nullified by decree."[8] Books were published that claimed to provide an evenhanded history by telling "the other side of the truth that is hidden, and that a partial truth (or a third or a quarter) is a virtual lie" (Márquez 2004:14). The authors argued that the government, the human rights movement, former guerrillas, and leftist intellectuals had silenced the victims of terrorism and had created political myths such as thirty thousand disappeared, state terrorism, and the theft of babies (Márquez 2006, 2008; Viotto Romano 2005). They entered Argentina's memory debate under the pretense of objective historical truth but, in fact, limited themselves to describing the armed violence between 1970 and 1976, the kidnapping of businessmen, the assassination of officers, and the rural guerrilla insurgency in Tucumán Province (Ranalletti 2010).

Scilingo's confession in 1995 and the coup d'état's twentieth anniversary in 1996 provided a fresh impetus to the memorialization of the repressive past begun in 1990. Students from the prestigious Colegio Nacional de Buenos Aires suggested in 1996 that a monument be erected in remembrance of the high school's disappeared (Tappatá de Valdez 2003:97). Most human rights organizations embraced the idea and on 10 December 1997 launched the plan to incorporate the monument in a Memory Park (Parque de la Memoria) at the edge of the La Plata River. President Menem's ill-timed proposal in January 1998 to tear down the notorious Navy Mechanics School (ESMA) and construct a monument to national unity in its place caused an uproar.[9] The proposal was seen as yet another attempt by the state to erase the national memory of the dictatorship. Menem's project was withdrawn when a judge ruled that the buildings belonged to Argentina's cultural patrimony. Instead, the plan for a memory park was submitted in March 1998 to the Buenos Aires legislature and approved in July 1998 in the reigning climate of accountability and memorialization. The ESMA was finally designated a memorial museum on 24 March 2004 by President Kirchner.

The forensic absence of most disappeared persons, the abundance of public testimonies by survivors, and the piecemeal confessions by perpetrators after their amnesty in the 1980s made the human rights movement pursue the preservation of memory sites and erect memorials, monuments, museums, and a memory park. Similar developments occurred worldwide under the influence of Holocaust commemorations and the global spread of Holocaust museums since the 1980s (Huyssen 2003:99; Williams 2007:7; Young 1993). The transmission of Holocaust memory served also as a model of how to remember Argentina's traumatic past (Guelerman 2001). The aim was to provide tangible proof, historical truth, and material representations for future generations. Sites of memory, as French historian Nora (1978, 1984) has coined them, were to prevent a national amnesia. However, this chapter is not concerned with the aesthetics, semiotics, and material culture of Argentina's hundreds of memorials and memory sites.[10] What interests me here are the controversies raised by the wave of memorializations in relation to the conflicting social memories.

The planning of Argentina's Memory Park, and especially the memorial walls of the granite Monument to the Victims of State Sponsored Terrorism with the names of those who died or disappeared between 1970 and 1983, revealed serious disagreements within the human rights movement. Several human rights organizations, including the Mothers de Plaza de Mayo Association, were opposed: "The Mothers do not want a monument that becomes a cemetery to bemoan our dead" (Vecchioli 2000:53). The project incorporated the memorial walls in a sinuous fissure that traversed part of the fourteen-hectare park to symbolize "the wound caused by the violent

acts perpetrated by the State" (Alegre 2005:62). Resembling the Vietnam
Veterans Memorial in Washington, DC, the design raised doubts because
the Argentine disappeared were neither soldiers nor confirmed dead. Nora
de Cortiñas therefore wanted a transparent wall because stone reminded
her of a tomb and the pantheons common in Argentine cemeteries (interview on 25 March 2010).

The proposal to eternalize Argentina's disappeared in five memorial
walls sparked a particularly sensitive issue: how many people had disappeared? The truth commission had documented almost nine thousand
disappeared (CONADEP 1986:447). Most human rights organizations persisted in putting that number at thirty thousand (Vecchioli 2000:1–2, 72–
73).[11] And what about the persons killed by guerrilla organizations? Should
they also be included in the list of victims? Opponents regarded the monument as a political move by the state and several human rights groups to
memorialize the past and solidify Argentina's collective memory. Should
persons be included who disappeared during democratic times or who had
died in armed confrontations with the Argentine military? Should victims
be listed chronologically, alphabetically, or by family? The memorial's thirty
thousand stone slabs remained empty for years because of these disagreements (Alegre 2005). Hebe de Bonafini contested the state's authority to
add the names of her sons to the memorial and threatened to remove them
with "a pickaxe, hammers and metal cutters" (Vecchioli 2001:100).

Despite these setbacks, the memorialization was well under way. In
another effort to influence Argentina's collective memory, the city council
of Buenos Aires decided in 2001 to turn 24 March into a Day of Memory
(Día de la Memoria) to commemorate the 1976 military coup. Every year
on this day, flags would fly at half-mast from official buildings. Schools
would offer educational programs about the dictatorship, and the city
would organize various public activities.[12] These were attempts to forge a
collective memory where there still existed discordance and provide a public space for an ever-distant past without forgetting the losses suffered.

In December 2001, a severe economic crisis led to nationwide food
riots, the death of protesters by police bullets, and a state of siege that
echoed the years of military rule (Auyero 2007). Calls for the derogation of
the amnesty laws became louder and strengthened the determination of the
human rights movement to make state terrorism the dominant discursive
frame of Argentina's collective memory. Exactly one year later, the Space
for Memory Institute (Instituto Espacio para la Memoria) was created for

"the preservation and transmission of the memory and history of the events that took place during State Terrorism, from the 1970s and the beginning of the 1980s till the recovery of the State of Law" (Careaga 2009:110). The organization included nine human rights organizations. The Founding Line mothers joined the institute, but the larger and more uncompromising Association mothers refused to memorialize the past.

The memorialization initiatives and judicial efforts to hold perpetrators accountable began to pay off in 1995 when Navy Captain Scilingo's admission of guilt set a dynamic of confession and reckoning in motion. The 1998 detention of junta commanders on kidnapping charges, and the political crisis of 2001, further strengthened the determination to bring the military to trial. Argentine President Kirchner, elected in 2003, embraced the human rights movement, idealized the guerrilla organizations, and supported the memorializations. He became the driving force behind the Supreme Court's derogation of the amnesty laws in 2005 and the presidential pardons in 2007, as will be elaborated in Chapter 6.

State terrorism had become the dominant discursive frame by the turn of the twentieth century. Not the political violence of the 1970s but the crimes against humanity stood at the center of Argentina's collective memory. It is telling that the government's secretary of human rights, Eduardo Luis Duhalde, added a new prologue to the CONADEP report that emphasized the state terrorism and rejected President Alfonsín's two-demons theory (Crenzel 2008:174–177; Duhalde 2006a, 2006b). Hebe de Bonafini supported Duhalde: "Our children were not demons. They were revolutionaries, guerrillas—wonderful and unique—who defended the Fatherland."[13] Shifting discursive frames had first turned guerrillas from subversives into terrorists, then into civilian victims of state terrorism, and now into insurgents, revolutionaries, and heroes. The diverse designations continued to circulate in Argentine society because different social groups produced other social memories and periodically elevated one discursive frame or another to national prominence.

Accountability and Revision

The fourth period of Argentine memory politics started in 2005 after the amnesty laws had been derogated. Accountability and revision constituted a dynamic opposition between social memories that brought increasingly more perpetrators to the stand and forced the military to finally admit fully to the human rights violations which a group of aging retired officers nevertheless continued to defend on moral, ideological, and geopolitical grounds. The competitive memory construction that had characterized earlier decades faded as attention turned to transnational discourses of human rights and victimhood. Despite the success of its state terrorism frame, the human rights movement began developing in the mid-2000s a parallel interpretive frame that focused on genocide. There was no compelling judicial reason to do so because crimes against humanity and genocide were equally without a statute of limitations.

The use of the term *genocide* was not new. The Argentine Human Rights Commission (CADHU), a vocal group of political refugees and exiled revolutionaries in Europe, denounced the Argentine military in March 1977 for "the genocidal acts of which the Argentine people are the victim" and for keeping thousands of citizens in "military and police barracks that have been transformed into genuine concentration camps" (CADHU 1977:9; Guest 1990:66–68). This chapter addresses the effect of the genocide frame on memory construction. The multiple uses of the term *genocide* in Argentina will be elaborated in Chapter 7.

The Argentine genocide discourse after 2005 made Holocaust studies directly relevant. Research about the social memories of a secret detention center (Bianchi 2009), labor relations under genocide (Cieza 2009), everyday life under repression (Caviglia 2006a, 2006b), and the role of rescuers (Casiro 2006) all echoed the Holocaust literature. Furthermore, the journal *Revista de Estudios sobre Genocidio (Journal of Genocide Studies)* was founded in 2007 to encourage an academic debate about the Argentine genocide. There were also effects on the sites of memory. The CONADEP report had in 1984 classified the clandestine detention centers (centros clandestinos de detención) into prisoner assessment centers (lugares de reunión de detenidos) and transit camps (lugares transitorios) (CONADEP 1986:76). By 2007, the human rights organizations preferred the term *clandestine detention, torture, and extermination centers (centros clandestinos de detención, tortura, y exterminio)*, which were identified as "genuine concentration camps" (Instituto Memoria 2008:8).

The discursive shift from state terrorism to genocide reflected a worldwide trend in what have been called transnational memories, multidirectional memories, and cosmopolitan memory cultures that arose during the accelerating globalization after the fall of the Berlin Wall in 1989. The

Holocaust became a universal paradigm of victimhood, evil, and testimony.[14] The correspondence between the Holocaust and Argentina's disappearances disclosed neglected remembrances and exposed new perpetrators
by altering "who counts as a subject of justice, and what is the appropriate
frame" (Fraser 2005:80; Rothberg 2009:19–21). The membership of the
social categories of victim, survivor, perpetrator, and bystander changed
when genocide emerged as a new discursive frame for recollecting and
interpreting the past.

The year 2007 galvanized several memorialization initiatives. President
Kirchner broke the stalemate about the Monument to the Victims of State
Terror by enforcing law 46/98, which stated that the names of the disappeared listed in the truth commission report and those of persons killed by
the military and police since 1969 had to be inscribed on the memorial
walls (CONADEP 1985; Careaga 2009:119). Kirchner unveiled the monument on 7 November 2007. The memorial plaque reads: "The list of this
monument comprises the victims of state terrorism, disappeared and assassinated detainees and those who died fighting for the same ideals of justice
and impartiality." The walls contain 8,727 names, including the names of
fallen guerrillas and the children of Hebe de Bonafini, who always opposed
the memorialization efforts. The names are grouped by year of disappearance or death and listed alphabetically with the victim's age at the time of
disappearance or death but without any other distinctions. More than
21,000 slabs remain empty.

In an important symbolic gesture, in 2007 the Argentine government
handed the infamous Navy Mechanics School (ESMA) to the human rights
organizations that had been designated for their use in 2004. Also in 2007,
the state began to provide funding to the Space for Memory Institute (Instituto Espacio para la Memoria) that had been created in 1999. This umbrella
of human rights organizations became a crucial force in the memorialization of Argentina's historical memory. Archives and sites of memory were
secured thanks to the Institute. By 2009, there were an estimated two hundred sites of memory in Buenos Aires alone (Memoria Abierta 2009). Other
activities included exhibitions, conferences, concerts, commemorations,
publications, human rights curricula for schools, and prizes for the best
multimedia designs about the military repression (Instituto Memoria
2008).

The memory work of the human rights movement has since the mid-
2000s become challenged by second-generation sympathizers of prosecuted

officers. Instead of denying the human rights violations, they began standing up for the forgotten victims of guerrilla operations, such as the relatives
of Major Larrabure, who had died in 1975 as a captive of the People's
Revolutionary Army (ERP). His son, Arturo Larrabure (2005), described
the anxious waiting for a sign of life, the negotiations, and the threats during his father's yearlong stay in the hidden people's prison. The testimonies
of family members revealed the psychological costs of living with the violent
death and the difficulties of keeping his memory alive in annual commemorations. A memorial to Major Larrabure was inaugurated at Plaza Mitre in
Buenos Aires in 1996.

What began in the year 2000 with a desire on the part of young sympathizers of indicted officers for an evenhanded history of Argentina's political violence evolved after 11 September 2001 into a move toward solidarity
with victims of terrorism worldwide. The term *subversion*, common among
veterans of the dictatorship, was rejected as archaic and replaced by *terrorism* to compare the Argentine insurgents to Osama bin Laden and to con-
nect the political violence of the 1970s to the terrorism of the twenty-first
century, in particular the attack on the World Trade Center in 2001 (Villarruel 2009:13). Attention was directed to the suffering and the PTSD of
survivors and bereaved relatives of Argentine victims of terrorism. The
young generation of military sympathizers has avoided mentioning the disappearances but has been seeking recognition for all victims of terrorism
and armed conflict.

In 2012, one year before former dictator Jorge Rafael Videla died from
multiple injuries after slipping on a shower floor in the Marcos Paz prison,
he finally confessed to the disappearances in several lengthy interviews: "A
large group of people had to be eliminated that could neither be taken to
court nor executed publicly" (Reato 2012:57). He admitted to the assassination of 7,000–8,000 people. "In order not to provoke domestic or foreign
protests, the conclusion was drawn in the course of events that these people
should disappear; every disappearance could certainly be understood as the
disguise, the concealment, of a death" (ibid.). Videla used just war as his
discursive frame. "It was a just war in the terms of Saint Thomas; a defensive war. I don't agree that it had been a dirty war, war is always something
horrible and dirty but Saint Thomas introduced this important nuance of
just wars, and this is what it was" (32). The just war frame had been
embraced by the military since their fall from power in 1983 and has persisted until today, but their social memories underwent major changes

through the decades, from a total denial of the enforced disappearances to a public admission of their occurrence.

Conclusion

The intertwined spirals of violence and trauma that characterized Argentina's political history between 1955 and 1983 turned memory into an important area of contestation in which periodically changing collective memories were created from different parts of social memories in conflicting discursive frames. Adversarial groups only trusted their own social recollections. They accused others, including the state that participated in the memory field through national and local organs, of betraying their history. These histories consisted of the ideals for which people had given their lives and the hardships they endured, of the victories won, and the social bonds forged during political struggles and combat operations. Former guerrilla insurgents and the Association mothers regarded the disappeared as revolutionaries who fought for a more just Argentina. Calling them terrorists and subversives, as the veterans of the dictatorship habitually did, was a betrayal of their history and the social relations that constituted them. These retired officers, in turn, did everything possible to keep the memory of their dead comrades alive and pay them tribute for their sacrifices to the nation and the preservation of Argentina's way of life. The mutual accusations of betrayal consisted of not acknowledging the histories of others with partisan social memories. Social bonds and attachments were denied existence, and the fallen might thus eventually be forgotten. Trustful social memories recognized these histories and attachments, and the various adversarial groups put great effort into confirming them in the public sphere with memorials and commemorations. The national government played an ambiguous role because it depended on whatever political winds were blowing during each administration. Memorialization, whether in stone, protest, or prayer, was thus an expression of trust that countered the oblivion and betrayal of social memory with or without the help of the state.

The changeable opposition of mutually constitutive social memories defined how Argentine society remembered its traumatic past. The dirty war and two-demons theory frames placed the responsibility on the guerrillas and the military. The state terrorism frame blamed the armed forces exclusively, whereas the genocide frame made Argentine society collectively responsible. Other discursive frames, such as just war, anti-revolutionary war, and civil war, never became prominent. Each discursive frame painted a starkly different picture of Argentina during the dictatorship, disclosed other repressive realities, and allocated different responsibilities to individuals, groups, and state institutions. The trustworthiness of the conflicting social memories in the eyes of the Argentine people changed through the decades, and became manifested by the dominance of one discursive frame over others. Trustworthiness is understood here as the credibility of the semiotic power, narrative coherence, and logical reasoning of the discursive frames. These interpretational frames have been formulated in Argentina mainly by the state, the human rights movement, and veterans of the dictatorship, whose internal disagreements and public conflicts have made memory a highly complex and volatile area of contestation. Their discursive and political influence on Argentina's collective memory has therefore fluctuated greatly between 1983 and the present.

The 1983–1987 period was very much dominated by a democratic government that had wrested state power away from a defeated armed forces. It asserted its historical narrative through retributive justice against military leaders and guerrilla commanders. These efforts to cast the blame exclusively on troops and insurgents failed to convince many Argentines. The CONADEP truth commission and the trial of the junta commanders provided key narratives that made the armed forces the chief culprit, while dwarfing the guerrilla insurgency in comparison to the monstrosity of military repression. Ex-disappeared and searching relatives were the principal public voices of social memory. Their testimonies gave content to the repression and helped shift the responsibility toward the armed forces. The mothers protesting at the Plaza de Mayo personified the nation's suffering in the public eye, and their moral stance towered above the destructive interests of the belligerents. The disclosure of atrocities, the sadism, assassinations, and disappearances effectively disproved the persistent denial of wrongdoing by the military and made the social memory of the mothers the most credible recollection of the traumatic past.

The Argentine military regained some of its lost political influence during the 1987–1995 period. The growing discontent with the prosecution of officers, who had attained military might via mutinies, resulted in amnesty laws and the pardoning of convicted officers and guerrillas. State terrorism surfaced as the most prominent discursive frame of Argentina's collective memory during this period. The different social memories in the public domain were directed more at themselves than against others. The military reiterated its master narrative for the proper ranks. Ex-guerrillas were trying to assume their old professional lives, joining political parties or becoming active in the human rights movement. Most human rights organizations expanded, each in their own way, from activism to memorialization. Sites of memory were preserved and memorials were erected to impress upon the Argentine people that the nation had suffered under state terrorism. Finally, the Argentine state kept away from memory politics, eager to turn the page and reform the faltering economy.

Open memory politics resurfaced again during the 1995–2005 period as perpetrator confessions obliged the armed forces and police to admit to past violations. Former junta commanders were arrested on kidnapping charges, and the human rights movement again took up its activism to campaign against the impunity laws. The social memories of ex-guerrillas finally became visible as accounts of their political struggle were published. The human rights movement received a boost when Néstor Kirchner won the presidential elections in 2003. He sympathized openly with the human rights movement and the political left. This collaboration made state terrorism the dominant discursive frame and helped overturn the impunity laws of the 1980s.

Since 2006, Argentine memory politics has been dominated by the trials against military perpetrators and civilian collaborators. The human rights movement and the judiciary have embraced genocide as an increasingly prominent discursive frame. The lengthy convictions of hundreds of perpetrators and the widening circle of suspects raised the stakes of memory. The social memories of human rights organizations and military interest groups have been developing into transnational directions instead of confronting each other in public. The Holocaust figures prominently in this interpretive frame. The trials have also raised renewed attention to personal recollections and have shown the importance of Ricoeur's categorical distinction between memory and remembrance. Witness testimonies reveal that emotions can erupt after decades and flood people's being. These strong sentiments find release in remembrances that may be so intimate and embodied that they are inexpressible in words, but there are also remembrances that can be narrated and thus influence social memories, as has happened in Argentina since the days when the disappearances became known to an unbelieving world.

CHAPTER 3

Testimony

"Many of the events described in this report will be hard to believe." So reads the opening sentence of *Never Again*, the 1984 report of the Argentine truth commission. "This is because the men and women of our nation have only heard of such horror in reports from distant places. . . . Month after month of listening to accusations, testimonies, and confessions, of examining documents, inspecting places, and doing all in our power to throw light on these terrifying occurrences have given us the right to assert that a system of repression was deliberately planned to produce the events and situations which are detailed in this report" (CONADEP 1986:9).

Facing a military master narrative that justified the coup d'état as being a national necessity and that dismissed accounts of enforced disappearances as fabrications, the CONADEP had visited military bases, mental institutions, prisons, and former secret detention centers in search of evidence. It had ordered the exhumation of mass graves and examined records of police stations, morgues, and cemeteries. The armed forces discredited the forensic methodology and the scant material evidence, arguing that bullet-ridden remains do not identify the executioner, despite the presence of army-issued Itaka ammunition. Narrative reconstructions therefore became essential because in April 1983 President Bignone had ordered the destruction of military documents related to the repression (*Boletín Público Ejército Argentino* 1984, 4524:673).

The witness testimonies were not unproblematic. They depicted a struggle with the representational complications analyzed in the previous chapters, namely the incommensurability of traumatic memories and everyday realities, incomplete recall, different personal remembrances, and conflicting social memories set in other discursive frames. Testimonies have therefore occupied an area of national contestation since the coup d'état of 1976.

This chapter analyzes the testimonies of torture survivors, former guerrillas, and the relatives of the disappeared. The next chapter discusses the testimonies of military and police.

The trustworthiness of witnesses was crucial to the international fact-finding missions that visited Argentina during the dictatorship and later to the Argentine truth commission and criminal courts. Diplomatic pressure on the military junta was only possible with truthful information, and plaintiffs and defendants could only be given a fair trial if the witnesses were reliable. Trustworthiness was also indispensable for the relatives of the disappeared. They hoped that the survivors of secret detention centers would share reliable information about other captives, however painful this might be. Yet, they were also suspicious of these same witnesses who might have owed their lives to the betrayal of their disappeared loved ones.

Just as former guerrilla commanders were considered traitors by the mothers and grandmothers of the Plaza de Mayo for enlisting their children in a hopeless insurgency and fleeing abroad when defeat was imminent, so former disappeared persons were suspected of having saved their skin by betraying their comrades. How could anyone have survived the horrendous conditions of captivity described in the human rights reports? Hebe de Bonafini could only conclude: "Those who are dead were all heroes, those who are alive are alive because they collaborated" (Longoni 2007:11; Park 2014:46). She has called them traitors, and former Montonero commander Fernando Vaca Narvaja accused them of collaboration: "They collaborated, all of them, and we know it and the comrades who are outside also know it. That's why some have a cleaner conscience and others a more guilty conscience" (interview on 2 October 1990). Vaca Narvaja's and de Bonafini's harsh judgment and their disregard of the complexities of collaboration (see Robben 2005a:248–255) are not widely shared, but others have nevertheless raised doubts about the witnesses and their testimonies in terms of disbelief, suspicion, and mistrust. Disbelief about the Dantesque horrors painted by survivors, suspicion about their role in the secret detention centers, and mistrust toward what are seen as self-serving testimonies and partial truths. Certain reservations dissipated as the witness accounts changed through the decades and more knowledge became available, but testimonies have never been accepted at face value.

Testimonies are narratives that provide coherence and chronology to past experiences and events that may be quite disparate. Unlike remembrances that may remain private, testimonies are public reflections about a personal past. Testimonial narratives are communicative modes that often combine several manifestations of the past to an audience through speech, gesture, emotion, and facial expression (Ochs and Capps 1996:20). Testimonies about violence are speech acts that allow witnesses to reconstruct themselves in public as trustworthy narrators. They create compassion among listeners, and provide legal evidence. Compared to social memories, testimonies give a more personalized content to larger political forces and structures by narrating everyday experiences and emotions. This subjectivity is often mistrusted by political adversaries. The facile use of words like *traitor*, *treason*, and *betrayal* in Argentina is a manifestation of the hostility among adversaries but also among former companions. Voicing a dissident opinion in a group might result in ostracism and an open condemnation for treason. Betrayal went beyond accusing witnesses of false testimony or the abuse of the right to silence. Betrayal was regarded as giving one-sided, partisan testimonies for self-serving reasons or with the intent to inflict legal, political, and emotional harm on others.

Oral testimonies are distinct from written accounts. Based on an analysis of Holocaust narratives, Langer (1991:160–161) observed that oral testimonies lack a preconceived narrative flow and structure. They are multivocal, and may include moments of silence. The discontinuities of oral testimonies are a consequence of the combination of story and plot. "The 'story' is the chronological narrative, beginning with 'I was born' and ending with 'I was liberated.' . . . The 'plot' reveals the witness seized by instead of selecting incidents, memory's confrontation with details embedded in moments of trauma" (174). These qualities can also be found in the court testimonies of former disappeared persons but not in their depositions to the truth commission because the oral accounts were written up by staff members who deleted the incongruities between story and plot and then presented the declaration to the testifier for authorization.

Testimonies about political violence have an added complexity when witnesses suffered from psychic trauma. Douglass and Vogler (2003:2) have pointed out that "it is by definition in the nature of a mental trauma to exceed and violate our normal mental processing ability and frames of reference. The more massive the traumatic impact, the more it will affect our ability to register it." Psychic trauma hampers the encoding of many facets of an assault and prevents complete recall (McNally 2003:190; Schacter 2001:174). Traumatic experiences disturb the ability to attribute meaning and therefore cannot be integrated into the everyday lifeworld, as was explained in Chapter 1. How reliable then is the firsthand knowledge of a violent event when its encoding is flawed and its mediation in speech can never fully reproduce the original traumatizing experiences? This epistemic vulnerability places doubt on the trustworthiness of witnesses and the truth value of survivor testimonies.

The complex relation between truth and trauma has crystallized, according to Leys (2000:298–307), into an unsolvable theoretical debate between mimetic and anti-mimetic positions. The mimetic position claims that trauma can never be reliably narrated because traumatic experiences bypass ordinary memory and are directly imprinted on the brain. Traumatic experiences exist in deep memory, in sense memory, and become manifest only in unmediated re-experiences such as dreams, flashbacks, and imaginations, although therapeutic and testimonial narration may attenuate the traumatic burden.[1] The anti-mimetic position instead maintains that a traumatic event impacts a person from the outside without restructuring the person's psyche. Traumatic experiences can be properly narrated once a sufficient amount of emotional distance has occurred.[2]

Both theoretical positions assume that there is a traumatic reality, whether knowable or unknowable, which establishes the testifier's authority but does not guarantee the testimony's reliability. Still, as LaCapra (2001:89–92) observes, this duality is too absolute because certain traumatizing experiences may be worked through and reconstructed accurately. Hirsch and Spitzer (2010) argue similarly that silence, embodiment, and affect may come closest to the unspeakable traumatic memory but have the troubling moral consequence of privileging muteness over narration. Such epistemic position stands in the way of gathering valuable knowledge. Furthermore, in my opinion, the two theoretical positions are not mutually exclusive because traumatic experiences undergo both mimetic or sensorial and anti-mimetic or cognitive processes. The embodied dimension of trauma is best expressed artistically, while the cognitive dimension can be described in testimonial accounts and scholarly writings.

Most Argentine psychologists and psychiatrists embraced a nuanced anti-mimetic position because they regarded torture as an external stressor that caused dissociation, thus allowing survivors to reconnect with their trauma through therapy (Kordon, Edelman, Nicoletti, Lagos, Bozzolo, and Kandel 1988:101). Furthermore, the anti-mimetic stance made Argentine psychologists emphasize the survivor's agency. Therapeutic testimonies raised political consciousness, and contributed to resistance against the dictatorship. For example, informal consultations and group therapies with searching mothers helped them understand that family crises, conjugal tensions, anger, anxiety, and guilt feelings were products of state terror and psychological warfare rather than the consequences of intrapsychic processes (Bozzolo and Lagos 1988; Kordon, Edelman, and Lagos 1988). The anti-mimetic position was therefore dominant in Argentina, precisely because power entered centrally into the testimony and treatment of relatives of missing persons and survivors of torture and disappearance.

This chapter analyzes the Argentine testimonies as dynamic narratives that changed in form and content over time and entailed other notions of truth and trustworthiness. The same witness might produce different testimonies in different contexts to achieve other objectives during decades of political undulation. Political opponents jumped on these changes as a means to brush aside the testimonies as false, and prompted the suspicion and mistrust of others.

Denunciations

The first account of a disappearance was often pieced together within the intimacy of the family. After overcoming their initial bewilderment, family members compared their recollection of the abduction or gathered information from eyewitnesses. Then the search began. Relatives called hospitals, visited police stations, and spoke with lawyers about submitting a writ of habeas corpus to the courts. If these efforts proved fruitless and it became apparent that the missing loved one might be in the hands of the Argentine military, then the social network would be activated. Catholics often approached their parish priest. They were generally deferred to the military bishop's private secretary, Monsignor Grasselli, who held office at Navy headquarters (Robben 2005a:284–288). Grasselli began receiving relatives in 1975. There is no record of these confidential conversations, but Grasselli recalled the emotional state of the anguished visitors at the 1985 trial of the junta commanders. He wanted to erase any doubt about their trustworthiness: "You, your Honor, are receiving in this place testimonies of events that occurred eight years ago. What you are hearing, I heard after a few hours or a few days, and I can assure you that people were not play-acting" (*El Diario del Juicio* 1985, 5:111).

Military Chaplain Grasselli listened but could not or would not help, and he was suspected of passing information to naval intelligence. Searching relatives would then overcome their fear and approach the commanding officers of military bases, who assured them that their son or daughter was not there. Some relatives were so well-connected that they succeeded in speaking with Lieutenant-General Videla or Admiral Massera but always to no avail. People also registered their disappeared relatives at an office opened in August 1976 by the Ministry of Interior and had to endure verbal abuse and veiled threats that destroyed their trust in the state and its agents. With the social and institutional channels exhausted, relatives sought each other's company at human rights organizations, such as the Permanent Assembly for Human Rights (APDH).

The APDH had been founded in December 1975 by people with various political backgrounds (including President-to-be Raúl Alfonsín) to defend human rights and halt political violence. Many relatives, most often mothers, went to the small APDH office in Buenos Aires to denounce the disappearances. A file card was created to register the denunciation, copies were made of habeas corpus requests, and a trustworthy volunteer who herself had a disappeared child would offer a sympathetic ear (Fernández Meijide 2009:43–48). Searching relatives had thus narrated the disappearance repeatedly at many different places by the time that their testimonies were published in human rights reports.

The first international fact-finding mission was conducted by Amnesty International in November 1976. The delegates recorded more than one hundred disappearances and included in their report portions of oral testimonies, such as that of seventy-two-year-old Rosa Daneman de Edelberg.

"At 1 o'clock in the morning of 15 July (1976), plainclothed persons came to my house, bringing my son-in-law, Hugo Tarnopolsky, who knocked on the door and asked us to open it saying, 'Open up, Nona, it's Hugo.' When I opened it, I met my son-in-law and the plainclothes men who said they were the police and, with threats and blows, they asked for my granddaughter, Bettina Tarnopolsky. . . . After they had violently locked me out on the patio, I heard them taking away my granddaughter, half-dressed, since most of her clothes were in her room" (Amnesty International 1977:28). Although the report concluded that "merely on the suspicion of subversion, a citizen may be arrested or abducted, held for a long period *incommunicado*, tortured and perhaps even put to death" (Amnesty International 1977:48), the method of disappearance was not entirely clear.

The first systematic description of Argentina's enforced disappearances was given in April 1979 after a fact-finding mission of the New York City Bar Association had investigated the fate of disappeared lawyers. The commission visited the APDH and the Mothers of the Plaza de Mayo and spoke with high-placed officials but was unable to visit prisons and military detention centers (Schell 1979). Although an important report, it lacks testimonial narratives and resembles a legal document. A subsequent visit in September 1979 by the Inter-American Commission on Human Rights (IACHR) of the Organization of American States (OAS) yielded a report that did reproduce testimonies, but most of them were rewritten in the third person, as in the case of Norberto Liwski, who was shot in both legs during the raid on his home: "He was kidnapped and tortured with electricity throughout his body, especially on the genitals; he was whipped for days, and burned with a branding iron also placed on his genitals" (IACHR 1980:chapter 4, case 3905). There were also some testimonies that appear to have been transcribed verbatim, as indicated by the temporal jumps and disjunctions, the minute details, and the reflective interludes typical of oral narratives, as in the following account by Sergio Hugo Schilman: "They began to apply electric shocks to me, I suppose it must have been the *picana* (cattle prod), I never experienced anything like it before. Unfortunately I still have many scars from it; at the same time as they applied the cattle prod, which they first used on my armpits, and then further down on much more sensitive zones, my genitals, they hit me; it was a very large group of people apparently judging from the uproar of voices in the room; they hit me over and over again; and also slapped me on the ears" (IACHR 1980:chapter 5, case 4674).

The IACHR spoke with thousands of people in Buenos Aires and five other cities, collecting 5,580 denunciations (Fernández Meijide 2009:112–115). The commission met President Videla, the military junta, former Argentine presidents, and the leaders of human rights organizations, religious congregations, and proscribed political parties and labor unions. The commission also visited the ESMA secret detention center, but it was empty because the captives had been temporarily moved to a former retreat of the Buenos Aires archbishop called The Silence on an island in the River Plate estuary (IACHR 1980:Introduction, section B; Verbitsky 2005). The IACHR report appeared in April 1980, and concluded that "due to the actions or the failure to act on the part of the governmental authorities and their agents, numerous serious violations of fundamental human rights, as recognized in the American Declaration of the Rights and Duties of Man, were committed in the Republic of Argentina during the period covered by this report—1975 to 1979. . . . The Commission is particularly concerned about the circumstances relating to the thousands of detainees who have disappeared and who, for the reasons set forth in the report, based on the evidence, may be presumed dead" (IACHR 1980:Conclusions and Recommendations, part A).

The Argentine authorities tried to prevent the report's distribution in Argentina, but the Center for Legal and Social Studies (CELS) succeeded in smuggling 2,500 copies into the country (CIDH 1984:5). In its rebuttal of November 1980, the Argentine government dismissed the findings: "When the Report refers to the denunciations, in no instance does it suggest even the slightest mistrust concerning the details that each contains, however suspicious or unrealistic they may seem at times. Every critical or negative opinion on the situation or the Government is made so assertively as not to admit dispute. On the other hand, much of the information provided by the Government or that simply casts it in a favorable light, is systematically placed in doubt" (Government of Argentina 1980:2).

The government criticized the report's rhetorical narrative, the absence of corroborating evidence, and the generalizations made on the basis of a few cases. The veracity of the testimonies was questioned because they came from terrorists who had gone into hiding, according to the Argentine government, and reappeared later to spread their fabricated stories. These witnesses made their accounts plausible with the following features: (1) Witnesses were able to talk to one another before they gave their public testimony and identified people they had not known before presenting their accounts; (2) They remembered the names, ages, and many personal details of these persons, despite the debilitating torture to which they had been subjected; (3) They remembered the names, rank, and functions of their tormentors, despite being hooded or blindfolded; and (4) The different testimonies of the witnesses concurred on key points to enhance their credibility (Government of Argentina 1980:54–55). The government was referring implicitly to a highly publicized testimony presented in October 1979 at the French National Assembly by three former captives. They had spent years at the ESMA for being members of the Montoneros. The women gave a detailed description of the ESMA's repressive infrastructure, identified their captors by name, and denounced for the first time the death flights that were to have such serious legal consequences three decades later (Martí, Pirles, and Osatinsky 1995).

Denunciations made during the dictatorship carried an inner tension between personal experiences and factual accusations that appealed to different truths, one narrative and the other evidential. Witnesses tried to convince public opinion with an empathetic narrative that their inconceivable torment had taken place. Fact-finding missions, however, required hard proof. After all, torture is not a clear-cut clinical category but rather a political and ethical reality whose qualification as torture varies between physicians and lawyers (Kelly 2012:91–99). The emotional narratives stood at odds with the neutral descriptions demanded by international organizations to undertake action against the dictatorship. Witnesses and survivors sought a solution in testimonio narratives that reconciled the personal and the political into a coherent account in which collective suffering came to stand for individual hardship.

Testimonios

A testimonio is a first-person account by a witness or protagonist who testifies to a violent event or oppressive situation for political reasons. Unlike Holocaust narratives that seek to document a traumatic past, testimonio is a resistance narrative written in the midst of repression with a clear political objective in mind. The 1980s were the heyday of this form of testimonial discourse when many Latin American countries were ruled by dictatorial regimes. Testimonio accounts should not be mistaken for autobiographies, memoirs, or life histories because the narrators speak in the name of others and intentionally address human and political conditions suffered by many (Beverley 2004:29–44; Gugelberger 1996). Finally, testimonio narratives are not all of one piece because they may address different audiences with different background knowledge and therefore require other narrative styles.

In the 1990s, a debate was held in comparative literature about whether testimonios were reliable witness testimonies or literary products that afforded stylistic liberties for political ends. This scholarly discussion turned bitter when David Stoll cast doubt on the canonical testimonio *I, Rigoberta Menchú: An Indian Woman in Guatemala* by Nobel laureate Rigoberta

Menchú (1991). Stoll (2008:65–70) claimed that Menchú (1991:173–180) had not personally witnessed the torture and death of her brother by Guatemalan military in 1979, although he did not dispute the tragic event itself. Menchú did concede eventually that she had not been present but had created a collective account based on multiple eyewitness testimonies. Taking a mimetic position, Stoll's critics argued that traumatic experiences are empirical realities that cannot be represented in language. A testimonio is therefore inevitably a narrative construct, irrespective of its political advocacy (Beverley 2004:63–73, 81; Gugelberger 1999).

Le diable dans le soleil (The Devil in the Sun) by Carlos Gabetta was the first Argentine testimonio about the dictatorship. Published in France in 1979 and directed primarily at a French audience, it appeared in Argentina in November 1983 under the title *Todos somos subversivos* (*We Are All Subversives*). In Paris, Gabetta (1983) recorded interviews with released prisoners, former disappeared, searching parents, and affected foreigners. They were representatives of all layers of Argentine society, thus making it clear that anyone—not just certain members of society—might be considered a subversive by the Argentine military. Being a senator, an upper-middle-class woman, or a French businessman meant as little as being a working-class woman, a Spanish nun, or a pregnant student.

The testimonio account by journalist Matilde Herrera is typical for Gabetta's book and is of additional interest because of her biography of her disappeared son José and my interviews with her in 1990. The testimonio in Gabetta's book is entitled "A woman searches for her smile." The smile is trope, metaphor, and description all in one. It describes Herrera's emotional state at the time of the interview and the insufferable pain over her disappeared children. The lost smile returns several times in the testimonio as a refrain: "a sad smile of large, even teeth" (Gabetta 1983:29, 30, 56, 57). It serves also as a metaphor for her disappeared children and a trope for her interminable search. She is not only searching for her three children and their spouses but also for the two grandchildren born in captivity.

In his introduction, interviewer Carlos Gabetta situates Matilde Herrera in the Montmartre district of Paris accompanied by her second husband, Roberto Aizenberg, an artist whose large sculpture of three geometric silhouettes is today on permanent display at the Memory Park in Buenos Aires. Matilde Herrera is presented as a soft-spoken woman with large, wide eyes who comes from a well-to-do Argentine family and has been moving heaven and earth to find her eight disappeared family members. In

July 1976, her son Martín and his pregnant wife Cristina disappeared. Matilde Herrera and Cristina's mother used their extensive contacts to find
them. Matilde described the social isolation from friends afraid to help her
and the blanket denials by high-placed military commanders and Church
authorities. In September 1976, she decided to spend a few months in Paris.
Intending to return to Buenos Aires in January 1977, Matilde Herrera heard
from a reliable source that her life would be in danger. She chose to remain
in France. Her pregnant daughter Valeria and her husband Ricardo disappeared in mid-May 1977. Her son José and his wife Electra made plans to
leave the country but disappeared two weeks later.

This testimonio was not constructed to evoke empathy, as were the
denunciations, but to provide identification. Matilde Herrera was not one
of the poor peasants who have commonly been the subject of Latin American testimonios but was an educated member of the Argentine upper
middle class. She could easily resemble her European readers. This identification was further enhanced by portraying the landlord of Matilde's son
Martín as an immigrant who "had fought the war in Spain and knew about
those things" (Gabetta 1983:32). Gabetta emphasized the link between the
Spanish Civil War and Argentina's political situation to draw the European
audience further into Herrera's account.

The narrative established Matilde Herrera's testimonial authority and
trustworthiness by presenting her as someone who had spoken with many
influential public figures, exchanged letters with Senator Edward Kennedy,
and founded COSOFAM (Solidarity Commission with Relatives of Prisoners and Disappeared), a European human rights organization. This information was intended to give credibility to her account, which was
corroborated in the book by two survivors of disappearance and torture:
the eighteen-year-old student, Ana María Careaga, and Julio, the father of
Matilde Herrera's daughter-in-law Electra. Careaga had seen José and Electra Herrera at the secret detention center where she had been held, and
Julio had heard from an officer that the young couple was still alive when
he was held captive for seven months. As if to dispel any doubt among the
readers, the testimonio reproduced two letters from Matilde's son José that
tell about the disappearance of his brother, sister, and their spouses. The
letters have an uncanny quality that enhances the testimonio's credibility
because the reader knows that José will disappear as well.

Typical of the testimonio literature, Matilde Herrera spoke for all families with disappeared children: "the problem exceeds by far my personal

situation. There are many thousands; so much suffering, so much horror. . . . Put in your book that I am only one case, that there are millions of Argentines who lost their smile, but we are going to recover it" (Gabetta 1983:56). She added that if the military would return her children, she would receive them with open arms, throw a big party, and then continue the next day with the search for the remaining disappeared. Her search was not a personal quest but a collective struggle.

Matilde Herrera had carefully avoided addressing her children's political activism when Carlos Gabetta asked in 1979 why they had been disappeared. She responded that she refused to enter into the military's logic by considering them guilty of working for political change in Argentina. This answer is understandable in the context of 1979, when the Argentine military were firmly in power. The emphasis was purely on the maternal right to know the whereabouts of one's children and the legal right of habeas corpus. Matilde Herrera published her son's biography in 1987, under the title *José*, and added a new discursive layer to the testimonio of 1979 by revealing her innermost feelings after all her children had disappeared: "They were no more. None of them. They had become disappeared. I was left stunned. I couldn't cry. I continued to eat, sleep, and talk to friends. I knew that if I gave in to my pain, then I would have been unable to continue living. I didn't cry, because I sensed that if I would sit down and cry, then I would never ever be able to get back on my feet again" (Herrera 1987:399). She also wrote that José had joined the People's Revolutionary Army (ERP) in April 1974 and that this membership caused his disappearance (181). In 1987, Argentina was a democracy, the CONADEP truth commission had presented its findings, and the junta commanders were still in prison. Herrera's trustworthiness as a witness would have suffered if she had persisted in her earlier testimony that eschewed her son's political activism.

Herrera's 1987 biography is indicative of the transformation of the testimonio genre into emotional portraits that tried to convey the maternal anguish of searching for one's missing children and the humanity of the disappeared. Testimonio's moment had passed in the mid-1980s because of a loss of political urgency with the return to democracy. Publications now served to humanize mothers who for years had been dismissed as crazy women or denounced as mothers of subversives but who had made an appeal to the universal attachment of mother and child. Common themes were the love and longing for the disappeared child, the silence at home, and the despair and discouragement of the interminable search (Diago 1988; Mellibovsky 1990; Sánchez 1985; Ulla and Echave 1986).

Jacobo Timerman's work *Prisoner Without a Name, Cell Without a Number* appeared in May 1981 in the United States and became internationally the most widely circulated testimonio about Argentina. The book is part personal ordeal, part political analysis, as will be explained in Chapter 7, and fits in the genre of personal testimonio narratives written in the mid-1980s (Vázquez and Vázquez 1984; Bondone 1985; Kozameh 1987; Buda 1988; Vázquez 1988). These books were intended to demonstrate the authenticity of the emotions and experiences of their authors during state terror. They belong to the testimonio genre as first-person accounts whose political objective was to disprove the denials by the Argentine military. Unlike autobiographies, they focused on the claustrophobic universe of the secret detention centers and the relations among the captives. They described vividly the dependency on the captors, the torture, and the inmates' small acts of resistance. The search for ways to represent what for many Argentines seemed unimaginable made some authors resort to creative nonfiction (Bonasso 1984; Portnoy 1986; Seoane and Ruiz Núñez 1986) or attempts to describe the nightmares after a torture session. "I saw myself twenty years later. . . . I had returned to life after this lapse of time. One of my sons had died. I suffered his death as if it was real. My husband had remarried and had several children with his new wife. My two other children had forgotten me. There are no words to describe the pain I felt. I had loved them more than ever during these years. It was impossible that I meant nothing to them anymore!" (Buda 1988:65). These emotions were precisely what the truth commission tried to elicit to give credibility to experiences that had been shielded from the Argentine people by the façade of normality erected by the dictatorship.

Depositions Before the CONADEP Truth Commission

The CONADEP truth commission provided a trusting environment in which witnesses could finally tell their story. They made confidential depositions at CONADEP's main office in Buenos Aires or at its regional branches. Depositions could also be made at Argentine embassies. The testifiers were aware that many Argentines were confused by the stories circulating in the media and encountered this bewilderment at the

CONADEP offices as well. Most early staff members were employees of the Ministry of Interior who could not handle the emotionally charged testimonies. Some even fainted. The effect on the witnesses was equally profound. A clerk's emotional collapse could make them doubt whether the truth commission could really communicate their experiences to the Argentine people in an atmosphere of disbelief. Many clerks resigned and were replaced by psychologists and volunteers from human rights organizations (CONADEP 1986:430; *El Diario del Juicio* 1985, 7:152–154; Hayner 2001:149–152).

Truth commissions have been praised for providing a forum for truth telling, personal healing, and social reconciliation. Minow (1998:61–74) emphasizes the restorative power of truth telling before sympathetic commissioners. Phelps (2004:55–73) argues that testimonies are healing because they turn victims into survivors, restore a humanity and dignity broken under torture, and recover the voice lost in pain. Becker (2006) concludes that truth telling can help the process of mourning, and Daly and Sarkin (2007:60–65) believe that truth commissions can promote cognitive healing through fact-finding and historical framing, while psychological healing may be achieved by inverting the power dynamics with the oppressors and understanding the traumas inflicted. Yet, these claims to emotional repair are not backed by hard evidence, according to Hayner (2001:133–153), Borer (2006), and Doak (2011). They point out that truth commissions offer only a single opportunity to speak and that testifying should not be equated with psychotherapy. Furthermore, revealing the truth may not provide psychological healing but instead may reopen emotional wounds, retraumatize victims, and lead to profound disillusionment and a sense of injustice when the commission's report constructs a truth that differs from personal understanding.

How was the Argentine truth commission to elicit credible testimonies from the ex-disappeared? Establishing the trustworthiness of the testifiers was the first step. Witnesses were asked to fill out a form about where and how they had been abducted (alone or with others), if there were witnesses, if property had been destroyed or stolen, who the captors were (number of persons and vehicles involved), how long the journey to the clandestine detention center had taken, and by which route. They were also asked where they had been held captive and under what circumstances, who was with them in captivity (family or friends), and whether they had been tortured. Next, they were asked detailed questions in an effort to (1) gather information about disappearances and incriminating evidence for the courts; (2) establish the whereabouts of disappeared persons; (3) locate kidnapped children and pass this information to juvenile courts; (4) denounce obstructions to the clarification of disappearances to the courts; and (5) publish the findings in a final report (San Martino de Dromi 1988, 2:597–598). The belief that there were still disappeared persons alive created a sense of urgency that defined the type of truth pursued by the commission, not a historical exegesis of the decades of political violence, not a restorative truth to heal society, and not a social truth based on a dialogue of perpetrators and victims, as was attempted in South Africa (Chapman and Ball 2001:10–12).

The CONADEP was seeking both an evidence-based forensic truth and a personal, narrative truth. This distinction would also be made by the South African Truth and Reconciliation Commission, according to Wilson (2001:37), who added that the forensic truth was given an epistemological status which the narrative truth lacked. In Argentina, however, the personal experiences of witnesses became of paramount importance because the forensic evidence was meager. Sensorial evidence became the most authentic expression of narrative truth. After testifiers had completed the CONADEP questionnaire, they were given free rein to narrate their experiences. "The evocation of smells, sounds, and tactile impressions, and the sight that succeeded in deceiving the blindfold or hood, were their instruments to reconstruct the topography of terror, and the identities of those responsible and those of other captives" (Crenzel 2008:72). Such testimonies maximized the empathy of the listener and added an emotional truth to the verbal accounts. Much attention was paid to a description of the excruciating pain, the length of the suffering, and the multiple methods of torture. Take for example the description by Norberto Liwski, who was abducted on 5 April 1978:

> For days they applied electric shocks to my gums, nipples, genitals, abdomen and ears. Unintentionally, I managed to annoy them, because, I don't know why, although the shocks made me scream, jerk and shudder, they could not make me pass out. They then began to beat me systematically and rhythmically with wooden sticks on my back, the backs of my thighs, my calves and the soles of my feet. At first the pain was dreadful. Then it became unbearable. Eventually I lost all feeling in the part of my body being beaten. The

agonizing pain returned a short while after they finished hitting me.
(CONADEP 1986:22)

According to the commissioners, such quotes were "selected solely in
order to substantiate and illustrate our main arguments" (CONADEP
1986:7). This explanation undervalues the impact on the readers. Set apart
from the main text, the report's rhetorical weight rests on the testimonies
and turns the victims into the report's main focus. Phelps (2004:89–90) has
pointed astutely at the report's polyphonic narrative that counterbalances
the commission's authoritative voice: "Thus there is a constant tension
between the stories themselves, which are stories of disorder and chaos, of
a world in which nothing was predictable, of 'voids' and phantasmagoric
sensations and images, and the report, which explicitly puts the stories in
an order." Highly emotional testimonial narratives were framed within a
description of the repressive infrastructure that through its detail enhanced
the credibility of the testimonies.

The CONADEP report demonstrated that the repression was meticu-
lously planned. The unbelievable was turned into the credible through a
narrative structure that responded to the dynamic of military denial versus
testimonial disclosure, as was analyzed in Chapter 2. After several hundred
pages, the conclusion could only be: "The evidence has now reached proportions unimaginable a few years ago, when a few isolated instances created the illusion that such things could not be representative of a general
practice" (CONADEP 1986:229). The literary hand of the commission's
president, the prominent Argentine novelist Ernesto Sábato, can be sensed
in the compelling way in which the testimonies were woven through the
report.

The CONADEP report made an unforgettable impression on Argentine society and led most Argentines to support the prosecution of the
culprits. The horrendous tales of torture and the appearance of survivors
in the media established a public platform for the 1985 trial against nine
junta commanders. Given the persistent denials by the retired military,
Argentine society had no position to fall back on other than the report's
confirmation or invalidation in court. Public truths carry less weight than
judicial truths in people's perception because of a belief in the court's
verification process. The Argentine truth commission acknowledged the
testimony of lived experiences but had limited means to establish their
veracity. The court made plausible incursions into the continued military

denials because of the legitimization of witness testimonies through the sentencing of perpetrators.

Court Testimonies

Many testifiers at the empathetic truth commission now had to face inquisitive judges and aggressive defense lawyers, lawyers who drew on information about the witnesses acquired through torture during their disappearance in secret detention centers (Fernández Meijide 2013:191). Unlike the truth commission that placed the victim-survivors at the center of attention to elicit a narrative truth and reliable proof about the disappeared, the court revolved around the accused. Witness testimonies provided incriminating evidence for the prosecution. This contrast becomes clear from two renditions by Adriana Calvo de Laborde of what must have been the most indelible day of her life.

Adriana Calvo de Laborde was abducted by policemen at around ten o'clock in the morning on 4 February 1977 in the town of Tolosa. Seven months pregnant with her third child, she was taken to a police station in La Plata, where her husband was being held. She was moved several times to other secret detention centers. On 15 April, as she was taken by squad car to another location by two policemen and a collaborating disappeared captive called Lucrecia, Adriana went into labor. She pleaded in vain to take her to a hospital and finally asked them to stop the car because the baby was coming. The policemen just laughed and told her that it didn't matter because they were going to kill her anyway and her child as well. Blindfolded and handcuffed, she succeeded in removing her underpants to give birth. "Thanks to the forces of nature, the birth was normal. The only assistance I received was when 'Lucrecia' tied the umbilical cord which was still linking me with the child as there was nothing to cut it with. No more than five minutes later we drove on, supposedly in the direction of a hospital. I was still blindfolded and my child was on the seat" (CONADEP 1986:291).

In the trial against the commanders, she gave the following rendition of this distressing ordeal. "My baby was born well, she was very tiny, she was hanging from the umbilical cord because she had fallen from the seat. She was on the floor. I asked them to, please, hand her to me so that I could have her with me, but they didn't give her to me. Lucrecia asked for a rag to the one sitting in front, who cut a dirty rag and with that they tied the umbilical cord, and continued on their way. Three minutes had passed. My baby was crying, I continued with my hands behind my back, with my eyes covered" (*El Diario del Juicio* 1985, 2:32).

The difference in tone and detail is remarkable, most likely because the first testimony was shared with a receptive CONADEP staffer and the second in the court's adversarial arena. The first testimony dates from early 1984, when this episode might have been hard to believe and a more emotional account was needed. In her court testimony, Adriana Calvo de Laborde tried to restrict herself to a matter-of-fact narration. The minute description of the birth in the trial testimony gave utmost attention to details to enhance its credibility and to stay as close as possible to the facts. Many other court testimonies were also precise about date, time, and location and, whenever possible, mentioned the (nick)names of the torturers and the military unit that held them captive.

The court testimonies were strictly directed by the presiding judges. For example, Norberto Liwski had described in the CONADEP testimony quoted earlier the bodily harm inflicted during his first days in captivity. The verbatim excerpt of his deposition is the longest torture account reproduced in the CONADEP report, occupying five pages in small print. Virtually none of that corporeal ordeal appears in his court testimony of 7 August 1985 because Judge Gil Lavedra was not so much interested in the physical torture of Liwski as in the psychological torment that involved his daughters. The judge asked the age of his daughters. Liwski responded that the youngest child was three and the eldest six, and then continued to describe the psychological torture of his captors. "During a break in the torture on the first or second day, they put me face down, take off my blindfold, and show me the underwear of my daughters, knickers that of course they showed me dirty and wet. . . . This went on and on, this torture of using the children in this way. At various occasions they told me that they had such control over my daughters that they had films of them on which I could ascertain myself—if I cared to see them—the degree of control they had over them" (*El Diario del Juicio* 1985, 30:549).

The court was primarily interested in testimonies that yielded solid, verifiable evidence to convict the junta commanders, while the authenticity and credibility of Liwski's testimony was more important for the truth commission. The extensive account in the CONADEP report is mainly about Liwski's personal experience of torture, and the reference to his children is limited to the following: "showing me more bloodstained rags, they said these were my daughters' knickers, and asked me whether I wanted them to be tortured with me or separately" (CONADEP 1986:23). Clearly, the narration of the same ordeal in different arenas influenced the testimony's form and content.

There was also suspicion about the witness testimonies. The judges forbade the defense lawyers to ask questions about the political affiliation of the witnesses because being a Montonero or ERP combatant did not justify torture and disappearance. Norberto Liwski was asked about his membership in the Revolutionary Communist Party (PCR). He responded that the question reminded him of his interrogation under torture, and thereupon defense lawyer Tavares was cut short by Judge Lavedra (*El Diario del Juicio* 30:551). Still, it made the military defendants discredit these testimonies. Relatives of disappeared persons might also be suspicious about the partial truths revealed in court, but most did not voice their skepticism in public, afraid to play into the hands of the indicted junta commanders.

Testimonial Chronicles

Some witnesses of the truth commission and the trial of the commanders had been involved in the guerrilla movement, but their combat experiences were not narrated to avoid self-incrimination. With the exception of Gasparini (1988), who had been held at the ESMA, books about the insurgency were only written by former guerrillas who had escaped capture. Their experience of the disintegrating revolutionary movement appeared in the form of interviews (Gutiérrez 1985; Mero 1987; Blixen 1988), creative nonfiction (Diez 1987), and monographs (J. Santucho 1988; Mattini 1990), as if they were struggling to find the right narrative form to understand their defeat.

The soul-searching tone of former guerrillas during the late 1980s was replaced one decade later by self-confident testimonial chronicles that sought to record, rather than analyze and interpret, the past with much attention to detail and emotion (Anguita and Caparrós 1997; Bonasso 1997; Diana 1997; Jauretche 1997; Perdía 1997). These narratives were prompted by the death flight confessions of Navy Captain Scilingo, the mea culpa by the armed forces, and the twentieth anniversary of the coup d'état in 1996.

An additional reason was to create a testimonial legacy "for the new generations . . . [as] an unavoidable moral duty" (Perdía 1997:back cover) and as "an appeal to the new generations so that they turn their gaze to the past in search of their own path" (Jauretche 1997:back cover). The title of the massive three-volume oral history of the Argentine revolutionary movement, *La voluntad*, which in Spanish means both *will* and *desire*, sums up the gist of these chronicles (Anguita and Caparrós 1997, 1998a, 1998b). The desire for revolution and the will to achieve fundamental change at the highest cost were what the authors wanted to convey to the second generation of activists who were rejuvenating the human rights movement and the political left.

Historical truth was not at stake in the testimonial chronicles but rather the agency and subjectivity of the protagonists, their revolutionary commitment, and the contingency of their actions in a volatile political environment. As one surviving Montonero commander wrote: "Our Montonero life was much more than a political rationality. It was a passion, a way-of-being-in-the-world, a profound solidarity, a commitment that involved the entire being, and the acting, thinking, feeling, and working for the construction of the 'new man' that dominated our utopias" (Perdía 1997:9). Anguita and Caparrós (1997:15) explained that they intended to show "the everyday life, the interests, hatreds, convictions, objectives, fears and satisfactions of those who chose this way." This genre of books combined oral history with original documents but did so— sometimes with nostalgic overtones (Mattini 2006, 2007)—in a way that emphasized the sacrifice of the historical protagonists who tried to create a more just society.

An illustration of this change from politically motivated testimonios to historicizing testimonial chronicles is the rendition of the disappearance of a group of seven high school students in La Plata. The repressive operation, code-named The Night of the Pencils (La Noche de los Lápices) had been conducted on 16 September 1976 and became emblematic of the Argentine military who abducted seven adolescents, tortured them, and assassinated six of them because they had protested against the price hike of student bus fares.[3] The operation was revealed by Pablo Díaz, the group's seventh member and its sole survivor, through his CONADEP deposition and court testimony (CONADEP 1986:318–320; *El Diario del Juicio* 1985, 3:62–66). The fate of the students was narrated by two journalists who warned the reader: "we know that whoever reads these pages cannot remain indifferent. One may or may not recover from the emotional impact of revealing the perversion that assassinated adolescence" (Seoane and Ruiz Núñez 1986:12–13). The book described how the group of seven had joined the tens of thousands of adolescents who became politically active in 1972–1973 during the fall of the Lanusse dictatorship and the return of Perón to Argentina. They became members of the Union of High School Students (UES) and the Guevarist Youth (JG) that were front organizations of the Montoneros and the Marxist PRT-ERP. The student unions were outlawed after the March 1976 coup, but the group of La Plata students continued their political activism clandestinely (Robben 2005a:213–214; Seoane and Ruiz Núñez 1986:132–141).

In a commentary, written twenty-four years later, Sandra Raggio (2010:159) argued that the book by Seoane and Ruiz Núñez had been written at a time that emphasized the exposure of human rights violations and the prosecution of perpetrators. The historical context made the book downplay the students' ideological support of a violent transformation of Argentina's political system. The portrayal of the seven students as adolescents who simply wanted cheaper bus tickets made them legally and symbolically innocent. Their political involvement, however, proved to have been much greater. Jorge Falcone, the brother of the disappeared María Claudia Falcone, revealed in 1999 that the students were not just members of the UES student union but also belonged to the Montonero militia: "in the apartment where my sister was taken, we kept the arsenal of the UES of La Plata" (Vezzetti 2009:111). In line with the testimonial chronicles by former guerrilla combatants, the picture of high school students was now redrawn in the image of determined political activists and militias. The fact that they were armed Montonero militias of course does not justify their abduction, torture, and assassination but does shed a different light on the repressive operation, the political motives of the students, and their transformation from victims into heroes and martyrs. According to Vezzetti (2009:115), it also raised uncomfortable questions about the responsibility of the guerrilla insurgency in arming adolescents and pursuing a violent political change.

The testimonial chronicles by former combatants who escaped Argentina into exile abroad also affected the testimonial narratives of former disappeared persons who had been involved in the armed insurgency. These disappeared had been described by the CONADEP report as "those who were proposing a social revolution, to aware adolescents who merely went

out to the shanty towns to help the people living there" (CONADEP
1986:4). As in the case of the Night of the Pencils, this profile was problematic when the idealistic victims were in fact revolutionary combatants. The
credibility gap was not resolved in the testimonial chronicles, and most
authors mentioned their political militancy only in passing. Some continued to add to the victim-survivor genre of the 1980s (e.g., Ramus 2000;
Tamburini 2002), while others reinterpreted their experiences within the
discursive frame of genocide (e.g., Calveiro 1998; Actis et al. 2001). The
latter emphasized the similarities between Nazi concentration camps and
Argentine secret detention centers and compared the mini-staff of trusted
ESMA captives to the Jewish Council (Judenrat) in a Polish ghetto (Actis
et al. 2001:296). This testimonial discourse articulated the transnational
correspondences between Argentina's disappearances and the Holocaust, as
was explained in the previous chapter.

The mothers of the disappeared who had written testimonios in the
1980s also began to produce testimonial chronicles. In the form of memoirs, they described their public lives as human rights activists, the anxieties of the search, and the piecemeal reconstruction of the disappearance
of their loved ones. Graciela Fernández Meijide (2009:309) finally reconciled herself with the loss of her son in a dream at a time when she was
finishing her memoirs: "I didn't awake sad but with a moving tenderness,
and immediately thought that writing this book had allowed me to bid
farewell to my son." Instead, the biographies of María Isabel Chorobik de
Mariani (Ramos Padilla 2006), known as Chicha Mariani, and Estela
Barnes de Carlotto (Petraglia 2008) remained open ended. The women
continued to be the driving force behind the Grandmothers of the Plaza
de Mayo and helped locate many grandchildren but not their own. Estela
de Carlotto wrote in an open letter to her disappeared grandson Guido:
"I am searching for you tirelessly from before you arrived in this world.
. . . Today you are already a man, and far from forgetting you I miss you
more every day, hour, and minute. How to explain that I feel so much
love for you without knowing you? You are the son of my daughter, blood
of my blood" (Petraglia 2008:301). Chicha Mariani ends her memoirs
with a somber reflection: "After thirty years, my hopes are diluted. I feel
that my life will end soon and I am no longer sure to find my granddaughter" (Ramos Padilla 2006:408). These two testimonial chronicles
create some order, coherence, and chronology to their lives as a function
of the search but cannot provide a narrative closure when the two women

and their grandchildren, Guido and Clara Anahí, are living parallel lives, perhaps in the same city, unbeknown to one another.

Conclusion

This chapter has analyzed five types of testimony by victims and survivors of state repression: denunciations, testimonios, depositions, court testimonies, and testimonial chronicles. The atrocities of the military and police were first denounced to Argentine human rights organizations in 1976 and later to international fact-finding missions. These oral testimonies carried an inner tension between representational shortcomings and factual accusations that made the Argentine regime question their credibility. The tales of suffering convinced world audiences through their emotional veracity, but international organizations needed dispassionate descriptions that provided sufficient grounds to accuse the Argentine dictatorship. Testimonios were an attempt to resolve this tension by writing first-person narratives that stood for the experience of others. Reconciling emotion with politics, the Argentine testimonio genre tried to achieve an identification between author and reader.

The creation of the CONADEP truth commission in December 1983 shifted the testimonial weight from denunciations and testimonios to depositions that accomplished a narrative truth through emotional accounts that remained as close as possible to the lived experiences. Their inclusion in the widely distributed report *Never Again* convinced many Argentines that the military had to be prosecuted.

The 1985 indictment against nine former Argentine junta leaders was based on the best-documented cases of the truth commission; the indictment meant that the witnesses had to testify again, but now in court. The adversarial questioning and the emphasis on legal evidence affected the testimonies in form and content because defense lawyers tried to dismiss the witnesses as untrustworthy. Five junta members were convicted in 1985 but pardoned in 1990. The climate of impunity made memorialization the new goal of witness testimonies. A genre of testimonial chronicles emerged in the mid-1990s that aimed to record almost ethnographically the decade of political violence and repression through a narrative emphasis on emotion, subjectivity, and lived experience. This historicization tried to convey the agency and subject position from which radical decisions had been taken and consequential events unfolded.

The political, legal, and emotional implications of testimonies about torture and disappearance made their credibility and the trustworthiness of the witnesses of paramount concern in Argentina but, as in the case of social memory, there existed several partial truths and degrees of trustworthiness to different audiences. Witness testimonies created chronology and coherence to the narration of past traumatic experiences and disparate violent events. People might agree on the course of events—whether or not the testifier was taken from his or her home and interrogated at a particular secret detention center—but disagreements arose about how these basic facts should be connected and interpreted by placing them in the proper historical and political context. What was an illegal abduction for one individual was a legitimate detention for another. Furthermore, the bewildering experiential origins of many testimonies raised the question of whether or not shattering experiences could be verbalized reliably. One group of scholars believes that traumatic experiences can by definition never be narrated because they are embodied rather than remembered, while another group argues that therapeutic distancing will evoke an accurate account. These dilemmas have persistently contributed to a mistrust of the testimonies given by adversary witnesses.

CHAPTER 4

Denial

Navy Lieutenant Adolfo Donda just smiled wryly when Leontina Puebla de Pérez, one of the founding members of the Grandmothers of the Plaza de Mayo, asked him if he could obtain information about her disappeared daughter, María Hilda. He pretended to know nothing. She must be dead, he said. On 26 March 1977, María Hilda Pérez de Donda was five months pregnant with her second child when she was overpowered at a railway station. She was hooded and brought to Morón Police Station No. 3 in Castelar, run by the 7th Air Brigade. Her husband, José María Donda, a member of the Montoneros and Lieutenant Adolfo Danda's younger brother, was abducted one month later and taken to the same secret detention center. After being tortured, he was forced to face his wife in a confrontation, but the two said they didn't know one another. José María Donda was then taken elsewhere, and María Hilda was moved to the maternity ward of the Navy Mechanics School (Donda 2009:41–45, 130; Mittelbach 1986:68).

Adolfo Donda and José María Donda were brothers who became enemies. Their father remarked once: "I had two sons. One is dead for having been a Montonero. The other is dead to me for having been an assassin" (Donda 2009:62). He never received any news about his disappeared son and could never have imagined the extent of his eldest son's betrayal.

Navy Lieutenant Adolfo Donda was head of operations at the ESMA when his sister-in-law María Hilda Pérez de Donda was taken to its maternity ward, which was nothing more than a bare room with dirty mattresses. María Hilda gave birth there in August 1977 with assistance from the gynecologist Jorge Luis Magnacco from the Naval Hospital. Fearing that the baby would be taken from her, she succeeded in passing a blue thread through each earlobe and named her Victoria. According to an eyewitness,

María Hilda's brother-in-law Adolfo "promised her that she would meet again with her husband, that the baby would be taken to her family, and that soon she would be reunited with all of them."[1] Instead, after fifteen days the baby was taken away by Coast Guard officer Héctor Febres, who was in charge of the maternity ward, and brought to the home of Juan Antonio Azic, who was also stationed at the ESMA. Azic and his wife raised Victoria together with another kidnapped girl. Febres became Victoria's godfather at her baptism.

The fate of Victoria's biological mother was revealed years later when Navy Lieutenant Adolfo Donda was intimidating the captive Alicia Ruscovsky to make her talk: "This is a war. And in a war one can't have mercy on the enemy. I didn't [have mercy] with my own brother, who was a Montonero. I didn't with my sister-in-law, who was like you disappeared [chupada] here in the ESMA. And she was killed [trasladada], like you will also if you don't do your chores. I didn't have any hurt feelings or guilt. Because this is a war, and they were with the other party. This is how it is: or we win or you win. So you better start telling everything you know."[2] Alicia Ruscovsky was eventually set free, but María Hilda had probably been sedated and put on a death flight. Ten years later, in another astounding twist, Adolfo Donda wrested legal custody of Eva Daniela, the eldest daughter of the disappeared María Hilda and José María Donda, from the hands of her grandmother Leontina Puebla de Pérez (Donda 2009:60).

In October 2004, Victoria's real identity was revealed through a blood test. Victoria, now twenty-seven years old, finally met her sister, Eva Daniela, who had been raised by her uncle Adolfo Donda. The brief meetings were tense. The blood relation of the two sisters proved to be emotionally weaker than the affective ties with their adopted parents. Victoria noted that Adolfo Donda "will always be her [Eva Daniela's] father. For me, he [Adolfo Donda] will always be responsible for the death of my own father," and she admitted that it was painful "to construct spaces of identification with those who were only tied to me by blood, before confirming my love and affection for those who I had always loved" (Donda 2009:202, 205). Adolfo Donda was handed a life sentence in October 2011 for one murder and eighteen cases of torture and disappearance. Juan Antonio Azic received a sentence of eighteen years for three instances of torture and disappearance, including the torture of a twenty-day-old baby who was placed on the stomach of his father as Azic gave him electric shocks (Donda 2009:51).[3]

This family tragedy shows how trust among close relatives can be betrayed, and how intimate ties may be based on deceit: Adolfo Donda betrayed his parents, brother, and sister-in-law but cultivated an affective bond with his adopted daughter and niece, Eva Daniela, while cynically refusing to meet his other niece Victoria because his brother José María "had never acknowledged her as his daughter" (Donda 2009:132). Victoria's adopted father, Juan Antonio Azic, raised two kidnapped children with loving care but concealed their real identity and at the same time exploited the basic trust between a captive and his baby to extract information during torture. The threat to the extended Donda family came from within, making us painfully aware "that intimacy is not just a haven of peace but also a lethal source of threat and betrayal" (Geschiere 2013:23). As Geschiere (2013) has shown in the case of African witchcraft, trust is not a given but a cultivated quality because betrayal may invade affective bonds and create mistrust in families.

There were more families in Argentina like the Donda family. Human rights lawyer Emilio Mignone, whose daughter Mónica was abducted, heard Colonel Roualdes snap to his sergeant about a colonel who wanted to see him: "'Tell him to go to hell.' And when he left, he said to me: 'Look, this man has a disappeared son. Here, here below,' and he jumped, 'I have thirty-three children of military officers and not one of them is ever going to see them again'" (interview on 14 December 1989). The repressive state enabled its agents to betray their families, friends, and the citizens who appealed to them for help. Donda and Azic, together with many state agents, violated people's political trust by misleading searching relatives and proved to be unreliable witnesses in court. Their word was set against the testimonies of their political adversaries. The conflicting testimonies form an area of national contestation in which opposite narrative accounts constitute one another reciprocally under changing historical circumstances. Both testimonies have changed through the decades, and have appealed to different discursive frames.

This chapter begins with a discussion of the betrayal of people's political trust by the authoritarian state and its agents. Next, the discourse of Argentine perpetrators and their supporters will be analyzed in terms of the logic and rhetoric of denial. It is important to realize that this denial was constituted at a time when the CONADEP truth commission, the courts, the human rights movement, and the news media were making great efforts to document the magnitude of the military repression. Finally, I will examine the complicated confession of Navy Captain Scilingo, who admitted to throwing sedated captives from a plane, and will reconstruct the intimidation of Coast Guard Prefect Febres to maintain the pact of silence.

Political Trust, Betrayal, and the State

Political trust differs from social trust. A functioning society is possible without the delegation of popular power to a state, but one can hardly imagine a society without at least some interpersonal trust. The degree of political trust depends on the state's trustworthiness as reliable and competent (Levi and Stoker 2000:476). People trust the state when their constitutional rights are respected and the state's obligations to its citizens are met by its agents. At the same time, the state needs to be able to trust its citizens in order to run an administration and dispense its services. The Argentine authoritarian state was less monolithic than the military junta pretended it to be and more closely resembled the state in late modernity, described astutely by Wendy Brown (1995:174) as "at once an incoherent, multifaceted ensemble of power relations and a vehicle of massive domination . . . the state is not a thing, system, or subject, but a significantly unbounded terrain of powers and techniques, an ensemble of discourses, rules, and practices, cohabiting in limited, tension-ridden, often contradictory relation with one another." For Argentine citizens, the state was the military junta that disseminated its power in prescriptive communiques; the armed police on horseback; the nightly raids; President Videla, who celebrated Argentina's victory euphorically at the World Cup soccer tournament in Buenos Aires; the small window at the end of a dark corridor at the Ministry of Interior to register missing people; and the personal meeting with Admiral Massera, who swore that he would try everything in his power to find a disappeared son or daughter.

The historical pendulum of democracy and dictatorship had made citizens wary of the state since the 1930s, and people's mistrust seemed to increase with each new coup d'état. The Argentine people were trapped in a major contradiction: they were constitutionally bound to cede the monopoly on violence to a state that periodically turned on its own citizens, like handing a gun to a repeat offender. People's political trust in the state was betrayed time and again during the last dictatorship, yet searching parents continued to appeal to an untrustworthy state out of desperation, as in the case of Julio Morresi, whose son Norberto vanished without a trace one month after the armed forces had taken power.

On 23 April 1976, late in the evening, Julio Morresi received a phone call asking why Norberto was not coming to the birthday party of a friend in Buenos Aires. Julio and his wife Irma were worried because they knew that their seventeen-year-old son was a member of a forbidden high school student union linked to the Montoneros. After spending hours waiting for a reassuring call from his son, Julio asked a retired police inspector for help, but his inquiries at hospitals and police stations yielded nothing. In the morning, the telephone rang again. An anonymous voice told Julio that his son and many other comrades had been detained the previous day.

Upon the advice of a lawyer, Julio Morresi submitted a request of habeas corpus at a Buenos Aires court. In the meantime, he visited police stations, military bases, prisons, morgues, and cemeteries, but he always came away empty-handed. The writ of habeas corpus was rejected after several days. It declared that Norberto Morresi was not in the custody of the Argentine authorities. On yet another fruitless visit to a police station, Julio noticed that the entry book of detainees showed dated blank lines without names or numbers. The attending policeman explained that some detainees were registered only in pencil. If they were placed under the responsibility of the state, then they turned from disappeared into prisoners and their names would be written in ink; otherwise their registration would be erased (interview on 29 March 1991; see also Robben 2005a:265–266).

The Argentine state betrayed its citizens by not honoring habeas corpus requests, not registering abducted detainees, and falsely promising to investigate all abductions through the Search for Missing Persons Division of the Federal Police. The entire state apparatus, including the armed forces, the police, the penitentiary system, the judiciary, and the corresponding ministries, pretended to provide a proper public administration but deliberately violated its political trustworthiness. Deceptively, Lieutenant-General Videla had justified the coup d'état against President Isabel Martínez de Perón as "the only possible alternative in the face of the deterioration provoked by misgovernment, corruption, and complacency" (Loveman and Davies 1989:198). Initially receiving the political support of many Argentines who wanted the country's chaos to end, the dictatorial state acted in bad faith by maintaining an appearance of good governance while blaming the disappearances on the guerrilla organizations and right-wing death squads. The junta commanders assured foreign diplomats that the disappeared were not in their hands and personally promised relatives that the state's powers would be mobilized to find the missing.

Unable to locate his son Norberto through state channels, Julio Morresi now entered a maze of rumors and shadowy contacts. In mid-1977, he finally received a sign of life. He was introduced to a woman only known as Nélida, who was said to be the illegitimate daughter of Admiral Guzzetti. She asked Julio to describe Norberto as best as he could and promised to make inquiries. Within days she sent him to a captain at the Palermo military base, but he told Julio to work only through Nélida. Some time later, Nélida came with the long-awaited news that Norberto was sharing a cell with the son of a high-ranking officer. He was being treated well. Julio and his wife Irma were euphoric. "She was our god, that's what that woman was at that moment. I believe that whatever that woman would have said, we would have done" (interview on 29 March 1991). Worries cast a shadow over their hopes when Nélida told them that the detainees were going to be executed in a week's time but that Norberto could be spared and sent to Switzerland with the officer's son if she could buy a false passport and bribe the guards. Julio gave her US$25,000, and Irma began to prepare the voyage in secret. "Because nobody was to know, nobody of the family, and because [Norberto] was going to a cold place, Irma spent all nights in bed knitting woolen clothing for him, pullovers, socks, vests, all through the night. . . . You could see her knitting with an enthusiasm, with a happiness" (interview on 29 March 1991). When Nélida asked for more money, Julio insisted on a letter from Norberto as proof. She agreed. That was the last he ever heard of her. "They [the extortionists] had gone up in smoke. This was the time that Irma almost died. That was the worst moment through which Irma passed. She was torn to pieces, destroyed, mentally and physically, destroyed" (interview on 29 March 1991; see also Robben 2005a:288–290). Thirteen years later, in July 1989, Norberto Morresi was exhumed from an anonymous grave at the General Villegas Cemetery.

Searching relatives like Julio Morresi had little choice but to deal with shady officers and anonymous intermediaries because the formal channels of the military state had proven to be impenetrable. They trusted people about whom they knew next to nothing in the desperate hope of finding a trace of their disappeared loved ones. The military authorities were obviously aware of the extortion schemes by unscrupulous state agents, who at the same time carried out the deceitful administration of an untrustworthy state, and warned the population "against false agents who, by charging large sums of money, promise parents of detainees allegedly held for a security check, to locate their whereabouts or places of detention."[4] Relatives therefore did not suspend their doubt about these intermediaries but entered into relationships of trust based on a suspicion of betrayal.

Secrecy and Denial

The turn to democracy did not bring the transparency that the Argentine people had hoped for. The Argentine military kept their repressive practices secret and thus reinforced the political mistrust that grew during the dictatorship, "because the secret designates that which has been deliberately withheld or has not yet been disclosed, it has been taken to breed a system of distrust" (Nuttall and Mbembe 2015:S318). Simmel (1906:462) and Herzfeld (2009:135) have pointed out that group secrets exist by virtue of their recognition by another group. Keeping the fate of the disappeared secret gave the Argentine military a sense of power by holding the searching relatives hostage to the hidden information. The Argentine military would gradually acknowledge their secrets through the decades.

In the 1960s and 1970s, the Argentine armed forces were convinced that they were waging an existential fight against a guerrilla insurgency and a large political opposition movement with revolutionary ambitions. Concealed operations were crucial to success because secrecy instilled fear, as Major Juan José Masi wrote in 1967: "One loses fear when one knows the cause producing it. This cause must therefore always remain hidden, must constantly change if possible, and must in all cases be part of reality" (Masi 1967:80). Secrecy provided a tactical edge over the enemy, strengthened the military's cohesion, and lessened the chance of legal accountability. The power of secrecy shrank when the dictatorship ended because the new Argentine government and the human rights organizations demanded accountability. Secrecy and silence turned into denial when the CONADEP truth commission was installed, and survivors of torture and disappearance revealed the hidden repression.

Silence and denial became different performative answers to the accusations brought forth by ex-disappeared, the courts, and human rights organizations. Silence had been a means to create uncertainty and fear in society during the dictatorship and was now presented by the deposed military as necessary to overcome the past. "Silence is healthier for the military than denial or remorse," Payne (2008:183) has argued. Silence simply ignores the past and may be justified as the only solution to reconcile a divided society or avoid accountability, while denial evokes the past through its negation. Denial might also produce internal divisions among the military and discord in society (173–179).

Denial can be conceptualized either through the rhetoric of deniers or the logic of denial. The sociologist Stanley Cohen (2001) has concentrated on individual deniers and denying nation-states through an analysis of the rhetorical devices used to challenge grave accusations. The historian Deborah Lipstadt (1993) has examined the logic of Holocaust denial. I will integrate both approaches to analyze the rhetoric and logic of denial in Argentina. This denial is not static because changing political circumstances, discursive frames, and multidirectional memories transformed the early blatant denials into justifications of the repressive violence, and finally into open confessions about procedures and practices that had been denied several decades earlier. The Argentine military engaged dynamically with the growing evidence against them in the ways described by Cohen (2001:103; emphasis in original): "Each variant of denial appears in the official discourse: *literal* (nothing happened); *interpretive* (what happened is really something else) and *implicatory* (what happened is justified). Sometimes, these appear in a visible sequence: if one strategy does not work, the next is tried."

The public denial of the systematic abduction, disappearance, torture, and assassination of citizens resembles the rhetoric of Holocaust denial. "Truth is mixed with absolute lies, confusing readers who are unfamiliar with the tactics of the deniers. Half-truths and story segments, which conveniently avoid critical information, leave the listener with a distorted impression of what really happened. The abundance of documents and testimonies that confirm the Holocaust are dismissed as contrived, coerced, or forgeries and falsehoods" (Lipstadt 1993:2). Lipstadt's analysis has allowed me to identify five elements of the Argentine military's denial: fate, moral relativism, self-defense, survival, and media manipulation (Robben 2011:171). Before discussing these five elements, it is important to emphasize that the Argentine military have always equated the political opposition movement with the guerrilla organizations as if armed insurgents and leftist civilians were of one stock. This has allowed them to exchange one for the other when it suited their argument.

First, the Argentine military argued that people disappear in every war. They muddled the issue by adding that people can also be missing in peacetime. Not military strategy but the fate of war explained Argentina's disappearances. Second, a moral equivalence was drawn with other armed conflicts. The military repression of the Argentine guerrilla organizations was not more brutal and did not cause more suffering than other counterinsurgency wars. Third, every sovereign nation has the right to defend itself against aggression and protect the democratically elected authorities. The Argentine armed forces were constitutionally mandated and empowered by a presidential decree in 1975 to eliminate the guerrilla insurgency. They acted in self-defense against armed assailants who were not victims of unlawful repression but legitimate targets of the Argentine armed forces. Fourth, the offensive military operations against the armed combatants and revolutionary ideologues were presented as essential for Argentina's economic and cultural survival. If the insurgents would have come to power, then the country would have been a Cuban-style satellite of the Soviet Union and would have lost control over its vast natural resources. Even more important was the ideological nature of the armed conflict. A communist government would install a planned economy, abolish private property, prohibit religion, and thus destroy Argentina's Christian, Western culture. Fifth, the Argentine military accused the ex-disappeared of fabricating their testimonies and planting these lies in the gullible news media.

The Argentine military also made use of the following rhetorical devices to buttress their denial. They stated that torture and disappearances did not take place; that the testimonies of the ex-disappeared and remorseful officers were false, subjective, and motivated by personal interests; and that the incriminating records and documents were forgeries. They also exploited discrepancies between testimonies or documents to dismiss all evidence and admitted some excesses as the inevitability of warfare but rejected any systematic wrongdoing (Robben 2011:171–172).

The Denial of Disappearances

The disappearance of armed combatants and political opponents between 1976 and 1983 was premeditated. Disappearances had occurred during the military government of President Lanusse between 1971 and 1973 and became a standard operating procedure in February 1975, when a counterinsurgency campaign was formed against a rural Marxist insurgency in Tucumán Province. The repressive method was applied nationwide in

March 1976. A network of secret detention centers covered Argentina. The dictatorship feigned ignorance during the first year of military rule. It blamed the disappearances on guerrilla organizations and right-wing death squads, but could not prevent people from witnessing raids and abductions by members of the armed forces and police (Robben 2005a:264–269).

News about the dictatorship's repressive methods was aired by Amnesty International after a fact-finding mission in November 1976. The American public relations company Burson Marsteller was hired in 1977 to improve the regime's reputation. The media offensive included paid trips to Argentina for journalists, ads in foreign newspapers, and a hurtful campaign against the human rights protests in Argentina under the slogan "We Argentines Are Right and Human" (Feitlowitz 1998:36, 42–45; Guest 1990:69–70). In 1979, President Videla spoke with confidence about the impending visit of the Inter-American Commission on Human Rights (IACHR): "Argentina has nothing to hide, and nothing about which we have to be ashamed. Some things have happened here, certainly, we have lived through a war. A war which we didn't call for and didn't want . . . In that war, as in every war, there were dead persons, there were prisoners, and there were disappeared persons."[5]

The IACHR concluded in April 1980 that thousands of people had disappeared in Argentina between 1975 and 1979. Argentina's official reply stated that terrorists created disappearances by going into hiding, after which the relatives reported them to the authorities as missing persons, submitted a habeas corpus request, and then raised the alarm with a human rights organization. Later, the terrorist reappeared and concocted a detailed story of abduction and torture. The Argentine government did not deny that there were people missing in Argentina, but blamed these disappearances mainly on the guerrilla organizations (Government of Argentina 1980:54). This explanation went against the evidence accumulated by Amnesty International, the IACHR, and Argentine human rights organizations.

Following the military defeat by the United Kingdom in the South Atlantic in June 1982, a transitional military government assumed power that confronted the incriminatory findings with a rhetoric of denial that consisted of four points. First, the Argentine armed forces had fought a dirty but just war with casualties on both sides because clean wars do not exist. Second, a counterinsurgency war conducted by small combat units made oversight difficult and excesses inevitable. Third, the fallen and missing guerrilla insurgents were not innocent victims but aggressors who had attacked the

Argentine nation. Fourth, the testimonies about enforced disappearances and the rumors about torture centers had been concocted by revolutionaries living in Europe during an international media campaign against Argentina (Agüero and Hershberg 2005; Marchesi 2005; Robben 2005b).

The National Commission on the Disappeared, or CONADEP, was to disprove the military by gathering thousands of testimonies. The military ignored the requests for information and refused to testify because the truth commission could not subpoena witnesses (CONADEP 1986:437). About a dozen allegedly repentant perpetrators came forward, but the commission was skeptical of their testimonies because of the perpetrators' efforts to plea-bargain a deal in exchange (Feitlowitz 1998:206–226). Nevertheless, the CONADEP collected much solid evidence, which was later used in the trial against the junta commanders. The military reacted in a predictable manner. They kept emphasizing that the armed forces had the constitutional right and obligation to defend Argentina's sovereignty and denied that torture and disappearance had been deliberate repressive methods. In addition, they resorted to a common strategy of trying "to avoid being counted among the perpetrators and to secure one's place among the victims" (Bartov, Grossmann, and Nolan 2002:xxiii). Fallen troops were celebrated in religious masses, a memorial was planned to honor them, and mothers of fallen troops were encouraged to gather at the Plaza de Mayo as a moral counterforce to the mothers of the disappeared. These efforts failed to convince, but the denial strategy continued in the courtroom.

The most systematically reasoned denial of the disappearances was written in 1984 by the defense counsel of General Ramón Camps, who was under investigation of the Armed Forces Supreme Council for thousands of disappearances in Buenos Aires Province. Retired General Osiris Villegas argued that the allegations concerned typical acts of war: "there are no excesses in war. Violence is used to the maximum possible, with the objective of causing the greatest physical, moral, and material destruction to the enemy, to hasten the outcome in order to minimize one's own losses. This is affirmed by the 150,000 dead, wounded and disappeared of the detonation of the atomic bombs in Hiroshima and Nagasaki" (Villegas 1990:67). Ignoring the existence of international war conventions, Villegas employed the just war argument that extreme means are allowed against an imminent danger that threatens a state's existence (Walzer 1977:252).

Villegas also tried to raise reasonable doubt about the thirty thousand disappeared mentioned by the human rights movement. Many disappeared were still alive, he argued, because they had fled abroad, were employed as mercenaries or instructors in Algeria, Lebanon, Yemen, El Salvador, and Nicaragua, were working as political agitators under false names in Brazil, Chile, and Peru, or had secretly returned to Argentina. Furthermore, there were combat casualties that had been buried anonymously, combatants who had fallen victim to violent disputes within the guerrilla organizations, and persons had been reported as disappeared even though they were known to be alive (Villegas 1990:182).

But how could Villegas substantiate his claim that there were missing people alive who somehow did not contact their relatives? Villegas employed the rhetorical device of generalizing a selective piece of information. In September 1985, Mexico City was hit by a major earthquake that caused thousands of fatalities. The list of Argentine survivors included sixteen names that matched with the names of disappeared persons listed in the CONADEP report. In addition, one hundred names showed a close resemblance (*Somos* 1985, 474(23):6–10). Without verifying whether the sixteen expatriates in Mexico were in fact reported missing in Argentina, Villegas concluded that many other disappeared persons must be alive and that the truth commission report was therefore unreliable (Villegas 1990:184).

Villegas could not ignore the fact that people had disappeared in Argentina and could ignore even less the following self-incriminatory declaration by General Camps: "About five thousand people disappeared when I was Chief of the Buenos Aires Provincial Police. I had some of them buried in anonymous graves" (*Somos* 1984, 384(27):7). Villegas argued that if there were missing persons in times of peace then they would certainly exist in times of war but added that "for the act of war as such, there are no disappeared but unidentified combat dead" (Villegas 1990:182). Most unidentified combatants had been killed in armed confrontations with the Argentine armed forces during assaults on police stations and military bases, during bank robberies and attempts to escape detention. There were also combatants who had swallowed cyanide pills to avoid capture or were assassinated by rival groups and right-wing death squads. Furthermore, the identification of the dead was not always easy because they might carry forged documents or had erased their fingerprints with pumice stone. According to Villegas (1990:182–185), the unidentified dead were not buried in clandestine graves, as the human rights movement claimed, but in unmarked war graves, as symbolized by the Tomb of the Unknown Soldier.

By treating all disappeared as armed insurgents and casting aside the eye-witness accounts about captives in secret detention centers as false, Villegas asked for the acquittal of his client (Robben 2011:176–177). Yet, the defense plea was never presented before the Armed Forces Supreme Council because the case against General Camps was taken to a federal court.

Captain Scilingo's Confession

The amnesty laws and presidential pardons of the 1980s ended the trials against the military and police, including that of General Camps, and ensured the memorialization of the past by the human rights movement and retired veterans of the dictatorship. The almost predictable mutual constitution of conflicting social memories was shaken up in March 1995 by a chilling interview by journalist Horacio Verbitsky with retired Navy Captain Adolfo Francisco Scilingo, who admitted to having thrown sedated captives from a plane. Scilingo had approached Verbitsky in 1994 when naval officers Pernías and Rolón had been denied promotion because of their participation in the military repression. In the Senate hearing, Captain Pernías admitted that the French nuns Alice Domon and Léonie Duquet, who had actively supported the Mothers of the Plaza de Mayo, had been abducted in December 1977 and held captive at the ESMA. Pernías and Rolón also admitted the use of torture (Robben 2005a:303–304; Verbitsky 1995:159–176). The treatment of the two officers may have prompted retired Captain Scilingo to make his confession, but it had been evolving for years. Elsewhere I have interpreted Scilingo's confession in the context of Argentina as a traumatized society (Robben 2005b), and in Chapter 6 I will focus on his account of the death flights, but here I will analyze the personal and political circumstances of his confession, and his vilification as a traitor of the armed forces.

Scilingo was suffering from a recurring nightmare in 1984. He dreamt that he was throwing naked bodies from a plane, stumbled, and fell through the hatch, only to wake up before hitting the water. The nightmare represented an unforgettable incident during a flight in June 1977 that occurred after Scilingo and a crew member had finished undressing the captives: "Next, we began lowering the subversives that way [through the hatch]. As I was quite nervous about the situation, I almost fell and tumbled into the abyss. . . . I slipped and they grabbed me" (Verbitsky 1995:58). A similar version of this incident appears in Scilingo's book, but several years earlier he had shared this story with the national prosecutor, Luis Moreno Ocampo, who heard a different version (Scilingo 2000:68). Moreno Ocampo remembered that Scilingo had told him that a person he had once abducted appeared on this death flight: "Despite [having received an injection of a sedative], this prisoner woke up, and half-conscious resisted being thrown out and almost dragged him into the abyss" (Verbitsky 1995:149). This different rendition is a reminder of the caution with which Scilingo's account must be treated. His confession is calculated and self-serving by placing himself in the role of a victim: ordered, if not duped, into dropping sedated captives from a plane; traumatized, stigmatized, and almost falling to his death while carrying out an act of duty. In his book, Scilingo tried to convey his moral misgivings after he and Lieutenant Vaca had undressed the captives sentenced to death by skyfall. "I saw the thirteen naked persons, half-sitting and sleeping, leaning against one another, on the left side of the plane. Similar to a scene from a concentration camp in the Second World War. If telepathy exists then it was at this moment. Vaca broke the silence and while looking at me said: 'It seems like a Nazi photo.' The silence became more intense. I will never forget this image. Especially that of two girls of 18–20 years old, blond, slender, with angel faces. What had they done? They didn't seem dangerous" (Scilingo 2000:68).

Scilingo shared his thoughts the next day with Father Luis Manseñido: "He talked about the importance of weeding. We had to do it for the wheat to grow. There was no sin. Neither did I have to repent. I had only carried out the orders of my superiors, which were the orders of God" (Scilingo 2000:69). In 1985, Scilingo shared his nightmares and flashbacks with a superior officer in relation to a possible promotion and was ordered to take a psychological examination at the Naval Hospital. He was considered to be in good mental health but was nevertheless not promoted (Verbitsky 1995:142–144). Disillusioned, he left the Navy in 1986 and became a businessman.

In the 1970s, Scilingo had accepted the ideological justification of the coup d'état. He also understood the tactical rationale behind the abductions and the importance of secrecy in war, but in the mid-1980s he began to disagree with the continued denial of the disappearances. Frustrated in his naval career, a failure in business, and apparently suffering from PTSD, he wrote in February 1991 to the pardoned Lieutenant-General Videla: "In response to the issue of the disappeared you said: There are subversives living under false names, others died in combat and were buried as NN [anonymously], and finally you did not rule out some excesses by your subordinates. Where do I fit in? Do you believe that these weekly transfers [death flights] were the result of unauthorized excesses? . . . Let's end this cynicism. Let us tell the truth. Make the death lists public, even though at the time you failed to take responsibility by not signing the execution order" (Verbitsky 1995:180).

Scilingo never received an answer. Admiral Ferrer and President Menem also failed to respond to similar letters. Scilingo felt betrayed by Videla because of his denial of the disappearances. Videla's unwillingness to assume responsibility for the repressive structure turned Scilingo into a war criminal for hurling sedated captives from a plane, even while acting under orders from his commanders. He faced the dilemma of breaking the pact of silence and being marked a traitor or swallowing his emotions and living with the traumatic consequences. The refusal of Congress to promote his comrades Pernías and Rolón, who had also carried out violent acts in the line of duty, made him seek out the prominent journalist and former Montonero Horacio Verbitsky in November 1994.

Scilingo's self-accusation gave his confession more credibility than the denials of his commanders. His account was corroborated by surviving ESMA captives, even though only he could describe the final stage of the death flights. Nevertheless, the interviews were highly problematic. Protected from prosecution by the amnesty laws, Scilingo used a rhetoric of confession that conferred the responsibility for his actions on his commanders. He also underplayed the suffering of his victims but gave detailed attention to his guilty conscience and troubled emotional life. He ignored the ethics of professional conduct and blamed a military culture of blind obedience. As if to comfort the relatives, Scilingo reassured his interviewer that the condemned captives did not know they were about to die because they had been given a powerful sedative: "They were completely asleep. No one suffered absolutely anything" (Verbitsky 1995:60). A self-serving discursive contrast was constructed between captives falling peacefully to their death and an emotionally torn executioner who hoped to evoke the empathy of his audience: "Nobody liked to do it, it wasn't something pleasant" (32). In fact, Scilingo presented himself as a victim of his superiors who had betrayed him repeatedly during his career and denied his PTSD and emotional suffering. Scilingo's deliberate lies, denials, half-truths, and silences about the death flights served to sanitize his confession of all too graphic details that would undermine the cultivated portrayal of the perpetrator as an honorable man caught in the wheelworks of an immoral military structure (Robben 2011:180).

Scilingo raised a public storm that intensified when Sergeant Víctor Ibáñez confirmed the death flights and said that he was also forced into retirement because of a severe mental depression (Almirón 1999:177–184; Feitlowitz 1998:206–207). Veteran generals persisted in their denial of human rights violations, but in April 1995, Army Commander General Martín Balza took the army's institutional responsibility for the "mistakes" of the dictatorship and promised to "initiate a painful dialogue about the past that has never taken place, and that hovers as a ghost over the collective conscience. As in these days, this ghost keeps returning inevitably from the shadows where it occasionally hides."[6] He explained that Argentina had been caught in a spiral of violence during the 1970s and that the armed forces tried to restore the peace with unjustifiable means and immoral orders.

Scilingo had been pressured by the Navy to remain silent before he went public. He was promised money, and when he rejected the offer, veiled threats were made to his family. He was also told that he was risking his Navy pension (Verbitsky 1995:148). When the interview finally broke the news, it shocked the nation. Afraid that Scilingo might further jeopardize the national reconciliation agenda, President Memem began to discredit him in public, saying that Scilingo intended to strike a profitable deal with some Hollywood producers for his fabricated story. Scilingo also received death threats. His former comrades at the Navy Mechanics School intimidated him to prevent more revelations: "We know about the book. Your days are numbered. Stop soon or we'll take you on a flight. We have people watching your steps. You know how we work" (Payne 2008:52). Scilingo was permanently branded as a traitor.

After spending two years in custody for passing a bad check, Scilingo was acquitted of the charge but not free from persecution. He was abducted on 11 September 1997 by four assailants who warned him to avoid the media. To further impress their threat on Scilingo, they cut the initials of the three journalists who had interviewed him into his forehead and cheeks.[7] Scilingo fled to Spain in October 1997 and testified in a judicial investigation by Judge Garzón about the disappearance of Spanish citizens in Argentina. To his shock, he was accused himself. Scilingo recanted his confession during his trial, but in April 2005 was sentenced to 640 years in prison for thirty assassinations. The Spanish Supreme Court raised the sentence to 1,084 years in 2007 because the willful deaths were considered to be crimes against humanity. The verdict translated into Spain's maximum penalty of twenty-five years' imprisonment.[8]

Intimidation of Defendants

Scilingo's prosecution in Spain and requests from several European countries for the extradition of junta commanders put international pressure on Argentina to hold its perpetrators accountable. Several officers who had been detained in 1998 on kidnapping charges were awaiting trial, but many others were protected by the impunity laws. The derogation of the amnesty laws in 2005 and the presidential pardons in 2007 finally allowed prosecutors to broaden their indictments. The question of the kidnapped babies was highest on the agenda for being an ongoing crime and because the grandparents were hoping to reunite with their grandchildren before dying of old age. The trial of retired Prefect Héctor Febres, who had been in charge of the maternity ward at the Navy Mechanics School and had also been commissioned as an intelligence officer under the aliases *Fat Orlando*, *Selva*, and *Daniel*, was therefore of particular urgency.

Héctor Febres belonged to the Argentine Naval Prefecture or coast guard and had been stationed at the ESMA. The naval officers looked down upon Febres and humiliated him in front of the inmates. His brutal way of torturing captives had earned him the nickname *Jungle* (*Selva*). Febres had been detained in 1986 but benefited from the Due Obedience Law of 1987. He was arrested again in December 1998 on the accusation of baby theft. Febres was held in custody in a comfortable one-bedroom apartment at the coast guard prison in Tigre, a town located in the River Plate delta. He had a computer, access to all means of communication, and could receive visitors freely.

Febres took the stand on 18 October 2007 and denied all charges. He claimed never to have been in the ESMA and refused to answer any questions or be present at the witness testimonies. Febres only returned to the courtroom on 21 November to hear the prosecutors seek a prison sentence of twenty-five years for the illegal deprivation of liberty, torture, and the enslavement of the four plaintiffs. The prosecutor Myriam Bregman called Febres "a key figure in the genocide that took place in Argentina."[9]

On 10 December 2007, four days before the judge would read the verdict, Héctor Febres was found dead in his prison cell. "We still had hopes for some sort of confession; that he would say what they did with the children," declared the human rights lawyer Rodolfo Yanzón.[10] The corpulent sixty-six-year-old coast guard officer was suffering from diabetes, had a heart condition, and was troubled by severe depressions during his eight years of incarceration. Although a heart attack seemed likely, the autopsy revealed that he had died in the early hours of Monday, 10 December, from a significant dosage of cyanide. Had he committed suicide or was he assassinated? Yanzón suspected murder. "This is a message so that nobody is going to talk (about the illegal repression); that there exists a pact of silence and that nobody is going to be convicted."[11]

The two prison guards in Tigre, and surprisingly also the wife, son, and daughter of Febres, were arrested within days of the unexpected death. Héctor Febres had spent the previous evening with his family. Apparently, his daughter had tried to break into his computer, possibly to access a confidential file or discover the number of a secret bank account. In January 2008, the prison guards Angel Volpi and Rubén Iglesias were indicted for murder after a forensic examination revealed that the cyanide had been ingested orally after dinner. The three members of the Febres family were released but charged with the cover-up of a crime. The investigating judge, Sandra Arroyo Salgado, suggested to the press that Febres might have been assassinated because he was determined not to be a scapegoat for the baby thefts. One indication was a manuscript, entitled "Martí-(children) tell everything," that was found in his cell and seemed to refer to the exile of the former captive Ana María Martí, who had given testimony about her time in the ESMA at the French parliament in 1979 (Martí, Pirles, and Osatinsky 1995).[12] In April 2009, the two prison guards were released for lack of proof. The judge did not rule out suicide but found assassination more probable because Febres had told several people that he was not going to take the blame. According to his physician, he was nervous but defiant as he showed him a large notebook: "this folder contains what I'm going to say at the trial. It'll serve to release me. It's going to be a bombshell."[13] Febres forewarned a final confession out of spite or revenge against his superiors, as Scilingo had done. He hoped to convince the court that he had only been following orders. The physician testified furthermore that he had overheard an angry high-ranking officer issue a death threat to Febres, telling him to keep his mouth shut. The judge eventually closed the case for lack of evidence.

The case of Prefect Héctor Febres demonstrates how secrecy, silence, denial, and confession can become intertwined, and how the relations among the different parties were influenced by radical shifts of trust and betrayal. His closest family members seem to have been conspiring against him, violating attachment relationships cultivated over many years. Allegedly, they were after his money or were in cahoots with or under pressure from naval officers to prevent him from talking. Naval officers with whom he had shared the nightly hunts for Montonero guerrillas were now threatening him to maintain the pact of silence, preserve the Navy's esprit de corps, and protect their comrades from prosecution. The state had entrusted the two prison guards with Febres's safety. They developed friendly relations but may have also poisoned him or averted their eyes when others did. Finally, the death allowed ESMA officers to persist in their denial of the scheme of forced baby adoptions and to prevent grandparents from knowing the truth about the fate of their grandchildren.

Febres might have been prevented from disclosing the secrets of ESMA's maternity ward, but then again he might not, as most grandmothers believed after having been betrayed so often. For example, Police Commissioner-General Miguel Etchecolatz promised during a trial in 2011 to "contribute facts and bits of evidence about the fate of Anahí Mariani, irrespective of whoever may feel harmed. I was an eyewitness of those circumstances generated by members of a pitiless and perverse terrorism."[14] Chicha Mariani had been searching for her granddaughter since November 1976, when the three-month-old baby had been taken from a destroyed home that contained a clandestine printing office of the Montoneros. Her mother and four comrades had been killed during a three-hour shootout with the Argentine army and Buenos Aires provincial police. Echecolatz did not keep his promise, as expected, but the Grandmothers of the Plaza de Mayo hoped that the commotion surrounding high-profile trials, such as those of Febres and Etchecolatz, would make Argentines born between 1976 and 1983 stop and think about their biological identity.

The search for Clara Anahí seemed successful when in December 2015 a woman came forward with a genetic test from a private lab in Córdoba that proved with a probability of 99.9 percent that she was the granddaughter of the ninety-two-year-old Chicha Mariani. The newspaper *Clarín*, on its front page, showed a picture of a cheerful Clara Anahí and a contemplative, faintly smiling Chicha. A press communiqué was released that called the discovery "one of the greatest achievements of Argentine society on the road to the restitution of grandchildren disappeared under the military dictatorship."[15] The disappointment was great when the National Genetic Data Bank (Banco Nacional de Datos Genéticos) determined that there was no genetic match. Despite this setback, the Grandmothers of the Plaza de Mayo had identified 122 grandchildren by April 2017, including eight who were reunited with their mothers.[16]

One of the recovered grandchildren is Ignacio Guido Montoya Carlotto, whose grandmother, Estela Barnes de Carlotto, is the hard-driving president of the Grandmothers of the Plaza de Mayo. Asked about their upcoming reunion on 6 August 2014, she responded: "I believe that there will be no room for words. There will be gestures, there will be embraces, and he will return this embrace. It's certain that there will first be silence and an embrace, the feeling of being together."[17] This embrace is the sensorial beginning of an affective relation based on a search of thirty-six years carried forward by the basic trust and love of a mother for her daughter and her grandchild. The two met in Estela de Carlotto's home, embraced, and talked for hours on end.[18] Such reunions confirmed the unconditional trust of the grandmothers in the grandchildren, and the transgenerational extension of basic trust from the disappeared mothers to the kidnapped children by way of the grandmothers, as Reina Esses de Waisberg explained: "We fight so hard because the disappeared children have to know that they were not thrown away, that their mothers did not abandon them, that they were conceived with love" (Arditti 1999:92).

The restitution of the family identity of kidnapped grandchildren is slowly loosening the perpetrators' hold on Argentine society and undoing their betrayal of the relatives. The many reasons for the appropriation of babies have been analyzed in my previous book (Robben 2005a:295–298). Important in relation to the issue of trust is that the baby thefts were for the military a victory over the enemy by interrupting their social, emotional, and ideological reproduction. General Vaquero had told human rights lawyer Emilio Mignone: "We have a big problem with the children of the subversives, and we have to find a way that the children are not educated with hatred toward the military institutions" (*El Diario del Juicio* 1985, 18:390). The children were generally given to members of the armed forces and police. Furthermore, the military believed that the grandparents were incapable of raising them. They were considered poor educators who had either fed their own children with revolutionary ideas or had been unable to prevent them from joining the guerrilla insurgency. In the eyes of the military, they had not instilled political trust in the state and a respect for authority in their children and had thus lost all grandparental rights. Locating the kidnapped children was therefore so important to the relatives and human rights movement because it restored the violently ruptured bonds of family and wrested power away from the Argentine military.

Conclusion

The Argentine military responded to the accusations of state terrorism and crimes against humanity with silence, denial, declarations of hierarchical responsibility, and individual confessions. They used a rhetoric and logic of denial to avoid prosecution during the years immediately following their fall from power in 1983, but ultimately they could not ignore the evidence stacked against them. Some persisted in their silence for decades. Most others preferred to deny the existence of a repressive structure with disappearances, torture, and the appropriation of babies and infants. The tenacious pursuit of the truth by the human rights movement and the military's defiant persistence in their denial or justification kept the issue alive and provoked Navy Captain Scilingo to make several detailed confessions. These confessions were just as much manifestations of perpetrator agency as the denials were, and they employed similar rhetorical devices through the use of inconsistent comparisons, vague allusions, and calculated pauses. Silence, denial, justification, and confession have been complementary discursive strategies united by a complicity in repressive structures and horrendous acts. Clearly, the perpetrators have operated in an area of contestation in which their diverse testimonies have changed through the decades.

Attempts by the Argentine state to silence the past through amnesties and pardons in the late 1980s failed because the Supreme Court overturned the legislation as unconstitutional in the 2000s, while the public defamation of men like Scilingo was unsuccessful. Intimidation and death threats from within the ranks of the armed and security forces were more effective. Captain Scilingo fled the country after a physical assault, and Prefect Febres died from cyanide poisoning just before his final day in court. Chapter 7 will describe other attempts to pressure witnesses for the prosecution against testifying. These obstructions of justice perpetuate the politics of silence and impunity that reigned during the dictatorship, and undermined the consolidation of the democratic state for inducing political mistrust among Argentines.

Nevertheless, the confessions by perpetrators made the active-duty commanders of the armed forces admit in 1995 the atrocious practices of military repression and made even Lieutenant-General Videla confess in 2012 to a truth that had been known to Argentine society for decades. Videla spoke only in general terms and did nothing to lift the veil of secrecy altogether. Graciela Mastrogiácomo, whose disappeared sister Marta was a noncombatant of the Montoneros and had been held at the Navy Mechanics School, expressed in court what many relatives had been thinking: "I demand answers about who abducted and how they abducted; who gave the orders, who carried them out, and who participated in the death flights, because this was not a war. My sister did not carry arms. She had her legal documents and was probably chosen at random to make up the death flight. . . . I would like to say that, after 37 years, if you have information or archives, then it is still time to repair something of the damage you have done, because for us this is important."[19]

Until today, these questions have not been answered by the former members of the military regime, not because they are afraid of incriminating themselves, since many perpetrators have been convicted to life sentences, but because secrecy is their only remaining means of power. The betrayal of this secret would undermine their cohesion as a group and take away the legitimacy of their acts for their relatives and supporters. Their knowledge about the whereabouts of the disappeared and the family identity of the kidnapped babies and infants is what remains of what they still perceive as a hard-won victory over the guerrilla insurgency and a revolutionary political movement.

CHAPTER 5

Sovereignty

"To maintain order and tranquility, the population is reminded that the state of siege is in force. All inhabitants must abstain from gathering in public places and spreading alarming news. Those who do so will be detained by the military, security or police authorities. Likewise, it is noted that every street demonstration will be repressed severely" (Graham-Yooll 1989:417). This second communiqué by the Argentine armed forces in the early hours of 24 March 1976 shut down public life and dictated the conditions of the state of siege. Two hours earlier, President María Estela Martínez de Perón had been arrested after the helicopter that was taking her from the Casa Rosada palace to her residence in Olivos made an emergency landing at Buenos Aires city airport under the pretense of mechanical failure. Following the coup d'état, army units took control of Congress and the presidential palace at the Plaza de Mayo. Road blocks were erected, travel restrictions imposed, and the territorial borders, waters, and airspace were sealed. A nocturnal curfew was enforced to limit the movement of people. This national lockdown was intended to secure the state's territorial integrity and political sovereignty (Dearriba 2001:257–268; Graham-Yooll 1989:417–426; Robben 2005a:192).

With the exception of a few remote pockets in Tucumán Province, where a dwindling company of guerrillas was roaming the Andean foothills, the Argentine armed forces controlled the country but not its citizens. The military were not waging primarily a terrestrial but an intelligence war intended to dismantle the cellular guerrilla forces, combative labor unions, and grassroots organizations. The military regime territorialized its repression of the Argentine population. The country was divided into five defense zones (Zonas de Defensa) commanded by five generals who had full control over the operations in their territories (see the map of Argentina at the front of this book). Each defense zone was subdivided into subzones and areas—and in the case of the city of Buenos Aires, into subareas—where task forces gathered intelligence, abducted suspects, assessed their degree of threat, and disposed of the dead (Robben 2005a:193–197). Military commanders decided about the lives of the people within their jurisdiction. The country's roads, waterways, airports, and public utilities were in the hands of uniformed troops. These regular forces would guard the perimeter of a so-called liberated zone when a task group in civilian dress carried out an operation against a designated target. Thus, the entire country and its population were subjected to a repressive structure, as indicated by the etymological roots of the word *territory*.

The word *territory* derives from the root *terra* (or *soil*), which made the Romans speak of a town's land as a *terrātōrium*, and from the root *terrēre*, or *to frighten and terrorize*. The conjunction of the two etymological roots formed the word *territōrium*, or "a place from which people were warned off" (*OED* 2nd ed., s.v. "territory"). An area thus becomes a territory through the exercise of power over its space and inhabitants. The Argentine dictatorship was determined to cleanse the national territory of revolutionaries, generally called *subversives*, who were regarded by General Ramón Díaz Bessone as a cancer to the nation that had to be extracted "however hard the surgery may be."[1] According to the military junta, the insurgents were supported by foreign communist regimes in pursuit of world hegemony. The guerrilla organizations were accused of corroding Argentina's Western, Christian culture with their revolutionary ideas and of trying to abolish the nuclear family, paternal authority, religion, and private property (Robben 2005a:178–180). The armed forces had taken power from President Martínez de Perón to protect the Argentine people and the country from communism and foreign domination. National and cultural sovereignty were at stake in the armed and political struggle over Argentina's independence and way of life. The violent conflict between the Argentine revolutionaries and the military was therefore not just about political power but about the power to determine the cultural confines and social conditions of the Argentine people.

According to the military, national and cultural sovereignty were to be achieved through a war against the insurrectional and ideological dimensions of the subversion. Subversion was not limited to the guerrilla insurgency, as Lieutenant-General Videla emphasized: "We understand by subversion the attempt to alter our essential values inspired by our historical tradition and

Christian conception of the world and of man. This man who inherited from God his freedom and dignity as a person as his most precious good."[2] General Díaz Bessone declared that "the coexistence of two value systems within one national society is impossible. That is why we fight the subversion that wants to impose another value system: a system without God, without religion; a system that builds walls to drown freedom; a system without private property."[3] Or, in the words of General Leopoldo Galtieri: "The subversive war . . . is the clash of two civilizations, ours and the Marxist, to determine which one will be dominant and thus inspire or direct the future organization of the world. More concretely, it is about discovering which scale of values will serve as the foundation of such organization" (*Somos* 1980, 4(186):43). Argentina's sovereignty could therefore only be secured by a strong regime that took absolute control over country and people through a state of siege.

Under the influence of the political philosophers Michel Foucault and Giorgio Agamben, anthropologists have come to define sovereignty as the power to rule over life and death in exceptional situations (Agamben 1998:8; Foucault 1998:135; Das and Poole 2004; Hansen and Stepputat 2006). Mbembe (2003) has captured the political and spatial dimensions of sovereignty with the terms *necropower* and *territoriality*. *Necropower* refers to the absolute political power over life and death. *Territoriality* refers to the absolute dominion over national territory that entitles authorities to decide who can live within its borders. "Space was therefore the raw material of sovereignty and the violence it carried with it" (Mbembe 2003:26). Argentine citizens could be abducted wherever they were—at work, at home, or in the street—and they could be disappeared, assassinated, or released according to the will and whim of individual military commanders.

Necropower and territoriality come together in anonymous graves filled with the enemy dead that literally and symbolically embodied sovereignty for the military rulers.[4] They also come together in the afterlife of the disappeared dead. The sovereignty of the body and the sanctity of life and death were violated when the assassinated disappeared were buried, cremated, dissolved in lye, or dumped in territorial waters. Thus, the dead were deprived of the common Judeo-Christian ritual accompaniment to the hereafter, and the bereaved relatives have been unable to express the attachment relationship through a comforting visit to a final resting place.

Sovereignty is a pivotal area of national contestation in relation to the dictatorship and its sequels that revolves around the power over the bodies and afterlives of the disappeared. Who owns the human remains, the burial grounds, and the continuing bonds between the living and the dead? State sovereignty is not only about the power over the residence and lives of citizens but also about the obligation to provide welfare for the living and care for the dead. The Argentine military decided over the lives of the disappeared and the destination of their dead bodies. They relinquished their necropower over Argentine citizens to the democratic state in 1983, as well as their influence on thought and culture, but never lost control over the dead. They prevented the democratic state from fulfilling its obligations to the dead and the bereaved. In fact, the military's unwillingness to open the archives and reveal the predicament of the disappeared and the kidnapped babies was a means to hold on to the vestiges of dictatorial power. The democratic state and the human rights movement have tried to wrest this power from the military through a truth commission, habeas corpus requests, criminal trials, and street protests, but the armed forces have refused to provide any information, and only a few officers have come forward.

The transitional military government also handed the power over the national territory to the democratic state. It could now decide who could reside in Argentina. Yet, the state is not in full control of who is interred in Argentina because the military have kept the burial places of the disappeared secret. They still possess a certain dominion over Argentina by concealing these markers of territoriality, namely the anonymous graves of the disappeared. Judicial inquiries, forensic exhumations, and the investigation of cemetery records have been ways by which the state and the searching relatives can reclaim the disappeared remains, but the military continue to hinder these efforts.

Aside from the treason of popular sovereignty by the coup d'état of 1976, the Argentine military have continued to betray the Argentine people and the democratic state by not handing over the national sovereignty of the dead and their burial grounds. They cling to these remnants of dictatorial power and the trusting relations forged through crimes against humanity. They are also betraying the corporeal sovereignty of the disappeared dead and by extension the bereaved relatives. The betrayal exists in the appropriation of the multiple social relations between the living and the disappeared dead, which entails an ongoing contestation over their political, territorial, and spiritual bonds. The state and the bereaved relatives try to recover the national and individual sovereign rights over the assassinated disappeared from the military in order to actively reproduce their basic, social, and political trust through national commemorations, cemetery visits, and genealogical ties, but they are impeded by the continued silence and denial of aging perpetrators.

Even though the Argentine dictatorship seemed to have acquired unlimited powers over country and people on 24 March 1976, it proved to be vulnerable to domestic protest and international pressure. This resistance shows the Achilles' heel of the conceptualization of sovereignty as absolute power during a state of exception. Jennings (2011) has criticized Agamben (1998, 2005) for this naturalization of sovereignty, which assumes that politics without sovereign authority is not possible. He argues that the sovereign state is a historical construction created by modernity. Political communities can exist beyond the state, however, as Hannah Arendt (1958:198) showed with her example of the Greek polis: "it is the organization of the people as it arises out of acting and speaking together, and its true space lies between people living together for this purpose, no matter where they happen to be." If we reintroduce this notion of political fellowship into the relation between state and society, then it shows that civic organizations may evade or curb the sovereign's power—defined mistakenly by Agamben as boundless—because "power springs up between men when they act together and vanishes the moment they disperse" (Arendt 1958:200). Furthermore, as anthropologists have demonstrated repeatedly, political agency can exist outside the state and influence sovereign powers from its margins.[5] Precisely for this reason, the Argentine people were forbidden to gather in public places and assemble in civic organizations independent of the authoritarian state. The searching relatives defied their public disenfranchisement at great personal risk, and created associations based on social trust that helped undermine the sovereignty of the military state. Their writs of habeas corpus, street protests, and later the demand for the human remains of the assassinated disappeared were ways to assert individual sovereignty over and against the national sovereignty held by the military and also the democratic state.

This chapter shows how the forensic exhumation of mass graves helped wrest the necropolitical and territorial grip over Argentina from the military and has contributed material evidence to their conviction in court. Graves are replete with symbolic meaning, as Laqueur (2015:106) has written: "The dead in the ground, or anywhere that they have been thoughtfully put, constitute a symbolic system that defies cultural nihilism and carries within itself a long, iterative, slowly changing history of meaning." This chapter provides an analysis of an unusual set of meanings attributed to burial places, namely the different symbolic meanings of Argentina's mass graves for the military, the state, and the bereaved relatives. I will describe these conflicting meanings through an examination of the multiple exhumations of one mass grave in the city of Córdoba and then illustrate how the symbolic meanings of anonymous graves became inverted through the exhumation, forensic identification, and reburial of a disappeared adolescent from Buenos Aires.

Mass Graves and Contested Sovereignty

In 1981, the brother of the abducted union leader Miguel Angel Sosa received a tip from an employee of the Ministry of Interior that valuable information about his disappearance might be found in the police archives. The police records described how Miguel Angel Sosa's body had been found floating in the Reconquista River in May 1976 and was buried at the park cemetery of Grand Bourg as an unidentified person, even though fingerprints had confirmed his identity. In October 1982, when Argentina was still under military rule, the search for the remains of Miguel Angel Sosa was approved by court order. The discovery of eighty-eight graves marked *NN* (Nomen Nescio, or No Name) at the Grand Bourg cemetery was reported in the press, and sent a shock wave through the country. Most graves held multiple corpses, and gravediggers estimated that around four hundred people were buried there (*Somos* 1982, 7(319):11). The Argentine people were horrified because this revelation presented them with the precariousness of life under dictatorial rule and the gruesome death of the exhumed, because the police records stated that Miguel Angel Sosa had been tortured and then killed with a strong blow to the head (Cohen Salama 1992:60–62). Searching relatives felt devastated. The ongoing uncertainty had at least maintained the hope that the disappeared might still be alive, but the discovery of the mass grave at Grand Bourg confirmed people's greatest fear.

In an exercise of territoriality, the military had for years prevented relatives from opening anonymous graves that could contain disappeared persons. And when the Argentine junta was finally forced to step down after the Falklands/Malvinas War, the court-ordered exhumations made "visible a formerly neglected cartography of terror and repression that encompasses many landscapes and localities throughout the country," as Ferrándiz (2010:311–312) observed about mass graves in Spain dating from the Civil War. The exhumed graves in Spain and Argentina caused relatives to be confronted with the broken skeletal remains of loved ones and provided judicial evidence for prosecution. The exhumations also expanded national memory with eyewitness accounts and revealed hidden territorial markers of the military's necropower (Robben 2010b, 2015). These relations between necropower, territory, and memory have also been observed in Guatemala: "The exhumation demands a coming to terms with space: physical space for the excavation, public space for memory, political space created by the exhumation, and the individual and collective giving of testimonies, each of which creates new space" (Sanford 2003:18). Such resignification of space demonstrates that concealed and exhumed graves have very different meanings for bereaved relatives and perpetrators. The disappeared were interred in anonymous graves to conceal the material evidence of unlawful killings, sow uncertainty, and affect the lives of searching relatives by depriving them and their dead loved ones of mortuary rituals that could attend to their emotional and spiritual needs. An analysis of three different symbolic meanings of anonymous graves and mass graves for perpetrators and relatives will demonstrate how exhumations relate to sovereignty and undo the military's grip on society (Robben 2015:56–60).

The distinction between individual anonymous graves and mass graves is a matter of definition. Archaeologists consider the condition and number of bodies in one grave as crucial, whereas legal scholars focus on the collective burial of victims of illegitimate execution or elimination (Jessee and Skinner 2005). In this chapter, I will treat anonymous individual graves and mass graves as one category of unceremoniously interred victims of political violence, unless indicated otherwise.

The treatment of enemy corpses in wars reveals how the enemy is perceived and what future relationship is imagined. Respect for the dead implies the possibility of peace and collaboration, whereas the abuse and destruction of enemy corpses emphasizes their absolute otherness (Capdevila and Voldman 2006:76; Dower 1986). Argentina's anonymous graves symbolized for the military a resounding victory over an enemy that was believed to pose an existential threat to the country's sovereignty, its Christian culture, and the spiritual health of the nation. The Argentine military demonized the insurgents and political opponents as a cancer, as something totally alien to Argentina: "The subversion serves an enslaving cause, and a conception that annihilates human rights: a nihilist conception, without God, without liberty, without human dignity and without loyalty. A conception reigned by the anti-values of treason, the rupture of family ties, the crime of sacrilege, cruelty and systematic deceit."[6] Enemies were therefore eliminated as persons, citizens, and human beings. They were not reincorporated into Argentine society as deceased members or given to their relatives for burial. They stopped being citizens of Argentina who had a say in the country's future. Ostracized from society and state, condemned to death, and defined as evil, most were interred in anonymous graves or dropped from planes into the ocean.

There were some attempts to regulate the return of bodies to relatives. An operational order in June 1977 by the commander of Zone 1 stated that the bodies should be sent first to the judicial morgue to determine the identity. The body would then either be released to the family or buried if no one claimed the corpse within thirty days (Ranalletti 2014:156). This bureaucratic procedure was seldom followed, but some relatives did receive their dead out of a rare display of compassion. The husband and four daughters of Elsa Sánchez de Oesterheld were abducted and assassinated in 1976 and 1977 by the Argentine army. Their bodies continue to be missing, except that of Elsa's eighteen-year-old daughter, Beatriz. Her body "was the only one I recovered because a police commissioner did not have the courage to bury her anonymously" (interview on 15 April 1991). The dumping of the overwhelming majority of the bodies epitomized their inhumanity. They had become outcasts whose expulsion from the junta's New Republic was emphasized by their burial in anonymous graves. The spatial separation in cemeteries of anonymous graves and grave sites with tombstones confirmed the classification of the dead into two fundamentally different social categories.

In contrast to the military, for whom the anonymous graves symbolized victory, the bereaved relatives and the human rights organizations regarded the anonymous graves as symbols of the personal sacrifice and political commitment of the disappeared. They had fought with revolutionary zeal against poverty and exploitation. These patriots deserved an honorable place of burial and had to be rescued from their emotional, political, and spiritual abandon in uncaring soil. This motivation added to the parents' need to search for the disappeared out of deep guilt feelings about their children's abduction and lonely death (Robben 2005b). Exhumation, identification, and reburial were personal and political obligations of trust that reversed the repressive sequence of abduction, assassination, and disappearance. The poorly exhumed Grand Bourg mass grave had shown the importance of advanced forensic expertise in Argentina, which first became available in 1984 when the American forensic anthropologist Clyde Snow visited the country and began training local experts. Also, a National Genetic Data Bank was founded in May 1987 that collected blood samples from relatives, at first to identify kidnapped babies and later to assist with the identification of exhumed skeletal remains when DNA testing became possible. By 2015, 637 successful forensic identifications had been made (Secretaría de Derechos Humanos 2015:1559).

The forensic investigations uncovered an intentionally buried past and gathered material evidence about pregnancies and close-range killings. The identified dead could then be restored to their proper place in society through mortuary rituals and memorials. During the first exhumations in the mid-1980s, Argentine forensic anthropologists would arrange the bones in several piles for the relatives to see and touch. They rejected an anatomical display of the remains as too scientific and detached (Joyce and Stover 1991:262). This practice was abandoned later when restored skeletal remains were presented to mourning family members as the body at rest before rising on Judgment Day, when the righteous will be separated from the wicked (Tumini, Garay, and Banchieri 2007:179).

The relation between society and territory in Judeo-Christian culture is expressed through the burial of the dead in native soil. Verdery (1999:104) traces this relation to Classical antiquity: "Ancestors were buried in the soil around the dwelling; their presence consecrated that soil, and continuous rituals connecting them with their heirs created a single community consisting of the dead, their heirs, and the soil they shared." National cemeteries, such as La Recoleta located in the wealthiest part of Buenos Aires, manifest this relation in sumptuous mausoleums erected for the nation's illustrious men and women.

Cemeteries have "four interlinked features: physical characteristics; ownership and meaning; the site's relationship to personal and community identities; and sacredness" (Rugg 2000:272). Secret burial places invert these characteristics. They have been concealed, are not owned by the Church or the bereaved, and disregard cultural meanings about death and the afterlife. They also cut the symbolic ties between the living and the dead and deprive both of mortuary rituals and memorial places. Aside from signifying victory, the anonymous graves symbolized for the military their reconquest of Argentina by burying the enemy dead in the defense zones and territorial waters. The symbolism of the dispersed anonymous graves as territorial markers was reinforced in Argentina by their concealment, whereas the visible presence of *NN*-marked graves at cemeteries such as Grand Bourg demonstrated the state's necropower. We can imagine how Argentine perpetrators felt empowered by the knowledge about the location of secret burial places as they drove around the areas where they had been stationed. Some may have become filled with remorse about concealing the dead or disappearing them altogether, as seems to have been the case for Navy Captain Scilingo, but many of the military I have spoken with through the decades were well satisfied with the assassinations.

The concealed graves commemorated the military's territorial grip as inconspicuous monuments. The English word *monument* derives from the earliest meaning of the Spanish word *monumento*, namely a burial place (el sepulcro) or a memorial in honor of a heroic act (*OED* 2nd ed., s.v. "monument"). The Argentine military celebrated their military victory and staked their claim over Argentina's national territory with anonymous graves. In the nineteenth century, when Argentina was embroiled in several civil wars, the belligerent caudillos abused enemy bodies for similar ends. The corpses of slain war lords were decapitated and dismembered, and the severed heads and limbs were exhibited in the conquered towns. Disappearances replaced beheadings in the twentieth century, and public display made way for concealment. The disappearance of Evita Duarte de Perón's embalmed body in 1955, upon orders from the Argentine rulers who had overthrown President Perón, and the body's secret burial in Italy in 1957 illustrate the historical shift in the treatment of deceased political opponents (Robben 2000a). Necropower and territoriality were substantiated through the secret interment of the disappeared. The concealed graves were mnemonic markers of the appropriation of land and life by the Argentine military. This sovereignty extended to the waters of the Atlantic Ocean, where sedated captives drowned to death after being thrown from a plane or helicopter.

The military's concealment of the dead and their usurpation of national territory were undone through forensic exhumations and reburials. Writing about the former Yugoslavia but equally relevant to Argentina, Verdery (1999:101–102) has interpreted these reversals as follows: "[G]raves laid out a geography of territorial claims and of personal commitment to those claims, for in these places 'our' dead were buried. Retrieving and reburying these nameless bones marked the territory claimed for a Greater Serbia, one that found its dead in the soil of most of the other republics. We might say that these corpses assisted in reconfiguring space by etching new international borders into it with their newly dug graves." Likewise, the Argentine reburials reclaimed the national territory with visible markers, often complemented by memorials and monuments. Hundreds of memory sites have been secured by neighborhoods and human rights organizations, frequently with financial support from state authorities (Memoria Abierta 2009). They exposed the military's repressive necropolitical structure and dissolved the symbolic meaning of anonymous graves as concealed monuments of territoriality.

Finally, the anonymous graves symbolized for the military the subjugation of the Argentine people to the authoritarian state, and the absolute power to remake civil society through the Process of National Reorganization. The practice of disappearing and assassinating guerrilla insurgents demoralized the combatants still at large and eliminated the guerrilla organizations. A similar treatment of grassroots organizations, combative labor unions, and human rights groups was intended to destroy a heterogeneous leftist movement and discourage further political action. The anonymous graves were material proof that the nation had been cleansed of undesirable citizens and that their revolutionary spirit had died with them.

As was already explained in this chapter's introduction, the military's sovereignty may have seemed absolute and equipped with unlimited repressive means, but the combination of trust and agency made searching relatives unite in human rights protests. The culture of fear spread by the disappearances failed to paralyze people emotionally and politically. Family bonds proved to be stronger than the threat of death. In particular, the mothers of the Plaza de Mayo symbolized the resistance against the authoritarian state. This movement was especially successful in gathering the support of international solidarity organizations and political parties in Europe, while slowly raising awareness in Argentina (Robben 2005a:306–310). Never backing down and never giving up the fight were emotional, political, and moral imperatives for searching relatives and human rights activists who refused to bow to the military authorities. They continued to clamor for information during democracy and turned the tables on the military through exhumations that provided forensic evidence for their conviction in court.

Anonymous Burials During the Dictatorship

Soon after the coup d'état of March 1976, dead bodies with signs of torture and gunshot wounds appeared along roads, riverbanks, and beaches. The Uruguayan Coast Guard reported in April 1976 that tortured bodies with multiple fractures had washed ashore. A maritime map showed that the prevailing sea currents had carried the bodies from Buenos Aires to Uruguay.[7] Mutilated bodies were also retrieved from Argentina's Paraná River. The director of the San Pedro cemetery wrote in October 1976 that the bodies had been delivered "blindfolded, gagged and with their hands tied behind their backs with wire. It was obvious at a glance that they had been maltreated" (CONADEP 1986:228). Similar observations were made in other parts of Argentina. Francisco Rubén Bossio gave the following impression of the dead that arrived in 1976 at the Judicial Morgue in Córdoba: "These corpses had the following characteristics: they had bullet wounds, some with a lot of perforations, sometimes so many as eighty, sometimes seventeen, for example. They all had painted fingers and bore clear marks of torture. They had marks on their hands as if they had been tied with cords. From time to time one would appear completely torn to pieces, split open" (CONADEP 1986:232). Some had died in shootouts with army troops, but many others arrived from political prisons and secret detention centers.

The number of dead deposited at Córdoba's Judicial Morgue, which had room for only six bodies, was so high that a mass transfer of sixty corpses to San Vicente Cemetery was organized between 14 and 16 December 1976. Another transport took place in March 1977 (Cohen Salama 1992:125). In June 1980, employees sent a petition to President Videla to request extra pay for their unsanitary working conditions. "It is impossible, Mr. President, to give a true picture of what we experienced when we opened the doors of the rooms where the corpses were kept. Some of the bodies had been stored for more than thirty days without any sort of refrigeration. There was a cloud of flies and the floor was covered in a layer about 10.5 centimeters deep in worms and larvae, which we cleared away with buckets and shovels. The only clothes we had were trousers, overalls, boots and gloves, while some people had to do the work in their ordinary clothes. . . . It should be noted that most of these bodies were of subversive delinquents" (CONADEP 1986:231).

The employees described how they had emptied the depositories, loaded the corpses onto trucks, and driven to San Vicente cemetery: "The sight which met us at the cemetery was too horrible to relate. The police cars lit up the common grave where the bodies were deposited, identified by number and using the pillars in a nearby wall as reference points. Behind this and even from roof tops the neighbours watched the macabre task in progress" (CONADEP 1986:231–232). The four petitioners added that they were "honest, Christian heads of household who believed in the Justice of God and Men" (Cohen Salama 1992:126). They did not receive a reply from President Videla but were fired for jumping the hierarchical chain (Cohen Salama 1992:125–126; Olmo and Salado Puerto 2008:50).

In general, bodies were disappeared in four ways: burials; destruction through cremation, with lye or explosives; death flights; and the deposit of bodies in barrels thrown in rivers (Ranalletti 2014:162–163). Burials in cemeteries consisted of individual anonymous graves and a few mass graves. Three mass graves were found outside cemeteries on the premises of army and police. Bodies were cremated in the ovens of cemeteries or incinerated in pits and oil drums at secret detention centers. Barrels containing bodies mixed with sand and cement were dropped in riverways. Finally, each of the three armed forces operated death flights to drop sedated captives from planes and helicopters over open water (CONADEP 1986:221–225; interview with Luis Fondebrider on 1 July 2011).[8]

The different burial practices deserve extra attention because of the implications for the question of military sovereignty. There were concealed graves and marked graves. Concealed individual graves and mass graves were located on and beyond cemetery grounds. Marked individual and mass graves were always in cemeteries and were registered in the cemetery records or identified by the abbreviation *NN*. Marked graves differed from concealed graves by their visible state of suspended reburial until the human remains could be exhumed and identified. Marked and concealed graves have other meanings for the military and the bereaved relatives. Marked graves were blatant exhibitions of sovereignty because the armed forces demonstrated that they had the power to decide over life and death, the burial of the dead, and the power to prevent relatives from recovering their loved ones. Instead, concealed graves were secret expressions of territoriality for the military, as markers known only to them.

Destructive exhumations were the ultimate demonstration of necropower. The clandestine exhumation and scattering of skeletal remains by the military were intended to remove the anonymous dead from public detection and obliterate their existence. The only confirmed destruction of a mass grave took place at the Arsenal Battalion of Azcuenaga in Tucumán Province (interview with Luis Fondebrider on 1 July 2011). According to the testimony of Lieutenant Ernesto Urien, a mass grave near Córdoba was exhumed in 1978 before the arrival of a fact-finding mission of the Organization of American States (*El Diario del Juicio* 1985, 11:233). The remains were dumped in oil drums and destroyed with lye. Forensic investigations have not yet been able to confirm the testimony. Destructive exhumations served obviously to obliterate incriminating evidence but also reinforced the first meaning of anonymous graves as signifying victory and affirmed the military's sovereign power by condemning the relatives to an interminable search for their twice disappeared loved ones.

Forensic Exhumations and Identifications During Democracy

Numerous anonymous graves were opened after democracy returned to Argentina in December 1983. These early exhumations were highly frustrating for the relatives because the limited forensic expertise in Argentina resulted in few identifications. The quality improved substantially when the truth commission and the Grandmothers of the Plaza de Mayo invited forensic anthropologist Clyde Snow in 1984. Snow gathered a handful of Argentine anthropology and medical students who in 1986 would form the Argentine Forensic Anthropology Team, or EAAF (Equipo Argentino de Antropología Forense) (Cohen Salama 1992:147–150; CONADEP 1986:311; Joyce and Stover 1991). Exhumations were no longer a haphazard unearthing of commingled human remains but a reliable means to identify assassinated civilians, establish pregnancies carried to completion, and raise hopes to reestablish violently broken family ties by locating kidnapped grandchildren. The repeated shocks of disclosure of concealed graves in 1982 and 1983, the positive identifications in 1984, the collection of criminal evidence against the military in 1985, and the confirmation of births in captivity increased the importance of exhumations. Exhumations in Argentina were approved by the courts and most human rights organizations. Funding came from international scientific and humanitarian organizations, while successive Argentine governments were neither openly against nor actively supportive of the forensic investigations.

In March 1984, Argentina's largest mass grave was found at San Vicente Cemetery in Córdoba, thanks to the testimony of Francisco Rubén Bossio of the Judicial Morgue to the truth commission. The grave measured 2.5 by 25 meters, and was 3.5 meters deep. A rudimentary excavation carried out with a power shovel uncovered an estimated four hundred dead, of which a limited number were exhumed. Contrary to any protocol and against common sense, the skulls were separated from the skeletons and stored in different bags. Twenty skulls were compared to dental records by Clyde Snow two months later. He could only identify Cristina Costanzo, twenty-five years old and a member of the outlawed Peronist Youth (Cohen Salama 1992:124–130). Her mother, Angela Morales de Costanzo, told the court about the recovery of her daughter's remains: "they gave me an urn with a heap of bones, with a skull, and I tell you that this was there because I opened the urn and there was a skull with a tuft of hair that I cut and kept. Here it is. I had a healthy, intelligent and beautiful daughter. They detained her and returned a heap of bones" (*El Diario del Juicio* 1985, 9:190).

The EAAF began to exhume the San Vicente mass grave in 2002 under complicated forensic conditions. The crude exploration of March 1984 had done damage to the site, and thirty-three bags containing skeletal remains had been lost. The new disinterment salvaged 123 bodies. Only about one-third were young people who had been the typical target of the armed forces, while two-thirds were older persons whose remains did not show any signs of violence. Four bodies in the latter group consisted of people who had been affected by leprosy. They must have come from a nearby lazaret. The commingling of lepers, aged paupers, and assassinated disappeared in one mass grave was proof that the so-called subversives were regarded as nonpersons who had been stigmatized and expelled from society. More than three hundred bodies were exhumed between 2002 and 2004, of which fifty-six were believed to be disappeared persons. By 2009, fourteen individuals had been identified (EAAF 2007:40–42, 2011:68; Olmo 2005).

The painstaking efforts the forensic anthropologists took to recover the disappeared demonstrate the emotional and political importance of the exhumations. Family members can finally bury their loved ones with honor and dignity, and make good on their basic trust. The reburials also remind the mourners that so many others are still interred in anonymous graves.

Alternatively, the reburials are political performances that convey the message that the disappeared were assassinated for ideological reasons and that the Argentine military must be brought to justice. Exhumations, identifications, and reburials negate the military's symbolic meanings of mass graves and anonymous graves, namely as symbols of victory, territoriality, and necropower. The following case study about Norberto Morresi provides an illustration of how these three symbolic meanings may be undone.

As was explained in this book's introduction, Norberto Morresi's disappearance was feared when he failed to appear at a birthday party on the night of 23 April 1976. His parents learned thirteen years later that he had been assassinated within two hours of being apprehended in Buenos Aires by the First Army Corps. Norberto Morresi was in the company of Luis María Roberto. They were in possession of the illegal magazine *Evita Montonera*. Norberto was shot in the head, Luis María was shot in the abdomen, both executed on empty terrain in La Matanza. An attempt had been made to set their Chevrolet station wagon on fire, but it failed. The local police found the bodies and the partially burned-out car that same day. They took photographs and fingerprints, and buried the bodies as unidentified persons at the General Villegas cemetery. Members of the Argentine Forensic Anthropology Team found the police report in 1989 and succeeded in identifying Luis María Roberto by the set of fingerprints. A grave was located through the cemetery register, and the skeletal remains of both men were identified in June 1989 (Cohen Salama 1992:228–232; Robben 2005a:266).

The remains of Norberto Morresi and Luis María Roberto were buried together on 7 July 1989 in a niche of a large raised tomb at the Bajo Flores cemetery. The Catholic funeral undid the military's first symbolic meaning of anonymous graves, and restored for Norberto Morresi's parents and Luis María Roberto's widow their place in society as deceased members after having been missing for thirteen years. The mortuary ritual accomplished a transition from a liminal existence on earth to the eternal peace of the afterworld. The joint reburial added a political significance to the funeral by emphasizing that they had been assassinated together (Cohen Salama 1992:232).

Two decades later, Irma Morresi recalled her sentiment about the reburial when she heard that her son Norberto had been found: "No, I don't want the cemetery. I want to cremate him; cremate him and then I'm going to take him to the park where he used to play, and there he's going to be" (Panizo 2012:235). She wanted to free him forever from the years of confinement to the mass grave: "To throw him in the air, so that he would remain on the land, that he would not be enclosed there. As if to liberate him, like something that is in the air, you see" (236). Even though Irma did not want to move her son to another enclosed space, her husband wanted to lay his son to rest and be able to visit him at the cemetery. Julio's wish had prevailed.

When I talked with Julio Morresi in March 1991, he spoke with pride about his son. Norberto had joined a small group of people who visited the slums of Buenos Aires to stop poor teenagers from taking drugs and to encourage them to attend school again. Their son's exhumation and reburial had given inner peace to Irma and Julio Morresi because they could finally fulfill their parental care to their dead son. "I know, unfortunately we have this little heap of bones at the Flores cemetery, no?" Julio told me. "It is like a ritual that we go there every Sunday to bring him even if it is only one flower. It is completely useless, but it helps spiritually. We go there, we kiss the photo hanging on the niche, and it makes us feel good" (interview on 29 March 1991).

On 23 April 1990, on the first anniversary of Norberto's identification, a documentary was shown about the forensic exhumation. It was standing room only at the community center José Hernández because about 450–500 persons had come to remember Norberto Morresi and Luis María Roberto. The widow Rosalina Cardozo de Roberto read aloud the telegrams and many messages of support sent by human rights organizations. The next speaker said that she was not going to give a speech because the disappeared were the ones who had already given many speeches to denounce social injustice. They had led the way, and would today be protesting against the unemployment, substandard housing, and poor schooling of Argentina's lower class. Julio Morresi was the last speaker to address the audience: "This is a sad occasion, but also an occasion of vindication. This is not an homage, because Norberto lives on in the ideals that we continue to carry forward." Morresi's speech, and especially his tireless work for the human rights organization Relatives of People Disappeared and Detained for Political Reasons, undid the military's third symbolic meaning of concealed graves. The forensic identification and reburial of his son Norberto motivated Julio Morresi to continue the human rights struggle and belie the political paralysis that the junta had tried to achieve with the disappearances. Furthermore, Julio Morresi's activism proved the Mothers of the Plaza de Mayo Association wrong in their belief that the exhumations and reburials would depoliticize the mourning relatives by allowing them to work through their losses and accept the deaths. Julio Morresi's efforts for the human rights movement led Argentine President Cristina Fernández de Kirchner to bestow upon him the Azucena Villaflor Prize on the National Day of Memory in March 2010.

The public recognition for Julio Morresi followed a long human rights struggle to instill an enduring national memory of the military dictatorship into the Argentine people. Memory sites were preserved, monuments and memorials were erected, and exhumations were conducted that together exposed the secret infrastructure of state repression and dismantled the second symbolic meaning of anonymous graves as concealed territorial markers. One important focal point of collective memory for the human rights movement became the Monument to the Victims of State Sponsored Terrorism at the Memory Park in Buenos Aires, which includes the names of Norberto Morresi and Luis María Roberto. The conspicuous memorial walls invert the concealed graves and confirm the indisputable truth of the disappearances that had been denied by the Argentine military.

Two decades after I had first spoken with Julio and Irma Morresi, they continued to visit the Bajo Flores cemetery, but somehow the sentiment was different. Julio commented that the Sunday visits were still giving him spiritual energy and emotional satisfaction, but something had changed after his son's name had been engraved on the memorial wall in 2007: "He [Norberto] is more present for us at the Memory Park because he is there with his comrades. Only his bones are at the cemetery, and even though they are mine, they are still only bones and not really Norberto for me" (interview on 22 March 2010). The separation of the jointly buried remains of Norberto Morresi and Luis María Roberto in 2010 must have added to the greater affinity with the memorial wall. The relatives of Luis María Roberto had decided to rebury his remains in the family grave of his deceased parents. Norberto's remains were also moved and placed in one of the tiny niches destined for children because of the urn's small size (Panizo 2012:233).

The memorial wall bears Norberto Morresi's name and his age on the day of his disappearance. Nothing else distinguishes him from the ten thousand other names, most of which belong to those who have not yet been exhumed and identified. They share their liminal existence in solidarity. The appeal of the Memory Park for Irma and Julio Morresi is their son's fellowship with other idealistic compatriots who sacrificed their lives for a better Argentina. The communitas sensed at the Memory Park is more inviting than their son's individual burial place at the cemetery. His grave symbolizes the family ties with his parents and brother but lacks the political significance of the memorial wall. The changing emotions of Irma and Julio Morresi about the remains and burial of their son Norberto demonstrate the semiotic transformations of the symbolic meanings of anonymous graves and how the struggle over exhumations has affected Argentine society.

Conclusion

Between 1976 and 1983, the Argentine military junta embarked on a cultural war against its own people, determined to secure national, cultural, and state sovereignty. Whereas the territorial sovereignty of the Argentine postcolonial state had been achieved in the late nineteenth century through the aggressive conquest of land and the extermination of its indigenous inhabitants, the dictatorship sought to gain cultural sovereignty through state terrorism, censorship, and an authoritarian control over Argentine society. Cultural sovereignty became extended into the bodies and minds of the enemies of state through disappearance, torture, and assassination. Just as state sovereignty is ultimately vested in the power to declare war and a state of siege, the Argentine military felt entitled to define the boundaries and conditions of Argentine society and culture. Argentines considered unfit for the coveted Christian nation were disappeared so that they could not be remembered as martyrs or reincorporated into society as deceased citizens.

Territoriality figured prominently in the Argentine military's repressive imagination because of the nationwide presence of the guerrilla organizations, while necropolitics was exercised within the five defense zones through a grid of areas of operation, each with its own special task forces and infrastructure to dispose of the assassinated disappeared. Corps commanders vied for moral superiority, ideological purity, and political influence by demonstrating that their defense zone was free of cancerous subversives, as they called the revolutionaries and political opponents. Territoriality and necropolitics went hand in hand in the national cleansing operation and materialized in mass graves and anonymous individual graves.

State sovereignty, as manifested in necropolitics and territoriality, is never as absolute as Foucault, Agamben, and Mbembe have suggested because societies harbor countervailing forces that can corrode authoritarian rule. The return to democracy allowed the Argentine people and the state to regain sovereignty. Forensic exhumations and identifications incorporated the reburied dead into national memory and commemoration and dismantled the military's hold on Argentina by means of concealed graves and unidentified disappeared citizens. The accountability of the military for their abuse of power was a necessary step for the human rights movement in the recuperation of state sovereignty. The Alfonsín government asserted its authority with a historic trial against the junta commanders in 1985 but soon gave in to military pressure, passing amnesties and pardons that made the military and police immune from prosecution. However, the continued exhumations, testimonies, and memory politics were instrumental for the renewed accountability of the Argentine military and police in 2005.

CHAPTER 6

Accountability

Miguel Osvaldo Etchecolatz, former director-general of investigations of the Buenos Aires Provincial Police, was the first defendant to stand trial after the amnesty laws had been derogated in 2005. Accompanied by the chant "Olé, olá, what happened to the Nazis is going to happen to them, wherever they go we are hunting for them," the seventy-seven-year-old handcuffed Etchecolatz entered the courtroom on the morning of 20 June 2006, facing a rowdy audience of more than four hundred people and a front row occupied by a dozen mothers of the Plaza de Mayo. The proceedings of Federal Oral Tribunal 1 were held in the town hall of La Plata, the capital of Buenos Aires Province. The presiding judge, Carlos Rozanski, read the accusation: six assassinations, eight counts of torture, and eight disappearances. Nilda Eloy and Jorge López were the two survivors. Judge Rozanski verified the defendant's identity and asked about his profession: "Assassin!" someone shouted from the audience. "Retired policeman," responded Etchecolatz. Clutching a rosary, he added that he was not going to cooperate with the court because he fell under military jurisdiction. At the end of the first trial day, Etchecolatz left the courtroom to a chorus of boos and hisses.[1]

The prosecution of Etchecolatz illustrates the roller coaster of Argentine transitional justice during more than three decades of democracy and helps us understand the mistrust of the accused and the accusers toward the Argentine state and its judicial branch. Etchecolatz had been denounced in the CONADEP report for running several secret detention centers. He was convicted in 1986 to twenty-three years in prison for ninety-one cases of torture but was released in 1988 in the wake of the Due Obedience Law. In 1998, he was the target of a street happening (escrache) at his home in

Buenos Aires.[2] Etchecolatz was called in 1999 to give testimony in a so-called truth trial to investigate disappearances in La Plata, but he refused to appear despite being protected by the amnesty law (González Leegstra 2011:131). He was arrested again in April 2001 after a federal judge had ruled that the Due Obedience Law was unconstitutional. Etchecolatz was accused of the theft and change of identity of Carmen Gallo Sanz, who had been born in captivity in 1977. He was convicted in March 2004 to seven years in prison but the sentence was reduced to three years by a court of appeals.[3] The years were spent under house detention because of his advanced age. Accused in June 2006 of new charges, Etchecolatz was sentenced in September 2006 to life in prison.

The successive indictments, convictions, releases, retrials, and public denunciations of military and police in Argentina have been unprecedented in the world. State officials are normally immune from prosecution since the state is held accountable for any wrongdoing by its agents. With the exception of the Nuremberg and Tokyo trials in the 1940s, in the twentieth century state officials enjoyed functional immunity from prosecution for acts of state until the trial in 1975 of the Greek colonels who had staged a military coup in 1967 and the conviction of members of the Portuguese secret police in 1976. The accountability of state officials gained international momentum after the trial of Argentina's former junta commanders in 1985. Sikkink (2011:24) traces this global trend to the wave of democratic transitions and human rights activism during the 1970s and 1980s. The end of the Cold War in the early 1990s accelerated the international call for the personal accountability of state agents accused of serious human rights violations.

On 13 June 2011, UN Secretary-General Ban Ki-moon visited the former torture center at the Navy Mechanics School (ESMA) in Buenos Aires and praised the Argentine government and human rights movement: "You have repealed laws that protected the guilty. You have built strong and enduring democratic institutions. . . . You have shown that there can be no safe refuge for those who commit crimes against humanity" (Ban 2011). The compliments were well deserved, but Ban Ki-moon neglected to mention the importance of nonlegal forms of accountability. Defendants as well as plaintiffs have argued that legal prosecution fails to do them justice. Many defendants are convinced that criminal law does not apply to them or consider themselves accountable only to history, as demonstrated by Admiral Massera, who declared during his trial in 1985: "My judges have the chronicle . . . but I have history, and there the final verdict will be heard" (*El Diario del Juicio* 1985, 20:25). Others put their faith in God, such as General Díaz Bessone, who told me in 1989: "I am a very religious man. And I know deep down in my heart that my conscience before God is clear" (Robben 1995:81). Also, for many victims, accountability is not confined to legal rulings because of the political and moral consequences of the criminal acts. They believe that trials can never deal with the extent of the crimes committed and have been searching for other forms of punishment. A comprehensive analysis of the local understanding of accountability in Argentina deserves therefore to include nonlegal forms of transitional justice.

Transitional justice comprises multiple types and instruments of justice, often in response to abuses of power and massive atrocities by a repressive state. Retributive, punitive, and restorative justice are the principal types, which aim respectively at reprisal, accountability, and accommodation. The instruments of justice include criminal trials, truth commissions, historical inquiries, amnesties, and administrative measures such as purging, lustration, and reparation. These responses affect the transition from one political system to another and influence how citizens will coexist in the wake of an authoritarian regime. Transitional justice varies from country to country because of historical legacies, the national balance of power, and international circumstances.[4] Latin America paved the way for transitional justice in the 1980s. A second wave of trials during the 2000s has been called *posttransitional justice*. The second wave has been attributed to the growing body of international laws and treaties, the so-called justice cascade; foreign prosecution, as in the case of Pinochet; proactive domestic human rights organizations; and a supportive state, as in the case of Argentina's Kirchner government.[5] I will argue that in addition to these four factors, the ongoing sequels of Argentina's sociocultural traumas help explain the persistent calls for the legal punishment and moral condemnation of perpetrators.

The difference between legal and moral justice rests on the distinction between accountability and attributability. In legal terms, *accountability* refers to "practices where some actors hold other actors to a set of standards and impose sanctions if these standards are not met" (Sikkink 2011:13). *Attributability* refers to people's causal responsibility for actions for which they do not necessarily have a moral responsibility, as in the case of victim-perpetrators such as child soldiers. They may have committed horrendous deeds and are therefore subject to legal sanctioning, but they are not held morally accountable because their violent conduct was rooted in an involuntary recruitment into soldierhood (Watson 2004:271–281; Honwana

2006:54–74). Argentina's Due Obedience Law was based on this reasoning: low-ranking officers were causally responsible for torturing people and were indicted but not tried because they had carried out orders for which high-ranking commanders had been legally responsible. Their moral responsibility was beyond the court's jurisdiction. Argentine victims of torture and disappearance had to accept this reasoning because of the political situation at the time, but they considered causal and moral responsibility inseparable.

What is the moral responsibility of perpetrators, and how can they be held accountable morally? Argentine officers, high- and low-ranking, were responsible as human beings for having acted in full knowledge of their actions. They might be declared not guilty according to the letter of the law, but for many Argentines they were guilty of having inflicted harm and injury. I will demonstrate in this chapter that Argentina's process of transitional justice emerged from the judiciary's engagement with a traumatized society and expanded accountability into a moral domain beyond legal confines.

The term *accountability* draws on the metaphor of an account, "a kind of moral bookkeeping of merits and demerits. . . . In this way, we move back to the semi-mythical figures of the great book of debts: the book of life and death" (Ricoeur 2000:14). This moral accounting extends beyond the legal liability of perpetrators and into their malevolence. The Argentine dictatorial regime violated society's social contract in ways that have been qualified during three decades of Argentine justice as crimes against humanity. Aside from the reinstatement of the rule of law in 1983, Argentine society required an acknowledgment of the traumatizing damage done and the reaffirmation of the social attachment, trust, and coexistence that constitute the foundation of human society. The moral judgment expressed in narratives, official reports, reparative measures, and artistic expressions authenticated the reality of past transgressions and reassured the recovery of humanness—were it not that military pressure undermined people's political trust in the state's power to serve justice.

This chapter analyzes an area of contestation that focuses on the accountability of state agents because the surviving guerrilla combatants fell outside the court's jurisdiction. The prosecution followed an erratic course that generated a political mistrust of the state and its judiciary among the Argentine military, police, ex-disappeared, and searching relatives. The latter two were indignant at the amnesties and pardons that benefited the

indicted and convicted belligerents in the late 1980s. The junta commanders felt betrayed by the state that prosecuted them in 1985 because they had
been given a legal mandate in 1975 to annihilate the guerrilla organizations,
had defended Argentina's sovereignty, and could not be tried in a civil
court. Low- and middle-ranking officers felt equally betrayed by the state
but also by the junta commanders for not assuming full responsibility for
the repressive practices. Finally, the armed forces argued that the military
were treated unfairly because the guerrilla insurgents were not prosecuted
and lost all trust in the state when the amnesties and pardons were derogated in the mid-2000s.

   The principal types of transitional and post-transitional justice that have
held Argentine perpetrators accountable are the truth commission, the
criminal trial of the junta commanders, truth trials, street happenings, and
human rights trials. The truth commission sought to acknowledge the suffering of the victims and survivors of state repression. The criminal and
human rights trials focused on the prosecution of perpetrators, whereas the
truth trials helped the mourning process of relatives searching for their
disappeared loved ones. Finally, the street happenings sought to denounce
perpetrators publicly and ostracize them from Argentine society. I will conclude that people's demand for accountability can never be fully satisfied by
the law because the moral significance of the traumatizing acts of violence
transcends their legal reckoning into a moral domain where good and evil
cannot be balanced but only remembered.

The National Commission on the Disappeared

The National Commission on the Disappeared (CONADEP) presented the
eagerly awaited report *Nunca Más* (*Never Again*) to President Alfonsín on
20 September 1984. The commission's president, Ernesto Sábato, emphasized in the report's prologue that the CONADEP "was set up not to sit in
judgment, because that is the task of the constitutionally appointed judges,
but to investigate the fate of the people who disappeared during those ill-
omened years of our nation's life" (CONADEP 1986:1). Thousands of testimonies and the discovery of hundreds of secret detention centers convinced
him nevertheless that a moral judgment was inescapable: "Although it must
be justice which has the final word, we cannot remain silent in the face of

all that we have heard, read, and recorded" (1–2). In his eyes, these violations were of such magnitude that they qualified as crimes against humanity. "Through the technique of disappearance and its consequences, all the ethical principles which the great religions and the noblest philosophies have evolved through centuries of suffering and calamity have been trampled underfoot, barbarously ignored" (2).

The report holds perpetrators responsible through a narrative that creates a moral contrast between innocent disappeared victims and culpable state agents. These state agents were mainly low- and middle-ranking members of the police and armed forces. The military juntas that implemented the state terror remain largely invisible in the report, other than a quote from General Riveros that says: "We waged this war with our doctrine in our hands, with the written orders of each high command" (CONADEP 1986:2) and the references to the military's doctrine of national security (442–445). Guerrilla combatants appear only as victims of torture and disappearance. Any mention of their political affiliation was avoided to prevent undermining the credibility of the depositions, to emphasize that the absence of due process made such information irrelevant, and to avoid corroborating the military's claim that the disappeared were terrorists. This framing made one officer remark that, according to the CONADEP: "the disappeared were peaceful citizens, writers, workers, and housewives who didn't know anything about politics. It seems as if one day they were detained by the armed forces just like that, without rhyme or reason" (*Somos* 1984, 408:11). Of course, the Argentine military had nurtured this impression by carrying out the repression without trials or sentences and by refusing writs of habeas corpus.

The disappeared are central in the report as Argentina's everyman because of society's "fear that anyone, however innocent, might become a victim of the never-ending witch-hunt. . . . The vast majority of them were innocent not only of any acts of terrorism, but even of belonging to the fighting units of the guerrilla organizations" (CONADEP 1986:3–4). This claim is most apparent for sick and disabled disappeared persons. Claudia Inés Grumberg had suffered from crippling osteoarthritis since the age of five; she was abducted in October 1976. In December 1977, British journalist Christopher Hitchens asked President Videla about her. He responded: "terrorism is not just killing with a bomb, but activating ideas. Maybe that's why she's detained. . . . We consider it a great crime to work against the Western and Christian style of life: it is not just the bomber but the ideologist who is the danger" (Hitchens 2011:195). Other disabled disappeared include the blind couple María Esther Ravelo Vega and Emilio Etelvino Vega and twenty-year-old Rosa Ana Frigerio, who was abducted on a stretcher because her body was in a cast due to back surgery (CONADEP 1986:334).

The physical inability to carry out violent acts made the sick and disabled the epitome of innocence, despite what Videla had suggested about their ideological danger. This innocence extended to all disappeared. When asked in January 1984 if her two disappeared sons had been guerrillas, Hebe de Bonafini replied: "They worked and studied. I believe that all that my children did, like thousands of disappeared, was to fight for a better country. They disappeared because there was nothing to accuse them of. Otherwise, they would have been tried and sentenced accordingly" (*Somos* 1984, 382:20). It would take two decades before she felt free to declare that many disappeared had been somehow involved in the guerrilla insurgency.[6]

CONADEP's discursive construction of the disappeared as innocent victims was threefold: they were innocent in causal and legal terms for not having raised any arms against the state and in moral terms for having been abused in inhuman ways. But if they were innocent, then why were they persecuted? Sábato argued that the military operations against the guerrilla insurgency "had become a demented generalized repression" against anyone labeled subversive: "*Marxist-Leninist, traitors to the fatherland, materialists and atheists, enemies of Western, Christian values . . .* from those who were proposing a social revolution, to aware adolescents who merely went out to the shanty towns to help the people living there" (CONADEP 1986:4; emphasis in original). The report regards the disappeared as scapegoats, victims of a "never-ending witch-hunt," who were sacrificed on the military's altar of Western civilization and Christian values (3). Girard's definition of a scapegoat fits CONADEP's usage clearly. "Scapegoat indicates both the innocence of the victims, the collective polarization in opposition to them, and the collective end result of that polarization" (Girard 1989:39). The Argentine military tried to rally the Argentine people behind their offensive against subversive enemies who threatened the Argentine state and the country's Western culture.

What explains CONADEP's portrayal of the disappeared as scapegoats? An open acknowledgment of the political agency of the disappeared would upset the moral contrast between innocent disappeared victims and culpable state agents. The admission that a number of the disappeared were guerrilla combatants would blur the report's discursive construct of binary oppositions between victim and perpetrator, democracy and dictatorship, fear-stricken civil society and terror-spreading armed forces, innocence and guilt, and ultimately good and evil. The inclusion of guerrillas as a subcategory of victims would taint all disappeared. They would become victim-perpetrators considered causally guilty but legally absolved because of their mistreatment by state agents. Such status would be in contradiction to the larger conclusion that anyone could have been a victim of military repression, that the disappeared stood for all Argentines, and that Argentine society as a whole was victimized.

The CONADEP commission served as a forum to make public the suffering of the victimized disappeared and their searching relatives. The report held up a mirror to Argentine society and revealed a subterranean world whose atrocities could have been suffered by anyone. It was an official acknowledgment of the survivors whose depositions were largely taken at face value, despite partial verification through testimonies, habeas corpus requests, exhumations, and site visits (CONADEP 1986:431–434). Claims of torture are difficult to verify years after the fact. Clinical diagnoses are fraught with interpretational challenges because the etiology of corporeal traces and mental health problems cannot be assessed easily. Ultimately, the credibility of a torture account comes down to its internal consistency, attention to detail, and the corroboration of external evidence (Kelly 2012:64). Furthermore, in the case of the CONADEP, the principal objective was to discover the fate of the disappeared and not the verification of witness testimonies. This task was left to the courts.

The CONADEP report's nationwide distribution shaped public opinion by casting a moral judgment that was credible because of the sheer volume of the testimonies, the systematic description of the repressive infrastructure, and the discursive frame of innocent disappeared victims versus culpable state agents. Who would not be moved emotionally by the accounts of the tortured survivors of disappearance? The bodily, mental, and legal defenselessness of the victims left no room for any conclusion other than that their human rights had been trampled and that the culprits had to be brought to court.

Trial of the Junta Commanders

The accountability of the Argentine military stood high on the political agenda when Raúl Alfonsín assumed the presidency in December 1983. On

13 December 1983, he issued Decree 158/83, which contained a weighty accusation: the commanders of the armed forces, who had usurped power on 24 March 1976, "conceived and implemented an operational plan against subversive and terrorist activities based on clearly illegal methods and procedures" (Decreto 158/83, 1983). Alfonsín ordered the Armed Forces Supreme Council to prosecute the three military juntas that had ruled between 1976 and 1982 for "the crimes of homicide, illegal detention, and the torture of detainees" (Decreto 158/83, 1983). The nine junta members were held accountable for masterminding a repressive infrastructure against "real terrorists as well as mere dissidents, and even those who limited themselves to criticizing the methods used" (Decreto 158/83, 1983). The military supreme court interrogated the junta members and heard the defense counsel but returned the case on 21 September 1984, the day after the CONADEP report had been submitted. The court indicated that it was unable to reach a verdict by the deadline of 21 October. In off-the-record conversations with high-ranking officers, I was told in 1990 that the court had deliberately delayed proceedings because they considered the trial to be political in nature. Also, some judges had received death threats. The Buenos Aires Federal Court of Criminal Appeals was now authorized to try the nine junta commanders.

Argentina has an inquisitional criminal law system in which judges are actively involved in truth finding. Judges interrogate the witnesses before the prosecution and defense counsel can raise questions that need approval from the bench. In the case of the trial of the junta commanders, oral proceedings replaced the written motions customary in Argentina. The six judges thus entered uncharted terrain by trying an unprecedented case before a public audience and facing nine men who had wielded unlimited power over Argentina only a few years earlier.

The prosecution retook the accusations raised in Decree 158/83 and selected the 709 most convincing cases from the CONADEP report, of which 281 were eventually examined by the court (Cámara Nacional 1987, 1:x). The cases were chosen on the basis of three features: the victims had all suffered crimes; the crimes were inflicted by members of the military or police; and these state agents had been guided by a criminal plan designed and ordered by the junta commanders (Moreno Ocampo 1999:683). The trial's objective was to establish the legal responsibility of the junta commanders for the criminal plan and the crimes committed by their subordinates. In 1985, there was little doubt in Argentina that the victim-survivors had been mistreated. The trial testimonies served mainly to authenticate in court what was already known in public through the CONADEP report. Not the victims or low-and middle-ranking officers but the junta commanders stood at the center of national attention in the trial that tried to establish their hierarchical responsibility as indirect perpetrators.

The first issue facing the court was to establish whether the military juntas had in fact acted outside of the law when fighting the guerrilla insurgency. Lieutenant-General Videla had declared before the military supreme court that on 6 October 1975, President Luder had signed Decree 2772, which authorized the armed forces "to execute the military and security operations necessary to annihilate the actions of the subversive elements throughout the country's territory" (PEN 1975). The mission was operationalized in battle plans that did not contain instructions about the torture or disappearance of armed insurgents or political opponents. Before the military supreme court, Videla had already rejected all accusations because the infractions of orders and directives had been brought before the proper judicial military authorities (Cámara Nacional 1987, 1:2–3).

The criminal trial began on the afternoon of 22 April 1985 with the testimony of former President Luder. Judge Arslanian asked Luder to explain the term *annihilation* used in Decree 2772: "it means to disable the combat capability of the subversive groups, but it means in no way whatsoever physical annihilation or the violation of the legal structure" (*El Diario del Juicio* 1985, 1:2). Implicitly, Luder followed the classic definition of annihilation as placing enemy forces "in such a condition that they can no longer carry on the fight" (Clausewitz 1984:90). Vice-Admiral Luis María Mendía disagreed. He defined annihilation as destroying the enemy physically. He differentiated annihilation from the less violent weakening or neutralization of the enemy (*El Diario del Juicio* 1985, 1:2). Witness testimonies about shackled captives penned up in secret detention centers and bodies that washed ashore with visible marks of torture provided convincing evidence that the armed forces had exceeded Decree 2772.

The Argentine military, however, reasoned away the brutal treatment by arguing that Argentina had been in a state of war. Excesses occurred in all wars, and especially in twentieth-century counterinsurgency wars. Officially, 323 members of the armed and security forces had been accused of excesses, of which 283 were convicted by military courts. Out of a total of 493 offenses committed, there were nine instances of torture, twenty cases of rape, thirty-seven illegal detentions or disappearances, twenty-five kidnappings, and forty murders; the remainder included theft, robbery, extortion, and the forgery of documents (Cerdá 1986/87). The criminal court that was trying the junta commanders defined an excess as "an intensification of an originally legal action," and reasoned that illegal detention, torture, and theft were not legal actions (Cámara Nacional 1987, 2:759–760). If the thousands of cases denounced before the CONADEP and the court would be considered excesses, then either the chain of command lacked proper oversight or the abusive treatment of detainees was a standard operating procedure. The question of whether the Argentine armed forces had been at war was tangential to the indictment because military forces at war are held to the national military code. The key question was whether the excesses were indeed accidental, as the defendants claimed, or intentional and planned, as the prosecutors argued.

The junta commanders presented their secret battle plans to prove that the offensive operations had been conceived correctly. The commanders of the Army, Navy, and Air Force were responsible for the operations executed by their force—the very men who also integrated the military juntas. Formally, the men on trial were not responsible as junta members but in their capacity as force commanders. The battle plans did not include any unlawful procedures but demonstrated the chain of command. The force commanders were therefore legally responsible for the orders, operations, and actions of their subordinate troops. Both Videla and Massera had confirmed before the Armed Forces Supreme Council that the execution of captives without a sentence had not occurred, except in rare instances (Camarasa, Felice, and González 1985:48–49). Other commanding officers affirmed in court that they had strictly followed the orders of their superiors, had command and control of their troops, and denied that the task groups had acted on their own account. Their statements implied that if the practices of abduction, torture, disappearance, and assassination were similar in the 117 defense areas, and the disappeared were held captive in buildings pertaining to the armed and police forces, then such repressive procedures could only have existed with the explicit approval of the junta commanders (Cámara Nacional 1987, 1:259–270).

The junta commanders argued that the nonconventional nature of the anti-revolutionary war hindered effective oversight, just as they had told U.S. President Carter's human rights emissary Patricia Derian at the time: "they all spoke to me about the difficulty to control lower-ranking personnel, especially those who had seen their comrades suffer at the hands of the terrorists; [Videla] explained that it was impossible to control them" (*El Diario del Juicio* 1985, 9:193). However, many officers testified that orders were given orally down the chain of command, and even Videla finally admitted in 2012 that decisions about life or death were approved by the five defense zone commanders (Cámara Nacional 1987, 1:274–275; Reato 2012:52).

After the prosecution's closing arguments had been read in September 1985, the defense counsel was heard. Aside from arguing that the trial lacked any legal foundation and was political in nature—thus suggesting that a verdict would not be based on convincing evidence and that the verdict was precooked under political pressure—the defense lawyers countered that the armed forces had fought with orders mandated by a constitutional government in a war against terrorism. They admitted that excesses had occurred, as could be expected of irregular warfare, but that the offenders had been court-martialed. The documentary evidence of the CONADEP was dismissed as inadmissible, and witnesses for the prosecution were discredited for being politically prejudiced against the military juntas or for having belonged to the guerrilla organizations (Amnesty International 1987:46–53; *El Diario del Juicio* 1985, 22–31).

Lieutenant-General Videla declined to speak in court, but Admiral Massera did and he did so in moral terms:

> I have not come to defend myself. Nobody has to defend himself for having won a just war. And the war against terrorism was a just war. Nevertheless, I am put on trial here because we won that just war. If we would have lost it, then we wouldn't have been here— neither you nor we—because the highest judges of this Chamber would have been replaced some time ago by turbulent people's tribunals, and a ferocious and unrecognizable Argentina would have replaced the old Fatherland. Unusual, but here we are because we won the war of arms and lost the psychological war. . . . The only thing I know is that here there was a war between the legal forces— when there were excesses these were rare—and the subversive terrorism—where excess was the norm. (*El Diario del Juicio* 1985, 20:25)

The verdict was given on 9 December 1985. The court considered six types of crime as proven: (1) illegal detentions aggravated by the use of violence and the concealment of detainees in clandestine detention centers; (2) torture to obtain information or break the captives' will; (3) death caused by torture; (4) aggravated homicide at no risk to the executioners because of the defenselessness of the victims; (5) the theft of goods belonging to detainees; and (6) additional crimes, in particular the concealment of the abovementioned offenses, the forced labor of captives, and the false response to habeas corpus requests (Cámara Nacional 1987, 2:723–731). The court recognized that terrorism had posed a threat to society and state but determined that the recourse to necessity, namely committing a smaller harm to prevent a greater harm, did not apply. The guerrilla insurgency did not constitute an imminent threat, the armed forces possessed ample legal means of combat, and the state's abductions and killings outnumbered by far those of the guerrillas (733–746). The court concluded that the armed forces had the constitutional right to respond to unjust aggression but was bound to the law when conducting operations. Instead, unjust means were employed to achieve a just end—unjust means that "neither answer[ed] to the ruling law, nor to the Argentine traditions, nor to the customs of civilized nations" (758). The court considered the emotional response of the Argentine people to these crimes as proof that they were contrary to Argentina's cultural norms, while the military's concealment of the crimes showed that the junta commanders knew they were inadmissible.

In the absence of the unity of command within the three military juntas, the court convicted the junta members individually as commanders of the Army, Navy, and Air Force. Two defendants (Videla and Massera) were sentenced to life in prison. Three defendants (Agosti, Viola, and Lambruschini) were given between four and seventeen years' imprisonment. Four defendants (Graffigna, Galtieri, Anaya, and Lami Dozo) were acquitted (Cámara Nacional 1987, 2:858–866). The epoch-making trial had ended. Victims and perpetrators had been defined, and knowledge about the systematic repression became part of the collective memory. What, in the end, had been so deeply condemnable in the conduct of the junta commanders?

Wars in the twentieth century have created time and again atrocity-producing situations where combat circumstances and troop deployments made soldiers prone to commit crimes. The term *atrocity-producing situation* was coined by Lifton (1973:41) in the context of Vietnam where guerrillas and civilians were seen as one by U.S. troops. Counterinsurgency tactics and superior American firepower, such as search-and-destroy missions and free-fire zones in which everyone was a target, led to a psychological willingness to kill indiscriminately, as happened in 1968 in the hamlet of My Lai. The Argentine junta commanders went one step further: they created an atrocity-producing structure that contained in its very design the systemic implementation of inhumane practices. The Federal Court had observed that the free-roaming task groups were not acting on their own account but were "just cogs in a gigantic machine" devised by junta commanders who could stop the system at will (Cámara Nacional 1987, 2:804). The atrocity-producing structure and the oral orders that turned the wheels of repression made the junta commanders deny any causal or legal responsibility for the disappearances. They accepted a perfunctory institutional responsibility but did not consider themselves guilty and invoked history or God as the final arbiter.

The court did not address the moral responsibility of the defendants because criminal guilt rests on the principle of intention (mens rea). In moral terms, the junta commanders were condemnable for violating people's human rights and their political trust in the state as its citizens. Mistrust was also sown into people's social relations as the atrocity-producing structure was inserted in the Argentine state and operated with impunity in civil society. There were no safe havens, as task groups forced their way into people's homes. This intrusion was not undone after the regime's fall from power. The persistent refusal to come clean about the enforced disappearances maintained the perpetrators as a specter in the lives of searching relatives and Argentine society.

Impunity, Popular Justice, and Truth Trials

The general mood in 1985 was one of punishment. The trial of the junta commanders was supported by 92.4 percent of the respondents in a November 1985 opinion poll (*El Diario del Juicio* 1985, 25:back page). This popular support has remained high because thirty years later, 84 percent of the people of Buenos Aires continued to approve of the historic trial.[7] In December 1985, 83 percent of the respondents wanted to prosecute all perpetrators (*Somos* 1985, 9(482):7). Accusations were pouring into the courts, and the names of nearly seven hundred tarnished officers were published by a human rights institute (CELS 1986). In the years 1985 and 1986, 481 officers were indicted, 16 tried, and 11 convicted (Moreno Ocampo 1999:669).

The Argentine military were embittered, and even the Full Stop Law of 23 December 1986 that placed a statute of limitations on new indictments failed to calm the growing animosity. What particularly distressed many middle-ranking officers, who had implemented the repression as junior officers, was the attitude of the junta commanders. The commanders had been negligent by not providing a proper legal framework for the operations, thus exposing their subordinates to prosecution. And now, they were feigning ignorance of the repressive practices, blaming the rank and file. As was explained in Chapter 2, a mutiny spread through the armed forces in April 1987. The demand for an end to the trials was met by the Due Obedience Law of June 1987, which relieved many officers of legal responsibility.

The military turmoil of 1986–1987 coincided with President Alfonsín's wish to bring about national reconciliation. This policy was maintained by President Menem with sweeping pardons benefiting indicted and convicted officers and guerrillas in October 1989 and December 1990. Argentine psychiatrists noticed the reappearance of traumatic symptoms among bereaved relatives and survivors of torture as a consequence of the impunity laws (Edelman and Kordon 1995a; Lagos 1994). The human rights movement was taken aback but not paralyzed by this reversal of justice because relatives of the disappeared had since 1987 filed complaints with the Inter-American Commission on Human Rights (IACHR) against the Argentine government for violating the right to judicial protection and a fair trial by issuing amnesty laws and presidential pardons. The IACHR agreed with the petitioners and concluded in October 1992 that the laws were incompatible with Inter-American conventions. It recommended that the Argentine government "clarify the facts and identify those responsible for the human rights violations that occurred during the past military dictatorship" (IACHR 1992). The commission confirmed the right to justice for crimes against humanity, and the right to truth of families about the disappearances, which were regarded as unresolved ongoing crimes. This landmark opinion gathered legal clout in 1994 when international human rights treaties received constitutional status in Argentina (Méndez and Mariezcurrena 1999:89–95; Sikkink 2011:79).

The call for truth and justice gained momentum in March 1995 when Navy Captain Francisco Scilingo confessed to having pushed sedated captives from a plane. The commanders of the armed forces and police issued public apologies to contain the national outcry. However, General Martín Balza's mea culpa, "I assume full responsibility for the present and full institutional responsibility for the past," sounded hollow in a climate of impunity (Balza 2001:262; Robben 2005a:351–352). A nationwide surge of protests surrounded the twentieth anniversary of the 1976 coup d'état in March 1996, which was rejuvenated by a new generation of activists about to play an important role in the struggle for accountability.

Children of the disappeared began seeking each other's company in 1993 with questions about their parents' past and their own identity. These groups united in April 1995 to form a national network with the acronym HIJOS (Hijos por la Identidad y la Justicia, contra el Olvido y el Silencio, or Children for Identity and Justice Against Oblivion and Silence) (Seidel 2014:144–150). In December 1996, the Buenos Aires chapter decided to target Jorge Luis Magnacco, who had worked as a gynecologist at the ESMA maternity ward. He delivered babies of abducted captives, including Victoria Donda, whose mother was later assassinated with the complicity of her brother-in-law, Navy Lieutenant Adolfo Donda, as was described in Chapter 4. Magnacco worked at the Mitre Clinic in Buenos Aires. A group of HIJOS arrived at the hospital to denounce him and then continued to his home to inform his neighbors. Weekly protests cost Magnacco his job, and he relocated to another neighborhood (Catela 2001:267; Seidel 2014:189–190).

This successful action developed into a new form of public protest, the *escrache*, or street happening—not to rail against perpetrators at the Plaza de Mayo but to expose them in their own neighborhood. Homes were spray-painted with slogans, dark pasts revealed by megaphone, photos distributed, and street signs were posted with sayings such as "Here lives a murderer." HIJOS aimed to ostracize the perpetrators from Argentine society until the day when they would all be in prison. As they declared during the escrache of a torturer, they wanted the neighborhood to shut him out, so that "tomorrow, the newsstand decides not to attend to him, the taxi driver decides not to take him, the baker chooses not to serve him, and the newsboy refuses him a paper" (De Mano en Mano 2002:47; Catela 2001:267–271). The street happenings tried to mobilize neighborhoods against perpetrators living in their midst by turning them into social outcasts, "to exclude them from society, to deny them any social life," as one activist said (Kaiser 2002:507). According to HIJOS, the street happenings deposited the accusations at the doorstep of repressors and torturers because justice could not be found inside the courtroom. Popular justice was exacted through a process of denouncement, sentencing, stigmatization, and ostracism.

In reality, neighbors were ambivalent. Some joined the protests. Others were disturbed by the noise and graffiti and did not consider it their business to give their neighbors the cold shoulder. Whatever their sentiment, publicly accused perpetrators would be seen with different eyes and regarded with other thoughts than before the escrache (Kaiser 2002:509–510). Even though the ostracism seldom succeeded, the media attention motivated the human rights movement to pursue the struggle for accountability and remind Argentina of the continuing impunity. As HIJOS stated: "without justice, there will be escraches" (De Mano en Mano 2002:35).

Two possibilities for holding perpetrators accountable arose in 1998. In February 1998, the Argentine Congress passed a motion to dismantle the amnesty legislation, and the Permanent Assembly for Human Rights (APDH) in La Plata petitioned the Federal Court in April 1998 to investigate the fate of disappeared persons. In September 1998, the first truth trial (Juicio por la Verdad) was held in La Plata, which summoned officers to testify about their knowledge of particular disappearances. A precedent had been set when Admiral Massera had given witness testimony in a Federal Court in 1996.[8]

The truth trials pursued restorative justice without forgoing punitive justice. Based on the legal right to truth, witnesses were summoned to speak under oath about the predicament of disappeared captives. In La Plata, the court also examined police records and visited police stations, cemeteries, and former secret detention centers. The entire atrocity-producing structure in La Plata was mapped, and the responsible state agents were identified. Eighteen hundred declarations were given about eleven hundred disappeared persons during years of proceedings.

Sessions began with the testimony of relatives, eyewitnesses to the abduction, and former disappeared persons. The testimonies resembled the depositions at the CONADEP truth commission where people had spoken their mind, and emotions were allowed to run free. Valuable premortem information was given that assisted forensic identifications of human remains exhumed in Buenos Aires Province. Finally, officers, policemen, and civilian collaborators were asked to take the witness stand (Andriotti Romanin 2013:14–19; Catela 2001:257–259; Centro de Información Judicial 2014). Although immune from prosecution because of the amnesty laws, several officers refused to appear in court, for fear of being accused of giving false testimony and thus risking a four-year sentence for perjury. They were charged with obstruction of justice, and jailed for two days to rethink their decision. Tight-lipped officers in Córdoba were arrested for refusing to appear in court but fought their detention successfully by appealing to the constitutional protection against self-incrimination. Many truth trials were inconclusive because witness-perpetrators either feigned ignorance or refused to appear in court. Nevertheless, the truth trials yielded much new evidence that would prove valuable once the amnesty laws had been derogated (Brett 2001:IV; Comisión de Educación 2004: 38–39; Roht-Arriaza 2005:102–107).

Relatives, ex-disappeared, and perpetrators related to one another differently in truth trials than in criminal trials. They were adversaries in criminal trials but witnesses in truth trials. However, the pursuit of truth placed them in other positions before the crime. Accountability was measured not in legal but in moral terms because not guilt but truth was at stake. The truth trial appealed to the moral responsibility of perpetrators to reveal when and how the disappeared had been assassinated and what had been done with the remains. Such information could help the personal mourning of the bereaved relatives and the national mourning of the Argentine people. Silence implied an ongoing hostility toward the dead and the living that would perpetuate the trauma of repression. In this sense, the escraches and the truth trials evoked moral judgments about the perpetrators inside and outside the courtroom, but where the street happenings attempted to ostracize them from society, the truth trials gave them an opportunity to be honest with the searching relatives. However, they refused to cooperate with the truth courts out of fear of future prosecution and because of the ideological conviction that the repression had been justified for the greater good of Argentina.

The review of the April 1998 petition to hold truth trials in La Plata coincided with an unexpected revelation. Army Commander Martín Balza remarked in June 1998 that babies captured during operations were passed to personnel of the police and armed forces.[9] Within days, Lieutenant-General Videla was detained because the kidnapping of children, next to rape and theft, had been excluded from the amnesty laws and presidential pardons. In July 2000, there were thirty-two officers in detention accused of baby snatching.[10]

In March 2001, Federal Judge Gabriel Cavallo ruled that the amnesty laws of 1986 and 1987 had been unconstitutional and incompatible with the American Convention of Human Rights. The pressure on the Argentine judiciary to prosecute was raised by extradition requests from Spain, France, Italy, and Germany in relation to the disappearance of their citizens in Argentina. The Argentine government decided in December 2001 that Argentines who had committed crimes on national soil were subject to Argentine law and thus supported the revocation of the impunity laws. Several judges confirmed the ruling of Judge Cavallo, Congress repealed the impunity laws, and newly elected President Néstor Kirchner accelerated the derogation process in 2003 by appointing new judges to the Supreme Court (Roht-Arriaza 2005:114–117).[11]

On 14 June 2005, the Supreme Court annulled the Full Stop Law of December 1986 and the Due Obedience Law of June 1987. Judge Ricardo Lorenzetti commented that, on moral grounds, human rights violations cannot be amnestied: "If the atrocious crimes remain unpunished, then society holds no promise for the future because its moral foundations will be contaminated."[12] Moral accountability was considered by Lorenzetti to be the foundation of legal accountability. When the judiciary failed to prosecute crimes, then society might exact accountability in culturally appropriate ways. The paralysis of the Argentine judiciary motivated HIJOS to denounce and stigmatize perpetrators with street happenings because the coexistence of victims and perpetrators was oppressive in moral and social terms, according to Estela de Carlotto: "The laws were issued and they exhausted us for years with their impunity. We have lived together with thieves and murderers [that] in reality should have been convicted."[13]

In line with the ruling from 2005, the Supreme Court declared on 13 July 2007 that the presidential pardons of October 1989 and December 1990 had also been unconstitutional. Former President Alfonsín supported the derogation of his amnesty laws as a sign of Argentina's mature democracy.[14] However, former President Menem disapproved of the annulment of his presidential pardons for reviving old hatreds by not prosecuting the guerrilla combatants together with the military: "This is a partial, unilateral vision that seems more like revenge than a balanced and prudent position."[15] Menem's opinion was certainly shared by more than two thousand members of the military and police who were to face court in the next decade. They felt betrayed by an untrustworthy state that retracted previous laws and did not hold the revolutionary organizations accountable for their violence against the democratic state between 1973 and 1976.

Human Rights Trials

The first human rights trial began on 20 June 2006 against retired Police Commissioner-General Miguel Osvaldo Etchecolatz. A total of 2,436 persons were accused between 2006 and 2016. By July 2016, 689 persons had been convicted, 68 persons had been acquitted, and 846 defendants had not yet been sentenced. There were 47 fugitives from justice. The remainder of 786 accused persons consisted of 395 persons who had died since 2006 (328 before being sentenced) and others who had not yet been indicted or were unfit to stand trial (Procuraduría de Crímenes contra la Humanidad 2016b:10–12).

The symbolic high point of the human rights trials was the life sentence of former dictator Jorge Rafael Videla on 22 December 2010 for the torture and execution of thirty-one political prisoners. Videla had refused to speak in his own defense in 1985 but did so now. His words sounded as if from another era, as if he was still addressing the nation as Argentina's president and supreme commander: "It was not a dirty war but a just war in which we saved the country from 'the young idealists' who wanted to impose an alien culture on our traditional, Western and Christian style of life."[16]

Videla's guilty verdict was the culmination of decades of painstakingly piecing together evidence from multiple sources. The crimes against humanity in Argentina were of such complexity and magnitude that the atrocity-producing structure became visible only gradually through the different types of transitional and post-transitional justice employed during thirty years of democracy. This slow discovery process is particularly clear in the case of the death flights. An estimated 2,000–3,500 captives at the Navy Mechanics School and the Campo de Mayo army base came to their end during these death flights (Somigliana and Olmo 2002:27). The flights from a landing strip at Campo de Mayo were described by Sergeant Víctor Ibañez, and conscript soldiers stationed there.[17] Here, I will focus on the Navy's death flights to demonstrate the process of accountability.

Disappeared captives held at the secret detention center of the Navy Mechanics School (ESMA) in Buenos Aires first heard about the death flights in February 1977. They already knew about the transfers on Wednesdays and sometimes Thursdays, when at 3:30 P.M. the building's basement was cleared and at 5:00 P.M. the numbers of captives were called out. They were said to be moved to a work camp or rehabilitation center. "A very tense climate reigned on the day of the transfers. We, the abducted, did not know whether or not it would be our turn that day. The guards took many more severe measures than usual. We couldn't go to the bathroom. Every one of us had to remain strictly in his place, hooded and shackled, without making any attempt to see what was going on" (Martí, Pirles, and Osatinsky 1995:40). The selected captives were taken from their cells, were lined up in single file, and were marched downstairs to be prepared for the voyage.

In February 1977, Emilio Carlos Assales Bonazzola told Juan Gasparini how he and twenty other inmates had received an injection in the infirmary, supposedly to vaccinate them for the transfer. Instead, they received the sedative Pentothal. Some vomited, others passed out. They were loaded on a truck and taken to the military zone of Aeroparque Jorge Newbery, the small city airport of Buenos Aires. When the drowsy Emilio Bonazzola was about to board the Fokker aircraft, he was taken aside and brought back to the ESMA, where he slept for twenty-four hours straight. He was told that he was wanted in Mendoza and was transferred there in March 1977.[18] Surviving inmates now understood that the marks they had noticed on the basement floor after the weekly transfer had been caused by the soles of rubber shoes and slippers of captives being dragged to the truck. They also understood why the clothes of recent transferees were found in the storage room. The Navy officers refused to talk about the transfers, but Coast Guard Officer Gonzalo Sánchez remarked that the captives on transport had been thrown in the South Atlantic Ocean (Martí, Pirles, and Osatinsky 1995:41–43).

My description of the death flights is mainly based on the press conferences held in Paris in October 1979 and in Madrid in February 1982 by five ESMA captives sent into exile (Martí, Pirles, and Osatinsky 1995; Daleo and Castillo 1982). The existence of the death flights was confirmed in March 1983 by former police inspector Rodolfo Peregrino Fernández, who declared that Irish-made Coast Guard planes were used, and that on one occasion, "a prisoner had dragged the NCO entrusted with his elimination in his fall into the sky" (Fernández 1983:71). The CONADEP commission also drew on these testimonies to report the death flights but could not hide its disbelief. "This is scarcely credible, but is mentioned by many witnesses: some because they had heard about it, others because of direct references made by their captors. Then there were the bodies washed up by currents on the shore. It is indeed difficult to believe, but in the general context of this savage repression one can imagine that for those who practiced it" (CONADEP 1986:221).

The CONADEP depositions were confirmed during the trial of the commanders in 1985 by former ESMA captive Carlos Muñoz (*El Diario del Juicio* 1985, 24:455). ESMA survivors also described how naval officers decided about life and death in "a sort of meeting of commanding officers, who were the ones who decided together about the fate of every captive" (*El Diario del Juicio* 1985, 26:490). According to Vice-Admiral Mendía, the military had consulted with Argentina's Church authorities about the death flights. They had told him that it was a humanitarian and Christian death (Scilingo 2000:35). Rear-Admiral Horacio Mayorga explained the procedure to me in an interview on 3 October 1990:

> One would detain a guerrilla combatant, obtain the information, and decide in a small committee without a trial or signature which fate he was going to run. It is a lie that there were no verdicts. There were verdicts. But it is true that nobody ever signed the verdict. The death of any guerrilla was always decided by at least five persons. But one thing yes, five persons who like you and me, sitting like this, said, "That one can't go on living." What did they do? I tell you what happened in the Navy, without any false sentiments. You will say, "but did they . . . ?" No, no, if not, I won't tell you anything and that's the end of it, isn't it? Very well, they injected them and threw them in the sea. They didn't . . . He didn't even know that he was going to die, I can assure you.

The opposite end of this gruesome trajectory was also known: tortured bodies had appeared on the beaches of Argentina and Uruguay since the dictatorship's first months in power and were reported in the regular as well as the clandestine press. In an open letter of March 1977 by Montonero Rodolfo Walsh, he accused the military junta of "carpeting the bottom of the River Plate with dead bodies or throwing prisoners into the sea from cargo planes of the First Air Brigade" (Walsh 1995:419; CADHU 1977:63–65). Clearly, assassinated disappeared persons were thrown into rivers and seas, but it was not yet proven that people had been thrown alive from planes because the bodies found on the beaches could have been lowered into the water from boats.

Despite the circumstantial evidence collected for nearly two decades, nothing was more convincing than the self-incriminatory confession of Navy Captain Scilingo that was analyzed in Chapter 4. Scilingo had participated in two death flights in June and July of 1977. The first flight with thirteen captives was carried out with a Skyvan plane from the Coast Guard, and the second flight of seventeen captives was made with an Electra plane from Naval Aviation. The prisoners were told that they would be flown to a prison in southern Argentina and required a vaccination (Verbitsky 1995:180). Navy Captain Jorge Acosta told the inmates to be happy and even turned on some music to make them dance. All did, except one captive who said it was a lie and that they were going to be killed. The music was turned up to drown his voice (Scilingo 2000:65).

Scilingo's description of the sedation of captives and their transport by truck to Buenos Aires city airport is identical to that of the ESMA survivors. The crew consisted generally of two pilots, two officers, two NCOs, and a physician. Once the sedated captives were aboard, the naval doctor gave them a powerful tranquilizer. Scilingo described the final stage of the operation as follows:

> They were undressed while being unconscious and when the flight commander gave the order, dependent on the location of the plane, the hatch was opened and they were thrown out naked, one by one. This is the story. A macabre but real story that no one can deny. They did it with Skyvan planes of the Coast Guard and Electra planes from the Navy. In the Skyvan through the rear hatch that opens from top to bottom. It's a large hatch without intermediate positions. It's closed or open, and therefore maintained in open position. The NCO stepped on the hatch, a sort of swivel hatch, so that there would be an opening of forty centimeters towards the void. Next, we began lowering the subversives that way. (Verbitsky 1995:58)

Survivors, witnesses, and perpetrators had by 1995 described the death flights accurately, but collecting the material proof would take another ten years. In 2005, the Argentine Forensic Anthropology Team identified the remains of five bodies that had washed ashore in December 1977 and had been buried anonymously at General Lavalle Cemetery. They belonged to the group of eight human rights activists who had been abducted on 8 and 10 December 1977 on the instigation of Navy Lieutenant Alfredo Astiz. Astiz had infiltrated the group under the name Gustavo Niño, pretending to be searching for his disappeared brother. The captives included the French nuns Léonie Duquet and Alice Domon, and Azucena Villaflor de De Vicenti, who had founded the Mothers of the Plaza de Mayo.[19] The women were taken to the Navy Mechanics School. About one week after the disappearances, the French embassy received a photo of the nuns Domon and Duquet posing as kidnap victims before a Montonero emblem. The photo was accompanied by a communiqué of the guerrilla organization and a letter by Alice Domon. The French authorities were not fooled by the Navy ploy but were unable to free the women. Several witnesses confirmed in 1984 that the nuns had been at the ESMA and that Alice Domon had been tortured so severely that she had to be carried to the bathroom. And even then, she asked her captors about the fate of Gustavo Niño, unaware that he was an undercover agent. She was also taken on a death flight in late 1977 (CONADEP 1986:343; Gasparini 1986:127–138; Robben 2005a:303–304). The forensic examination in 2005 of the five bodies reached the following conclusion: "During the laboratory study the team established that the fractures on the bodies were consistent with those of people who had fallen from a great height onto a hard surface (even though water is not a 'hard' surface, when a body falls from a great height, it acts as a hard surface). This case is important because it is the first forensic investigation providing evidence indicating that kidnapped people who had been seen alive in ESMA and remained disappeared were actually dropped into the ocean" (EAAF 2006:18).

Forensic proof of the death flights had finally been given, but the evidence was still insufficient to prosecute any suspects. The situation changed in September 2009 when a witness remembered how Navy Corporal Rubén Ricardo Ormello had told him how captives had been dragged from a bus into a DC-3 aircraft. Also, Navy helicopter pilot Emir Sisul Hess had bragged about how captives had begged for their lives and fallen into the sky like ants. Finally, two Dutch pilots reported that over dinner in Bali with colleagues from a Dutch airline company, former Navy pilot Julio Alberto Poch had defended the throwing of prisoners into the sea because Argentina had been at war. He had added that the searching relatives should not complain because they knew that the inmates had been terrorists. Poch was detained in Spain in September 2009 and extradited to Argentina on the accusation of his participation in the death flights.[20]

Set on the trail of these pilots, the flight records at Jorge Newbery Airport between 1976 and 1978 were analyzed in terms of four variables: (1) duration (only flights over 2.5 hours were considered); (2) destination (departure from and arrival at Jorge Newbery Airport); (3) nocturnal flights (between 6 P.M. and 6 A.M.); and (4) purpose (for example, transport of officers; maintenance; training mission). The investigation yielded eleven suspicious flights. The flight of three hours and ten minutes on Wednesday, 14 December 1977, departing at 9:30 P.M. with Skyvan PA-51, was suspected of having carried Azucena Villaflor de De Vicenti and Léonie Duquet to their deaths. The plane was operated by Coast Guard pilots Mario Daniel Arru, Alejandro Domingo D'Agostino, and Enrique José De Saint Georges. The pilots stated during their questioning that the flight had been a nocturnal training mission without passengers.[21] In further investigations, the court examined the support structure of Naval Operations Command (Comando de Operaciones Navales) that supplied the planes, helicopters, and crews for the alleged death flights.[22]

The trial against the three Coast Guard pilots, Arru, D'Agostino, and De Saint Georges, the Navy pilots, Poch and Hess, and the Navy mechanic, Ormello, began on Wednesday, 28 November 2012. The indictments were part of the major ESMA trial in which 68 defendants were accused of crimes against 789 victims, of whom about one-third were survivors. Navy pilot Poch based his defense on four arguments. First, he had never been at the ESMA. Second, he was a fighter pilot who could not fly small passenger planes. Third, he had not been involved in the anti-subversive war. Fourth, he had been misunderstood by his Dutch colleagues at the restaurant in Bali. In relation to the last point, Judge Sergio Torres observed that friends of Poch had asked the two witnesses to retract their earlier testimonies and declare instead that Poch had spoken in general about the death flights, not in the first person.[23] Aside from presenting documentary proof that Poch was capable of flying passenger planes, had participated in a repressive operation, and that his log books were incomplete, the prosecution reconstructed the organizational structure of the death flights to demonstrate the complicity of the six defendants. The Navy Mechanics School, Naval Aviation Command (Comando de Aviación Naval), and the Coast Guard's Aviation Division (División de Aviación de Prefectura) were separate organizations within Naval Operations Command. The ESMA did not have planes and crews, which explains why the six defendants might never have visited the ESMA. Airborne support for death flights had to be requested by the ESMA at Naval Operations Command.[24] The perpetrators were held personally, legally, and morally accountable for the death flights. The final verdict was still forthcoming at the time of writing.

Conclusion

This chapter has analyzed Argentina's convoluted process of transitional and post-transitional justice that began in 1983 with the CONADEP truth commission. The various types of justice were all predicated on the notion of individual accountability. This accountability has in the Argentine understanding of justice been differentiated into the causal, legal, and moral responsibilities for massive crimes. These responsibilities have been sanctioned in different ways, depending on national political circumstances and developments in international law. Mainly state agents were subjected to the changing judicial standards. The guerrilla insurgents did not fall under this judicial regime because they were nonstate armed actors and were not entrusted with the protection of the Argentine people.

The cultural significance of moral accountability helps explain why the conviction of more than two thousand perpetrators will not end the pursuit of justice in Argentina. Whereas criminal trials close the books on perpetrators by making them pay for their crimes with a prison sentence, their moral responsibility exists in the realm of good and evil, a realm that continuously reassesses people's moral accountability as new pieces of evidence and new discursive frames emerge. Derrida (1992:22–25) has deconstructed the unsolvable tension between law and justice by arguing that a just verdict does not exist simply in applying the law but that a just verdict appeals to a boundless sense of justice that cannot be reduced to the law. This means that each revelation, each new understanding of the past, is another entry on the moral ledger that alters what justice is, even though the law remains the same. Some disclosures may affect the process of justice in decisive ways, as happened when General Balza spoke about the kidnapping of children or when Captain Scilingo confessed to his participation in the death flights. If the truth perception of crimes changes, then this will show the past in a different light and identify crimes and responsibilities that were invisible before. The sense of justice of citizens and interest groups may then call for renewed prosecution.

The preoccupation with the moral injustice of legal impunity started a new wave of prosecutions in the 2010s against civilians that included corporate executives and factory owners. Furthermore, nonmilitary state organs, the economic and educational system, the mass media, and cultural institutions were accused of complicity with the military repression. Individual accountability and retributive justice became almost impossible to satisfy for the large number of people suspected of collaboration with the dictatorship. They were often not legally responsible but nevertheless regarded as morally accountable. Was Argentina not facing the dilemma Hannah Arendt (1958:241) had posed about radical evil in postwar Germany: "men are unable to forgive what they cannot punish and they are unable to punish what has turned out to be unforgivable." Arendt's dilemma of legal and moral accountability is unsolvable, unless justice in terms of individual responsibility is abandoned and moral accountability is assigned collectively. The question of collective guilt has been raised about postwar Germany. The responsibility for World War II and the Holocaust was attributed during the Nuremberg trials to culpable state agents but became assumed by the German people as a whole in later decades. Multiple individual responsibilities became dissipated into a collective responsibility. This shared sense of guilt about the past developed as well in Argentina during the 2010s, when genocide emerged as a new interpretive frame to historically understand and morally judge the past.

CHAPTER 7

Guilt

On 25 September 1979, Jacobo Timerman was stripped of his Argentine citizenship and forced onto a plane bound for Israel. Timerman had been the director of the newspaper *La Opinión*, a critical follower of the military regime, until he was abducted on 15 April 1977 on suspicion of having financial ties to the Montoneros. He was taken to the Buenos Aires Provincial Police Headquarters in La Plata and was interrogated by Colonel Ramón Camps and Police Commissioner Etchecolatz (Camps 1983:133–135; CONADEP 1986:153, 238). Timerman remained disappeared for four days and was then legalized as a prisoner of the military junta. He was tortured repeatedly, court-martialed, and acquitted. Nevertheless, he remained in prison until April 1978 and was then placed under house arrest. International pressure and a Supreme Court ruling secured his release in September 1979. The military junta immediately deported Timerman to Israel (*El Diario del Juicio* 1985, 2:44–47; Timerman 1981:128, 160).

Timerman celebrated his arrival in Tel Aviv as a homecoming from a diaspora of many centuries. He narrates in his book, *Prisoner Without a Name, Cell Without a Number*, that his ancestors had escaped the Netherlands from Spanish occupation and the Inquisition in the sixteenth century. They traveled eastward and settled in the small town of Bar in the Ukraine. Many of Bar's Jews were massacred by the Cossack chief Chmielnitski in the mid-seventeenth century, but the community recovered until the Nazis murdered the Jewish inhabitants in October 1942. Jacobo Timerman was living in Buenos Aires at the time because he and his family had fled the anti-Semitism in his native Ukraine in 1928. But Jacobo Timerman was not safe there, either. "In 1977, in Argentina, the same ideological conviction that impelled Chmielnitski and the Nazis reverberated in the questions posed by my interrogators inside the army's clandestine prisons. And in their methods of torture as well" (Timerman 1981:viii).

Timerman explained that right-wing military officers were convinced that they were fighting World War III against a global communist hegemony, just as the Nazis had done during World War II. They believed that Jews and communists conspired in Argentina, as they had done during the Russian Revolution. His captors accused Timerman of acting as a liaison between the Argentine guerrilla organizations and Israel to seize Patagonia. Timerman saw several parallels between dictatorial Argentina and Nazi Germany: anti-communism and anti-Semitism reigned in both countries; communists were considered guilty by ideology, Jews by birth; and both regimes held the belief that they were fulfilling a historical mission for the sake of humanity (Timerman 1981:72–75, 101–103).

Timerman thought that someday the Argentine commanders would be held accountable, just like the Nazis. "The Argentine military at present perceive the Nuremberg Trials in the Latin American context not as a historic event but as an actual possibility. They still feel justified historically, but foresee the improbability of being pardoned by their contemporaries" (Timerman 1981:154). Timerman's denunciation of the military's crimes was complemented by an imputation of the Argentine people's complicity and moral accountability: "How can a nation reproduce in every detail, though employing other forms, in every argument, though employing other words, the same monstrous crimes explicitly condemned and clearly expounded so many years before?" (157).

Timerman's perplexity about the collective guilt of the Argentine people was raised again when the transitional military government suggested introducing democracy with a clean slate. In April 1983, Bishop Quarracino expressed his support for an amnesty law, although he preferred to speak of a law to forget. He believed that criminal trials would lead to a "poisoning of human relations in this country . . . because one way or the other we are all guilty" (*Esquiú* 1983, 24(1199):10). His pronouncement might have been self-serving because many bishops had provided ideological and pastoral support to the military (Burdick 1995; Mignone 1988; Verbitsky 2006), but Quarracino articulated a majority opinion that was confirmed weeks later when the episcopacy called for a reconciliation with God that implied "the full acknowledgment and abomination of one's sins, the resolve not to commit them again, and the reparation of the wrong done through penitence and the adoption of an entirely new conduct [that] will

finally lead to fraternal Love with its capacity for repentance and forgiveness, offered with generosity, and accepted with humility" (Conferencia
Episcopal Argentina 1988:94). These words might be in line with the Christian faith of reconciliation and forgiveness but went against the wish of
most Argentines to try the military for their horrendous crimes. Leaving
aside rhetorical uses, the issue of Argentina's collective guilt was not prominent in public discourse during the 1980s but became relevant in the mid-
2000s as genocide emerged as an important discursive frame to interpret
the past and as civilians were accused of aiding or abetting the dictatorship.

Guilt refers in this chapter to immoral or unlawful acts (actus reus) and
not to a guilty conscience (mens rea). It is important to understand this
distinction in order to grasp the meaning of collective guilt in Argentina
in terms of individual responsibility. "Guilt is linked to individual responsibility, and whether individuals feel guilt for a violation committed by a
member of their group depends on whether they regard the violation as
ascribable to particular acts over which they had some control" (Moses
2007:20). The attempt to cast a collective guilt on the Argentine people
departs from the assumption that the Argentine people could have somehow influenced the political process that led to the dictatorship and that
Argentines shared a degree of personal responsibility for the political
violence.

The question of guilt in the sense of individual responsibility became
an important area of national contestation in Argentina when in 1983 President Alfonsín decreed the prosecution of junta and guerrilla commanders
with the argument that both were equally responsible for the political violence. Subsequent efforts to bring their combatants to trial were cut short
by amnesties and pardons in the late 1980s. The shift from the two-demons
theory to state terrorism as the principal discursive frame in the 1990s
resulted in the renewed prosecution of military and police in the 2000s,
while guerrilla insurgents continued to benefit from legal immunity. This
chapter shows how guilt came to be addressed in the mid-2000s in terms
of a collective responsibility for the political violence and military repression of the 1970s.

Collective responsibility is a disputed concept, and collective guilt even
more so. Some philosophers argue that only individuals have agency and
intentionality (Lewis 1948; Narveson 2002). Others believe that social processes and organizations cannot be reduced to individual responsibilities
because the underlying social dynamics make the entire group—not the

individual members—accountable (Cooper 1968, 2001; May 2005). Apologies and reparations are therefore made in the name of the group. The next issue is whether entire societies can be held responsible for actions carried out by particular persons. Jaspers (2001:30) conceptualized political collective guilt in terms of people's liability as citizens for crimes committed by state agents. French (1984) stated that only identifiable groups are accountable, while Held (1970) argued that even an amorphous group can be held responsible for a passive attitude toward injustice. Although important for conceptual clarity, I sidestep these debates and concentrate on how local understandings of collective guilt and responsibility have influenced public discourse and legal action in Argentina.

In this chapter, I begin with an analysis of genocide as a discursive frame and explain its relation to public debates in Argentina about collective guilt and responsibility. Next, I address the corporate complicity of Argentine businessmen and foreign multinationals with the dictatorship as a manifestation of the expansion of guilt from military and police to civilians and corporations. As an illustration, I analyze the indictment of the owner of an agribusiness accused of collaborating with the Argentine army to repress rural protests. I conclude that genocide and collective guilt have emerged in public discourse as commensurable interpretations of the multiple losses, betrayal, and traumatization of Argentine society.

Genocide

Argentines in exile charged the Argentine military with genocide as early as 1977. Terms such as *concentration camp, extermination,* and *genocidal perpetrator* (genocida) also appeared in several publications abroad (CADHU 1977; Timerman 1981; Duhalde 1983; Gabetta 1983). The word *genocide* was used during the dictatorship as a hyperbole to touch Europe's raw nerve about the Holocaust and influence international public opinion.

The word *genocide* also appeared in Argentina after the dictatorship. The Mothers of the Plaza de Mayo called the military genocidal perpetrators in its magazine *Madres* and described a secret detention center in Tucumán as if it resembled Auschwitz: "on an adjacent piece of land, a Nazi concentration camp was constructed: a perimeter surrounded by two barbed wire fences, observation towers, guards with dogs" (*Madres* 1985, 1(4):15). The human rights lawyer Emilio Mignone argued that the legal definition of genocide applied to Argentina because the military "committed a true genocide, that is to say the assassination en masse without any trial of a sector of society" (Frontalini and Caiati 1984:7). The CONADEP commission stated that "behind the façade of a fight against a terrorist minority lurked genocide" (CONADEP 1986:234). Finally, public prosecutor Julio Strassera referred in his closing argument at the trial of the junta commanders to "the chilling number of victims that caused what we can qualify as the greatest genocide that our country's young history has recorded" (*El Diario del Juicio* 1985, 20:1).

References to genocide, the Holocaust, and concentration camps remained common in human rights circles after the amnesties of the 1980s. Marcos Weinstein, whose son Mauricio disappeared in 1978, told me with a reasoning similar to Timerman's: "When one part of a population kills another part of a population then it is genocide or it is a holocaust. . . . Why, I think, yes, it is important to refer to the Holocaust is that it was the same ideology that took the Nazis or the Germans to make concentration camps and to kill the Jews—and not only the Jews—in concentration camps; this is also what reigned here in the concentration camps. . . . The same Holocaust policy was transferred to here" (interview on 21 April 1990).

Around the same time, the former Montonero commander Fernando Vaca Narvaja touched on Argentina's collective responsibility for the political violence of the 1970s: "nobody is without responsibility in Argentina. . . . I believe that there are indeed individual responsibilities . . . but we did not form ourselves at the margins of Argentine society; we are the products of Argentine society" (interview on 31 May 1990). Nevertheless, state terrorism was the dominant discursive frame in the 1990s, and neither genocide nor collective responsibility were concepts that demanded much public attention.

Matters changed when Spanish courts decided to prosecute Argentine officers for the torture and disappearance of Spanish citizens. The process was set in motion by Spanish prosecutor Carlos Castresana after watching coverage on television of a massive protest against impunity in Buenos Aires. Determined to bring the perpetrators to justice, he asked Spain's national court on 28 March 1996 to initiate proceedings against Argentine commanders for genocide or state terrorism (Asociación Progresista de Fiscales de España 1996). The criminal complaint was assigned by lot to Judge Baltasar Garzón (Roht-Arriaza 2005:2–3).

On 25 March 1997, Judge Garzón presented an extradition request for General Leopoldo Galtieri for implementing a "systematic plan for the disappearance and elimination of members of national groups, imposing on them forced displacements of identity and heritage, and torture and death, which constitute the crime of genocide" (Garzón 1997). Exactly one year later, he provided the legal reasoning behind the genocide charge. The Argentine junta, like Adolf Hitler in Nazi Germany, had tried to establish a new social order through the elimination of a national group. The Argentine disappeared could be defined as a national group on the basis of their shared opposition to the military's Process of National Reorganization. Leaning heavily on the CONADEP truth commission report, Garzón observed that the repression was not directed just toward the guerrilla insurgency and combative labor unions but toward anyone—doctor, lawyer, or artist—who was perceived as a threat to the New Republic. The fact that the perpetrators and the victims had the same nationality did not invalidate the legal argument because the massive disappearances in Argentina constituted an autogenocide, similar to the killing of ethnic Khmer in Cambodia who were regarded by the Red Khmer as class enemies (Hinton 2005:15; Garzón 1998).

The Argentine military had a second motive for committing genocide, according to Garzón; this motive had received the blessing of many conservative Argentine bishops. They wanted to systematically destroy an ideological group that was hostile to Argentina's Western, Christian civilization. This group included not only revolutionaries and communists but also progressive Catholic clergymen and Jews. Jews received an especially brutal treatment from anti-Semitic officers. Garzón acknowledged that the United Nations Genocide Convention excluded ideological and political groups, but he reasoned that any group that shares a particular faith or ideology, whether Christianity, Judaism, Islam, atheism, or communism, resembles a religious group. In sum, the Argentine military committed autogenocide against a national group for their resistance to a new sociopolitical order and genocide against a religious-ideological group for not adhering to the authoritarian state's official religion and national culture (Garzón 1998).

The genocide frame acquired further legal endorsement when another court established on 4 November 1998 that Spain had jurisdiction over crimes such as genocide and terrorism committed outside Spain, as in the case of Navy Captain Adolfo Scilingo, who had confessed to his participation in death flights. "It was an act of extermination that was not committed at random, in an indiscriminate way, but it responded to the decision to destroy a specific sector of the population, a highly heterogeneous but differentiated group. . . . The repression did not seek to change the group's attitude about the new political system but intended to destroy the group through detentions, deaths, disappearances, the theft of children from the group's families, and the intimidation of group members. These imputed acts constitute the crime of genocide" (González 1998).

With the legal reasoning in place, Argentine scholars began to provide the conceptual foundation of the Argentine genocide. Pilar Calveiro compared Argentina's secret detention centers to Nazi concentration camps. Inspired by Hannah Arendt, she concluded that the military had created a mechanism that resulted in "the bureaucratization, routinization, and naturalization of death" (Calveiro 1998:34). The human rights lawyer Mirta Mántaras followed Judge Garzón's lead to prove the autogenocide thesis. She argued that the military and the ruling elite had sealed a pact to restructure the country's economic system and exterminate an emergent national group of opponents to its policies: "workers, students, politicians, adolescents, children, employees, housewives, journalists and everyone else who for whatever circumstance was suspected by the genocidal perpetrators of obstructing the realization of their goals" (Mántaras 2005:68). Mántaras did not confine the term *autogenocide* to the killing of the disappeared but included the iron control over Argentina's social institutions and the exploitation of the working class as important elements.

The sociologist Daniel Feierstein conceptualized the Argentine genocide by elaborating on Garzón's comparison of Nazi Germany and dictatorial Argentina. Argentina and Nazi Germany shared ideological, structural, and processual similarities that articulated a comparable combination of "genocidal social practices" and "a mode of reorganizing social relations" (Feierstein 2008a:26). This so-called reorganizing genocide consisted of the imposition of a particular economic model and the annihilation of a heterogeneous opposition consisting of unions, political and armed organizations, and neighborhood and student movements (Feierstein 2008a:358). Both regimes exterminated particular groups to create a new social order. Feierstein (2006:159–160) emphasized the ideological relation between the two regimes: "Argentine perpetrators identify with Nazi perpetrators, no matter how we try to explain the differences between the two. And the Jews themselves suffered because of these models of identification, these genealogies, in the Argentine concentration camps." Argentina's national group consisted of guerrilla combatants and social militants who "had in common not their political identity, but rather the fact that they participated in the social movements of that time. These ranged from Peronist groupings, to the entire scope of the left, and even several independent movements without any clear partisan affiliation" (Feierstein 2006:150). They were attacked as group members, not as individual political actors, and were therefore victims of genocide, not crimes against humanity (Feierstein 2008b). Feierstein drew heavily on Lemkin's two-phase definition of genocide as the "destruction of the national pattern of the oppressed group," a destruction not limited to physical extermination but that might also consist of political, cultural, or economic oppression, and "the imposition of the national pattern of the oppressor" (Lemkin 2002:27). In other words, Feierstein concluded that the Argentine military committed genocide against a heterogeneous national group to impose a particular economic structure and to reorganize Argentine society.

As I have argued elsewhere (Robben 2005a:172–174), the Argentine military did indeed try to impose their cultural project on Argentine society, but they did so in a cultural war with a guerrilla movement and a much larger heterogeneous political opposition that also worked to impose their revolutionary project on Argentine society, even though the power of the former to achieve its objective surpassed by far that of the latter. The intertwined counterinsurgency war and state terrorism were thus directed at armed insurgents who wanted to achieve their goal with violence and political opponents who pursued their objectives through protest crowds, labor strikes, and grassroots mobilization. Argentine critics have argued that the term *genocide* therefore does not apply, precisely because of the different actions conducted by specific actors.

Vezzetti (2003:153–164) has rejected the notion of an Argentine genocide and the comparison with the Holocaust. He has stated that the Argentine victims were massacred for what they did, thought, or were believed to do and think politically, while the Holocaust victims were assassinated for who they were. Using the term *genocide* in the Argentine context denies that many disappeared captives died because of their political ideals, according to Vezzetti, whereas equating genocide with economic exploitation trivializes Argentina's disappearances and the extermination campaigns of the twentieth century. Furthermore, while the genocide of the Jewish people rested on a bureaucratic rationality and a banality of evil, Argentina's state terrorism was inspired by sociopolitical vengeance and ideological volition. Like Vezzetti, the judges Rafecas (2011:170) and Lozada (2008:73–75) have preferred the term *crimes against humanity* because the elimination of political groups does not fall under the UN genocide definition. Crimes against humanity have been defined in the Rome Statute as "a widespread or systematic attack directed against any civilian population," including murder, torture, rape, extermination, enforced disappearance, and "persecution against any identifiable group or collectivity on political, racial, national, ethnic, cultural, religious, gender . . . or other grounds" (International Criminal Court 1998). Lozada has emphasized that the junta's victims did not constitute a national group because they were targeted for their individual political convictions, not for their national identity. Finally, the legal scholar Schabas (2009:171) has objected strongly to an ad hoc creation of national and political groups that turns all mass slaughters into genocide: "In the end, such reasoning leads to an absurdity that trivializes the very nature of genocide: the human race itself constitutes a protected group, and therefore genocide covers any mass killing. From a legal standpoint, the principal drawback of this approach is that it can in no way be stretched to apply to the [Genocide] Convention."

Aside from these conceptual objections, the term *genocide* has also been dismissed on factual grounds. Conversations in March 2010 with Argentine lawyers, forensic anthropologists, ex-disappeared, and former guerrilla combatants yielded nine points of criticism:

1. The regime did not abduct people as members of a national group but handpicked specific members of oppositional organizations. In contrast to the Holocaust and the Armenian, Cambodian, and Rwandan genocides, relatives of the disappeared who did not fit the enemy definition were generally not assassinated. Relatives were frequently abducted, tortured, or held hostage but most often were released after they had been assessed as harmless.
2. The captives were not immediately eliminated but tortured for information about their comrades to dismantle the guerrilla organizations and front organizations.
3. Many disappeared were not victims of genocide but revolutionaries who fought and were defeated. The term *genocide* takes away their political agency and depoliticizes their revolutionary struggle and death.

4. Many disappeared were released and forced into exile after officers had decided that they did not pose a threat. In fact, much valuable testimony during the dictatorship about the secret detention centers came from exiled disappeared persons.

5. The repression was selective because members of the Argentine Communist Party were not persecuted systematically, despite being leftist opponents to the regime and its economic plans.

6. Thirty thousand assassinated disappeared do not qualify as a partial extermination of a political left that numbered into the millions. The massive human rights protests in 1983 demonstrated that the left had not been destroyed.

7. If the targeting of guerrilla insurgents and political opponents counts as genocide, then the assassination of military officers, industrialists, and their family members for belonging to a loosely defined national or ideological group might also be considered genocide.

8. Genocide is not necessary to reorganize society and impose an economic plan, as has been shown in other Latin American countries.

9. The children of the disappeared were either handed to neighbors and relatives or kidnapped and adopted by military families, instead of being killed for belonging to a national group as would be common in the case of genocide.

This diffuse criticism has been unable to compete with the moral appeal by human rights lawyers and activists eager to prosecute civilians and the military for genocide. Their public discourse influenced post-transitional justice after the derogation of the amnesty laws in 2005 and, in particular, after the trial of Etchecolatz. Etchecolatz was indicted in June 2006 for the abduction, torture, and assassination of six disappeared persons and the abduction and torture of the ex-disappeared Nilda Eloy and Jorge López, who were both giving testimony at the trial.

Alejo Ramos Padilla, the lawyer for the plaintiff María Isabel Chorobik de Mariani, asked the three judges to hand Etchecolatz a life sentence for acts that "qualify as genocide according to the constitution" (Ramos Padilla 2006:394). The defense lawyers dismissed the plea, arguing that Argentina had been involved in a war against subversive terrorists who had tried to install a totalitarian regime. The accused had acted in defense of a nation at war because a democratic government had mandated the armed forces

in October 1975 to annihilate the guerrilla insurgency. The charge of genocide was therefore incorrect: "Here, they did not try to destroy or annihilate
a national, ethnic, racial or religious group . . . the subversives . . . were
almost all Argentines, and they were attacked for being terrorist delinquent
subversives; not for belonging to a national group or a certain class because
they were of all social classes" (Ramos Padilla 2006:395). Adolfo Casabal
Elía, another defense lawyer, lamented that a true patriot was being prosecuted. He asked for an end to the opening of wounds and called for reconciliation, but the lawyer Verónica Bogliano, herself the daughter of
disappeared parents, responded: "We had to wait thirty years to arrive at
this trial in search of justice, and as long as they do not give all the answers,
we will not forget, we will not forgive, and we are not going to become
reconciled" (Ramos Padilla 2006:399).

The courtroom in La Plata was packed with a restless audience on 19
September 2006, waiting to hear the verdict. When Judge Carlos Alberto
Rozanski convicted Miguel Osvaldo Etchecolatz to life in prison for six
homicides and eight disappearances, the accused rose to his feet, kissed the
rosary clenched in his hands, and looked to heaven. Red paint balls were
thrown from the audience, and Etchecolatz was escorted outside to a
shower of insults.[1] The judge threatened to clear the courtroom and continued reading the sentence. He considered Etchecolatz guilty of "human
rights violations committed in the framework of a genocide that had taken
place in the Argentine Republic between 1976 and 1983" (Rozanski, Isaurralde, and Lorenzo 2006:101). When the verdict was ratified by the
Supreme Court in March 2009, Judge Rozanski commented: "This sentence
means a paradigm shift, it is a watershed."[2] The La Plata ruling was not
automatically underwritten by other judges. The bench of four judges that
handed Lieutenant-General Videla his first life sentence on 22 December
2010 convicted him by majority vote for crimes against humanity. One
judge dissented, pleading to charge Videla with genocide (Gavier 2012:
317–341).

The La Plata court based its argumentation on United Nations Resolution 96(1) of 11 December 1946, in which the General Assembly defined
genocide as the destruction of any group in whole or in part, including
political groups. The exclusion of voluntary associations, and in particular
political groups, from the 1948 UN Genocide Convention made the court
in La Plata redefine the assassinated-disappeared as constituting a national
group. The court also drew legal inspiration from the 1985 verdict of the

five junta commanders for their systematic plan of elimination. Additional support was found in Judge Garzón's legal opinion and the above cited ruling by the Spanish national court on 4 November 1998. Scholarly confirmation was found in the work of Feierstein (Rozanski, Isaurralde, and Lorenzo 2006:section IV-b).

Judge Rozanski observed later that "here, a part of a national group was persecuted and annihilated. This defines the genocidal perpetrator: the one who decides to annihilate."[3] Yet, Etchecolatz was convicted for homicides and disappearances, not for genocide. O'Donnell (2009:367) praised this Solomon's judgment that contained "a troubling and discordant definition of genocide that has the potential to undermine the integrity of current genocide jurisprudence," but at the same time the court "was able to satisfy the victims' desire that the genocide label be used while stopping short of convicting defendants for violating the [Geneva] Convention." The verdict's legal argumentation implied a category shift from state terrorism to genocide that had been spearheaded by the human rights movement and supported by politicians, lawyers, and scholars since the late 1990s. A new discursive frame was emerging that made Argentines see the past from a different point of view and forced them to examine their own role during the dictatorship.

And how did Etchecolatz respond to his conviction? He considered himself a political prisoner, "a participant in a war that we won with weapons and are losing politically" (Ramos Padilla 2006:400). This opinion was shared by the thousands of officers who had been indicted or were imprisoned. They regarded themselves as victims of justice who were tried for following orders, were humiliated in court by civilian judges, and were without guilt or remorse about a war they considered just (Van Roekel 2016:126). A solidarity movement arose in the wake of the Etchecolatz trial. The most important support organization became the Association of Family and Friends of Argentina's Political Prisoners (Asociación de Familiares y Amigos de los Presos Políticos de la Argentina) run by Cecilia Pando, the wife of a retired officer. This group began organizing protests outside courtrooms where human rights trials were held. They also painted slogans on memorials and coordinated a monthly protest at the Plaza de Mayo. Protesters showed photographs of the victims of guerrilla violence, just as the mothers of the Plaza de Mayo used to carry pictures of the disappeared until they decided to expand their motherhood to all victims of political violence and exploitation.

The perimeter of the pyramid at the Plaza de Mayo was declared an official memory site in March 2005. Silhouettes depicting white scarves and the text "victims of state terrorism" were painted on the pavement to immortalize the courageous mothers. On 9 March 2010, I attended a protest there led by Cecilia Pando. The manifestation began at 6:45 P.M. after the presidential guard had finished the flag-folding ceremony. Around sixty to eighty persons had gathered, carrying photos of the prominent union leader José Rucci, who was assassinated in 1973 by the Montoneros; Major Julio Larrabure, who had died of asphyxiation in 1975 while being held captive by the People's Revolutionary Army; and Vice-Admiral Lambruschini's daughter Paula, who was killed in 1978 by a bomb planted by Montoneros in an apartment adjacent to the family's residence. The group of protesters walked slowly around the pyramid that commemorated Argentina's independence, stopping each time to allow Cecilia Pando to spray-paint a black mourning band next to a white scarf and add the text "victims of Montonero and ERP terrorism." She had done this for the first time in October 2006, just weeks after Etchecolatz had been sentenced to life in prison.[4]

Cecilia Pando closed the event with a speech in which she denounced Argentina's one-sided justice. Why were only the military in prison, and not the guerrillas, she asked rhetorically? Instead, Argentina needed reconciliation, and leaders like Nelson Mandela and Uruguayan President José Mugica. Mugica used to be a Tupamaros guerrilla commander who spent years in prison, yet he did not prosecute the Uruguayan military. After the applause died down, I struck up a conversation with the wife of a retired army sergeant held in Campo de Mayo prison for human rights violations. She did not deny that there had been torture and disappearances during the dictatorship but demanded the prosecution of former guerrilla commanders like Firmenich, Perdía, and Vaca Narvaja because everyone should be treated equally before the law.

The human rights trials have considerably hardened the public confrontation between proponents and opponents of the dictatorship. Human rights lawyers, such as Guadalupe Godoy, who provided counsel to plaintiffs in the Etchecolatz trial, have stated that they pursue a collective conviction for genocide of the armed forces, resembling the blanket sentence of the SS and Gestapo at the Nuremberg trial as criminal organizations (Heller 2011:11). Furthermore, the genocide discourse has raised questions about Argentina's collective responsibility for the political violence of the 1970s.

The question of guilt has changed since human rights, academic, and judicial circles began talking about an Argentine genocide. The issue of the legal and especially moral guilt of the guerrilla commanders has also been raised, albeit reluctantly.

The guilt of the guerrilla organizations for the political violence underwent several changes since the dictatorship. The revolutionaries turned from terrorists into victims when state terrorism replaced the two-demons theory as the dominant discursive frame in Argentina. Later, the guerrillas became heroes in leftist circles and in the eyes of some human rights leaders and the Presidents Néstor Kirchner and Cristina Fernández de Kirchner. They were admired, if not romanticized, for sacrificing their lives to their ideals and enduring the consequences with their heads held high. Not these disappeared revolutionaries, but the guerrilla commanders who guided them toward political violence after the fall of the military dictatorship in May 1973, came under attack in the 2010s. The betrayal of cadres and sympathizers by failing or even refusing to protect them against the military repression was part of the criticism, but more fundamental has been the charge that the guerrilla commanders chose a violent road to revolution after democracy had been restored in 1973. Former Peronist Congressman Julio Bárbaro stated that the Peronist movement should take responsibility for the violence of the 1970s, in particular for "not channeling the revolutionary force of hundreds of thousands into a path of peace and progress. . . . The armed struggle made sense until it succeeded in evicting the dictatorship in 1973. But once popular sovereignty was restored and the historical popular demand of Perón's return was fulfilled, it [the armed violence] was a fundamental and fatal mistake" (Bárbaro 2009:159–160). A similar criticism was made by the human rights leader Graciela Fernández Meijide (2013), whose son Pablo was abducted in 1976, most likely for sympathizing with the forbidden Guevarist Youth. She argued that the idealization of the disappeared was necessary during the dictatorship to prevent the military from labeling them as terrorists but that the time had come to see them as human beings with errors and weaknesses who cast themselves in the image of Che Guevara and led by guerrilla commanders who saw the Cuban Revolution as a blueprint for Argentina. Former Montonero Héctor Leis searched his conscience at the end of his life. He concluded that the Montoneros had been a terrorist organization that assassinated Peronist union leaders and provoked the ire of the military by executing former General Aramburu. He rejected the term *state terrorism* and emphasized that the armed forces, the guerrilla organizations, and the right-wing death squads had all practiced terrorism against Argentina's political community (Leis 2012).

In Chapter 2, I explained the growing influence of multidirectional and cosmopolitan memory cultures on the Argentine human rights movement. The term *genocide* has great historical and moral weight because of its association with the Holocaust, and this significance will influence Argentina's collective memory if the genocide frame will become dominant. According to the genocide frame, the political violence neither took place between the armed forces and the guerrilla insurgency nor could it be attributed exclusively to a repressive state, but everyone carried a degree of responsibility, military as well as civilian. The military were no longer the only culprits, but Argentine society as a whole was considered complicit in the dictatorship, as Luis Miguel Baronetto, the director of the Cordoban human rights office, observed: "The magnitude of the genocide would not have been possible without the approval and applause of hegemonic sectors of Cordoban society: businessmen, members of the judiciary and Church, politicians, academics and unionists who have not yet been tried or convicted."[5]

Corporate Complicity

The genocide discourse has made an expanding group of civilians suspect of complicity with the military regime because it is difficult to understand how the repression could have functioned without their involvement. The human rights movement has therefore been calling for the criminal prosecution of complicit civilians. In 2010, the press, the judiciary, and the corporate world came under increased legal and public scrutiny. The human rights leader Hebe de Bonafini organized a political-ethical trial in April 2010 at the Plaza de Mayo at which journalists and newspaper publishers were condemned for "having exploited the people, allowing that people were killed and tortured, and that the horror was silenced."[6] In July 2010, three judges from Mendoza were denounced for having failed to investigate hundreds of habeas corpus requests and cases of torture and sexual abuse. One judge fled to Chile and asked in vain for political asylum.[7]

Businessmen and multinationals were also investigated, even though according to Argentine law only individuals can be charged with criminal offenses. On 19 November 2010, the Argentine government created a special unit for the investigation of crimes against humanity committed for economic motives (Ministerio de Justicia, Seguridad y Derechos Humanos 2010). Argentine courts have since 2010 paved the way for trials against civilians who had not been part of the armed forces and police. Judicial functionaries and businessmen are the two principal categories of civilians accused of complicity. By January 2016, fifty-four judicial functionaries (including twenty-five judges) and nineteen businessmen were under indictment. Two defendants of each group have been convicted, while the charges against five businessmen have been dropped (Procuraduría de Crímenes Contra la Humanidad 2016a:17–19).

The human rights movement rallied behind the pursuit of companies and businessmen on the Day of Memory of 24 March 2012 with the slogan "Economic Groups Were Also the Dictatorship."[8] The accompanying speech denounced corporate complicity: "With the genocidal perpetrators in power, an economic, political, social, and cultural plan against the people was implemented. Large economic groups were supporting and instigating this coup d'état. We demand trials and convictions because they were among those who financed and benefited from the coup. They enriched themselves with the dictatorship and were participants: without them the genocide would not have been possible."[9] Four years later, on the Day of Memory in 2016, the human rights movement made Argentine businessmen and the military coresponsible for the repression: "The genocidal civilians did not play a secondary role: they were at the same table with Videla at the hour of planning the terror. They even used the offices of [the newspapers] *Clarín* and *La Nación* to commit their crimes, and the installations of Ford to abduct, torture, and interrogate. Almost all of these civilians, like Blaquier and Massot, remain unpunished."[10]

Corporate complicity "refers to indirect involvement by companies in human rights abuse—where the actual harm is committed by another party, whether state agents or nonstate actors, but the company contributes to it" (Ruggie 2013:98). A scale of increasing complicity runs from silent and beneficial involvement to direct corporate complicity (Clapham 2006:220–222). The prosecution of direct corporate complicity, in which a company willingly participates in human rights violations, is traced historically to several court cases in the wake of the Nuremberg trials in which German owners and managers but not their factories were held accountable by the military tribunal. For example, thirty-six defendants of the chemical company Farben and the steel company Krupp were indicted for crimes against peace, war crimes, and crimes against humanity. They were charged with corporate criminal responsibility in Nazi Germany's wars of aggression, the plunder of occupied territories, and the exploitation of forced labor. Eleven Farben defendants were convicted for plunder and slave labor at Auschwitz, and eleven Krupp defendants were sentenced for slave labor and the mistreatment of workers. In addition, the Krupp company was forfeited (Heller 2011:93–94, 100–101, 253). Six decades later, the International Commission of Jurists argued that companies and their representatives "could be held responsible under criminal law and/or the law of civil remedies, for complicity in gross human rights abuses committed by a government, armed group, or other actor," when they benefited from or had knowledge of such violations (ICJ 2008:9).

This legal history informed the accusations against Citibank and Bank of America for collaborating with the Argentine dictatorship. The junta was strapped for funds when its aggressive monetarist reform of 1977 failed. It required large foreign loans to shore up the economy and finance the increased defense spending (Smith 1991:237–242). Foreign banks loaned US$20 billion to Argentina at a time when the disappearances were being denounced by the United Nations and Amnesty International. Also, the Carter administration was pursuing an active human rights agenda and cut military aid to authoritarian regimes in Latin America, including Argentina. Bohoslavsky and Opgenhaffen (2010:192) conclude about Argentina that, "although military expenditures increased, spending on arms imports actually decreased, indicating that financial resources were directed in large part toward the support of the internal fight against 'subversion,' which was the very framework within which crimes against humanity were perpetrated." It is uncertain whether this argument would stand up in court, if the Argentine legislature would someday allow the prosecution of businesses, but it does indicate that silent corporate complicity with a repressive regime can be substantiated by circumstantial evidence.

The prosecution of Carlos Blaquier, the owner of the agribusiness Ledesma in Jujuy Province, demonstrates the difficulty of trying suspects of corporate complicity in Argentina. The first mention of the Ledesma sugar mill in relation to state repression was made by a worker who testified at the Argentine truth commission about his abduction on company premises (CONADEP 1986:379). No legal action was undertaken in 1984, but in November 2011, Carlos Blaquier and his general manager, Alberto Lemos, were accused of being instrumental to the arrest and disappearance of the physician Luis Arédez in May 1977. Arédez had been mayor of the company town Libertador General San Martín in 1973 and in the years thereafter provided social and medical assistance to workers employed by Ledesma. Labor protests and strikes against the poor living conditions led to mass arrests in 1974 and 1975, which provoked the Montoneros to bomb Lemos's house in 1975 (Dirección Nacional 2015:133). Blaquier and Lemos were also charged with lending company trucks to army and police for transporting four hundred detainees to various police stations and the secret detention center Guerrero. The abductions took place between 20 and 27 July 1976 under total darkness because electricity had been cut at the Ledesma distribution substation. Fifty-five captives remain disappeared.[11]

Blaquier and Lemos were indicted on 15 November 2012 for the abduction of Luis Arédez and two union leaders on 24 March 1976 and for the abduction of twenty-six persons during the so-called Night of the Blackout in July 1976. The indictment stated that there was a causal relation between the abductions and the provision of company vehicles because Gendarmerie troops were stationed at the Ledesma sugar mill "to contain the growing union protests organized in the region," a presence that resulted in "a symbiotic relation between the Company and the police forces participating in the state repression that would keep those persons at bay who were considered—even potentially—to be opposed to their plan of economic growth" (Poviña 2012:184). The case dragged on in court for years but ended abruptly in March 2015 through an unusual intervention in an ongoing legal proceeding. The Federal Penal Appeals Court ruled that Ledesma trucks had indeed been used to transport captives in 1976, but that "from this it cannot be deduced that there had been knowledge of an illegal operation," and that therefore there was insufficient ground to prosecute Blaquier and Lemos. In December 2016, the attorney general asked the Supreme Court to revoke the decision of the Appeals Court.[12]

The prosecution of the Ledesma executives may have been cut short, but a public condemnation of their moral responsibility could not be prevented. In fact, Argentina's National Secretary of Human Rights had implied precisely this in July 2012 by planting a large sign on the road leading to the Ledesma company that read: "Ledesma Sugar Mill: Here crimes against humanity were committed during state terrorism."[13] Adriana Arédez, the daughter of the disappeared physician Luis Arédez, situated the condemnation in a much larger historical frame: "The Blaquiers are responsible for three genocides: the indigenous population, state terrorism, and the natural environment."[14] She accused the company of ravaging the region's natural and human resources for profit.

The public denunciation of Blaquier and the Ledesma corporation transcends their involvement in the repressive operations of 1976 and is part of a general condemnation of Argentina's industrial elite for masterminding the coup d'état and the regime's economic policies to exploit the Argentine working class.[15] Dandan and Franzki (2013:229–230) have argued that the violence against Ledesma workers expressed the historical conflict between labor and capital. This analysis echoes a political-economic history of Argentina published in 2010 by a group of human rights organizations, which stated that "State Terrorism was the means through which the control of capital over labor was consolidated" (Bayer, Borón, and Gambina 2010:217; Basualdo 2013). For this reason, a collection of essays about corporate complicity in Argentina rejected the term *military dictatorship* in favor of *civil-military dictatorship* because of the support of businesses, banks, publishers, the news media, and Argentina's Catholic Church (Verbitsky and Bohoslavsky 2013:12). The list can be expanded easily with construction companies, real estate firms, food suppliers, transportation companies, producers of cattle prods, and a host of professionals who dealt directly with the military authorities.

In November 2015, a bicameral congressional committee was created to examine this economic and financial complicity. Comparable to the CONADEP truth commission, the committee was only mandated to identify possible suspects and pass this information to the courts.[16] Taking large numbers of civilians to court will be difficult, and their legal liability will be hard to establish, but the moral accusation of their complicity with the dictatorship buttresses the charge that Argentine society as a whole was responsible for the repressive regime.

Genocide and Collective Guilt

German philosopher Karl Jaspers analyzed the many horrors of World War II in an August 1946 lecture at Heidelberg University. Starting from the assumption that in Germany "no one is guiltless," he emphasized the importance of a national soul-searching about collective guilt: "The guilt question is more than a question put to us by others, it is one we put to ourselves. The way we answer it will be decisive for our present approach to the world and ourselves" (Jaspers 2001:16, 22). Jaspers (25–26) distinguished four types of guilt. Criminal guilt refers to crimes for which people are held individually accountable in court, as in the case of the Argentine junta commanders convicted in 1985. Political guilt addresses a nation's collective liability for crimes committed by state agents. Every citizen is thus liable, even if he or she had actively opposed the repressive state. The financial, legal, and symbolic reparations awarded to victims of the dictatorship by the Argentine government express such liability. Moral guilt involves a judgment of conscience about one's own deeds, such as looking away or remaining silent when someone was taken away in plain view. This moral evaluation follows personal standards, which can imply that a torturer may continue to believe that his actions were justifiable. Finally, metaphysical guilt is based on people's fundamental human solidarity and refers to their attitude rather than their actions toward the world's injustices. The term has religious overtones by making people accountable only to God. As Olick (2005:289) has observed astutely, Jaspers's four types of guilt prevented any German from casting blame on others or claiming innocence. Perpetrators had a criminal responsibility that was determined in court, whereas everyone else was politically guilty, including those courageous individuals who had resisted the Nazi regime.

Philosophically speaking, Jaspers (2001:27) may be right to conclude: "No one can morally judge another." Nevertheless, moralities overshadow theoretical understandings and conceptual boundaries. Political circumstances may make people pass moral judgments because morality is not a contained cultural system, as is religion, law, or ideology, but morality "may be better conceived as a modality of action in any domain [that is] always present whenever humans are present" (Csordas 2013:435–536). This transcendence of morality was manifested in Argentina when the discursive frame of genocide was embraced by the human rights community. Guilt was no longer apportioned into circumscribed individual responsibilities and legal liabilities because of the moral magnitude and complexity of the crime. The expansion of guilt from legal accountability to moral accountability and the category shift from crimes against humanity to genocide were casting collective responsibilities on an entire society.

The substitution of collective for individual guilt dilutes the legal complicity of civilians with the dictatorship into moral collective guilt. Broad layers of the middle class supported the coup d'état in 1976, and many

Argentines remained silent about the disappearances. The comparison of Argentina's disappeared with Holocaust victims has contributed to a growing public discourse about collective guilt. The punishment of individual perpetrators no longer measures up to the infinity of the crime because a verdict cannot settle the account between perpetrators and victims, as Ricoeur (2006:473) observed: "There is no punishment appropriate for a disproportionate crime. In this sense, a crime of this sort constitutes a de facto instance of the unforgivable." Nevertheless, Arendt (1994:200) wrote in 1946, "It is as necessary to punish the guilty as it is to remember that there is no punishment that could fit their crimes."

Why did some Argentine judges, scholars, and most bereaved relatives and human rights activists pursue a conviction for genocide when crimes against humanity covered all atrocities committed? First of all, as "the crime of crimes" (Schabas 2009:11), genocide is situated higher on the hierarchy of harms than crimes against humanity. Genocide is directed toward groups while crimes against humanity are aimed at individuals. The qualification of genocide expresses a greater moral outrage because people were killed for who they were. Genocide is the betrayal of human beings by fellow humans to alter the diversity and reproduction of society by exterminating particular social groups.

The second reason for embracing the genocide frame corresponds to the ensuing sociocultural trauma. As much as the historical, political, and sociopsychological causes of mass killings are delineated and eyewitness accounts are recorded and as much as empathetic narratives are written, there will always remain an inaccessible background of meaning, a dark matter whose existence can only be inferred from psychic and sociocultural trauma. The term *genocide* fits better for such open-ended conceptualization than crimes against humanity, which are directed at individuals instead of groups.

A third reason is that the bereaved relatives, friends, and comrades continue to suffer from the ongoing crime of disappearance and want the Argentine people to feel collectively guilty about the past. In this sense, collective guilt means that people "accept that their ingroup is responsible for immoral actions that harmed another group" (Branscombe and Doosje 2004:3). This guilt implies a moral collective guilt, as in the case of young Germans who are assigned a collective guilt for the acts of their grandparents (Wohl and Branscombe 2004). The proponents of the genocide frame do not want the Argentine people to look away, but they want them to assume their share of collective responsibility and support the call for justice.

Finally, unlike crimes against humanity, genocide attributes a collective guilt that can be expiated only by denouncing, punishing, and remembering the crime. Convicting individuals, state organs, and business corporations for genocide, providing scientific arguments to buttress the legal and moral reasoning, showing compassion to genocide victims, and remembering them in annual commemorations are some of the ways in which people make amends for the irreparable wrongs inflicted. The genocide frame is then a guarantee that the disappeared will not be forgotten, and that the collective memory will be passed to future generations. The underlying assumption is that people can save themselves from collective guilt only by denouncing and remembering the crime.

Conclusion

Guilt and responsibility have assumed several forms in Argentina since the human rights trials began in 2006. These trials concentrated at first on the individual accountability of more than two thousand members of the armed forces and police, which included civilians working in secret detention centers, such as priests and physicians. Other civilians, mainly judicial functionaries and businessmen, have been prosecuted since 2010. The expansion of legal liability from military and police to civilians, and the emergence of genocide as a legal and discursive frame, have given rise to a public discourse about collective responsibility and guilt. Rather than dividing Argentine society into victims, perpetrators, and a silent majority, as was common within the framework of state terrorism, the genocide frame imagines Argentine society as a heterogeneous universe in which people chose different courses of action as perpetrators, resisters, naysayers, collaborators, bystanders, and refugees. According to the proponents of the genocide frame, Argentine society is collectively guilty, and all Argentines carry a responsibility for the past, albeit to different degrees.

If a society believes that it carries a collective responsibility for genocide, and if guilt cannot be established in a court of law for every citizen, how can society then be held accountable? Hannah Arendt's response to postwar Germans who professed to bearing a collective guilt for the Holocaust seems to apply also to Argentina: "the cry 'We are all guilty' that at first hearing sounded so very noble and tempting has actually only served to exculpate to a considerable degree those who actually were guilty. Where all are guilty, nobody is. Guilt, unlike responsibility, always singles out; it is strictly personal. It refers to an act, not to intentions or potentialities" (Arendt 2003:147). The reason for the difficulty in establishing people's guilt is that outbursts of massive violence, like the Holocaust and Argentina's decades of political violence, are overdetermined wholes that have multiple causes and exist on multiple interconnected levels of social complexity. Stewart (2012:35) has pointed out the dilemma of legal accountability for such crimes: "Overdetermination poses serious problems for international criminal justice, where the individual agency upon which criminal responsibility depends tends to diminish in direct proportion to the scale of mass violence." The higher the number of people with some degree of guilt or complicity, the more difficult it becomes to take legal action against them.

However, conversely, Arendt's point is still relevant for understanding Argentina's local use of the term *genocide*: the dissipation of individual guilt into collective guilt intertwines the collective responsibility for Argentina's disappearances and sociocultural trauma as cause and consequence because it is not the crime but the intention and context that determine the legal qualification genocide. "The exact same underlying act—for instance, murder or rape—can variously qualify as a war crime, crime against humanity, or genocide, depending only on the context within which it was committed" (Akhavan 2012:30). Once the Argentine people accept the genocide frame and assume a collective guilt, then the boundless violence and trauma are on a par. This internalization of collective guilt by the Argentine people has important moral and political implications. Collective guilt has an effect on people's social and political trust, and instills a mistrust toward Argentina's unpredictable political forces. Collective guilt also leads to ontological insecurity because of the belief that anyone can betray or turn on another individual under certain historical circumstances. These assumptions about the betrayal of social and political trust sow mistrust in society.[17]

Argentina's condition as a traumatized society is making people receptive to the genocide frame. The massive killings are morally and emotionally best described with the term *genocide* for the proponents, even though its application is questionable in the terms of international law. The losses are experienced as being so immense that only this local interpretation of the term *genocide* can fill the void left by the disappearances, and only the term *genocide* will make people understand how such carnage was possible in Argentina. Inevitably, the mental images evoked by other genocides, such as the extermination camps of Nazi Germany, spill over into the Argentine context and give meaning to its sociocultural trauma. Genocide counterbalances trauma writ large as an equally unresolvable and existentially disturbing loss. Traumatized groups reexperience their losses repeatedly and formulate new interpretations of past events that involve society in their public protests, legal initiatives, and memory politics. The proponents of the genocide frame face adversaries, particularly military interest groups and solidarity organizations, that have come to acknowledge the existence of torture and disappearance but justify them out of military necessity. These opponents hold each other collectively responsible for the political violence of the 1970s, and thus contribute to the construction of collective guilt.

This chapter has shown how, in the eyes and sentiment of bereaved relatives and human rights activists, *genocide* has become the only suitable term to describe the massive crime and sociocultural trauma that affected Argentine society. The legal limits of establishing the individual guilt of an expanding group of civilians complicit to the genocide turned collective guilt into the moral reckoning of Argentine society. But collective guilt, let alone the collective responsibility of an entire nation, has no place in a court of law, and this moral impunity will continue to trouble Argentine society and complicate the process of national mourning.

CHAPTER 8

Mourning

The national mourning of Argentina's violent past has been undergoing considerable transformations since 1983, when a traumatized society confronted its massive losses and tried to bring those responsible to justice. National mourning processes do not have clear time spans or developmental stages. Societies differ in how and when they address their losses. Argentina's national mourning was not influenced by the repression of painful memories, as has been common in other countries, because Argentine society immediately faced the deaths and disappearances through public testimonies, exhumations, a truth commission, and the trial of former junta commanders, all within two years of the military regime's fall from power. The ways in which Argentina should acknowledge and come to terms with the dead and disappeared has constituted a crucial area of contestation because of the affective, legal, political, and historical implications. Times of prosecution alternated with times of impunity, and contested memories of heinous crimes cleared the way for a nationwide acknowledgment that systematic abduction, torture, assassination, and disappearance had taken place. The national mourning process was dominated by sociocultural traumas, antagonistic memory politics, and decades of troubled civil-military relations because of the mistrust among the state and contesting social groups in civil society.

How do traumatized societies mourn sociocultural traumas, and how are its members capable of forging a national coexistence with regard to the past? Anthropological analyses of national mourning have implicitly addressed these questions through the grief work hypothesis and so have studies about the Holocaust.[1] Developed by Freud (1968a), Lindemann

(1944), and Bowlby (1981), the grief work hypothesis assumes that mourning entails the unraveling of the emotional ties to the deceased, the acceptance of the finality of their death, and the separation of the world of the living from the world of the dead. In therapy, people are encouraged "to let go" of the deceased and to leave the death behind during a painful process of working through and eventually accepting the loss. This psychological insight has been taken to the collective level to explain how the relation of postwar societies to the dead becomes expressed in memorials, historicized in narratives, and ritualized in commemorations.

Freud's grief work hypothesis has become criticized by constructivist psychology (Neimeyer 2001; Valentine 2006), and this criticism deserves to be heeded by analyses of national mourning. Stroebe and Schut (1999, 2001) have developed a Dual Process Model of Coping with Bereavement that describes mourning as an oscillation between an intermittent attention to primary losses revolving around the bond with the deceased (loss orientation) and a complimentary attention to secondary losses to deal with life's challenges without the deceased (restoration orientation). Mourners are not permanently enveloped in this dual mourning process because the flow of everyday life provides repose and distraction. Stroebe and Schut (1999:214) emphasize that the term *restoration* does not refer to a desirable outcome but to the problems bereaved persons need to address as they recompose their shattered lives. Each of the two coping strategies contains positive and negative effects, depending on the meaning of the death. Loss and restoration processes may therefore be beneficial but can also be harmful for bereaved persons (Stroebe and Schut 2001:66–69). The model's departure from the grief work hypothesis, and its accommodation of prolonged loss and restoration orientation, have been corroborated in sociology and anthropology.

Loss orientation does not necessarily imply severing the relation with the deceased through grief work because mourners may refashion the affective tie into an active bond with the dead. The bereaved may incorporate the dead into their lives through narration, active remembrance, and ongoing conversation.[2] The sociologist Tony Walter (1999:205) has analyzed the social integration of the dead into the lives of the living through two positions: "One is that the living must leave the dead behind and move on without them. The other is that the dead are always with us and the bereaved continue to bond with them; indeed the dead must be incorporated in some way if families, other groups and indeed entire societies are to have any sense of their past." This loss- and restoration-oriented coping of mourners is supported by numerous ethnographic studies of how mortuary rituals serve to receive the bereaved into the community after the bond with the dead has been forged.[3]

The dual attention to loss and restoration is in Argentina reflected in the relation of mourning and trust. Bereaved relatives do not sever their attachment to the dead and disappeared because that would be a betrayal of basic and social trust and would condemn the unceremoniously buried dead to a liminal afterlife, forever abandoned by remembrance. Mourning expresses the trusting relationship between the dead, the disappeared, and the living and how the living continue to care for the deceased in their memories and recollections. Furthermore, the public presence of the dead and disappeared in Argentine society and national memory was gained at great cost through a relentless struggle for their recognition in memorials and commemorations, the demands for justice and truth, and the pursuit of their political agendas.

My analysis of Argentina's national mourning process is inspired by social psychology's model of oscillatory mourning. This model has been designed to address intrapersonal and interpersonal processes of mourning, and it needs to be adapted to mourning on the social and national levels. Furthermore, the term *restoration orientation* needs to be replaced by *recovery orientation* to distinguish the psychological from the anthropological meaning of coping with secondary losses.

Mourning is a multidimensional concept that denotes processes of coping with manifold losses, whether on the personal, interpersonal, group, or supragroup level. I conceptualize mourning as the oscillatory process of loss and recovery orientation, and in this chapter I make an analytical distinction between personal, social, and national mourning. Personal mourning refers to individual coping. The personal mourning of the dead and disappeared of political violence by relatives and friends is only touched upon incidentally because my main concern is with collective processes. Social and national mourning are forms of collective mourning that differ in their relation to the dead. Social mourning concerns people with close attachments to the deceased as members of particular social groups. The Mothers of the Plaza de Mayo and other family-based organizations are involved in social mourning processes concerning the dead and disappeared, the repression, and the damage done to Argentine society. Veterans of the military dictatorship and their support groups are concerned with the deaths inflicted by the guerrilla insurgency, the sequels of the repressive regime, and the accountability of the armed forces and police.

National mourning refers to the oscillatory mourning process between the state and civil society as represented by conflicting social groups that have positive or negative emotional investments in the dead and disappeared. Civil society includes bereaved relatives and human rights organizations as well as military veterans and their supporters who dispute Argentina's national mourning among themselves and with the Argentine state. Please note that Argentine perpetrators are also bereaved in their capacity as members of a society that incurred massive human losses, the disruption of social and political institutions, and the widespread fear and mistrust in society. Perpetrators have to face the losses they inflicted on society and bear the societal consequences. They live in the same neighborhoods as the relatives of the disappeared and participate together as citizens in Argentina's public and political arenas. They will try to influence the national mourning process to suit their historical narrative. National mourning therefore constitutes a politics of oscillation through which a multifaceted state and a divided civil society contest the mourning of the dead and the recovery of social coexistence.

Trust and betrayal enter centrally into this politics of oscillation. The varying degrees of trust, the suspicion of hidden agendas, and a past of so much betrayal affected the varying emphasis on either loss or recovery in Argentina's dual mourning process. It might seem obvious that bereaved family members gave greater attention to loss orientation and that perpetrators preferred to forget about the past and move forward through recovery orientation, but the persistence of relatives in pursuing issues surrounding loss was influenced by the silence and secrecy of the military, the periodic impunity of the perpetrators favored by the state, and the inability to integrate traumatic experiences into collective understandings. The state and the conflicting social groups were, of course, not unwavering in their dual mourning orientations, as Chapters 6 and 7 showed. For example, the Argentine armed forces acknowledged in due time their past wrongdoing and grudgingly accepted the human rights trials. Furthermore, the Argentine state successfully pushed the dual national coping process in directions that were rejected by perpetrators and bereaved relatives and vice versa. This chapter will demonstrate that the national mourning of Argentina's losses can thus be understood through an analysis of the oscillatory politics of loss and recovery orientation that was

influenced by a considerable degree of mistrust among the state and rival
social groups.

Pacification and Reconciliation

The transitional military government that assumed power in June 1982
after the Falklands/Malvinas War was well aware that Argentine society had
to come to terms with the dictatorship and in particular with the disappeared whom the military knew to be dead. The ecclesiastical authorities
had been encouraging a dialogue about a transition to democracy among
major sectors of Argentine society since 1981 through their Reconciliation
Service (Servicio de Reconciliación). In July 1982 the Argentine bishops
determined that Argentina was on the verge of collapse, not necessarily
because of the defeat in the South Atlantic, "but because of older and more
enduring wounds on the economic, social and political level" (Conferencia
Episcopal Argentina 1988:37). On 19 December 1982, National Reconciliation masses were held in churches throughout the country to reconcile the
Argentines with God, ask Him for forgiveness, and then restore peace with
one another (65). A plan to announce the amnesty of troops that had committed human rights violations failed because of insufficient political support (Verbitsky 2006:340–344). Nevertheless, the largely pro-military
episcopacy continued to toll the bells of forgiveness and reconciliation.

Bishop Quarracino went one step further by declaring repeatedly in
early 1983 that there should be a "law of oblivion" (ley del olvido) in the
legal sense of the term to achieve "an atmosphere of true reconciliation in
Argentine society" (*Somos* 1983, 7(342):12; Verbitsky 2006:345). Quarracino explained that he was not suggesting that people should forget their
losses emotionally but that, in a spirit of forgiveness, they should admit to
their share of responsibility in the political violence, instead of holding
others legally accountable, because then Argentina would be poisoned
by hatred and revenge: "we are all guilty in one way or the other," he
said (*Esquiú* 1983, 24(1199):10). In April 1983 the episcopacy wrote in a
communiqué that reconciliation should not be taken for granted but
required truth, justice, sincere soul-searching, the recognition of one's own
mistakes, and fraternal love with its capacity for repentance and forgiveness:
"Only by accepting these principles, our people can face such grave situations as the painful problem of the 'disappeared,' and the problem of the

victims of subversion that also tears at homes, and affects the coexistence of Argentines" (Conferencia Episcopal Argentina 1988:94). These edifying words came straight from the heart of the Christian faith in the divine harmony of God and humankind but fell on barren soil in a country that had witnessed bishops and cardinals blessing the junta commanders. After all, these dignitaries themselves did not reveal a truth they so piously asked of others. The episcopacy had for years drawn attention to the plight of the poor and the aged but had failed to address society's preoccupation with the disappeared. The human rights movement, the bereaved relatives, and numerous politicians did not trust the sincerity of the episcopacy's unctuous message and suspected a hidden agenda to cover up its complicity with the disappearances. The theological notion of universal reconciliation was incompatible with the anguish of many Argentines, however hard the Argentine bishops tried to harmonize them spiritually.

In anticipation of the uncertain democratic times ahead, the junta, led by General Bignone, issued a final accounting on 28 April 1983. Presented as a historical analysis of two decades of "terrorist aggression," the document urged the Argentine people to let bygones be bygones and concentrate on rebuilding the torn nation: "The time has come to face the future: it will be necessary to mitigate the wounds that every war produces, confront a new phase with a Christian spirit, and look towards tomorrow in sincere humility" (Junta Militar 1983:1). After summarizing the many violent acts by the guerrilla insurgency and the nonconventional military operations, the document observed "that many wounds of Argentine society have not closed," and especially the wound caused by the "physical disappearance of persons" (10). The junta acknowledged that the disappearances were devastating to people's emotional well-being and decided to resolve this anguish by pronouncing all disappeared dead: "it must be absolutely clear that those who appear on the lists of disappeared and who are not in exile or in hiding, are considered dead in legal and administrative terms, even though the cause and occasion of their unexpected death or the place of their burial cannot yet be determined" (13). In other words, the junta took away the hope that the disappeared were still alive, tried to set the bereaved relatives on a path of mourning, and encouraged an arduous reconstruction process that absolved the military of the injuries inflicted. The military junta offered a combination of loss-oriented and recovery-oriented policies based on an appeal to a Christian spirit of reconciliation and the plea to leave the verdict about the decades of violence to history: "Reconciliation is the difficult beginning of an era of maturity and responsibility accepted with realism by all. The scars are a painful memory but also the foundation of a strong democracy for a free and united people" (14).

Political parties, human rights organizations, and foreign governments, including the Vatican, reacted with anger and disbelief (*Somos* 1983, 7(346):14–17). The decision to pronounce the disappeared dead and expect searching relatives to simply stop asking about their fate was unacceptable. Only the executive committee of the Argentine episcopacy praised the junta's document for its "positive aspects, which may constitute a step toward reconciliation" (Mignone 1988:39). As a matter of fact, Cardinals Aramburu and Primatesta had worked closely with the military in imbuing the junta's final document with the spirit of reconciliation.[4] Most Argentine bishops shared this pastoral ambition, but several bishops who worked with human rights organizations objected strongly, such as Bishop Hesayne, who called the document "false and immoral because it justifies criminal methods, and maintains that the end justifies the means" (*Esquiú* 1983, 24(1202):3).

The military's final document foreshadowed the Law of National Pacification of 23 September 1983 that gave amnesty to troops and guerrillas for criminal acts committed between May 1973 and June 1982 (Robben 2005a:319–320). Rumors about such self-declared amnesty had circulated in the press in the preceding months, and more than forty thousand people had gathered in protest on 19 August 1983, but the transitional military junta went ahead anyway because at that time already around 2,500 legal complaints had been launched against military personnel (*Somos* 1983, 8(367):24–26). The recovery-oriented amnesty law went entirely against the Argentine people's sense of justice and became one of the key issues of the upcoming elections. Raúl Alfonsín, the Radical Party's presidential candidate, promised to overturn the law, but there was talk that the Peronist candidate Italo Luder had made a secret pact with the military not to prosecute them—a deal that was confirmed years later by declassified U.S. embassy cables.[5]

Contested Exhumations

On 10 December 1983, President Bignone handed power to Raúl Alfonsín, who had won the October elections on a message of truth and justice. Alfonsín created the National Commission on the Disappeared

(CONADEP) to discover the truth about the disappeared, thus unhinging the junta's declaration that they were dead. Meanwhile, Congress advanced the pursuit of justice by abrogating the Law of National Pacification. The military's twofold recovery orientation paved the way for loss orientation as now it was not the reconciliation of Argentine society that was central to national mourning but the whereabouts of the disappeared and the accountability of the perpetrators.

In his electoral campaign, Alfonsín had proposed to prosecute only high-ranking officers. Everyone else would be regarded as having acted under due obedience. Thus, Alfonsín hoped to reinsert the military into Argentine society and achieve social peace (Giussani 1987:238–240; Malamud-Goti 1990). The term *reconciliation* was avoided because it implied forgiveness and was tainted by the military's final document and the conciliatory message of the Argentine bishops. Instead, Alfonsín's due obedience proposal paid equal attention to loss and recovery.

President Alfonsín's social peace plan foundered when the truth commission reported in September 1984 that all disappeared should be presumed dead, with the exception of several hundred kidnapped babies (CONADEP 1986:447–449). The human rights movement rejected the making of amends with the Argentine armed forces, and insisted on loss-oriented retributive justice and truth finding that maintained society's attention on the dead and the disappeared. Active remembrance through public testimonies and street demonstrations reinforced this loss orientation. The majority of the Argentine people rallied around the human rights movement to suspend the state's recovery-oriented policies until past losses had been dealt with adequately. It was the first dispute about Argentina's national mourning between the state and civil society. In an oscillatory response, the Argentine government redefined its measures. The concern for secondary losses became limited to removing the administrative measures of dictatorial rule, reinstating the rule of law, and embracing the truth commission's finding that the disappeared were dead and the military their executioners. Loss orientation became focused on the documentation of human rights violations, the exhumation of anonymous graves, and the prosecution of perpetrators.

The military's loss orientation was less prominent. They held religious masses to honor the 497 members of the police and armed forces who had been killed between 1960 and 1979 (Díaz Bessone 2001), and they encouraged civic organizations to manifest their solidarity through demonstrations, publications, and testimonies. Loss orientation was combined with recovery orientation by erecting memorials on military premises, and calling for the amnesty of indicted troops. Retired officers articulated a memorialization of past violence by presenting the dictatorship as a necessary stage of nation building set within the ideological struggles of the Cold War.

Loss orientation dominated national mourning in the mid-1980s, in part because the human rights movement convinced the political opposition to delay the congressional approval of reparation legislation. They argued that Argentina could attend neither to the legal and financial problems of persons with disappeared breadwinners nor to the transitional problems of the country's budding democracy; before relatives could rebury their missing dead, the armed forces had taken their responsibility and the perpetrators had been convicted. The Alfonsín government maintained that the CONADEP commission had transformed the disappeared from being alive yet missing into being dead yet unaccounted for. They could now be mourned as victims of state terror. However, the government's proposed legislation to normalize their legal status was not accepted. Recovery-oriented policies were weakened or revoked, and loss orientation revolved around the primary loss of the assassinated disappeared, the exhumation of their bodies, the prosecution of perpetrators, and the presence of the dead and disappeared in public events and the media. These issues divided Argentine society for decades and made Argentina focus more often on past losses than on contemporary and future problems emanating from the past.

One consequence of the reigning loss orientation was a dispute about the exhumation of anonymous graves that would recover the disappeared for burial and allow relatives to get on with their lives. In Chapter 5, I explained how the forensic exhumations contributed to wresting away the military's necropolitical and territorial hold on Argentina. Most human rights organizations supported the exhumations, but a majority faction of the Mothers of the Plaza de Mayo began to have misgivings in December 1984. These Mothers were infuriated that the exhumations did not result in criminal convictions. Hebe de Bonafini accused President Alfonsín of breaking yet another electoral promise: "We told him *no to the exhumation of cadavers* as long as we did not know who the assassins were. And they began to conduct exhumations of cadavers as if these were football matches" (*Madres* 1984, 1(1):2; emphasis in original). Exhumations would

turn the disappeared into assassinated citizens and imply a twenty-year statute of limitations on the crime, thus endangering the prosecution of perpetrators. De Bonafini also suspected the Argentine government of trying to
close the book on the disappeared: "Convert the mothers of the disappeared
into the mothers of the dead. And so, close the problem of the disappeared"
(*Madres* 1984, 1(1):2). A minority faction of the Mothers of the Plaza de
Mayo, with unanimous support from the Grandmothers of the Plaza de
Mayo, favored exhumations because they provided legal proof that the disappeared had been assassinated, and yielded forensic evidence that pregnant captives had given birth (Gorini 2008:305–313, 331–334).

The first open disagreement among the Mothers concerned the right to
approve exhumations. In March 1985, Judge Pedro Hooft ordered the
opening of three anonymous graves at the Park Cemetery of Mar del Plata
against the wishes of Walfrida de Torti, one of the three parents involved.
The Argentine Forensic Anthropology Team established the identity of Néstor Fonseca and Liliana Pereyra, who was proven to have given birth before
her execution. The anthropologists intended to return the next morning to
exhume the third person. When they arrived at the cemetery, they were
confronted by Hebe de Bonafini, who had come to support Walfrida de
Torti's opposition to the exhumation. De Bonafini declared: "We don't
want deaths by decree, and don't accept either anthropologists or scientists
from anywhere else in the world to come and tell us that the packages of
bones are our children" (Gorini 2008:308). Amid shouts and insults of
complicity with the dictatorship, cemetery workers closed the half-opened
grave after Judge Hooft suspended the procedure. The forensic anthropologists withdrew from the cemetery, unwilling to proceed against the will of
the family members. A few days later, grave diggers carried out the court
order but could not identify the remains for lack of forensic expertise
(Cohen Salama 1992:160–167; Gorini 2008:303–314; Joyce and Stover
1991:256–263).

More parents began to oppose the forensic identifications in the following months. When his son had been exhumed, the father of Juan Carlos
Vera responded: "I know that you can identify the remains of my son but
that would destroy my wife. I will always refuse an identification" (Cohen
Salama 1992:195). Likewise, when Lucrecia Cervino was told by forensic
anthropologist Mercedes Doretti that her daughter had been found, she
started crying, fainted, and, after regaining consciousness, "She said it was
the most terrible thing to tell her, she would prefer to go on thinking that

her daughter had disappeared, that she would reappear someday, and that's the way she wanted things to remain" (Doretti cited in Joyce and Stover 1991:296). Lucrecia Cervino did not claim her daughter's remains, and they were eventually reburied at the cemetery where they had been exhumed.

The second disagreement among the Mothers of the Plaza de Mayo concerned the personal and political consequences of mourning the identified disappeared. The Alfonsín government was accused of trying to induce personal mourning. The forensic identifications and the ritual reburial of the exhumed remains would loosen the affective ties between relatives and their assassinated loved ones—a reasoning that closely followed Freud's grief work hypothesis—and violate the basic trust and care between mother and child. Mourning is generally understood in Argentina as the process of working through and eventually accepting a significant loss by creating emotional distance. Freud's grief work hypothesis guided the therapeutic treatment of affected family members after the dictatorship. Disappearances were assumed to demand much grief work because the loss could not be confirmed by reality, as two Argentine psychiatrists wrote: "in this case one doesn't know what it is that one has to accept, and what the nature of the loss is. This has a destructuring effect on the psyche and is confusing for the person who has to accompany this process of working through. It is worth remembering that the presence of a corpse is an important element that helps a person to escape denial mechanisms when trying to work through a death. Moreover, when there are no [death] certificates, funerary rituals cannot be performed" (Edelman and Kordon 1995b:107). This interpretation was embraced by bereaved parents, such as Graciela Fernández Meijide, who knew rationally that her son Pablo was dead but who felt emotionally that he was still alive: "the fantasy of the unconscious never meets with reality . . . it is a road which I don't know if it will ever end. It is what psychoanalysts call 'unelaborated grief.' Because you don't know how to elaborate it. For those who are religious or who want to have a place on earth where they have their dead to take flowers to, to say a prayer, whatever, this is denied to them" (Ulla and Echave 1986:34–35).

There was also a political dimension to the mourning induced by forensic exhumations, according to the opponents. The personal acceptance of death would break the social solidarity of the searching relatives and thus undermine their political activism. The desire for the accountability of the perpetrators would diminish, and the grieving relatives would become open to the state's pursuit of social peace. Hebe de Bonafini suspected a sinister political scheme to demobilize and depoliticize the vocal Mothers of the Plaza de Mayo organization that was very critical of the Alfonsín government. One group of Mothers retorted that reburials were as much mortuary rituals that satisfied emotional needs as political rituals that drew public attention to their struggle. The tens of thousands of disappeared still unaccounted for encouraged them to continue demanding accountability (Robben 2000a:328–330).

The two disagreements about the exhumations added to several other quarrels among the Mothers, as was explained in the introductory chapter, that amounted to irreconcilable differences. In April 1986, the organization was divided into the larger Mothers of the Plaza de Mayo Association and the smaller Mothers of the Plaza de Mayo Founding Line. The grief work hypothesis was so firmly embedded in Argentine culture, with its predilection for psychoanalysis, that it guided the discourse of both factions. Their conduct and emotions demonstrated, however, that the affective ties with the reburied disappeared were not cut but rather reshaped and prolonged as an expression of enduring parental trust. Founding Line mothers who received their exhumed loved ones remained active in the human rights movement, continued the weekly protests at the Plaza de Mayo, held public commemorations, and erected memorials. Association mothers argued that exhumations and reburials destroyed the living remembrance of the disappeared and interred them in an enclosed memory. They rejected memorialization in museums and sites of memory and proposed an active remembrance in marches and protests.

The Association mothers took a radical turn in 1988. They began to adopt the suffering of all victims of political violence in the world (*Madres* 1988, 48:17). "When we understood that our children were not going to appear, we socialized motherhood and felt that we are the mothers of everybody, that all are our children" (*Madres* 1989, 53:17). Political activism and the refusal to accept the death of their abducted children were their ways of continuing a relationship with the disappeared. They objected to the separation of body and spirit through reburials. The disappeared had died for the betterment of Argentine society, so they argued, and remained endowed with a generative political force that allowed Association mothers to turn personal losses into their children's spiritual and ideological rebirth. Furthermore, the Association mothers did not accept any economic compensation for their disappeared children. Just as was the case with the exhumations, such reparation payments were seen as political instruments to individualize social mourning and demobilize their radical protests. The Association's loss orientation around their children's spiritual life and the collectivization of their loss existed alongside the loss orientation on the physical death of the disappeared and the individual losses by the Founding Line mothers. The Association mothers' rejection of recovery-oriented measures was unusual in Argentina because exhumations, reparations, and personal mourning were accepted by most human rights organizations.

Accountability, Amnesty, and Reparations

President Alfonsín had been struggling to achieve social peace in Argentina since his 1983 electoral proposal to prosecute only a small number of senior officers, but he was faced time and again with strong opposition. The discovery of mass graves, the testimonies about the cruel treatment in secret detention centers, death flights, and the findings of the CONADEP truth commission had made the Argentine people unforgiving. The upcoming trial of the junta commanders in April 1985 received overwhelming public approval, but the Minister of Defense Raúl Borrás declared that "the country cannot live forever with an open wound. A final full stop has to be put to this" (*Somos* 1985, 8(447):8). Verdicts were read in December 1985, and many more trials were expected.

People were dumbfounded when in 1986 President Alfonsín introduced his plan to put a halt to the growing number of indictments. The government was accused of betraying its electoral promises, and the political trust in the state and its agents suffered with it, but President Alfonsín had more pressing worries on his mind. Fearing that years of trials would destabilize the transitional democracy, he successfully passed the Full Stop Law through Congress in December 1986. The law placed a statute of limitations of sixty days on new accusations. To express their disapproval, judges and legal clerks canceled their traditional January holidays and registered complaints against more than four hundred mostly middle-ranking officers. President Alfonsín's recovery-oriented law had backfired. In reaction, six army bases rose in mutiny in April 1987. President Alfonsín met with rebel leader Lieutenant-Colonel Aldo Rico, and Rico explained that the rebels were not staging a military coup but that they wanted an end to the trials and wanted Argentina to begin a process of national reconciliation (Robben 2005a:331–335). In June 1987 Congress approved the Due Obedience Law, which freed most officers from prosecution, despite opposition from the human rights movement. The assassinated-disappeared had become negotiable losses by absolving the material authors and sacrificing society's right of redress, to benefit democratic consolidation and social peace. The government shifted from loss-oriented to recovery-oriented national mourning under pressure of a powerful state institution.

The surprise was great when two more military mutinies occurred in January and December 1988 and even greater when fifty Marxist guerrillas attacked the Third Infantry Regiment at La Tablada on 23 January 1989, supposedly to prevent an imminent military coup. Twenty-eight guerrillas and eleven members of the police and armed forces died during thirty hours of intense fighting before the base was retaken (Robben 2005a:335–336). Five years of democracy had not brought peace to Argentina, and there was fear of more political violence because of a serious economic crisis, tense civil-military relations, and the upcoming general elections of May 1989. There was talk of more amnesty legislation to appease the country.

In April 1989, a group of unusual political players made a call for reconciliation. Aware that the guerrilla attack on La Tablada had resuscitated concerns about a resurgence of violence, former Peronist guerrillas presented a notarized statement to Bishop Ogñenovich to be deposited at the feet of the Virgin Mary of Luján, Argentina's patron saint. The declaration characterized the political violence of the last few decades as "an intermittent civil war," because "the historical truth is that not one sector is without guilt or mistakes for the violent political confrontations among Argentines" (Consejo Federal del Peronismo Revolucionario 1989:1). The former Montoneros denounced the use of armed force and promised to achieve their political goals through democratic means. "National pacification is an indispensable requirement for creating the minimal conditions to suture the wounds of the national popular body, and achieve reconciliation" (1). The motivation behind these lofty words was the desire to participate again in Argentine politics, free the incarcerated ex-commander Mario Firmenich, and allay people's suspicion about the democratic commitment of the former guerrillas. They tried to organize a Mass of Reconciliation, but the retired generals of the dictatorship rejected the proposal, and so did Bishop Ogñenovich and Cardinal Primatesta, who argued that there is a difference between a Mass as a prayer for reconciliation and a Mass as the culmination of reconciliation (interview with Ogñenovich on 29 May 1990).

The Catholic authorities tried to reconcile Argentine society in their own way. Cardinal Primatesta proposed a general amnesty without any atonement by the former belligerents. According to reliable sources, "The cardinal spoke about the need to achieve an authentic reconciliation as soon as possible by putting the national interest above those of social sectors" (*Somos* 1989, 12(658):17). Bishop Hesayne added that amnesty was purely a political measure because spiritual reconciliation was only possible after repentance (Giúdice 1989). The incompatibility of personal forgiveness and national mourning that had troubled the call for reconciliation since 1981 and had made human rights activists consistently reject the term was verbalized clearly by the Founding Line mother, Nora de Cortiñas: "Everyone can forgive insofar as one's intimate belief will make one say: 'but I have forgiven them.' Many mothers have perhaps already forgiven them. But one cannot forgive politically. Because if not, then let's forget about the world's holocausts. That is impossible. Here in Argentina, reconciliation cannot be possible with assassins, torturers and those who disappear people. There are prisons for them" (interview on 16 November 1990). The refusal to forgive was for Association mother Hebe de Bonafini motivated by hate: "I believe that hate is a sentiment that should not be repressed. Because when one represses hate, one becomes a hypocrite. I therefore cannot say that I do not hate those who tore more than thirty thousand people to pieces; who raped them, who raped pregnant women, and who stole our children and grandchildren; who became God and master of life and death. Well then, if I would say that I do not hate them, I would be a hypocrite. I hate them from the bottom of my heart. And that's why I'm not going to forgive, and I'm not going to forget" (*Madres* 1991, 73:20). National reconciliation, let alone forgiveness, was just as much out of the question for the Grandmothers of the Plaza de Mayo until all kidnapped children had been recovered.

Yet Carlos Saúl Menem, Alfonsín's presidential successor, continued to advance the cause of social peace. He was determined not only to deal with the dictatorship but to weed out Argentina's social discord completely by ending the historical enmity festering in Argentine society since the nineteenth century. According to Menem, "Nobody, absolutely nobody has the legitimate right to continue to arrest our development because of bygone events, for history cannot be a heavy load, an insupportable burden, a painful memory or a petty opinion. History must be a chain of union, stronger than frustration, than war, than death."[6] The remains of Brigadier General

Juan Manuel de Rosas, a tyrant for liberals and a patriot for nationalists, were exhumed from his grave in Southampton, England, and reburied on 1 October 1989 at La Recoleta Cemetery in Buenos Aires. Descendants of the nineteenth-century dictator and his onetime enemies were present to symbolize the national reconciliation.

Seven days later, President Menem pardoned hundreds of military officers and former guerrillas. Vice-President Eduardo Duhalde justified the decision: "We have to occupy ourselves with the human rights of the living to be able to bury the past and dedicate ourselves 24 hours a day to the present and the future" (Granovsky 1989:6). President Menem continued to make other public gestures of social peace, such as attending a Mass on 2 November 1989 at the Navy's Stella Maris Chapel for all soldiers who had died for the fatherland and reviewing a military parade on 9 July 1990 in the name of national reconciliation. Menem said that he wanted "to heal without more ado the bleeding wound of the Argentine body."[7] An opinion poll of November 1990 showed that 63 percent of the respondents were against a presidential pardon.[8] Nevertheless, the junta commanders were released from prison in December 1990, despite large protest demonstrations in 1989 and 1990.

The social peace agenda of Alfonsín and Menem was accompanied by recovery-oriented administrative and reparative measures. Public servants, teachers, and bank employees who had been dismissed during the dictatorship were reincorporated through laws passed in 1984 and 1985. Pensions were given to spouses and children of the disappeared in 1986, and reparation and compensation payments were made to former political prisoners in 1991 and 1992. An indemnification of US$224,000 was finally given for a disappeared relative in 1994. The latter economic reparation touched an open nerve in Argentine society. The law did not include a presumption of death and only acknowledged the enforced disappearance, but many relatives had emotional difficulty in petitioning for reparations on behalf of the disappeared. They felt guilty about accepting payments and feared that the law would discourage the prosecution of perpetrators. Despite these misgivings, eight thousand claims were approved by 2004. The Mothers of the Plaza de Mayo Association rejected the payment as hush money (Guembe 2006). President Menem had certainly succeeded in shifting the weight of national mourning from loss orientation to recovery orientation. His government had succeeded in appeasing the armed forces, persuaded most relatives to receive reparation

payments for the disappeared, and had sidelined the human rights movement as measured by the absence of major street protests during the first
half of the 1990s.

Memorialization and Accountability

The human rights movement paid less attention to primary losses after
the presidential pardons of 1989–1990 and began a recovery-oriented
memorialization to turn its historical interpretation of the violent past
into Argentina's hegemonic national narrative, as was analyzed in Chapter 2. Memorialization is recovery-oriented because, according to Young
(1993:5), "For once we assign monumental form to memory, we have to
some degree divested ourselves of the obligation to remember. In shoul-
dering the memory-work, monuments may relieve viewers of their memory burden." Memorialization provided searching relatives with a new
identity as bereaved relatives and instilled in Argentine society the historical truth of state terror and disappearance. Paradoxically, this ritualiza-
tion of past memories heightened instead of lessened memory politics in
Argentina because it motivated competing groups to memorialize their
distinct rendition of the past.

Captain Scilingo's confession in March 1995 to his involvement in
death flights again centered the public debate on the disappeared and
shifted national mourning from recovery to loss orientation. President
Menem tried to discredit Scilingo, fearing that he might endanger the budding social peace. The armed forces and police admitted in April 1995 to
their past mistakes as a sign of remorse and reconciliation, despite the public justification of the repression by seventy retired generals.[9] This discord
between retired and active-duty generals peaked in June 1998 when Army
Commander Balza confessed that the military had used a standard operating procedure for separating guerrillas from their children and giving them
up for adoption. Lieutenant-General Videla and many officers were arrested
on kidnapping charges, reminding Argentina again of unresolved issues
from the past. The public clamor about the kidnapped children exposed
the state's reluctance to assume official responsibility for its abducted citizens. The Alfonsín government did establish a National Genetic Data Bank
in 1987, but the search for the grandchildren was left entirely to the Grandmothers of the Plaza de Mayo. The organization had to wait until 1998

before the Argentine government would provide financial support through the Historical Reparation Fund.

Lieutenant-General Videla's detention encouraged the human rights movement to appeal the amnesty laws and presidential pardons, as was explained in Chapter 7, and revealed that the armed forces and the veterans of the dictatorship were no longer of one stock. Instead of defending the arrested high-ranking officers, Army Commander Brinzoni suggested in mid-2000 a roundtable dialogue among members of the armed forces and human rights organizations to resolve the issue of the disappeared and bring about national pacification. The human rights organization HIJOS rejected the gesture during an escrache in September 2000: "We don't want to reconcile either with the genocidal perpetrators or with those who want to rescue them from the bonfire of a social verdict. Their unpunished names burn in this bonfire. There is neither forgetfulness nor forgiveness in this blaze. The escrache is therefore our most sincere answer to this crowing over reconciliation" (De Mano en Mano 2002:46). One congressional representative proposed a truth commission, in which priests would take the confession of perpetrators to guarantee the anonymity of their information. The suggestion amounted to nothing because the derogation of the amnesty legislation was imminent.

Argentina's oscillatory process of national mourning changed considerably when Néstor Kirchner assumed Argentina's presidency in May 2003. Twenty years after Alfonsín, Kirchner revitalized the social peace agenda and steered the course of national mourning toward a more evenly balanced combination of loss-oriented accountability and recovery-oriented memorialization. He actively supported the Space for Memory Institute, which preserved many memory sites, and gave new impetus to the Memory Park with the completion of the Monument to the Victims of State Sponsored Terror, as was described in Chapter 2. Kirchner was equally active in the accountability issue. The forty-four highest-ranking officers were sent into retirement in order to make a clean break with the past. Kirchner declared on 7 July 2003: "It was painful that we Argentines came face to face, but we must find a rapprochement that helps us overcome this sad history," and he added that "the rapprochement cannot come from silence or complicity."[10] Kirchner implied that social peace could only be achieved through accountability. He presented the armed forces with the choice to either swallow the derogation of the amnesties and pardons or accept the extradition of accused officers to Spanish courts eager to prosecute them for disappearing Spanish citizens. President Kirchner succeeded in appointing politically loyal judges to the Supreme Court and thus accomplished the derogation of the amnesty laws in June 2005, and the presidential pardons in April 2007.

The indicted military did not accept their prosecution passively. They began to interfere with the legal process and intimidate witnesses, right from the start of the first human rights trial. On 17 or 18 September 2006, the seventy-seven-year-old Julio López disappeared. Julio López and Nilda Eloy were the two key witnesses in the trial against retired Police Commissioner-General Etchecolatz. López failed to appear in the La Plata courtroom on 18 September when the prosecutor and defense counsel were making their final pleas. He was also absent the next day when Etchecolatz was handed a life sentence. Fear set in that López had been abducted by retired policemen out of revenge or to stop him from issuing further accusations against the Buenos Aires Provincial Police. The other witness, Nilda Eloy, declared that days before López's disappearance she had received several phone calls with the sound of a mock torture session.[11] According to the ex-disappeared Adriana Calvo, "It's a clear message about the life sentence of Etchecolatz and a threat against the witnesses in the trials against genocidal perpetrators."[12]

The first trace of Julio López was found in January 2009. An abandoned Volkswagen was located near the home of a close friend of Etchecolatz; it was the vehicle in which López had probably been transported, just hours after his disappearance. A police investigation did not yield any further leads, and neither did the examination of a waste land in February 2011 where López was supposedly buried. Etchecolatz did not stop intimidating witnesses because, during a subsequent trial in October 2014, he ostensibly held a slip of paper in his hand with the name *Julio López* written on it. Julio López has remained disappeared to this day.[13] The harassment of witnesses took other forms. For example, on 26 July 2010, a military solidarity organization posted a list of names and addresses of trial witnesses on the Internet, accompanied by this menacing text: "Know the names of the terrorists and their addresses: They could be your neighbors and teachers, and approach you as friends. . . . They live among us" (Presos Políticos de la Argentina 2010).

Animosities around the human rights trials alternated with proposals for social peace. The convicted Generals Videla, Bignone, and Riveros and hundreds of indicted officers petitioned the government for amnesty on the day of the bicentennial celebrations of Argentina's May Revolution. They presented the 1976–1983 dictatorship as just one of many "internal fights" during two centuries of Argentine history and suggested "a reciprocal act of forgetting through which Argentines recognize themselves in the suffering, dignity and mutual acceptance of human errors."[14] The proposal did not stand a chance and lacked support from the armed forces. According to Badaró (2009) and Frederic (2013), the Argentine armed forces had shed their political mission during the 2000s through professionalization and modernization. Furthermore, the Argentine military was better integrated into the democratic state by allowing the rule of martial law only in times of war and through curriculum changes in the military academy that included a course on human rights. Frederic (2013:409) suggests that the human rights trials accelerated this process of democratization by revealing the division between the politicized armed forces of the twentieth century and the professional armed forces of the twenty-first century.

Another approach to social peace was suggested by José Manuel de la Sota, the governor of Córdoba Province. He accused the government of President Cristina Fernández de Kirchner in May 2013 of a politics of resentment because of the continued human rights trials. He proposed lesser prison sentences if the convicted perpetrators came forward with information about the disappeared. De la Sota received severe criticism from the human rights movement for trying to gain electoral support from the political right and protect civilians from being prosecuted for their complicity with the military regime.[15]

Argentine bishops also continued to raise the issue of reconciliation. In August 2015, only two months before the general elections, retired Bishop Jorge Casaretto remarked: "Today not one political force talks about reconciliation. It is a taboo subject during the elections. But reconciliation must be on Argentina's agenda in the near future," and he added that there existed in Argentina an inverse relation between truth and justice: "the more justice we administer, the less truth we seem to recover, and the more truth we want to recover, the softer we have to be in the administration of justice."[16] The comments were condemned as conceptually misguided and historically false. Justice and truth were not opposites but were complementary. The trial against the junta commanders in 1985 and the human rights trials during the 2000s yielded much valuable information that the perpetrators had always refused to give. Archbishop José María Arancedo distanced himself from Casarreto's words and responded in the name of the episcopacy that reconciliation is essential to the Catholic Church, but that it can only be achieved on the basis of respect for the law, accountability, and truth: "reconciliation is not 'wipe the slate clean,' and even less, impunity. What is needed is the commitment to search for the truth, the admission of what is deplorable, the repentance of those who are guilty, and the legal reparation of the damage done."[17]

The most radical reconciliation proposal has come from a former Montonero combatant in conversation with the mother of a disappeared son. Héctor Leis and Graciela Fernández Meijide met in May 2013 to exchange thoughts about the political violence of the 1970s. The dialogue appeared later as a documentary and a book.[18] Terminally ill, Leis had written a political testament in 2012 in an attempt to explain the periodic eruptions of violence in Argentina. "My hypothesis is that the nation was cradled during a civil war that was internalized in the collective consciousness; that Argentines became accustomed to living in a state of permanent war, manifest or latent; and that peace bores them" (Leis 2012:66). This origin story, which easily glosses over the historical circumstances of each violent outburst and the different political options available, led Leis to advocate forgiveness and sacrifice to break the cycle of civil war: forgiveness for past wrongs, and the sacrifice of a confession to the wrongs committed, were the two necessary steps to achieve reconciliation (79). Fernández Meijide (2013:202–204) sympathized with Leis. She shared his critique of the idealization of the disappeared insurgents and activists but refused to forgive the perpetrators of violence and repression. Supporters of convicted military officers applauded the attempt to step over the shadow of the past and look toward the future. Critics denounced Leis and Fernández Meijide for betraying the disappeared.[19] Forgiveness and reconciliation were unimaginable for most bereaved families and human rights activists.

Conclusion

This chapter has argued that not only did Argentina's national mourning revolve around people's relation to the assassinated-disappeared and the legacies of the repressive regime, as the grief work hypothesis would have it, but also that such loss orientation has been accompanied by a recovery orientation that attended to the challenge of rebuilding the post-authoritarian society. Successive governments, the armed forces, human rights organizations, political coalitions, and military interest and solidarity groups have for decades been tangled in political, legal, and memory disputes about how to cope with the massive violent deaths suffered during Argentina's last dictatorship. Loss orientation and recovery orientation coexisted in an oscillatory process since 1983, but the former prevailed during the periods 1983–90 and after 1998, whereas the latter was dominant between 1987 and 1998.

National loss orientation has been concerned with the following issues: truth finding about the disappeared; the forensic exhumation of anonymous graves; the accountability of perpetrators; and the active public remembrance of the dead and the disappeared in street protests. National recovery orientation has focused on the coexistence of the military, former guerrilla combatants, bereaved relatives, and ex-disappeared; the memorialization of the state repression through sites of memory, memorial museums, and commemorations; and the social assistance and financial reparations to victims of torture, exiled Argentines, and family members of the assassinated-disappeared. The relative importance of loss and recovery orientation has depended on the distribution of political forces during the various periods, and the pervasive mistrust toward one another. Each party to the politics of oscillation tried to steer national mourning toward a particular combination of loss- and recovery-oriented mourning. There were periods in which the human rights movement, occasionally beset by internal disagreements, or veterans of the dictatorship and rebel officers, succeeded in influencing the national dual mourning process. At other times the Argentine state forced its hand, for instance when amnesty laws and presidential pardons were pushed through Congress or when these measures were undone two decades later.

There were crucial times when the weight of national mourning shifted from one orientation to another. President Alfonsín's recovery-oriented policies and national pacification discourse of 1983 and 1984 were supported by the Catholic episcopacy but were quickly dislocated by the loss orientation on the disappeared and the accountability of the perpetrators championed by the human rights movement. However, the state's national recovery orientation gathered momentum with the amnesties and pardons between 1986 and 1990. Most human rights organizations finally accepted the state's reparation laws and began to memorialize the dictatorial past. The sudden arrest of former dictator Videla in 1998 gave new impetus to the subdued loss orientation. Talks between adversarial civil and military groups were rejected outright in the year 2000, and legal pressure was exerted by a heterogeneous opposition movement to overturn the impunity laws. This pendular swing of the national dual mourning process can be explained through a growing force accumulation in the politics of oscillation by the human rights movement. Truth trials and the public denunciation of amnestied perpetrators through street happenings had by 1998 shifted the distribution of loss and recovery orientation toward a loss-oriented accountability. In 2003 President Néstor Kirchner stabilized the oscillatory shifts. Hundreds of trials and the preservation of sites of memory combined loss-and restoration-oriented national mourning. Retributive justice and memorialization became government policies in 2003 that remained in place between 2007 and 2015 during the presidency of Kirchner's wife, Cristina Fernández de Kirchner.

The dominant loss orientation of national mourning turned the disappeared and the reburied victims of state terrorism into participants of Argentine society. Their presence in graves, trials, and human rights protests is a continuous reminder of losses that influence Argentine society, especially when the disappearances are described as genocide. Argentina's sociocultural trauma made the bereaved relatives, ex-disappeared, and human rights movement susceptible to the genocide frame. This frame began reinforcing the loss orientation of national mourning in the mid-2000s by raising collective responsibilities and accusing Argentine society of complicity with the dictatorship. Meierhenrich (2006:230) has poignantly described the impact of such change in interpretation: "Representations of the past . . . structure strategic interaction between adversaries. They open—and foreclose—opportunities for the peaceful resolution of disputes. The menu of choices available to victims and survivors—from reconciliation to revenge—is filtered through representations of the past." The frame shift from crimes against humanity to genocide complicates national mourning because the implications of collective guilt make recovery-oriented policies and the acknowledgment of the fathomless crime harder to accept.

The CONADEP truth commission was established to discover the truth about the disappeared and thus make the searching relatives and Argentine society confront these losses—however painful the reality of mass graves and thousands of dead might be—and as a consequence come to terms with the past. However, this truth did not contribute to national reconciliation, defined by Hayner (2001:161) as "building or rebuilding relationships today that are not haunted by the conflicts and hatreds of yesterday." Neither did the commission's truth lead to a national coexistence, "where former enemies may continue to disagree, but respect each other as citizens with equal rights" (Gloppen 2005:20). And even Payne's (2008:281) notion of "contentious coexistence . . . [that] rejects infeasible official and healing truth in favor of multiple and contending truths that reflect different political viewpoints in society" fails to account for the open hostility within Argentine society. Instead of debate and dialogue, the prevailing mistrust and the disagreements over the past have become entrenched in irreconcilable positions. The veterans of the dictatorship feel betrayed by a state that is prosecuting them and are provoked by the escraches and barrage of indictments. These veterans accuse the human rights movement of a vindictive misrepresentation of the armed insurgency and the state's armed response in the 1970s. The former guerrilla commanders have remained beyond the public eye for decades but have recently drawn the attention of several critics from within their own circle. Former disappeared combatants and activists cannot forgive their tormentors or support national reconciliation because of the damage to their social trust inflicted in the military's torture chambers. Bereaved relatives demand truth, accountability, and remorse as necessary conditions for social peace, and the grandmothers of kidnapped babies will not rest until their grandchildren have been reunited with their biological kin. Finally, the human rights movement is indignant over the judiciary's reluctance to prosecute businessmen and corporations and is permanently on guard against the harassment of court witnesses and the apologia about state terrorism. It denounces the military veterans and support groups for reviving the dictatorship's repressive practices by threatening judges and disappearing witnesses.

The recent disappearances and intimidation practices have awakened fears among Argentines committed to human rights, not of another coup d'état but of society's indifference to these violations. The human rights movement, bereaved relatives, judges, lawyers, and ex-disappeared have therefore been emphasizing loss orientation in their politics of national mourning, in which the understanding of the political violence as genocide is of growing importance. If reconciliation is defined as "the process of healing the traumas of both victims and perpetrators after violence, providing a closure of the bad relation" (Galtung 2001:3), then Argentina still has a long road to travel because of the ongoing mistrust in Argentine society and its particular dual national mourning process.

This chapter does not imply a value judgment about how Argentines should mourn their dead and disappeared, and whether or not its path should be followed by other societies struggling over their past.[20] Elsewhere (Robben 2014), I compared the oscillatory mourning processes of Chile and Argentina. The two countries passed through similar political processes during the Cold War with military coups d'état in 1973 and 1976 respectively, revolutionary insurgencies and activism, labor protests, state terrorism, torture, enforced disappearances, and assassinations. Post-authoritarian Chile and Argentina had comparable transitional justice instruments, such as truth commissions, criminal trials, escraches, amnesties, and reparation laws. There were of course differences as well, such as the economic success of the prolonged Pinochet dictatorship (1973–1990) and the economic failure of the shorter Argentine dictatorship (1976–1983). Also, the Chilean military maintained their political influence on the democratic government in 1990 after a negotiated transition, while the Argentine military had been defeated in the Falklands/Malvinas War of 1982, and had to swallow the prosecution of the junta commanders. The dual process model of national mourning is able to explain the different oscillations in Chile and Argentina between loss orientation and recovery orientation, fluctuations and sudden changes that are inexplicable and even contradictory from the perspective of the grief work hypothesis. Attention to loss and recovery has existed side by side in different combinations in the two countries. Argentina has had a predominant emphasis on loss-oriented mourning through exhumations, street protests, and retributive justice with some attention to memorialization and reparation, whereas Chile has mainly pursued recovery-oriented mourning through reconciliation policies, amnesties, memorialization, and restorative justice, while exhumations, accountability, and public protests have been less prominent. I believe that the dual process model of national mourning can be applied to other societies trying to come to terms with massive losses but that each society attends in a unique way to loss and recovery, especially when it has to face sociocultural traumas and continuing political discord over the past.

Conclusion

More than three decades after the decisions that had defined his life, Admiral Isaac Rojas received me in his spacious apartment on Austria Street in Buenos Aires. Admiral Rojas and General Aramburu had conspired against President Perón in September 1955 and, as Argentina's new leaders, were responsible for the execution of eight men at the garbage dump of José León Suárez in June 1956, allegedly for their participation in a military rebellion organized by General Valle and General Tanco. The rebellion failed, and it was Rojas who insisted on the execution of General Valle a few days later, despite the objection of Aramburu, who wanted to give the general a life sentence (Robben 2005a:92). Perón wrote from his exile in Panama: "The day that Aramburu, Rojas, and the last of their murderers have died, we will have taken not only revenge for our brothers but then the Republic can sleep peacefully, free of the tremendous nightmare that weighs it down. Killing these infamous men is not only a matter of patriotism but also of self-defense" (Perón 1973:396–397). Retired General and former President Aramburu was abducted on 29 May 1970 by the Montoneros from his Buenos Aires apartment. He was executed for overthrowing Perón, ordering the execution of General Valle and the eight men at José León Suárez, and for the disappearance of Evita Perón's embalmed body. Understandably, Admiral Rojas was vigilant when protesters appeared at his residence on 25 May 1973, just after the release of hundreds of political prisoners who included many guerrilla combatants. They had been given amnesty by newly elected President Cámpora. Refusing to leave the Recoleta neighborhood for a more secluded location, Rojas received lifelong protection.

The two petty officers in civilian dress standing outside the building where Admiral Rojas and his wife lived were expecting me on 9 October 1990 at 6:00 P.M. One officer announced my arrival through the intercom and was told to let me through. He first checked my briefcase and then accompanied me into the elevator to the fourth floor. He rang the bell, and the door swung open. Admiral Rojas invited me in, and we sat down in the large living room. Eighty-four years of age now and of small stature, he still possessed the sharp features and piercing eyes that had characterized him in 1955. We discussed the rise of Peronism and the overthrow of Perón and inevitably turned to the events of 9 and 10 June 1956.

The secret service had been aware of the precise start of the armed rebellion but, just the same, Vice-President Rojas and his wife attended a classical ballet performance at the Colón Theater that evening. Toward the end of the performance, Rojas was informed that the uprising had begun. His wife was taken home, and he assumed responsibility of the situation because President Aramburu was in the city of Santa Fe. The necessary decrees had been prepared and signed in advance. With the state of siege still in place since Perón's overthrow, Rojas installed martial law and military tribunals, thus allowing officers to decide upon the summary execution of disturbers of the peace (San Martino de Dromi 1988, 2:37). Rojas sent out the following order to all commanders: "Do not carry out any capital punishment without my permission [cúmplase], and never before daybreak." Admiral Rojas assured me that he was certain that this order was sent to everybody. "But General Cuaranta, who was the head of the SIDE [secret service], didn't receive this order in time. And they had found a group of troublemakers in José León Suárez. It was truly a revolution, wasn't it? Several sentries of the regiments here had already died. . . . General Cuaranta had not received the order. He acted on his own will. He was acting within martial law" (interview on 9 October 1990).

I tried to understand what had taken place in the early hours of 10 June 1956. Rojas's answer vacillated between a miscommunication that relieved him of any personal responsibility, and a justified death penalty, as suggested by his remark about the rebels: "There was a pact, something really macabre: we all had to be killed. All members of the government and their families had to be killed. That was very clear" (interview on 9 October 1990).

Several Peronist interviewees had stressed that the men assassinated at José León Suárez had no connection to the military rebellion whatsoever but were listening to a boxing match. And there was of course the investigation by reporter Rodolfo Walsh who had spoken with several survivors only six months after the nighttime shooting. Walsh discovered that the men had been arrested before martial law went into effect at midnight and that the order to execute them was given by General Cuaranta to Lieutenant-Colonel Fernández Suárez. "There will now be no balancing acts capable of erasing the terrible evidence that the government of the Liberating Revolution applied retroactively a martial law, enacted on 10 June, to men detained on 9 June. And this is not execution. It is assassination" (Walsh 1988:191–192). Walsh considered Aramburu and Rojas to be ultimately responsible for the massacre (Walsh 1988:150, 194; Baschetti 1994:148).

Finally, the authoritative American historian Robert Potash (1980:233) concluded that the "executions were an emergency response designed to create shock and to prevent the rebellion from escalating into civil war. This would explain the government's hastiness in authorizing and publicizing the executions, a hastiness that was reflected in the absence of anything like orderly hearings, in the inclusion among those who faced the firing squads of men who had been captured prior to the public proclamation of martial law." Once more, as so often during my fieldwork in Argentina, I was stuck between competing versions of a violent event.

Whom was I to trust? Should I believe Admiral Rojas, who had given me a black book about Perón (*República Argentina 1987*) in which he wrote the dedication "to Don Antonius Robben with all consideration and special sympathy," signing off with "your friend Isaac Francisco Rojas"? And what was I to make of his offer to put me in touch with his close friend, Navy Captain Alfredo Astiz, who had betrayed the mothers of the Plaza de Mayo in an undercover operation in 1977? Did I have a trusting relationship with Admiral Rojas? We certainly had an unspoken understanding, wrapped in courtesies and civilities, in which I played the neutral outsider and he the openhearted gentleman-protagonist. This was not a case of good rapport but of ethnographic seduction in which the research participant leads the ethnographer away from his or her intended path of questioning and "tries to seduce the anthropologist into accepting his or her discourse as the only discourse and as the only correct discourse" (Robben 1996:100). In fact, one retired officer had cautioned me in advance about my meeting with Admiral Rojas, "because he can be very seductive." I suspect that Admiral Rojas had an ingrained mistrust about outsiders after having been threatened so often since 1955, a mistrust that became visible when my briefcase was inspected by the petty officer before allowing me into the apartment.

The mistrust of General Díaz Bessone was closer to the surface of our relationship because during our interviews he was under indictment for crimes against humanity as former commander of Defense Zone 2. He was accused in 1985, pardoned in 1989, indicted in 2004, and given a life sentence in 2012. We had long conversations at the Officers Club (Círculo

Militar) in Buenos Aires and sometimes at his apartment. As he was in the habit of reflecting extensively on Argentine history, I asked him once what a book in the year 2020 would write about the dictatorship. "Look, I believe that a good historian is a person who tries to be respectful of the truth. But let's not forget one thing: the truth means describing the events as they have been, and clearly the truth cannot be gathered in full because it exists in the testimonies of people who have their own values and write the truth accordingly. But the historian in turn has his values. You who come from another country have your values. Thus, when you judge this situation here you will do so on the basis of your values; you are neither neutral" (interview on 26 June 1989). General Díaz Bessone clearly understood the interest-driven selection of data, as he wrote in his book about Argentina's guerrilla insurgency: "It is a fallacy to pretend that before social phenomena one can assume the same attitude taken by an investigator before a phenomenon of natural science" (Díaz Bessone 1988:xviii). He had learned this Weberian distinction during his studies in sociology and admitted that he was a historical protagonist who did not have the dispassionate view of a foreign researcher but that nevertheless his interpretation relied on verifiable documents. General Díaz Bessone of course knew perfectly well that many repressive orders had been given orally, that the bodies of the disappeared had been cremated or buried anonymously, and that many compromising documents had been destroyed in April 1983. Historical truth thus depended greatly on the trustworthiness of witnesses and interviewees.

General Díaz Bessone never admitted in our interviews that Argentina's disappearances had been premeditated, but he did mention several political reasons that might explain this repressive practice, such as the pariah status of the Pinochet dictatorship in 1973 after worldwide protests against the mass arrests in Chile, the plea of Pope Paul VI in 1975 to General Franco not to execute five ETA combatants, and especially the release in Argentina of hundreds of convicted guerrilla insurgents in May 1973 by Héctor Cámpora when he replaced Lieutenant-General Lanusse as president of Argentina (Robben 2005a:188, 278–280). General Díaz Bessone eventually let his guard down when he told French journalist Marie-Monique Robin (2005:441–442) in a secretly recorded conversation: "with regard to the disappeared, let's say there were 7,000. I don't believe that there were 7,000, but okay, what would you have wanted us to do? Do you think that one can execute 7,000 persons? If we would have executed three persons, then the Pope would have come down on us like he did with Franco. The entire world would have come down on us. What could we have done? Put them in prison? And later when the constitutional government would come, they would be freed and have started anew." I only talked to Díaz Bessone briefly on the phone in March 2010 when he was under house arrest, but I spoke with his wife in person. She complained about the betrayal of the French journalist whose off-camera recording was accepted in court as evidence against her husband.[1]

As ethnographers of violence, we are not pursuing criminal investigations. We enter into an ethnographic relationship with mutual consent and try to grasp the research participant's knowledge, subjectivity, and latent discourse. We cannot expect perpetrators to incriminate themselves, and we are therefore as suspicious of their answers and observations as they are of our questions and writings. At the same time, we are hesitant to doubt the words of people who have been tortured or lost loved ones. Yet, I have spoken to enough survivors and victims of repression to know that many are conscious of the impact of their words and tears on us. Some have told me candidly that they know which experiences to share and which emotions to show in particular settings. They know that the display of intimate feelings is persuasive because such vulnerability belongs generally to trusting relationships. Openly questioning these emotions would be callous and a betrayal of trust when empathy and acknowledgment are expected (Robben 1996:79–82), but mistrust may also come from the interviewee, as in the case of Poema Akselman, whose eighteen-year-old daughter Leticia had been abducted on 12 June 1976 and whose remains were identified in 1987 (Cohen Salama 1992:198–202).

Poema Akselman looked fragile and filled with sorrow when we spoke at her home about her daughter's disappearance. She must have noticed how her story was affecting me. Still, at the end of our conversation she told me: "Make sure that my story can never be used by those who killed my daughter," and "Do not use the things I have told you against us" (interview on 4 June 1990). There is a subtle mistrust here, as if she doubted that the narrative about her daughter's death, the abduction of her son-in-law, and the tragic death by cancer of her husband within one year of Leticia's disappearance had convinced me. Her caution was directed at the heart of our relationship, one that did not end when we departed but that carried on in my writings. Poema Akselman implied that by entrusting me with her story, with her past and her emotions, she was offering her attachment to Leticia. She gave what was "really part and parcel of [her] nature and substance," as Marcel Mauss (1990:12) phrased it, but with some doubt whether I would leave the relationship unharmed by returning it in a narrative that reflected her truth. Misrepresentation would betray our trusting relation forged during the emotional interview and betray her attachment relation to Leticia.

Both General Díaz Bessone and Poema Akselman seemed conscious of the possibility of betrayal but from different political and moral positions. The general openly denied but privately approved of torture and disappearance, as was revealed during the conversation with the French journalist, and he mistrusted the bereaved relatives for stating to the world that their abducted children were nonpolitical, while conceding years later that they had been revolutionaries. The general knew that I had read the truth commission report *Never Again* and was speaking with torture victims. He must have also concluded from my questions that I was reading him between the lines. There existed a tension between his entrusting me selectively with his knowledge about the dictatorship and my interpretation and contextualization of his answers afterward. In turn, Leticia Akselman's assassination was a forensic fact, but her mother, Poema, worried that her narration of the abduction and the relation to her daughter could be manipulated. I had told her that I was interviewing former military and guerrilla commanders and had spoken to leaders of the two Mothers of the Plaza de Mayo organizations. In sum, Díaz Bessone feared the debunking of his answers, whereas Poema Akselman was wary about the consequences of my rendition and historical interpretation of her daughter's life and death.

Poema Akselman's sensitivity to betrayal was founded on her experience with an authoritarian state that had abducted her daughter and refused to honor habeas corpus requests even though Leticia's inert body had been found, registered, and subjected to an official autopsy. Furthermore, the military had betrayed the searching relatives by burdening them with guilt feelings. A media campaign was launched around questions such as: "How do you bring up your child?" and "Do you know what your child is doing at this precise moment?" (Kordon and Edelman 1988:34). Poema Akselman knew at the time that her daughter was an active member of the forbidden UES (Union of High School Students), a front organization of the Montoneros. She urged her daughter to abandon her activism when the military took over because people began to disappear and she was certain that the UES had been infiltrated. Knowing that Leticia and her comrades were painting antigovernment slogans, Poema told her in tears, "Look, if I had the strength I would break your leg so that you would be in a cast and could not leave the house" (interview on 4 June 1990). Instead, her daughter responded with the idealism taught at home by her mother. Poema had raised Leticia "as I believe one should raise a child, with humanism, without repression, so that she will show solidarity and become a good human being, but this [disappearance] was not what I expected, in no way whatsoever. This is what hurts me most. . . . It can't be that we raise our children in this way to then have them killed unjustly. This can't be" (interview on 4 June 1990). She added that if she had educated Leticia as a reactionary then she would have still been alive. This bitter conclusion added to the guilt feelings about having been unable to protect her daughter from harm and having somehow failed to live up to her basic trust. It also explains her mistrust toward me. I assume that she feared I might play up Leticia's leftist education and militancy and thus make mother and daughter both culpable of the abduction while providing evidence to the military's persistent accusation that the disappeared had been subversives.

The Argentine military blamed the disappearances at first on the guerrilla insurgency and right-wing death squads, which seemed credible to Argentines who had not been affected directly because these armed groups had kidnapped people and carried out political assassinations in the years preceding the 1976 coup. Soon, the military junta claimed that the disappeared were guerrilla insurgents who had died in internal disputes or armed combat with government forces. Later, subversives were defined by General-Brigadier Agosti (Agosti 1978:68) as "fundamentally different from us, some in their behavior, others conceptually and ideologically." These changing enemy definitions were directed at public opinion, nationally and abroad.

But who was really the enemy? The secret battle orders of 1975 and 1976 targeted the revolutionary insurgency and a heterogeneous political opposition. The revolutionary insurgency was composed of guerrilla organizations such as the Montoneros and the People's Revolutionary Army (ERP) with their front organizations, such as ERPs Guevarist Youth (JG) and the Union of High School Students (UES) of the Montoneros. The counterinsurgency war against the guerrilla insurgency had almost been won by the end of 1975. The state terrorism against a much larger, heterogeneous opposition movement was planned to begin after the coup d'état of March 1976 with the objective of reforming Argentine society through the Process of National Reorganization. This political opposition was located in large industries, educational institutions, the Roman Catholic Church, and working-class neighborhoods. The disappeared included combative leaders of labor unions, shop floor representatives in factories, teachers and student activists in high schools and universities, progressive clergymen, members of grassroots organizations, and community leaders and demobilized guerrillas. Many disappeared were thus noncombatant but politically active civilians (Robben 2005a:198–205). What united the enemy, according to Lieutenant-General Videla, was their existential threat to Argentine culture: "We understand by subversion the attempt to alter our essential values inspired by our historical tradition and Christian conception of the world and of man."[2] With such broad enemy definition, many Argentines on the political left feared becoming a victim.

The state's concealed repression affected people's social trust because the threat became interiorized. Argentines became mistrustful of anyone outside the familiar circle of close friends and relatives, according to a survey conducted secretly. Fear had pervaded Argentine society, and nobody was trusted. The contact with neighbors and colleagues became more superficial, and new friends were rarely made. A process of social atomization had taken hold of Argentine society that provoked a sense of loss among people about their impoverished social lives (O'Donnell 1986).

The parents of the disappeared felt this social isolation even more intensely because relatives and friends might cut off all contact, afraid to put their families at risk. Julio Morresi, who was searching for his son Norberto, felt as if "me and my wife were sowing fear around us with our despair and anguish because I realized that there were friends who were even afraid to talk to me" (interview on 15 March 1990). They had been deserted by the state, the Church, and even by friends and relatives. The human rights organizations therefore became sanctuaries of social trust for relatives surrounded by a culture of fear and besieged by a repressive state. These organizations did not doubt the stories of disappearance told by their members, and they operated on the basis of social trust in a society pervaded by mistrust.

The military junta's branding of the disappeared as subversives, guilty of undermining Argentine society and culture, made the searching relatives deny that their missing loved ones were involved with the armed insurgency or had been in any other way politically active. They were afraid that an admission of their militancy might endanger them in captivity and undermine the moral right to know about their whereabouts. Hebe de Bonafini explained the reasoning as follows: "At first we used to deny they were politically involved. 'Politics' was a dirty word for us. Some Mothers said, 'my son didn't do anything, he only defended convicts, my son was a lawyer,' others said 'she was a poet, a writer,' but they weren't taken away because they wrote pretty poems. Nor were they taken, as the military say, because they were all terrorists. If there had been an army of 30,000 guerrillas, the military would have been defeated. They were taken because they made a stand against the military and against injustice, whether it was in their factories, schools or universities" (quoted in Fisher 1993:134). In 2004, Hebe de Bonafini was less ambiguous: "We cannot deny that many of our children were involved in the armed revolution. It seems healthy to me that I say so; there are some who deny it."[3] The contradictory statements of the military and the relatives through the decades enhanced their mutual mistrust because both knew about other truths that had been concealed during the dictatorship.

The mistrust continued in democratic times. The military, the bereaved relatives, and the ex-disappeared remained hostage to each other's suspicion of betrayal. The indicted officers and junta commanders kept silent during the trials of the mid-1980s and then benefited from amnesties and pardons. This impunity enhanced people's mistrust of the military, and prevented Argentine society from overcoming its sociocultural traumas. Psychiatrists observed "[t]he persistence of sentiments of fear, defenselessness and insecurity, such as persecutory experiences, in large social groups that are reactivated in certain situations" (Edelman and Kordon 1995a:32). These troubled feelings extended to a younger generation born during the dictatorship. "In the present 20/25-year-old generation, a deep feeling of failure and skepticism about the future can be observed. . . . they have grown up first in the context of *state terrorism* and later of generalized expectation about just *punishment* for the crimes. This justice—promised and canceled as an ideal—produced a fall in trust in the viability of such social ideals" (Lagos 1994:14; emphasis in original). Argentina lived on as a traumatized society that struggled with its contested memories, disturbing revelations, and multiple losses.

The relation between the military and the human rights movement seemed to change in the late 1990s because of the mea culpa of the armed forces and the renewed trials on kidnapping charges. However, the mutual mistrust remained. The military mistrusted the bereaved relatives who had emphasized during the dictatorship that the disappeared were innocent of

any wrongdoing and now admitted that they had in fact been armed revolutionaries and political activists. In turn, the relatives accused the military
of first denying the enforced disappearances, and now admitting grudgingly
to their repressive practices but without coming clean by opening the books
and helping grandparents find the hundreds of grandchildren living under
mistaken identities. This ambiguity increased the suspicion of betrayal that
became manifest every time the various parties confronted one another in
the areas of contestation examined in this book.

The ambiguous status of the disappeared as victims, heroes, and revolutionaries helps explain the appeal of genocide as a frame of interpretation
for Argentina's political violence and the sociocultural trauma of the disappearances. *Genocide* is used in Argentine public discourse, on the one hand,
as a legal term and, on the other, as a moral term. As an international
legal concept, *genocide* describes the assassination of people who are seen
as members of a social group; this definition includes political and national
groups, according to its Argentine proponents. The disappeared were revolutionaries who fell victim to an indiscriminate extermination that conjures
up images of the Holocaust. This legal discourse maintains that they were
exterminated by the Argentine armed forces to impose an oppressive economic model and a new social order and that the military therefore deserve
a conviction in court for the crime of genocide.

As a moral term, *genocide* describes the enforced disappearances as the
elimination of a heterogeneous political or national group for pursuing a
social revolution aimed at ending social inequality, exploitation, and injustice in Argentina. They were revolutionaries who sacrificed their lives for a
better world, which in their eyes could not be realized without bloodshed.
The surrounding emotions are understandable when the cruelty and vin-
dictiveness of the Argentine military are considered. Bereaved relatives and
former guerrilla combatants portray the assassinated disappeared as young
adults full of compassion, generosity, and idealism. They cannot accept that
their benevolence and humanitarianism are misconstrued by the military
as the subversion of Argentine culture and society.

The legal and moral notions of genocide share the ultimate betrayal of
one human being by another and the betrayal of a political movement by
the state's armed forces and a complicit society. The moral significance of
the term *genocide* is that it expresses the violation of people's social and
political trust. It implies that human beings can turn on one another when
the circumstances for excessive violence are present and that the state can

attack its citizens. This transgressive violence is impossible to accept and has infused mistrust among Argentines, especially when the democratic state took an erratic course, perpetrators failed to make amends, and the victim-survivors felt that the enormity of the crime was not being acknowledged sufficiently by Argentine society and the armed forces.

The veterans of the dictatorship and some former guerrilla insurgents deny that genocide took place in Argentina. General Díaz Bessone became angry when I told him that the father of a disappeared son had compared Argentina's disappearances to the Holocaust: "Do you realize that comparing the Holocaust in Europe—the Jews that were turned into soap, the gas chambers, and whatever more—with what has happened in Argentina . . . But that is an enormous absurdity! . . . There, millions of people, Jews and non-Jews died in the concentration camps of the Nazis. Here, what? No comparison. Here, there were no gas chambers, there was nothing that looked like it" (interview on 21 June 1989). The genocide frame was also rejected by Luis Mattini, the former secretary-general of the People's Revolutionary Army. He criticized the human rights movement for depoliticizing the disappeared as suffering victims, while they had been revolutionaries who had fought to achieve their ideological dreams. He also argued that the Argentine military had been justified in fighting the insurgency because the guerrillas tried to attain a revolution with armed violence. "The action of the Argentine armed forces was not irrational. . . . it was of course inhuman, it was bestial. But they knew how to destroy a dangerous process in the bud" (interview on 14 September 1990). The armed forces did not kill people indiscriminately, Mattini concluded, but targeted combatants and political activists. Rather than for genocide, the military should be tried for war crimes (interview on 22 March 2010).

Ultimately, the understanding of the disappearances as genocide expresses a way of mourning by bereaved relatives, former disappeared, and the human rights movement. The genocide frame allows them to cope with the immensity of the crime and the sociocultural trauma of the disappearances in a moral and emotional universe. Political violence and sociocultural trauma come together in genocide, a frame that expresses people's condemnation of the inexcusable violation of the trust upon which family relations, society, and state are built. The relation between the living, the dead, and the disappeared is therefore fashioned through continued social bonds. These bonds have found collective expression in public commemorations, memorials, and works of art, and have been incorporated in human

rights protests and the demands for truth, memory, and justice. Mourning
in terms of working through, accepting the death, and severing the attachment, is felt as a betrayal of the basic and social trust toward the dead and
disappeared. The trust nurtured between relatives and the disappeared
loved ones is maintained and reproduced in their enduring memory in
Argentine society. These trusting relations are passed on to the next generation of activists, who have promised not to abandon them. The betrayal by
fellow Argentines is intolerable and unacceptable on a deep human level
because attachment and trust are what help people to become moral human
beings.

APPENDIX

Timeline of Argentine Political History

1810	Revolution against Spanish colonial rule of Argentina (25 May)
1810–1820	Wars of Independence against Spain
1816	Independence from Spain (9 July)
1814–1880	Civil wars between Centralists (Unitarios) and Federalists (Federales)
1852–1862	Process of National Organization
1872	Chapter of First International founded in Argentina
1878–1884	Extermination campaigns against Native American population
1919	Tragic Week (la Semana Trágica) (9–14 January)
1930–1932	Military dictatorship of General Uriburu
1932–1943	Conservative governments of Presidents Justo, Ortiz, and Castillo
1943–1946	Military dictatorships of Generals Rawson, Ramírez, and Farrell
1945	Day of Loyalty to Juan Domingo Perón (Día de la Lealtad) (17 October)
1946–1955	Democratic government of President Perón
1955	Bombardment of Plaza de Mayo (16 June)
1955	Military coup against President Perón (16 September)
1955–1958	Military dictatorships of Generals Lonardi and Aramburu
1956	Military rebellion by Generals Tanco and Valle (9–10 June)
1956	Execution of Peronists at José León Suárez (10 June)
1958–1966	Democratic governments of Presidents Frondizi, Guido, and Illia
1966–1973	Military dictatorships of Generals Onganía, Levingston, and Lanusse
1969	Urban uprising in Córdoba (Cordobazo) (29 May)
1970	Kidnapping and execution of former President Aramburu by Montoneros (29 May)
1972	Execution of guerrillas at Trelew naval airbase (22 August)
1973	Héctor Cámpora sworn in as president of Argentina, and release of political prisoners (25 May)
1973	Violent clashes between right-wing and left-wing Peronists at Ezeiza Airport (20 June)
1973	Juan Domingo Perón sworn in as president of Argentina (12 October)
1974	Death of President Perón, and succession of presidency to his widow, Vice-President Isabel Martínez de Perón (1 July)
1976–1982	Military dictatorships of Generals Videla, Viola, and Galtieri

1977	First public protest at the Plaza de Mayo, Buenos Aires, by mothers of disappeared children (30 April)
1982	Argentina invades Falkland/Malvinas Islands (2 April)
1982	Surrender of Argentine forces to British forces at Falkland/Malvinas Islands (14 June)
1982–1983	Transitional military government of General Bignone
1983	Raúl Alfonsín sworn in as president of Argentina (10 December)
1983–1984	National Commission on the Disappeared (CONADEP) (installed on 15 December 1983)
1985	Trial of nine junta commanders (April–December)
1986	Final Stop Law (Ley de Punto Final) (23 December)
1987	Military mutiny (15–19 April)
1987	Due Obedience Law (Ley de Obediencia Debida) (4 June)
1989	President Alfonsín resigns as president of Argentina (8 July)
1989–1999	Government of President Menem
1989–1990	Presidential pardons of convicted perpetrators, including the junta commanders
1995	Public confession to death flights by Navy Captain Scilingo (2 March)
1995	Mea culpa by Army Commander Balza about human rights violations during the dictatorship (25 April)
1998	Arrest of Lieutenant-General Videla on kidnapping charges (9 June)
2003–2007	Government of President Kirchner
2005	Derogation of Final Stop Law and Due Obedience Law by Supreme Court (14 June)
2006	Disappearance of Julio López, witness at the trial of Police Commissioner-General Etchecolatz (18 September)
2007	Derogation of presidential pardons by Supreme Court (13 July)
2007–2015	Government of President Fernández de Kirchner
2010	Lieutenant-General Videla receives life sentence for crimes against humanity (22 December)
2015	Mauricio Macri sworn in as president of Argentina (10 December)

NOTES

Introduction

1. The terms *Mothers of the Plaza de Mayo* and *Grandmothers of the Plaza de Mayo* will refer in this book to the two formal organizations and their members, while *mothers of the Plaza de Mayo* and *grandmothers of the Plaza de Mayo* will refer to all mothers and grandmothers of disappeared children and grandchildren protesting at the Plaza de Mayo, whether or not they were members of the two organizations.

2. "Cristina dijo que 'si no hay justicia' irá a tribunales internacionales," *Clarín*, 25 March 2010.

3. "Entre kirchneristas y la izquierda, la Plaza quedó partida en dos," *Clarín*, 25 March 2010.

4. In addition, Appendix 1 provides a timeline of Argentina's most important political events.

5. Around one-quarter of the assassinated-disappeared were women, and three-quarters were men. The age group of young adults between 20 and 29 years comprised nearly 60 percent of the assassinated-disappeared (Secretaría de Derechos Humanos 2015:1551–1552).

6. "'Macri mostró desprecio y desinterés,'" *Página/12*, 11 August 2016.

7. "'Se trata de una campaña de bastardeo,'" *Página/12*, 9 November 2016.

8. "'Quieren devaluar moralmente los juicios,'" *Página/12*, 16 August 2016.

9. "Miles y miles con una misma bandera," *Página/12*, 25 March 2017.

10. The psychological explanation of trust by Erik Erikson (1963), and also Ronald Laing (1960), has influenced the work on social trust by anthropologists such as Eisenstadt and Roniger (1984), Robben (2000b), Scheper-Hughes (2014), and Ystanes (2011).

11. Trust may seem self-evident in the social attachment of mothers and children. They want to remain close to one another, provide each other with comfort, and may suffer distress when separated (Ainsworth 1989; Bowlby 1998; Mikulincer and Shaver 2007). This classical understanding of attachment has been criticized for its neglect of contextual and cultural variations in child development (Hrdy 2011; LeVine and Norman 2001; Otto and Keller 2014; Quinn and Mageo 2013). These anthropologists do not question attachment as a universal human need, but they criticize the exclusive focus on the mother-infant relationship. Children may also become socialized by networks of multiple caregivers, with or without corporeal closeness, and with intense or sparse verbal contact (Keller 2014:6–14).

12. For an elaborate analysis of torture in Argentina, see chap. 11, "The Operating Theater: Torture, Dehumanization, and Traumatization," in Robben (2005a).

13. In a recent collection of ethnographic studies of trust, Broch-Due and Ystanes (2016) argue that trust is not an individual quality of human beings but constructed between people

who attribute different cultural meanings to trust. This book will not discuss such cultural notions of trust (confianza) in Argentina but use trust as an analytical tool to understand repressive state violence and its long-term effects on Argentine society.

14. See Beck (1992), Hardin (2006), Luhmann (1979), Misztal (1996), and Sztompka (1999).

15. Möllering (2001:404) has argued that sociologists have taken trust for granted, and the same goes for anthropologists, according to Broch-Due and Ystanes (2016:1). The concept of trust has appeared in ethnographic studies about reciprocity (Lévi-Strauss 1969; Malinowski 1961; Mauss 1990; Sahlins 1979), child-rearing (Weisner 2014), friendship and clientelism (Bailey 1970; Boissevain 1974; Eisenstadt and Roniger 1984; Grimen 2009), witchcraft (Geschiere 2013), corporate responsibility (Corsín Jiménez 2011; Strathern 2000), gift and commodity economies (Gregory 1982; Parry 1986; Strathern 1988), hunter-gatherer, pastoral, and peasant societies (Aguilar 1984; Banfield 1958; Gellner 1988; Ingold 2000; Shipton 2007); and repressive states (Daniel and Knudsen 1995; Robben 2000b; Scheper-Hughes 1992; Ystanes 2011).

16. See, e.g., Banfield (1958), Daniel and Knudsen (1995), Gambetta (1988), Geschiere (2013), Thiranagama and Kelly (2010), and Ystanes (2016).

17. Akerström (1991) has elaborated Simmel's (1906) interpretation of betrayal as the breaking of a secret.

18. The Mothers of the Plaza de Mayo split into two groups over the following issues: the truth commission, the trial against the junta commanders, the style of leadership of its president Hebe de Bonafini, the forensic exhumations, the reparation payments to relatives of disappeared persons, and the posthumous homages to the disappeared (Gorini 2008:553–557). There were also political differences between the two groups. The group presided over by Hebe de Bonafini was much closer to parties on the political left, while the group headed by Antokoletz, Epelbaum, and de Cortiñas was closer to Alfonsín's UCR. There also seem to be differences in class, with the former group more working class and the latter group more middle and upper class, but I did not examine the class background of the two groups and believe that such explanation cannot account for the disagreements about the aforementioned issues.

19. The names of the people interviewed during my main fieldwork period from 1989 to 1991 are listed in appendix 1 of Robben (2005a).

Chapter 1

1. Numerous authors have argued that trauma as a concept or human experience is a cultural construct (Bracken, Giller, and Summerfield 1995; Hinton and Good 2016; Kirmayer 1996; Last 2000; Merridale 2000; Robben and Suárez-Orozco 2000; Summerfield 1995, 1999; Young 1995). Others have pointed to cultural variations in the idioms of distress but conclude that psychic traumas are universal disorders (Alexander 2012:30; Droždek and Wilson 2007; Hinton and Lewis-Fernández 2010; Kleber, Figley, and Gersons 1995). McNally (2012) offers a way out of this unending debate by proposing a causal system interpretation that regards the symptoms of PTSD as mutually reinforcing autonomous entities.

2. I want to stay clear of the controversy over Freyd's claim (1996:9) that betrayal trauma in abusive parent-child relations may "necessitate a 'betrayal blindness' in which the betrayed person does not have conscious awareness, or memory, of the betrayal," due to the child's

dependence on the abusive caregiver. McNally (2003:176; 2007) has argued that there is insufficient evidence for amnesia among abused children, and suggests that they may not have recognized, understood, or disclosed the abuse when it occurred at an early age. For a rebuttal, see Freyd, DePrince, and Gleaves (2007).

3. My understanding of sociocultural trauma combines ideas from sociology about the disintegration of communality (K. Erikson 1994, 1995), cultural disorientation (Alexander 2012; Eyerman 2001; Smelser 2004), and temporality (Neal 1998; Sztompka 2000) with psychodynamic insights about complex trauma (Herman 1997) and the incommensurability of inner and outer worlds (Freud 1968b; Gampel 2000).

4. See also Martín-Baró (1989), Kleinman (1999), Fassin and Rechtman (2009), Hinton and Hinton (2014), and Somasundaram (2014).

5. Theidon (2013:27) warns about "assuming a 'traumatized' population that homogenizes victims and perpetrators into a morally elastic category," while Fassin and Rechtman (2009:277–284) point to a moral economy of trauma that emphasizes the different experiences and subject positions of victims and perpetrators.

6. The ERP had of course put its combatants in harm's way when it refused to demobilize on 25 May 1973. The decision was met with disbelief by the Peronist guerrilla organizations, the labor unions, and the political parties at the time, but I did not hear relatives of disappeared combatants accuse ERP commanders of betrayal during my interviews, perhaps because the Argentine armed forces had not yet unleashed its massive terror on them in 1973.

7. There exists an extensive literature in English on Latin American protest movements of women, e.g., Agosin (1993), Eckstein (1989), Jaquette (1994), Kampwirth (2010), Maier and Lebon (2010), Nash and Safa (1986), Shayne (2014), and Stephen (1997). Key studies on Argentina about the mothers and grandmothers of the Plaza de Mayo have been written by Agosin (1992), Arditti (1999), Bouvard (1994), Fisher (1989, 1993), Simpson and Bennett (1985), and Taylor (1997).

8. See, e.g., Adorno (1986), Friedlander (1993), LaCapra (1996), Santner (1990), Segev (2000), and Alexander and Margarete Mitscherlich (1975).

Chapter 2

1. Numerous anthropological studies have analyzed these manifestations of social memory. See, e.g., Cappelletto (2003), Climo and Cattell (2002), Fabian (2007), Rasmussen (2002), Slyomovics (1998), and Watson (1994).

2. Similar ideas have been put forth by Argenti and Schramm (2010), Boyarin (1994), and Lambek and Antze (1996) in anthropology, and Huyssen (1995), Olick (2007), and Zemon Davis and Starn (1989) in related disciplines.

3. "Alfonsín: 'Grave error y retroceso,'" *La Nación*, 10 October 1989.

4. See Buda (1988), Diago (1988), Herrera (1987), Mellibovsky (1990), and Vázquez (1988).

5. "Documento del Jefe del Ejército Teniente General Martín Balza," 25 April 1995, http://www.desaparecidos.org/arg/doc/arrepentimiento/balza.html, accessed on 12 November 2016.

6. "Conocer y comprender el pasado," *La Nación*, 6 May 1995.

7. "Detienen a Videla en un caso por robo de bebés," *Clarín*, 10 June 1998; "El Ejército argentino tenía un reglamento para separar a los hijos de los insurgentes," *El País Internacional* (Spain), 13 June 1998.

8. Argentinos por la Memoria Completa, *¿Quienes Somos?* (2007), http://www.memoria completa.com.ar/Quienes.htm; accessed 24 July 2007, defunct website, hard copy in author's possession.

9. "Activa un juez un recurso por el traslado de la ESMA," *La Nación*, 14 January 1998.

10. See Barela (2002), Bianchi (2009), Brodsky (2005), Gates-Madsen (2011), Huyssen (2003), Sarlo (2009), Tappatá de Valdez (2003), Vezzetti (2009), and Williams (2007).

11. "Una duda histórica: no se sabe cuántos son los desaparecidos," *Clarín*, 6 October 2003.

12. "El 24 de marzo será el Día de la Memoria," *Clarín*, 14 March 2001.

13. "Controversia por el prólogo agredado al informe 'Nunca más,'" *La Nación*, 19 May 2006.

14. See Alexander (2002), Baer and Sznaider (2017), Huyssen (2003:12–16), Levy and Sznaider (2006), and Rothberg (2009).

Chapter 3

1. See Caruth (1995), Felman and Laub (1991), Langer (1991), Van der Kolk, McFarlane, and Weisaeth (1996), and Scarry (1985).

2. See Agger and Jensen (1996:90–93), Danieli (1988), and Herman (1997:175–187).

3. Nine high school students had already been abducted on 4 September 1976 (CONADEP 1986:319). They survived, as did Pablo Díaz, who was abducted on 21 September 1976.

Chapter 4

1. "La historia de Donda Tigel, el marino que mató a su cuñada y le robó a sus hijos," *Página/12*, 25 November 2001. See also "'Donda fue el responsible directo,'" *Página/12*, 24 October 2004. See further Donda (2009:50); Martí, Pirles, and Osatinsky (1995:45).

2. "La historia de Donda Tigel, el marino que mató a su cuñada y le robó a sus hijos," *Página/12*, 25 November 2001.

3. "Astiz, el Tigre y el grupo de tareas de Massera," *Página/12*, 27 October 2011; "Los condenados," *Página/12*, 6 July 2012.

4. "Advertencia del Comando Militar," *La Nación*, 25 July 1976.

5. "Videla sobre derechos humanos," *La Nación*, 31 August 1979.

6. "Documento del Jefe del Ejército Teniente General Martín Balza," 25 April 1995, http://www.desaparecidos.org/arg/doc/arrepentimiento/balza.html, accessed on 12 November 2016. Balza's use of the term *collective conscience*, and his allusion to psychological repression, is not exceptional in Argentina. Concepts such as trauma, repression, neurosis, and the unconscious have pervaded popular idioms in Argentina since the 1950s, and were also used by the military junta, due to the influence of psychoanalysis as the country's foremost interpretive model of the human condition (Hollander 1990; Plotkin 2001).

7. Payne (2008:300); "Vicious Reminder of 70s Atrocities in Argentina," *New York Times*, 12 September 1997.

8. "La condena de Scilingo es irrevocable," *Página/12*, 24 February 2014.

9. "ESMA: piden veinticinco años de cárcel para el represor Febres," *Página/12*, 22 November 2007.

10. "Apareció muerto el represor Febres, el primer acusado por el caso ESMA," *Clarín*, 11 December 2007.

11. "El represor Febres tenía cianuro en la sangre e investigan si fue asesinado," *Clarín*, 14 December 2007.

12. "Para la jueza, a Febres lo mataron porque estaba decidido a hablar," *Clarín*, 5 January 2008. See also "La plancha," *Página/12*, 10 February 2008.

13. " 'No surgen elementos de riesgo suicida,' " *Página/12*, 26 April 2009.

14. "Anuncio que provoca más sospechas," *Página/12*, 4 October 2011.

15. "Encontraron a Clara Anahí, la nieta de Chicha Mariani," *Clarín*, 24 December 2015. See also "La Abuela que sigue buscando a su nieta," *Página/12*, 26 December 2015.

16. "Otro nieto que recuperó su identidad," *Página/12*, 23 April 2017.

17. " 'No me quería morir sin abrazarlo,' " *Página/12*, 6 August 2014.

18. " 'Estamos felices, hablamos de todo y nos superentendimos,' " *Página/12*, 7 August 2014.

19. "El impacto de la muerte del dictador," *Página/12*, 20 May 2013.

Chapter 5

1. "Discurso de Díaz Bessone al asumir como Ministro de Planeamiento," *La Nación*, 23 October 1976; see also Robben 2015:54.

2. "Estado de subversión," *La Nación*, 14 December 1976.

3. "Díaz Bessone sobre 'el planeamiento,' " *La Nación*, 24 November 1976.

4. In Robben (2015), I have argued that Argentina and neighboring Chile had other repressive state structures with different combinations of territoriality and necropower. Nationally, there was an emphasis on necropower in Chile because of the unified command under Pinochet, and on territoriality in Argentina because of the parceling out of military authority among five defense zone commanders. The difference between the two countries was one of degree rather than kind because the Argentine territorialization of repression created defense zones with similar necropolitical infrastructures in terms of task forces, secret detention centers, and the disappearance of bodies through cremation, anonymous burials, or death flights.

5. See, e.g., Biehl (2005), Das (2007), Das and Poole (2004), Hansen and Stepputat (2001), Scheper-Hughes (1992), and Skidmore (2004).

6. "La subversión," *La Nación*, 8 July 1976.

7. "Imágenes que prueban los vuelos de la muerte," *Página/12*, 15 December 2011.

8. "El trabajo de nombrar a los desaparecidos," *Página/12*, 17 November 2010.

Chapter 6

1. "El ex represor Etchecolatz se negó a declarar y apeló a la Constitución," *Clarín*, 21 June 2006; "Cerca del fin de una larga impunidad," *Página/12*, 21 June 2006.

2. "Graves incidentes en el repudio a un represor," *Clarín*, 10 September 1998.

3. "Robo de bebés: siete años de prisión para Etchecolatz y Bergés," *Clarín*, 30 March 2004.

4. See Daly and Sarkin (2007), De Greiff (2008), Kritz (1995, 1996), Minow (1998), Orentlicher (1991), and Teitel (2000).

5. See Arthur (2009), Collins (2010), Davis (2013), Hinton (2010), Roht-Arriaza (2005), and Sikkink (2011), who coined the term *justice cascade*.

6. "Bonafini reivindicó la lucha armada," *Clarín*, 3 April 2004.

7. "La memoria de los juicios," *Página/12*, 20 December 2015.

8. "Por qué siguen y qué puede pasar con los juicios a militares," *Clarín*, 23 July 2000.

9. "El Ejército argentino tenía un reglamento para separar a los hijos de los insurgentes," *El País Internacional* (Spain), 13 June 1998.

10. "Por qué siguen y qué puede pasar con los juicios a militares," *Clarín*, 23 July 2000.

11. "Anulan el punto final y la obediencia debida," *Clarín*, 7 March 2001; "Leyes del perdón," *Clarín*, 18 December 2003.

12. "Una decisión en la que cada juez buscó dejar un sello propio," *Clarín*, 15 June 2005.

13. "'Hemos convivido con ladrones y asesinos,' dijo Estela Carlotto," *Clarín*, 14 June 2005.

14. "Leyes de impunidad: la respuesta de Alfonsín a una transición condicionada," *Clarín*, 15 June 2005.

15. "Menem: 'Firmé los indultos para cerrar una etapa de odios,'" *Clarín*, 14 July 2007.

16. "El dictador volvió a reivindicar sus crímenes," *Página/12*, 22 December 2010.

17. "Escenas del final," *Página/12*, 24 March 2015; see also Almirón (1999:176–184).

18. Anguita and Caparrós (1998b:384), Daleo and Castillo (1982:33–34), Gasparini (1988:106), Martí, Pirles, and Osatinsky (1995:41–42), and Robben (2005a:267–269).

19. "Además de los restos de la fundadora de Madres, hallan otros seis cuerpos," *Clarín*, 9 July 2005.

20. "Aviones de la muerte," *Página/12*, 6 September 2009; "Las hormiguitas del capitán Hess," *Página/12*, 7 September 2009; "'Tiró gente vivo al mar y se jactaba,'" *Página/12*, 24 September 2009.

21. "El último eslabón en la cadena del terror," *Página/12*, 24 March 2011; "Navegación nocturna," *Página/12*, 12 April 2011; "Entrenamiento criminal," *Página/12*, 12 May 2011.

22. "La estructura que se oculta detrás de los vuelos de la muerte," *Página/12*, 21 October 2014.

23. "Los pilotos," *Página/12*, 25 November 2012; "El megajuicio por la ESMA, episodio 3," *Página/12*, 29 November 2012; "Los vuelos de la ESMA y los que falta investigar," *Página/12*, 3 December 2012; "Secretos y confesiones," *Página/12*, 3 December 2012.

24. "'Está probada la participación de Poch,'" *Página/12*, 3 September 2015; "Una estructura armada para matar," *Página/12*, 27 September 2015.

Chapter 7

1. "Condenan a reclusión perpetua a Etchecolatz por genocida," *Clarín*, 20 September 2006.

2. "La Corte ratificó la prisión perpetua para Etchecolatz," *Página/12*, 24 March 2009.

3. "'El juicio fue la suma de la historia,'" *Página/12*, 1 October 2006.

4. "Crespones que agravian a los pañuelos," *Página/12*, 11 March 2010.

5. "Juicio al fin," *Página/12*, 3 July 2010.

6. "Bonafini hizo su 'juicio ético' a la prensa y ahora irá por los jueces," *Página/12*, 30 April 2010.

7. "La Justicia pone la lupa sobre la Justicia," *Página/12*, 10 July 2010; "Con pedido de captura internacional," *Página/12*, 10 September 2010; "Preso en una cárcel común de Mendoza," *Página/12*, 6 September 2013.

8. "Con el eje en el poder económico," *Página/12*, 25 March 2012.

9. Ibid.

10. "'Sin derechos no hay democracia,'" *Página/12*, 25 March 2016.

11. "Un fiscal pidió indagar a Blaquier," *Página/12*, 21 February 2012.

12. "Dictaminaron que deben dejarse sin efecto las sentencias de la Cámara Federal de Casación Penal que revocaron los procesamientos de Carlos Pedro Tadeo Blaquier y Alberto Enrique Lemos," Ministerio Público Fiscal, https://www.fiscales.gob.ar/lesa-humanidad/di ctaminaron-que-deben-dejarse-sin-efecto-las-sentencias-de-la-camara-federal-de-casacion -penal-que-revocaron-los-procesamientos-de-carlos-pedro-tadeo-blaquier-y-alberto-enrique -lemos/, accessed on 23 February 2017.

13. "La marca indeleble del mal," *Página/12*, 12 July 2012.

14. " 'Se está rompiendo el miedo,' " *Página/12*, 20 May 2012.

15. For an official report on the alleged complicity of national and foreign corporations with the dictatorship, see Dirección Nacional (2015).

16. "Por más memoria y justicia," *Página/12*, 26 November 2015.

17. See Moses (2007) about the lengthy process to nurture people's trust in the political institutions of postwar Germany.

Chapter 8

1. See, e.g., Kwon (2006), Nelson (2008), Nordstrom (1997), Sant Cassia (2007), and Schwenkel (2009). Crucial studies of postwar Germany and the Holocaust have been written by Buruma (2009), Alexander and Margarete Mitscherlich (1975), Friedlander (1993), LaCapra (1996), Moses (2007), Santner (1990), and Young (1993).

2. See, e.g., Francis, Kellaher, and Neophytou (2005), Green (2008), Hallam and Hockey (2001), Klass and Goss (2003), Klass, Silverman, and Nickman (1996), Miller and Parrott (2009), and Walter (1996).

3. The integrative function of mortuary rituals was first argued by Durkheim (1995), Hertz (1960), and Van Gennep (1960), and has been applied to massive violent death by Kwon (2006), Nelson (2008), Oushakine (2009), and Sanford (2003).

4. See Burdick (1995:228–231), Dri 91987:239–250), Gorini (2006:579–584), and Verbitsky (2006:347–348).

5. "Para Estados Unidos, en 1983 existió un pacto sindical," *Clarín*, 22 August 2002.

6. " 'Los hermanos sean unidos . . . ,' " *La Prensa*, 1 October 1989.

7. "El Presidente en Salta," *La Nación*, 17 June 1990.

8. "El indulto no tiene hinchada," *Página/12*, 21 November 1990.

9. "Conocer y comprender el pasado," *La Nación*, 6 May 1995.

10. " 'Hay que separar la paja del trigo,' " *Página/12*, 8 July 2003.

11. "Una búsqueda que despierta fantasmas," *Página/12*, 23 September 2006.

12. "Masiva marcha por la aparición del testigo clave del caso Etchecolatz," *Clarín*, 23 September 2006.

13. "Etchecolatz: buscan a un testigo," *Clarín*, 21 September 2006; "Una búsqueda con esperanza y escepticismo," *Página/12*, 2 February 2011; "Intimidación y perturbación pública," *Página/12*, 29 October 2014; "Diez años sin López," *Página/12*, 18 September 2016.

14. "Si algo no existe es el olvido," *Página/12*, 30 May 2010.

15. "Un baño de repudios," *Página/12*, 23 May 2013.

16. "Un pedido de explicaciones a la Iglesia," *Página/12*, 22 August 2015.

17. " 'La justicia es el primer paso,' " *Página/12*, 5 September 2015.

18. The documentary was directed by Pablo Racioppi and Carolina Azzi, and appeared in 2014 under the title *El diálogo*. The text of the conversation appeared in print one year

later (Fernández Meijide and Leis 2015). In its wake, the Catholic University in Buenos Aires organized a public debate between Senator and former Montonera Norma Morandini and Arturo Larrabure, the son of Major Larrabure who had died in 1975 during his captivity by the ERP ("El tabú de la reconciliación," *Página/12*, 14 August 2016).

19. "'Documental El diálogo'—Leis y Fernández Meijide," Pacificación Nacional Definitiva, 22 May 2014, http://pacificacionacionaldefinitiva.blogspot.nl/2014/05/documental-el-dialogo-leis-y-fernandez.html, accessed on 2 March 2017; "'El diálogo' entre Graciela Fernández Meijide y Héctor Leis no es tal diálogo sino un monólogo al unísono de dos traidores," Taller La Otra blog, 29 April 2014, http://tallerlaotra.blogspot.nl/2014/04/el-dialogo-entre-graciela-fernandez.html, accessed on 2 March 2017; "Tema del traidor y del héroe," *Página/12*, 30 April 2013, accessed on 6 March 2017.

20. For comparative analyses of national reconciliation processes, see Daly and Sarkin (2007), Johnston and Slyomovics (2009), Lederach (1997), Minow (1998), Skaar, Gloppen, and Suhrke (2005), and Wilson (2003).

Conclusion

1. "'Usted no puede fusilar 7000 personas,'" *Página/12*, 31 August 2003.
2. "Estado de subversión," *La Nación*, 14 December 1976.
3. "Bonafini reivindicó la lucha armada," *Clarín*, 3 April 2004.

BIBLIOGRAPHY

Actis, Munú, Cristina Aldini, Liliana Gardella, Miriam Lewin, and Elisa Tokar. 2001. *Ese infierno: Conversaciones de cinco mujeres sobrevivientes de la ESMA*. Buenos Aires: Editorial Sudamericana.

Acuña, Carlos Manuel. 2000. *Por amor al odio: La tragedia de la subversión en la Argentina*. Buenos Aires: Ediciones del Pórtico.

Adorno, Theodor W. 1986 [1959]. What Does Coming to Terms with the Past Mean? In *Bitburg in Moral and Political Perspective*, ed. Geoffrey H. Hartman, 114–129. Bloomington: Indiana University Press.

Agamben, Giorgio. 1998. *Homo Sacer: Sovereign Power and Bare Life*. Stanford, CA: Stanford University Press.

Agamben, Giorgio. 2005. *State of Exception*. Chicago: University of Chicago Press.

Agger, Inger and Søren Buss Jensen. 1996. *Trauma and Healing Under State Terrorism*. London: Zed Books.

Agosin, Marjorie. 1992. *Circles of Madness: Mothers of the Plaza de Mayo*. Fredonia: White Pine Press.

Agosin, Marjorie, ed. 1993. *Surviving Beyond Fear: Women, Children and Human Rights in Latin America*. Fredonia: White Pine Press.

Agosti, Orlando Ramón. 1978. *Discursos del Comandante en Jefe de la Fuerza Aerea Argentina Brigadier-General Orlando Ramón Agosti*. Buenos Aires: Author's edition.

Agüero, Felipe and Eric Hershberg. 2005. Las Fuerzas Armadas y las memorias de la represión en el Cono Sur. In *Memorias militares sobre la represión en el Cono Sur: Visiones en disputa en dictadura y democracia*, ed. Eric Hershberg and Felipe Agüero, 1–34. Madrid: Siglo Veintiuno de España Editores.

Aguilar, John L. 1984. Trust and Exchange: Expressive and Instrumental Dimensions of Reciprocity in a Peasant Community. *Ethos* 12(1): 3–29.

Ainsworth, Mary D. Salter. 1989. Attachments Beyond Infancy. *American Psychologist* 44(4): 709–716.

Akerström, Malin. 1991. *Betrayal and Betrayers: The Sociology of Treachery*. New Brunswick, NJ: Transaction Publishers.

Akhavan, Payam. 2012. *Reducing Genocide to Law: Definition, Meaning, and the Ultimate Crime*. Cambridge: Cambridge University Press.

Alegre, Gabriela, ed. 2005. *Proyecto Parque de la Memoria*. Buenos Aires: Gobierno de la Ciudad de Buenos Aires.

Alexander, Jeffrey C. 2002. On the Social Construction of Moral Universals: The "Holocaust" from War Crime to Trauma Drama. *European Journal of Social Theory* 5(1): 5–85.

Alexander, Jeffrey C. 2012. *Trauma: A Social Theory*. Cambridge: Polity Press.

Almirón, Fernando. 1999. *Campo Santo*. Buenos Aires: Editorial 21.

Améry, Jean. 1980. *At the Mind's Limits: Contemplations by a Survivor on Auschwitz and Its Realities*. Bloomington: Indiana University Press.

Amnesty International. 1977. *Report of an Amnesty International Mission to Argentina, 6–15 November 1976*. London: Amnesty International Publications.

Amnesty International. 1987. *Argentina: The Military Juntas and Human Rights*. London: Amnesty International Publications.

Andriotti Romanin, Enrique. 2013. Decir la verdad, hacer justicia: Los Juicios por la Verdad en Argentina. *European Review of Latin American and Caribbean Studies* 94(April): 5–23.

Anguita, Eduardo and Martín Caparrós. 1997. *La Voluntad: Una historia de la militancia revolucionaria en la Argentina*. Vol. 1: 1966–1973. Buenos Aires: Editorial Norma.

Anguita, Eduardo and Martín Caparrós. 1998a. *La Voluntad: Una historia de la militancia revolucionaria en la Argentina*. Vol. 2: 1973–1976. Buenos Aires: Editorial Norma.

Anguita, Eduardo and Martín Caparrós. 1998b. *La Voluntad: Una historia de la militancia revolucionaria en la Argentina*. Vol. 3: 1976–1978. Buenos Aires: Editorial Norma.

Arditti, Rita. 1999. *Searching for Life: The Grandmothers of the Plaza de Mayo and the Disappeared Children of Argentina*. Berkeley: University of California Press.

Arendt, Hannah. 1958. *The Human Condition*. Chicago: University of Chicago Press.

Arendt, Hannah. 1975 [1948]. *The Origins of Totalitarianism*. San Diego: Harcourt Brace and Company.

Arendt, Hannah. 1994. *Essays in Understanding, 1930–1954*, ed. Jerome Kohn. New York: Harcourt Brace and Company.

Arendt, Hannah. 2003. *Responsibility and Judgment*. New York: Schocken Books.

Argenti, Nicolas and Katharina Schramm, eds. 2010. *Remembering Violence: Anthropological Perspectives on Intergenerational Transmission*. New York: Berghahn.

Arthur, Paige. 2009. How "Transitions" Reshaped Human Rights: A Conceptual History of Transitional Justice. *Human Rights Quarterly* 31: 321–367.

Asociación Progresista de Fiscales de España. 1996. Denuncia. 28 March. http://www.derechos.org/nizkor/arg/espana/inicial.html. Accessed on 4 February 2016.

AUNAR. 1999. *Subversión: La historia olvidada*. 2nd ed. Buenos Aires: Asociación Unidad Argentina.

Auyero, Javier. 2007. *Routine Politics and Violence in Argentina: The Gray Zone of State Power*. Cambridge: Cambridge University Press.

Badaró, Máximo. 2009. *Militares o ciudadanos: La formación de los oficiales del Ejército Argentino*. Buenos Aires: Prometeo Libros.

Baer, Alejandro and Natan Sznaider. 2017. *Memory and Forgetting in the Post-Holocaust Era: The Ethics of Never Again*. London: Routledge.

Bailey, F. G. 1970. *Stratagems and Spoils: A Social Anthropology of Politics*. Oxford: Basil Blackwell.

Bakhtin, M. M. 1981. *The Dialogic Imagination*. Austin: University of Texas Press.

Balza, Martín Antonio. 2001. *Dejo constancia: Memorias de un general argentino*. Buenos Aires: Planeta.

Ban, Ki-moon. 2011. Secretary-General, at Argentina's "Dirty War" Memorial, Says World Can No Longer Have Safe Havens for Violators of International Human Rights, Humanitarian Law. Press release SG/SM/13639 on 14 June 2011. http://www.un.org/press/en/2011/sgsm13639.doc.htm. Accessed on 23 December 2014.

Banfield, Edward C. 1958. *The Moral Basis of a Backward Society*. New York: Free Press.

Bárbaro, Julio. 2009. *Juicio a los 70: La historia que yo viví*. Buenos Aires: Editorial Sudamericana.

Barela, Liliana. 2002. Límites de la representación artística en la construcción del Parque de la Memoria. *Voces Recobradas* 5(14): 4–11.

Bartov, Omer, Atina Grossmann, and Mary Nolan. 2002. Introduction. In *Crimes of War: Guilt and Denial in the Twentieth Century*, ed. Omer Bartov, Atina Grossmann, and Mary Nolan, ix–xxxiv. New York: New Press.

Baschetti, Roberto, ed. 1994. *Rodolfo Walsh, Vivo*. Buenos Aires: Ediciones de la Flor.

Basualdo, Eduardo M. 2013. El nuevo patrón de acumulación de capital, la desindustrialización y el ocaso de los trabajadores. In *Cuentas pendientes: Los cómplices económicos de la dictadura*, ed. Horacio Verbitsky and Juan Pablo Bohoslavsky, 81–99. Buenos Aires: Siglo Ventiuno.

Bayer, Osvaldo, Atilio A. Borón, and Julio C. Gambina. 2010. *El Terrorismo de Estado en la Argentina: Apuntes sobre su historia y sus consecuencias*. Buenos Aires: Instituto Espacio para la Memoria.

Beck, Ulrich. 1992. *Risk Society: Towards a New Modernity*. London: Sage.

Becker, David. 2006. Confronting the Truth of the Erinyes: The Illusion of Harmony in the Healing of Trauma. In *Telling the Truths: Truth Telling and Peace Building in Post-Conflict Societies*, ed. Tristan Anne Borer, 231–257. Notre Dame, IN: University of Notre Dame Press.

Benjamin, Walter. 1999. *Illuminations*. London: Pimlico.

Bernard, H. Russell. 2006. *Research Methods in Anthropology: Qualitative and Quantitative Approaches*. 4th ed. Lanham: Altamira Press.

Bernstein, Rosemary E. and Jennifer J. Freyd. 2014. Trauma at Home: How Betrayal Trauma and Attachment Theories Understand the Human Response to Abuse by an Attachment Figure. *Attachment* 8(March): 18–41.

Beverley, John. 2004. *Testimonio: On the Politics of Truth*. Minneapolis: University of Minnesota Press.

Bianchi, Silvia. 2009. *"El Pozo" (ex Servicio de Informaciones): Un centro clandestino de detención, desaparición, tortura y muerte de personas de la ciudad de Rosario, Argentina*. 2nd ed. Rosario: Prohistoria Ediciones.

Biehl, João. 2005. *Vita: Life in a Zone of Social Abandonment*. Berkeley: University of California Press.

Blixen, Samuel. 1988. *Treinta años de lucha popular: Conversaciones con Gorriarán Merlo*. Buenos Aires: Contrapunto.

Bohoslavsky, Juan Pablo and Veerle Opgenhaffen. 2010. The Past and Present of Corporate Complicity: Financing the Argentinean Dictatorship. *Harvard Human Rights Journal* 23: 157–203.

Boissevain, Jeremy. 1974. *Friends of Friends: Networks, Manipulators and Coalitions*. Oxford: Basil Blackwell.

Bonasso, Miguel. 1984. *Recuerdo de la Muerte*. Mexico City: Ediciones Era.

Bonasso, Miguel. 1997. *El presidente que no fue: Los archivos ocultos del peronismo*. Buenos Aires: Planeta.

Bondone, Luis José. 1985. *Con mis hijos en las cárceles del "proceso."* Buenos Aires: Editorial Anteo.

Borer, Tristan Anne. 2006. Truth Telling as a Peace-Building Activity: A Theoretical Overview. In *Telling the Truths: Truth Telling and Peace Building in Post-Conflict Societies*, ed. Tristan Anne Borer, 1–57. Notre Dame, IN: University of Notre Dame Press.

Bouvard, Marguerite Guzman. 1994. *Revolutionizing Motherhood: The Mothers of the Plaza de Mayo*. Wilmington, DE: Scholarly Resources.

Bowlby, John. 1981. *Attachment and Loss*. Vol. 3: *Loss: Sadness and Depression*. Harmondsworth: Penguin.

Bowlby, John. 1998 [1973]. *Attachment and Loss*. Vol. 2: *Separation: Anger and Anxiety*. London: Pimlico.

Boyarin, Jonathan, ed. 1994. *Remapping Memory: The Politics of TimeSpace*. Minneapolis: University of Minnesota Press.

Bozzolo, Raquel C. and Darío M. Lagos. 1988. Clinical Approach to Relatives of Missing People. In *Psychological Effects of Political Repression*, ed. Diana R. Kordon, Lucila I. Edelman, Darío M. Lagos, Elena Nicoletti, and Raquel Bozzolo, 49–55. Buenos Aires: Sudamericana/Planeta.

Bracken, Patrick J., Joan E. Giller, and Derek Summerfield. 1995. Psychological Responses to War and Atrocity: The Limitations of Current Concepts. *Social Science and Medicine* 40(8): 1073–1082.

Branscombe, Nyla R. and Bertjan Doosje. 2004. International Perspectives on the Experience of Collective Guilt. In *Collective Guilt: International Perspectives*, ed. Nyla R. Branscombe and Bertjan Doosje, 3–14. Cambridge: Cambridge University Press.

Brett, Elizabeth A. 1993. Psychoanalytic Contributions to a Theory of Traumatic Stress. In *International Handbook of Traumatic Stress Syndromes*, ed. John P. Wilson and Beverley Raphael, 61–68. New York: Plenum Press.

Brett, Sebastian. 2001. Reluctant Partner: The Argentine Government's Failure to Back Trials of Human Rights Violations. *Human Rights Watch* 13(December): 5(B).

Broch-Due, Vigdis and Margit Ystanes. 2016. Introducing Ethnographies of Trusting. In *Trusting and Its Tribulations: Interdisciplinary Engagements with Intimacy, Sociality and Trust*, ed. Vigdis Broch-Due and Margit Ystanes, 1–36. New York: Berghahn.

Brodsky, Marcelo. 2005. *Memoria en construcción: El debate sobre la ESMA*. Buenos Aires: La Marca Editora.

Brown, Wendy. 1995. *States of Injury: Power and Freedom in Late Modernity*. Princeton, NJ: Princeton University Press.

Buda, Blanca. 1988. *Cuerpo I-Zona IV (el infierno de Suárez Mason)*. Buenos Aires: Editorial Contrapunto.

Burdick, Michael A. 1995. *For God and the Fatherland: Religion and Politics in Argentina*. Albany: State University of New York Press.

Buruma, Ian. 2009 [1994]. *The Wages of Guilt: Memories of War in Germany and Japan*. London: Atlantic Books.

CADHU (Comisión Argentina por los Derechos Humanos). 1977. *Argentina: Proceso al genocidio*. Madrid: Elías Querejeta, ediciones.

Calveiro, Pilar. 1998. *Poder y desaparición: Los campos de concentración en Argentina*. Buenos Aires: Ediciones Colihue.

Cámara Nacional de Apelaciones en lo Criminal y Correccional Federal de la Capital Federal. 1987. *La Sentencia*. 2 vols. Buenos Aires: Imprenta del Congreso de la Nación.

Camarasa, Jorge, Ruben Felice, and Daniel González. 1985. *El Juicio: Proceso al horror*. Buenos Aires: Sudamericana/Planeta.

Cambareri, Horacio. 1990. Proyecto de ley. *Tributo* January–April: 27–29.

Camps, Ramón J. A. 1983. *El poder en la sombra: El affaire Graiver*. Buenos Aires: RO.CA. Producciones.

Canetti, Elias. 1966. *Crowds and Power*. New York: Viking Press.

Capdevila, Luc and Danièle Voldman. 2006. *War Dead: Western Societies and the Casualties of War*. Edinburgh: Edinburgh University Press.

Cappelletto, Francesca. 2003. Long-Term Memory of Extreme Events: From Autobiography to History. *Journal of the Royal Anthropological Institute* 9: 241–260.

Carassai, Sebastián. 2014. *The Argentine Silent Majority: Middle Classes, Politics, Violence, and Memory in the Seventies*. Durham, NC: Duke University Press.

Careaga, Ana María. 2009. *Leyes: Principales instrumentos legales sobre derechos humanos y memoria*. 2nd ed. Buenos Aires: Instituto Espacio para la Memoria.

Caruth, Cathy. 1995. Introduction. In *Trauma: Explorations in Memory*, ed. Cathy Caruth, 3–12. Baltimore: Johns Hopkins University Press.

Casiro, Jessica. 2006. Argentine Rescuers: A Study on the "Banality of Good." *Journal of Genocide Research* 8(4): 437–454.

Catela, Ludmila da Silva. 2001. *No habrá flores en la tumba del pasado: La experiencia de reconstrucción del mundo de los familiares de desaparecidos*. La Plata: Ediciones Al Margen.

Caviglia, Mariana. 2006a. *Dictadura, vida cotidiana y clases medias: Una sociedad fracturada*. Buenos Aires: Prometeo Libros.

Caviglia, Mariana. 2006b. *Vivir a oscuras: Escenas cotidianas durante la dictadura*. Buenos Aires: Aguilar.

Cazes Camarero, Pedro, ed. 1986. *Hubo dos terrorismos?* Buenos Aires: Ediciones Reencuentro.

Cazes Camarero, Pedro. 1989. *El Che y la generación del '70*. Buenos Aires: Ediciones Dialéctica.

CELS. 1986. *Terrorismo de estado: 692 responsables*. Buenos Aires: Centro de Estudios Legales y Sociales.

Centro de Información Judicial. 2014. Cámara Federal de la Plata, Juicio por la Verdad. 28 November. http://www.cij.gov.ar/nota-14492-CAMARA-FEDERAL-DE-LA-PLATA---JUICIO-POR-LA-VERDAD.html. Accessed on 6 March 2015.

Cerdá, Carlos Horácio. 1986/87. La lucha contra la subversión. Anexo 4: Condenas, procesos y sanciones a personal de las FFAA y de Seguridad. Unpublished report in author's possession.

Cerruti, Gabriela. 2001. La historia de la memoria. *Puentes* 1: 14–25.

Chapman, Audrey R. and Patrick Ball. 2001. The Truth of Truth Commissions: Comparative Lessons from Haiti, South Africa, and Guatemala. *Human Rights Quarterly* 23: 1–43.

Charmaz, Kathy. 2006. *Constructing Grounded Theory: A Practical Guide Through Qualitative Analysis*. Los Angeles: Sage.

Charmaz, Kathy and Richard G. Mitchell. 2008. Grounded Theory in Ethnography. In *Handbook of Ethnography*, ed. Paul Atkinson, Amanda Coffey, Sara Delamont, John Lofland, and Lyn Lofland, 160–174. Los Angeles: Sage.

Charuvastra, Anthony and Marylene Cloitre. 2008. Social Bonds and Posttraumatic Stress Disorder. *Annual Review of Psychology* 59: 301–328.

Cháves, Gonzalo Léonidas. 2005. *La masacre de Plaza de Mayo*. La Plata: De la Campana.

CIDH (Comisión Interamericana de Derechos Humanos). 1984 [1980]. *El informe prohibido: Informe sobre la situación de los derechos humanos en Argentina*. Buenos Aires: OSEA and CELS.

Cieza, Daniel. 2009. La dimensión laboral del genocidio en la Argentina. *Revista de Estudios sobre Genocidio* 2(3): 66–80.

Clapham, Andrew. 2006. *Human Rights Obligations of Non-State Actors*. Oxford: Oxford University Press.

Clausewitz, Carl von. 1984 [1832]. *On War*. Princeton, NJ: Princeton University Press.

Climo, Jacob J. and Maria G. Cattell, eds. 2002. *Social Memory and History: Anthropological Perspectives*. Walnut Creek, CA: AltaMira Press.

Cohen Salama, Mauricio. 1992. *Tumbas anónimas: Informe sobre la identificación de restos de víctimas de la represión ilegal*. Buenos Aires: Catálogos Editora.

Cohen, Stanley. 2001. *States of Denial: Knowing About Atrocities and Suffering*. Cambridge: Polity Press.

Collins, Cath. 2010. *Post-transitional Justice: Human Rights Trials in Chile and El Salvador*. University Park: Pennsylvania State University Press.

Comisión de Afirmación de la Revolución Libertadora. 1985. *A 30 años de la Revolución Libertadora*. Buenos Aires: Edición de la Comisión.

Comisión de Educación. 2004. *Memoria y Dictadura: Un espacio para la reflexión desde los Derechos Humanos*. Buenos Aires: APDH.

CONADEP. 1984. *Nunca más: Informe de la Comisión Nacional sobre la Desaparición de Personas*. Buenos Aires: EUDEBA.

CONADEP. 1985. *Anexos del Informe de la Comisión Nacional sobre la Desaparición de Personas*. Buenos Aires: EUDEBA.

CONADEP. 1986 [1984]. *Nunca Más: The Report of the Argentine Commission on the Disappeared*. New York: Farrar, Straus, Giroux.

Conferencia Episcopal Argentina. 1988. *Documentos del Episcopado Argentino, 1982–1983*. Buenos Aires: Oficina del Libro.

Consejo Federal del Peronismo Revolucionario. 1989. *Compromiso solemne por la pacificación y reconciliación nacional sustentadas en la justicia social y la autocrítica nacional*. 17 April. Unpublished document in author's possession.

Cooke, John William. 1973. *Perón-Cooke Correspondencia*. 2 vols. Buenos Aires: Granica Editor.

Cooper, David E. 1968. Collective Responsibility. *Philosophy* 43(July): 258–268.

Cooper, David E. 2001. Collective Responsibility, "Moral Luck," and Reconciliation. In *War Crimes and Collective Wrongdoing: A Reader*, ed. Aleksandar Jokić, 205–215. Malden, MA: Blackwell.

Corsín Jiménez, Alberto. 2011. Trust in Anthropology. *Anthropological Theory* 11(2): 177–196.

Crenzel, Emilio. 2008. *La historia política del Nunca Más: La memoria de las desapariciones en la Argentina*. Buenos Aires: Siglo Veintiuno Editores.

Csordas, Thomas J. 2013. Morality as a Cultural System? *Current Anthropology* 54(5): 523–536.

Curutchet, Ricardo. 1974. Editorial. *Cabildo* 1(11): 3.

D'Andrea Mohr, José Luis. 1999. *Memoria Debida*. Buenos Aires: Ediciones Colihue.

Daleo, Graciela and Andrés Ramón Castillo. 1982. *Informe*. Madrid: CADHU.

Daly, Erin and Jeremy Sarkin. 2007. *Reconciliation in Divided Societies: Finding Common Ground*. Philadelphia: University of Pennsylvania Press.

Dandan, Alejandra and Hannah Franzki. 2013. Entre análisis histórico y responsabilidad jurídica: el caso "Ledesma." In *Cuentas pendientes: Los cómplices económicos de la dictadura*, ed. Horacio Verbitsky and Juan Pablo Bohoslavsky, 217–234. Buenos Aires: Siglo Ventiuno.

Daniel, E. Valentine and John Chr. Knudsen, eds. 1995. *Mistrusting Refugees*. Berkeley: University of California Press.

Danieli, Yael. 1988. Treating Survivors and Children of Survivors of the Nazi Holocaust. In *Post-Traumatic Therapy and Victims of Violence*, ed. Frank M. Ochberg, 278–294. New York: Brunner/Mazel.

Darwin, Charles. 1988. *Charles Darwin's Beagle Diary*, ed. Richard Darwin Keynes. Cambridge: Cambridge University Press.

Das, Veena. 2007. *Life and Words: Violence and the Descent into the Ordinary*. Berkeley: University of California Press.

Das, Veena and Deborah Poole. 2004. State and Its Margins: Comparative Ethnographies. In *Anthropology in the Margins of the State*, ed. Veena Das and Deborah Poole, 3–33. Santa Fe, NM: School of American Research Press.

Davis, Coreen. 2013. *State Terrorism and Post-transitional Justice in Argentina: An Analysis of Mega Cause I Trial*. Houndmills: Palgrave Macmillan.

De Greiff, Pablo, ed. 2008. *The Handbook of Reparations*. Oxford: Oxford University Press.

De Mano en Mano. 2002. *Situaciones 5: Mesa de escrache popular*. Buenos Aires: Ediciones De Mano en Mano.

Dearriba, Alberto. 2001. *El golpe: 24 de marzo de 1976*. Buenos Aires: Editorial Sudamericana.

Derrida, Jacques. 1992. Force of Law: The "Mystical Foundation of Authority." In *Deconstruction and the Possibility of Justice*, ed. Drucilla Cornell, Michel Rosenfeld, and David Gray Carlson, 3–67. New York: Routledge.

Diago, Alejandro. 1988. *Hebe: memoria y esperanza*. Buenos Aires: Ediciones Dialéctica.

Diana, Marta. 1997. *Mujeres guerrilleras: La militancia de los setenta en el testimonio de sus protagonistas femeninas*. Buenos Aires: Planeta.

Díaz, Diego. 2002. El mapa de la memoria. *Puentes* 2(7): 34–39.

Diaz Araujo, Enrique. 1988. *La semana trágica de 1919*. Vol. 2. Mendoza: Universidad Nacional de Cuyo.

Díaz Bessone, Ramón Genaro. 1988. *Guerra Revolucionaria en la Argentina (1959–1978)*. Buenos Aires: Círculo Militar.

Díaz Bessone, Ramón Genaro, ed. 2001. *In Memoriam*. 3 vols. Buenos Aires: Círculo Militar.

Diez, Rolo. 1987. *Los Compañeros*. Mexico City: Leega.

Dirección Nacional del Sistema Argentino de Información Jurídica. 2015. *Responsabilidad empresarial en delitos de lesa humanidad: Represión a trabajadores durante el terrorismo de Estado*. Vol. 1. Buenos Aires: Editorial Ministerio de Justicia y Derechos Humanos de la Nación.

Doak, Jonathan. 2011. The Therapeutic Dimension of Transitional Justice: Emotional Repair and Victim Satisfaction in International Trials and Truth Commissions. *International Criminal Law Review* 11: 263–298.

Donda, Victoria. 2009. *Mi nombre es Victoria*. Buenos Aires: Editorial Sudamericana.

Douglass, Ana and Thomas A. Vogler. 2003. Introduction. In *Witness and Memory: The Discourse of Trauma*, ed. Ana Douglass and Thomas A. Vogler, 1–53. New York: Routledge.

Dower, John W. 1986. *War Without Mercy: Race and Power in the Pacific War*. New York: Pantheon.

Dri, Rubén R. 1987. *Teologia y Dominación*. Buenos Aires: Roblanco.

Droždek, Boris and John P. Wilson, eds. 2007. *Voices of Trauma: Treating Psychological Trauma Across Cultures*. New York: Springer.

Duhalde, Eduardo Luis. 1983. *El estado terrorista argentino*. Buenos Aires: Editorial El Caballito.

Duhalde, Eduardo Luis. 2006a. Prólogo a la edición del 30⁰ aniversario del golpe de estado. http://www.iade.org.ar/modules/noticias/print/php?storyid = 1487. Accessed on 8 August 2016.

Duhalde, Eduardo Luis. 2006b. "De los dos demonios al terrorismo de Estado." *Página/12*, 15 May.

Duncan Baretta, Silvio R. and John Markoff. 1978. Civilization and Barbarism: Cattle Frontiers in Latin America. *Comparative Studies in Society and History* 20: 587–620.

Durkheim, Emile. 1995 [1912]. *The Elementary Forms of Religious Life*. New York: Free Press.

EAAF (Equipo Argentino de Antropología Forense). 2006. *2006 Mini Annual Report: Covering the Period January to December 2005*. Buenos Aires: EAAF.

EAAF (Equipo Argentino de Antropología Forense). 2007. *2007 Annual Report: Covering the Period January to December 2006*. Buenos Aires: EAAF.

EAAF (Equipo Argentino de Antropología Forense). 2011. *2007–2009 Triannual Report*. Buenos Aires: EAAF.

Eckstein, Susan Eva, ed. 1989. *Power and Popular Protest: Latin American Social Movements*. Berkeley: University of California Press.

Edelman, Lucila I. and Diana R. Kordon. 1995a. Efectos psicosociales de la impunidad. In *La impunidad: Una perspectiva psicosocial y clínica*, ed. Diana R. Kordon, Lucila I. Edelman, Darío M. Lagos, and Daniel Kersner, 27–41. Buenos Aires: Editorial Sudamericana.

Edelman, Lucila I. and Diana R. Kordon. 1995b. Trauma y duelo. Conflicto y elaboración. In *La impunidad: Una perspectiva psicosocial y clínica*, ed. Diana R. Kordon, Lucila I. Edelman, Darío M. Lagos, and Daniel Kersner, 101–110. Buenos Aires: Editorial Sudamericana.

Eisenstadt, S. N. and L. Roniger. 1984. *Patrons, Clients and Friends: Interpersonal Relations and the Structure of Trust in Society*. Cambridge: Cambridge University Press.

Eloy Martínez, Tomás. 1997 [1973]. *La pasión según Trelew*. Buenos Aires: Planeta.

Erikson, Erik H. 1963. *Childhood and Society*. 2nd ed. New York: W. W. Norton and Company.

Erikson, Kai T. 1976. *Everything in Its Path: Destruction of Community in the Buffalo Creek Flood*. New York: Simon & Schuster.

Erikson, Kai T. 1994. *A New Species of Trouble: Explorations in Disaster, Trauma, and Community*. New York: W. W. Norton and Company.

Erikson, Kai T. 1995. Notes on Trauma and Community. In *Trauma: Explorations in Memory*, ed. Cathy Caruth, 183–199. Baltimore: Johns Hopkins University Press.

Eyerman, Ron. 2001. *Cultural Trauma: Slavery and the Formation of African American Identity*. Cambridge: Cambridge University Press.

Fabian, Johannes. 2007. *Memory against Culture: Arguments and Reminders*. Durham, NC: Duke University Press.

FAMUS. 1988. *Operación Independencia*. Buenos Aires: FAMUS.

Fassin, Didier and Richard Rechtman. 2009. *The Empire of Trauma: An Inquiry into the Condition of Victimhood*. Princeton, NJ: Princeton University Press.

Feierstein, Daniel. 2006. Political Violence in Argentina and Its Genocidal Characteristics. *Journal of Genocide Research* 8(2): 149–168.

Feierstein, Daniel. 2008a. *El genocidio como práctica social: Entre el nazismo y la experiencia argentina*. Buenos Aires: Fondo de Cultura Económica.

Feierstein, Daniel. 2008b. La Argentina: ¿Genocidio y/o crimen contra la humanidad? Sobre el rol del derecho en la construcción de la memoria colectiva. *Nueva Doctrina Penal* (A): 211–230.

Feitlowitz, Marguerite. 1998. *A Lexicon of Terror: Argentina and the Legacies of Torture*. New York: Oxford University Press.

Feld, Claudia. 2002. *Del estrado a la pantalla: Las imágenes del juicio a los ex comandantes en Argentina*. Madrid: Siglo Veintiuno.

Feldman, Allen. 1991. *Formations of Violence: The Narrative of the Body and Political Terror in Northern Ireland*. Chicago: University of Chicago Press.

Felman, Shoshana and Dori Laub. 1991. *Testimony: Crises of Witnessing in Literature, Psychoanalysis, and History*. New York: Routledge.

Fernández, Rodolfo Peregrino. 1983. *Autocrítica policial*. Buenos Aires: El Cid Editor.

Fernández Meijide, Graciela. 2009. *La historia íntima de los derechos humanos en la Argentina*. Buenos Aires: Subamericana.

Fernández Meijide, Graciela. 2013. *Eran humanos, no héroes: Crítica de la violencia política de los 70*. Buenos Aires: Editorial Sudamericana.

Fernández Meijide, Graciela and Héctor Ricardo Leis. 2015. *El diálogo: El encuentro que cambió nuestra visión sobre la década del 70*. Buenos Aires: Editorial Sudamericana.

Ferrándiz, Francisco. 2010. The Intimacy of Defeat: Exhumations in Contemporary Spain. In *Unearthing Franco's Legacy: Mass Graves and the Recovery of Historical Memory in Spain*, ed. Carlos Jerez-Farrán and Samuel Amago, 304–325. Notre Dame: University of Notre Dame Press.

Firmenich, Mario and Norma Arrostito. 1974. Como murió Aramburu. *La Causa Peronista* 1(9): 25–31.

Fisher, Jo. 1989. *Mothers of the Disappeared*. Boston: South End Press.

Fisher, Jo. 1993. *Out of the Shadows: Women, Resistance and Politics in South America*. London: Latin American Bureau.

Foucault, Michel. 1977. *Language, Counter-Memory, Practice*. Ithaca, NY: Cornell University Press.

Foucault, Michel. 1998 [1976]. *The Will to Knowledge*. Harmondsworth: Penguin.

Francis, Doris, Leonie Kellaher, and Georgina Neophytou. 2005. *The Secret Cemetery*. Oxford: Berg.

Fraser, Nancy. 2005. Reframing Justice in a Globalizing World. *New Left Review* 36: 69–88.

Frederic, Sabina. 2013. *Las trampas del pasado: Las Fuerzas Armadas y su integración al Estado democrático en Argentina*. Buenos Aires: Fondo de Cultura Económica.

French, Peter A. 1984. *Collective and Corporate Responsibility*. New York: Columbia University Press.

Freud, Sigmund. 1968a [1917]. Mourning and Melancholia. *The Standard Edition of the Complete Psychological Works of Sigmund Freud* 7: 243–258. London: Hogarth Press.

Freud, Sigmund. 1968b [1920]. Beyond the Pleasure Principle. *The Standard Edition of the Complete Psychological Works of Sigmund Freud*. 18: 7–64. London: Hogarth Press.

Freyd, Jennifer J. 1996. *Betrayal Trauma: The Logic of Forgetting Childhood Abuse*. Cambridge, MA: Harvard University Press.

Freyd, Jennifer J., Anne P. DePrince, and David H. Gleaves. 2007. The State of Betrayal Trauma Theory: Reply to McNally—Conceptual Issues and Future Directions. *Memory* 15(3): 295–311.

Friedlander, Saul. 1993. *Memory, History, and the Extermination of the Jews of Europe*. Bloomington: Indiana University Press.

Frontalini, Daniel and María Cristina Caiati. 1984. *El mito de la "guerra sucia."* Buenos Aires: CELS.

Gabetta, Carlos. 1983. *Todos somos subversivos*. Buenos Aires: Editorial Bruguera.

Galimberti, Rodolfo. 1974. ¿Quién votó a Isabel-López Rega? *La Causa Peronista* 1(8): 2–3.

Galtung, Johan. 2001. After Violence, Reconstruction, Reconciliation, and Resolution: Coping with Visible and Invisible Effects of War and Violence. In *Reconciliation, Justice, and Coexistence: Theory and Practice*, ed. Mohammed Abu–Nimer, 3–23. Lanham, MD: Lexington Books.

Gambetta, Diego, ed. 1988. *Trust: Making and Breaking Cooperative Relations*. New York: Basil Blackwell.

Gampel, Yolanda. 2000. Reflections on the Prevalence of the Uncanny in Social Violence. In *Cultures Under Siege: Collective Violence and Trauma*, ed. Antonius C. G. M. Robben and Marcelo M. Suárez-Orozco, 48–69. Cambridge: Cambridge University Press.

Garzón, Baltasar. 1997. Orden de prisión provisional incondicional. Madrid, 25 March. http://www.derechos.org/nizkor/arg/espana/autogalt.html. Accessed on 4 February 2016.

Garzón, Baltasar. 1998. Auto confirmando la jurisdicción de la corte y las órdenes emitidas. Madrid, 25 March. http://www.derechos.org/nizkor/arg/espana/compe.html. Accessed on 5 February 2016.

Gasparini, Juan. 1986. *La pista suiza*. Buenos Aires: Editorial Legasa.

Gasparini, Juan. 1988. *Montoneros: Final de Cuentas*. Buenos Aires: Puntosur.

Gasparini, Juan. 1990. *El crímen de Graiver*. Buenos Aires: Editorial Zeta.

Gassino, Francisco E. and Enrique B. Bonifacino. 2001. *Los 70: Violencia en la Argentina*. Buenos Aires: Círculo Militar.

Gates-Madsen, Nancy. 2011. Marketing and Sacred Space: The Parque de la Memoria in Buenos Aires. In *Accounting for Violence: Marketing Memory in Latin America*, ed. Ksenija Bilbija and Leigh A. Payne, 151–178. Durham, NC: Duke University Press.

Gavier, Jaime Díaz. 2012. Sentencia. Tribunal Oral Federal No 1, Córdoba, 22 December, pp. 317–241. http://apm.gov.ar/sites/default/files/Sentencia%20Videla.pdf. Accessed on 5 February 2016.

Gellner, Ernest. 1988. Trust, Cohesion, and the Social Order. In *Trust: Making and Breaking Cooperative Relations*, ed. Diego Gambetta, 142–157. New York: Basil Blackwell.

Geschiere, Peter. 2013. *Witchcraft, Intimacy, and Trust*. Chicago: University of Chicago Press.

Giddens, Anthony. 1991. *Modernity and Self-Identity: Self and Society in the Late Modern Age*. Stanford, CA: Stanford University Press.

Gillespie, Richard. 1982. *Soldiers of Perón: Argentina's Montoneros*. Oxford: Clarendon Press.

Girard, René. 1989. *The Scapegoat*. Baltimore: Johns Hopkins University Press.

Girard, René. 1992 [1972]. *Violence and the Sacred*. Baltimore: Johns Hopkins University Press.

Giúdice, Diego. 1989. Monseñor Miguel Hesayne: "La paz no es arbitraria." *Derechos Humanos* 6(24): 11–14.

Giussani, Pablo. 1984. *Montoneros: La soberbia armada*. Buenos Aires: Sudamericana/Planeta.

Giussani, Pablo. 1987. *¿Por qué, doctor Alfonsín?* Buenos Aires: Sudamericana/Planeta.

Glaser, Barney G. and Anselm L. Strauss. 1967. *The Discovery of Grounded Theory: Strategies for Qualitative Research*. Chicago: Aldine.

Gloppen, Siri. 2005. Roads to Reconciliation: A Conceptual Framework. In *Roads to Reconciliation*, ed. Elin Skaar, Siri Gloppen, and Astri Suhrke, 17–50. Lanham, MD: Lexington Books.

Gobin, Robyn L. and Jennifer J. Freyd. 2014. The Impact of Betrayal Trauma on the Tendency to Trust. *Psychological Trauma: Theory, Research, Practice, and Policy* 6(5): 505–511.

González, Carlos Cezón. 1998. Auto de la Sala de lo Penal de la Audiencia Nacional confirmando la jurisdicción de España para conocer de los crímenes de genocidio y terrorismo cometidos duranta la dictadura argentina. Madrid, 4 November. http://www.derechos.org/nizkor/arg/espana/audi.html. Accessed on 5 February 2016.

González Bombal, Inés. 1995. "Nunca Más": El Juicio más allá de los estrados. In *Juicio, Castigos y Memorias: Derechos humanos y justicia en la política Argentina*, ed. Carlos H. Acuña, 193–216. Buenos Aires: Nueva Visión.

González Leegstra, Cintia. 2011. El juicio a Etchecolatz: Nuevos y viejos actores en la lucha por la justicia. *Intersticios* 5(2): 129–144.

Gorini, Ulises. 2006. *La rebelión de las Madres: Historia de las Madres de Plaza de Mayo*. Vol. 1: 1976–1983. Buenos Aires: Grupo Editorial Norma.

Gorini, Ulises. 2008. *La otra lucha: Historia de las Madres de Plaza de Mayo*. Vol. 2: 1983–1986. Buenos Aires: Grupo Editorial Norma.

Government of Argentina. 1980. *Observations and Criticisms Made by the Government of Argentina with Regard to the Report of the Inter-American Commission on Human Rights on the Situation of Human Rights in Argentina (April 1980)*. Washington, DC: Organization of American States.

Graham-Yooll, Andrew. 1989. *De Perón a Videla*. Buenos Aires: Editorial Legasa.

Granovsky, Martín. 1989. ¿La Argentina era una fiesta? *Derechos Humanos* 6(24): 6–7.

Grecco, Jorge and Gustavo González. 1988. *¡Felices Pascuas! Los hechos inéditos de la rebelión militar*. Buenos Aires: Planeta.

Green, Bonnie L. 1990. Defining Trauma: Terminology and Generic Stressor Dimensions. *Journal of Applied Social Psychology* 20: 1632–1642.

Green, James W. 2008. *Beyond the Good Death: The Anthropology of Modern Dying*. Philadelphia: University of Pennsylvania Press.

Gregory, C. A. 1982. *Gifts and Commodities*. London: Academic Press.

Grimen, Harald. 2009. Power, Trust, and Risk: Some Reflections on an Absent Issue. *Medical Anthropology Quarterly* 23(1): 16–33.

Guber, Rosana. 1996. Las manos de la memoria. *Desarrollo Económico* 36: 423–442.

Guelerman, Sergio J., ed. 2001. *Memorias en presente: Identidad y transmisión en la Argentina posgenocidio*. Buenos Aires: Grupo Editorial Norma.

Guembe, María José. 2006. Economic Reparations for Grave Human Rights Violations: The Argentinean Experience. In *The Handbook of Reparations*, ed. Pablo de Greiff, 21–54. Oxford: Oxford University Press.

Guest, Iain. 1990. *Behind the Disappearances: Argentina's Dirty War Against Human Rights and the United Nations*. Philadelphia: University of Pennsylvania Press.

Gugelberger, Georg M. 1996. Introduction: Institutionalization of Transgression: Testimonial Discourse and Beyond. In *The Real Thing: Testimonial Discourse and Latin America*, ed. Georg M. Gugelberger, 1–19. Durham, NC: Duke University Press.

Gugelberger, Georg M. 1999. Stollwerk or Bulwark? David Meets Goliath and the Continuation of the Testimonio Debate. *Latin American Perspectives* 26(6): 47–52.

Gutiérrez, Roger. 1985. *Gorriarán: Democracia y Liberación*. Buenos Aires: Ediciones Reencuentro.

Halbwachs, Maurice. 1992 [1925]. *On Collective Memory*. Chicago: University of Chicago Press.

Hallam, Elizabeth and Jenny Hockey. 2001. *Death, Memory and Material Culture*. Oxford: Berg.

Hansen, Thomas Blom and Finn Stepputat, eds. 2001. *States of Imagination: Ethnographic Explorations of the Postcolonial State*. Durham, NC: Duke University Press.

Hansen, Thomas Blom and Finn Stepputat. 2006. Sovereignty Revisited. *Annual Review of Anthropology* 35: 295–315.

Hardin, Russell. 2006. *Trust*. Cambridge: Polity Press.

Hayner, Priscilla B. 2001. *Unspeakable Truths: Confronting State Terror and Atrocity*. New York: Routledge.

Held, Virginia. 1970. Can a Random Collection of Individuals Be Morally Responsible? *Journal of Philosophy* 67(14): 471–481.

Heller, Kevin Jon. 2011. *The Nuremberg Military Tribunals and the Origins of International Criminal Law*. Oxford: Oxford University Press.

Herman, Judith Lewis. 1997. *Trauma and Recovery*. New York: Basic Books.

Herrera, Matilde. 1987. *José*. Buenos Aires: Editorial Contrapunto.

Hertz, Robert. 1960 [1909]. *Death and the Right Hand*. London: Cohen and West.

Herzfeld, Michael. 2009. The Performance of Secrecy: Domesticity and Privacy in Public Spaces. *Semiotica* 175: 135–162.

Hinton, Alexander Laban. 2005. *Why Did They Kill? Cambodia in the Shadow of Genocide*. Berkeley: University of California Press.

Hinton, Alexander Laban. 2010. Introduction: Toward an Anthropology of Transitional Justice. In *Transitional Justice: Global Mechanisms and Local Realities After Genocide and Mass Violence*, ed. Alexander Laban Hinton, 1–22. New Brunswick, NJ: Rutgers University Press.

Hinton, Devon E. and Byron J. Good, eds. 2016. *Culture and PTSD: Trauma in Global and Historical Perspective*. Philadelphia: University of Pennsylvania Press.

Hinton, Devon E. and Alexander Laban Hinton, eds. 2014. *Genocide and Mass Violence: Memory, Symptom, and Recovery*. Cambridge: Cambridge University Press.

Hinton, Devon E. and Roberto Lewis-Fernández. 2010. Idioms of Distress Among Trauma Survivors: Subtypes and Clinical Utility. *Culture, Medicine, and Psychiatry* 34: 209–218.

Hirsch, Marianne and Leo Spitzer. 2010. The Witness in the Archive: Holocaust Studies/ Memory Studies. In *Memory: Histories, Theories, Debates*, ed. Susannah Radstone and Bill Schwarz, 390–405. New York: Fordham University Press.

Hitchens, Christopher. 2011. *Hitch-22: A Memoir*. London: Atlantic Books.

Hollander, Nancy Caro. 1990. Buenos Aires: Latin Mecca of Psychoanalysis. *Social Research* 57(4): 889–919.

Honwana, Alcinda. 2006. *Child Soldiers in Africa*. Philadelphia: University of Pennsylvania Press.

Hoy, David Couzens. 1978. *The Critical Circle: Literature, History, and Philosophical Hermeneutics*. Berkeley: University of California Press.

Hrdy, Sarah Blaffer. 2011. *Mothers and Others: The Evolutionary Origins of Mutual Understanding*. Cambridge, MA: Belknap Press.

Huyssen, Andreas. 1995. *Twilight Memories: Marking Time in a Culture of Amnesia*. New York: Routledge.

Huyssen, Andreas. 2003. *Present Pasts: Urban Palimpsests and the Politics of Memory*. Stanford, CA: Stanford University Press.

IACHR (Inter-American Commission on Human Rights). 1980. *Report on the Situation of Human Rights in Argentina*. Washington, DC: Organization of American States.

IACHR (Inter-American Commission on Human Rights). 1992. *Report No. 28/92, Argentina, 2 October*. Washington, DC: Organization of American States.

ICJ (International Commission of Jurists). 2008. *Corporate Complicity and Legal Accountability*. Vol. 1: *Facing the Facts and Charting a Legal Path*. Geneva: International Commission of Jurists.

Ingold, Tim. 2000. *The Perception of the Environment: Essays on Livelihood, Dwelling and Skill*. New York: Routledge.

Instituto Memoria. 2008. *Nuestra Memoria*. Buenos Aires: Instituto Espacio para la Memoria.

International Criminal Court. 1998. Rome Statute. Rome, 17 July. https://www.icc-cpi.int/nr/rdonlyres/ea9aeff7-5752-4f84-be94-0a655eb30e16/0/rome_statute_english.pdf. Accessed on 5 February 2016.

Irwin-Zarecka, Iwona. 1994. *Frames of Remembrance: The Dynamics of Collective Memory*. New Brunswick, NJ: Transaction Publishers.

James, Daniel. 1988. *Resistence and Integration: Peronism and the Argentine Working Class, 1946–1976*. Cambridge: Cambridge University Press.

Jaquette, Jane, ed. 1994. *The Women's Movement in Latin America: Participation and Democracy*. 2nd ed. Boulder, CO: Westview Press.

Jaspers, Karl. 2001 [1947]. *The Question Concerning German Guilt*. New York: Fordham University Press.

Jauretche, Ernesto. 1997. *Violencia y política en los 70: No dejés que te la cuenten*. Buenos Aires: Ediciones del Pensamiento Nacional.

Jennings, Ronald C. 2011. Sovereignty and Political Modernity: A Genealogy of Agamben's Critique of Sovereignty. *Anthropological Theory* 11(1): 23–61.

Jessee, Erin and Mark Skinner. 2005. A Typology of Mass Grave and Mass Grave-Related Sites. *Forensic Science International* 152(1): 55–59.

Johnston, Barbara Rose and Susan Slyomovics, eds. 2009. *Waging War, Making Peace: Reparations and Human Rights*. Walnut Creek, CA: Left Coast Press.

Jones, Kristine L. 1993. Civilization and Barbarism and Sarmiento's Indian Policy. In *Sarmiento and His Argentina*, ed. Joseph T. Criscenti, 35–43. Boulder, CO: Lynne Rienner Publishers.

Jones, Warren H., Laurie Couch, and Susan Scott. 1997. Trust and Betrayal: The Psychology of Getting Along and Getting Ahead. In *Handbook of Personality Psychology*, ed. Robert Hogan, John Johnson, and Stephen Briggs, 465–482. San Diego: Academic Press.

Joyce, Christopher and Eric Stover. 1991. *Witnesses from the Grave: The Stories Bones Tell*. London: Bloomsbury.

Junta Militar. 1983. *Documento Final de la Junta Militar sobre la Guerra contra la Subversión y el Terrorismo*, p. 1. http://www.memoriaabierta.org.ar/materiales/documento_final_junta.phpwww.institutomemoria.org.ar. Accessed on 26 February 2015.

Kaiser, Susana. 2002. *Escraches*: Demonstrations, Communication and Political Memory in Post-Dictatorial Argentina. *Media, Culture and Society* 24: 499–516.

Kalyvas, Stathis N. 2006. *The Logic of Violence in Civil War*. Cambridge: Cambridge University Press.

Kampwirth, Karen, ed. 2010. *Gender and Populism in Latin America: Passionate Politics*. University Park: Pennsylvania State University Press.

Keller, Heidi. 2014. Introduction: Understanding Relationships—What We Would Need to Know to Conceptualize Attachment as the Cultural Solution of a Universal Developmental Task. In *Different Faces of Attachment: Cultural Variations on a Universal Human Need*, ed. Hiltrud Otto and Heidi Keller, 1–24. Cambridge: Cambridge University Press.

Kelly, Tobias. 2012. *This Side of Silence: Human Rights, Torture, and the Recognition of Cruelty*. Philadelphia: University of Pennsylvania Press.

Kelly, Tobias and Sharika Thiranagama. 2010. Introduction: Specters of Treason. In *Traitors: Suspicion, Intimacy, and the Ethics of State-Building*, ed. Sharika Thiranagama and Tobias Kelly, 1–23. Philadelphia: University of Pennsylvania Press.

Kirmayer, Laurence J. 1996. Landscapes of Memory: Trauma, Narrative, and Dissociation. In *Tense Past: Cultural Essays in Trauma and Memory*, ed. Paul Antze and Michael Lambek, 173–198. New York: Routledge.

Klass, Dennis and Robert Goss. 2003. The Politics of Grief and Continuing Bonds with the Dead: The Cases of Maoist China and Wahhabi Islam. *Death Studies* 27: 787–811.

Klass, Dennis, Phyllis R. Silverman, and Steven L. Nickman, eds. 1996. *Continuing Bonds: New Understandings of Grief*. Washington, DC: Taylor and Francis.

Kleber, Rolf J., Charles R. Figley, and Berthold P. R. Gersons, eds. 1995. *Beyond Trauma: Cultural and Societal Dynamics*. New York: Plenum Press.

Kleinman, Arthur. 1999. Experience and Its Moral Modes: Culture, Human Conditions, and Disorder. In *The Tanner Lectures on Human Values*, ed. Grethe B. Peterson, 355–420. Salt Lake City: University of Utah Press.

Kordon, Diana R. and Lucila I. Edelman. 1988. Psychological Effects of Political Repression, I. In *Psychological Effects of Political Repression*, ed. Diana R. Kordon, Lucila I. Edelman, Darío M. Lagos, Elena Nicoletti, and Raquel C. Bozzolo, 33–40. Buenos Aires: Sudamericana/Planeta.

Kordon, Diana R. and Lucila I. Edelman. 1995. Efectos psicosociales de la impunidad. In *La impunidad: Una perspectiva psicosocial y clínica*, ed. Diana R. Kordon, Lucila I. Edelman, Darío M. Lagos, and Daniel Kersner, 27–41. Buenos Aires: Editorial Sudamericana.

Kordon, Diana R., Lucila I. Edelman, and Darío M. Lagos. 1988. On the Guidance Group's Experience with the Relatives of Missing People. In *Psychological Effects of Political Repression*, ed. Diana R. Kordon, Lucila I. Edelman, Darío M. Lagos, Elena Nicoletti, and Raquel C. Bozzolo, 41–47. Buenos Aires: Sudamericana/Planeta.

Kordon, Diana R., Lucila I. Edelman, Elena Nicoletti, Darío M. Lagos, Raquel C. Bozzolo, and Ester Kandel. 1988. Torture in Argentina. In *Psychological Effects of Political Repression*, ed. Diana R. Kordon, Lucila I. Edelman, Darío M. Lagos, Elena Nicoletti, and Raquel C. Bozzolo, 95–107. Buenos Aires: Sudamericana/Planeta.

Kordon, Diana R., Lucila I. Edelman, Darío M. Lagos, Elena Nicoletti, and Raquel C. Bozzolo, eds. 1988. *Psychological Effects of Political Repression*. Buenos Aires: Sudamericana/Planeta.

Kowalski, Robin Marie. 2009. Betrayal. In *Encyclopedia of Human Relationships*, ed. Harry T. Reis and Susan Sprecher, 174–176. Los Angeles: Sage.

Kozameh, Alicia. 1987. *Pasos bajo el agua*. Buenos Aires: Editorial Contrapunto.

Kritz, Neil J., ed. 1995. *Transitional Justice: How Emerging Democracies Reckon with Former Regimes*. Vol. 1: *General Considerations*. Washington, DC: United States Institute of Peace Press.

Kritz, Neil J. 1996. Coming to Terms with Atrocities: A Review of Accountability Mechanisms for Mass Violations of Human Rights. *Law and Contemporary Problems* 59(4): 127–152.

Kwon, Heonik. 2006. *After the Massacre: Commemoration and Consolation in Ha My and My Lai*. Berkeley: University of California Press.

LaCapra, Dominick. 1996. *Representing the Holocaust: History, Theory, Trauma*. Ithaca, NY: Cornell University Press.

LaCapra, Dominick. 1998. *History and Memory After Auschwitz*. Ithaca, NY: Cornell University Press.

LaCapra, Dominick. 2001. *Writing History, Writing Trauma*. Baltimore: Johns Hopkins University Press.

Lagos, Darío. 1994. Argentina: Psychosocial and Clinical Consequences of Political Repression and Impunity in the Medium Term. *Torture* 4(1): 13–15.

Laing, R. D. 1960. *The Divided Self: A Study of Sanity and Madness*. London: Tavistock Publications.

Lamas, Raúl. 1956. *Los Torturadores: Crímenes y tormentos en las cárceles argentinas*. Buenos Aires: Editorial Lamas.

Lambek, Michael and Paul Antze. 1996. Introduction: Forecasting Memory. In *Tense Past: Cultural Essays in Trauma and Memory*, ed. Paul Antze and Michael Lambek, xi–xxxviii. New York: Routledge.

Langer, Lawrence L. 1991. *Holocaust Testimonies: The Ruins of Memory*. New Haven, CT: Yale University Press.

Laplanche, J. and J.-B. Pontalis. 1973. *The Language of Psycho-Analysis*. New York: W. W. Norton and Company.

Laqueur, Thomas W. 2015. *The Work of the Dead: A Cultural History of Mortal Remains*. Princeton, NJ: Princeton University Press.

Larrabure, Arturo C. 2005. *Un canto a la patria*. Buenos Aires: Edivérn.

Last, Murray. 2000. Reconciliation and Memory in Postwar Nigeria. In *Violence and Subjectivity*, ed. Veena Das, Arthur Kleinman, Mamphela Ramphele, and Pamela Reynolds, 315–332. Berkeley: University of California Press.

Lederach, John Paul. 1997. *Building Peace: Sustainable Reconciliation in Divided Societies*. Washington, DC: United States Institute of Peace Press.

Leis, Héctor Ricardo. 2012. *Testamento de los años 70*. Bonk.com.ar/tpfile_download/12/testamento-leis-print.pdf. Accessed on 28 February 2017.

Lemkin, Raphaël. 2002 [1944]. Genocide. In *Genocide: An Anthropological Reader*, ed. Alexander Laban Hinton, 27–42. Malden, MA: Blackwell.

Levi, Margaret and Laura Stoker. 2000. Political Trust and Trustworthiness. *Annual Review of Political Science* 3: 475–507.

LeVine, Robert A. and Karin Norman. 2001. The Infant's Acquisition of Culture: Early Attachment Reexamined in Anthropological Perspective. In *The Psychology of Cultural Experience*, ed. Carmella C. Moore and Holly F. Mathews, 83–104. Cambridge: Cambridge University Press.

Lévi-Strauss, Claude. 1969 [1949]. *The Elementary Structures of Kinship*. Boston: Beacon Press.

Levy, Daniel and Natan Sznaider. 2006. *The Holocaust and Memory in the Global Age*. Philadelphia: Temple University Press.

Lewis, H. D. 1948. Collective Responsibility. *Philosophy* 24(84): 3–18.

Leys, Ruth. 2000. *Trauma: A Genealogy*. Chicago: University of Chicago Press.

Lifton, Robert Jay. 1973. *Home from the War. Vietnam Veterans: Neither Victims nor Executioners*. New York: Simon & Schuster.

Lindemann, Erich. 1944. Symptomatology and Management of Acute Grief. *American Journal of Psychiatry* 101(2): 141–148.

Lipstadt, Deborah E. 1993. *Denying the Holocaust: The Growing Assault on Truth and Memory*. New York: Free Press.

Longoni, Ana. 2007. *Traiciones: La figura del traidor en los relatos acerca de los sobrevivientes de la represión*. Buenos Aires: Grupo Editorial Norma.

López, Ernesto. 1988. *El último levantamiento*. Buenos Aires: Legasa.

Lorenz, Federico Guillermo. 1999. The Unending War: Social Myth, Individual Memory and the Malvinas. In *Trauma and Life Stories: International Perspectives*, ed. Kim Lacy Rogers, Selma Leydesdorff, and Graham Dawson, 95–112. London: Routledge.

Lorenz, Federico Guillermo. 2002. ¿De quién es el 24 de marzo? Las luchas por la memoria del golpe de 1976. In *Las conmemoraciones: Las disputas en las fechas "in-felices,"* ed. Elizabeth Jelin, 53–100. Madrid: Siglo Veintiuno.

Loveman, Brian and Thomas M. Davies, Jr., eds. 1989. *The Politics of Antipolitics: The Military in Latin America*. Lincoln: University of Nebraska Press.

Lozada, Martín. 2008. *Sobre el genocidio: El crimen fundamental*. Buenos Aires: Capital Intelectual.

Luhmann, Niklas. 1979. *Trust and Power*. Chichester: John Wiley and Sons.

Luhrmann, T. M. 2006. Subjectivity. *Anthropological Theory* 6(3): 345–361.

Luna, Félix. 1973. *El 45: Crónica de un año decisivo*. Buenos Aires: Editorial Sudamericana.

Lynch, John. 1993. From Independence to National Organization. In *Argentina Since Independence*, ed. Leslie Bethell, 1–46. Cambridge: Cambridge University Press.

Maier, Elizabeth and Nathalie Lebon, eds. 2010. *Women's Activism in Latin America and the Caribbean: Engendering Social Justice, Democratizing Citizenship*. New Brunswick, NJ: Rutgers University Press.

Malamud-Goti, Jaime. 1990. Transitional Governments in the Breach: Why Punish State Criminals? *Human Rights Quarterly* 12: 1–16.

Malinowski, Bronislaw. 1961 [1922]. *Argonauts of the Western Pacific*. New York: E. P. Dutton.

Mántaras, Mirta. 2005. *Genocidio en Argentina*. Buenos Aires: Autores Editores.

Marchesi, Aldo. 2005. Vencedores vencidos: las respuestas militares frente a los informes "Nunca Más" en el Cono Sur. In *Memorias militares sobre la represión en el Cono Sur:*

Visiones en disputa en dictadura y democracia, ed. Eric Hershberg and Felipe Agüero, 175–210. Madrid: Siglo Veintiuno de España Editores.

Márquez, Nicolás. 2004. *La otra parte de la verdad: La respuesta a los que han ocultado y deformado la verdad histórica sobre la década del '70 y el terrorismo.* Mar del Plata: Author's edition.

Márquez, Nicolás. 2006. *La mentira oficial: El setentismo como política de Estado.* Mar del Plata: Author's edition.

Márquez, Nicolás. 2008. *El Vietnam argentino: La guerrilla marxista en Tucumán.* Buenos Aires: Author's edition.

Martí, Ana María, María Alicia Milia de Pirles, and Sara Solarz de Osatinsky. 1995 [1979]. *ESMA "Trasladados." Testimonio de tres liberadas.* Buenos Aires: Abuelas de Plaza de Mayo.

Martín-Baró, Ignacio. 1989. Political Violence and War as Causes of Psychosocial Trauma in El Salvador. *International Journal of Mental Health* 18(1): 3–20.

Martín-Baró, Ignacio. 1994. *Writings for a Liberation Psychology*, ed. Adrianne Aron and Shawn Corne. Cambridge, MA: Harvard University Press.

Masi, Juan José. 1967. Lucha contra la subversión. *Revista de la Escuela Superior de Guerra* 45(373): 36–90.

Mattini, Luis. 1990. *Hombres y Mujeres del PRT-ERP.* Buenos Aires: Editorial Contrapunto.

Mattini, Luis. 2006. *Los Perros: Memorias de un combatiente revolucionario.* Buenos Aires: Ediciones Continente.

Mattini, Luis. 2007. *Los Perros 2: Memorias de la rebeldía femenina en los '70.* Buenos Aires: Ediciones Continente.

Mauss, Marcel. 1990 [1925]. *The Gift: The Form and Reason for Exchange in Archaic Societies.* London: Routledge.

May, Larry. 2005. Collective Responsibility, Honor, and the Rules of Law. *Journal of Social Philosophy* 36(3): 289–304.

Mbembe, Achille. 2003. Necropolitics. *Public Culture* 15(1): 11–40.

McNally, Richard J. 2003. *Remembering Trauma.* Cambridge, MA: Harvard University Press.

McNally, Richard J. 2007. Betrayal Trauma Theory: A Critical Appraisal. *Memory* 15(3): 280–294.

McNally, Richard J. 2010. Can We Salvage the Concept of Psychological Trauma? *Psychologist* 23(May): 386–389.

McNally, Richard J. 2012. The Ontology of Posttraumatic Stress Disorder: Natural Kind, Social Construction, or Causal System? *Clinical Psychology: Science and Practice* 19(3): 220–228.

Meierhenrich, Jens. 2006. A Question of Guilt. *Ratio Juris* 19(3): 314–342.

Mellibovsky, Matilde. 1990. *Círculo de amor sobre la muerte.* Buenos Aires: Ediciones del Pensamiento Nacional.

Memoria Abierta. 2009. *Memorias en la ciudad: Señales del terrorismo de estado en Buenos Aires.* Buenos Aires: EUDEBA.

Menchú, Rigoberta. 1991. *I, Rigoberta Menchú: An Indian Woman in Guatemala*, ed. Elisabeth Burgos-Debray. London: Verso.

Méndez, Eugenio. 1988. *Aramburu: El crimen imperfecto.* Buenos Aires: Sudamericana/Planeta.

Méndez, Juan E. and Javier Mariezcurrena. 1999. Accountability for Past Human Rights Violations: Contributions of the Inter-American Organs of Protection. *Social Justice* 26(4): 84–106.

Mero, Roberto. 1987. *Conversaciones con Juan Gelman: Contraderrota, Montoneros y la revolución perdida*. Buenos Aires: Editorial Contrapunto.

Merridale, Catherine. 2000. *Night of Stone: Death and Memory in Twentieth-Century Russia*. New York: Viking.

Mignone, Emilio F. 1988. *Witness to the Truth: The Complicity of Church and Dictatorship in Argentina*. Maryknoll: Orbis Books.

Mikulincer, Mario and Phillip R. Shaver. 2007. *Attachment in Adulthood: Structure, Dynamics, and Change*. New York: Guilford Press.

Miller, Daniel and Fiona Parrott. 2009. Loss and Material Culture in South London. *Journal of the Royal Anthropological Institute* 15: 502–519.

Ministerio de Justicia, Seguridad y Derechos Humanos. 2010. *Resolución 3216/2010*. 19 November. http://www.infoleg.gov.ar/infolegInternet/anexos/175000-179999/175667/norma.htm. Accessed on 29 February 2015.

Minow, Martha. 1998. *Between Vengeance and Forgiveness: Facing History After Genocide and Mass Violence*. Boston: Beacon Press.

Minow, Martha. 2002. *Breaking the Cycles of Hatred: Memory, Law, and Repair*. Princeton, NJ: Princeton University Press.

Misztal, Barbara A. 1996. *Trust in Modern Societies: The Search for the Bases of Social Order*. Cambridge: Polity Press.

Mitscherlich, Alexander and Margarete Mitscherlich. 1975. *The Inability to Mourn: Principles of Collective Behavior*. New York: Grove Press.

Mittelbach, Federico. 1986. *Punto 30: Informe sobre desaparecidos*. Buenos Aires: Ediciones de la Urraca.

Mohamed, Saira. 2015. Of Monsters and Men: Perpetrator Trauma and Mass Atrocity. *Columbia Law Review* 115(5): 1157–1216.

Möllering, Guido. 2001. The Nature of Trust: From Georg Simmel to a Theory of Expectation, Interpretation and Suspension. *Sociology* 35(2): 403–420.

Möllering, Guido. 2006. *Trust: Reason, Routine, Reflexivity*. Oxford: Elsevier.

Moreno Ocampo, Luis. 1999. Beyond Punishment: Justice in the Wake of Massive Crimes in Argentina. *Journal of International Affairs* 52(2): 669–689.

Moses, A. Dirk. 2007. *German Intellectuals and the Nazi Past*. Cambridge: Cambridge University Press.

Moyano, María José. 1995. *Argentina's Lost Patrol: Armed Struggle, 1969–1979*. New Haven, CT: Yale University Press.

Narveson, Jan. 2002. Collective Responsibility. *Journal of Ethics* 6(2): 179–198.

Nash, June and Helen Safa, eds. 1986. *Women and Change in Latin America*. South Hadley, MA: Bergin and Garvey.

Neal, Arthur G. 1998. *National Trauma and Collective Memory: Major Events in the American Century*. Armonk, NY: M. E. Sharpe.

Neimeyer, Robert A. 2001. Meaning Reconstruction and Loss. In *Meaning Reconstruction and the Experience of Loss*, ed. Robert A. Neimeyer, 1–9. Washington, DC: American Psychological Association.

Nelson, Christopher. 2008. *Dancing with the Dead: Memory, Performance, and Everyday Life in Postwar Okinawa*. Durham, NC: Duke University Press.

Nora, Pierre. 1978. Mémoire collective. In *La nouvelle histoire*, ed. Jacques Le Goff, Roger Chartier, and Jacques Revel, 398–401. Paris: Retz-C.E.P.L.

Nora, Pierre. 1984. Entre Mémoire et Histoire: La problématique des lieux. In *Les Lieux de Mémoire*. Vol. 1: *La République*, ed. Pierre Nora, xvii–xlii. Paris: Gallimard.

Norden, Deborah L. 1996. *Military Rebellion in Argentina: Between Coups and Consolidation*. Lincoln: University of Nebraska Press.

Nordstrom, Carolyn. 1997. *A Different Kind of War Story*. Philadelphia: University of Pennsylvania Press.

Nuttall, Sarah and Achille Mbembe. 2015. Secrecy's Softwares. *Current Anthropology* 56(Supplement 12): S317–S324.

O'Donnell, Guillermo. 1986. On the Fruitful Convergences of Hirschman's *Exit, Voice, and Loyalty* and *Shifting Involvements: Reflections from the Recent Argentine Experience*. In *Development, Democracy, and the Art of Trespassing: Essays in Honor of Albert O. Hirschman*, ed. Alejandro Foxley, Michael S. McPherson, and Guillermo O'Donnell, 249–268. Notre Dame, IN: University of Notre Dame Press.

O'Donnell, Margarita K. 2009. New Dirty War Judgments in Argentina: National Courts and Domestic Prosecutions of International Human Rights Violations. *New York University Law Review* 84: 333–374.

Ochs, Elinor and Lisa Capps. 1996. Narrating the Self. *Annual Review of Anthropology* 25: 19–43.

Olick, Jeffrey K. 2005. *In the House of the Hangman: The Agonies of German Defeat, 1943–1949*. Chicago: University of Chicago Press.

Olick, Jeffrey K. 2007. *The Politics of Regret: On Collective Memory and Historical Responsibility*. New York: Routledge.

Olmo, Darío, ed. 2005. *Cementerio de San Vicente: Informe 2003*. Equipo Argentino de Antropología Forense. Córdoba: Ferreira Editor.

Olmo, Darío and Mercedes Salado Puerto. 2008. Una fosa común en el interior de Argentina: el Cementerio de San Vicente. *Revista del Museo de Antropología* 1(1): 3–12.

Orentlicher, Diane F. 1991. Settling Accounts: The Duty to Prosecute Human Rights Violations of a Prior Regime. *Yale Law Review* 100(8): 2537–2615.

Osiel, Mark. 2000. *Mass Atrocity, Collective Memory, and the Law*. New Brunswick, NJ: Transaction Publishers.

Otto, Hiltrud and Heidi Keller, eds. 2014. *Different Faces of Attachment: Cultural Variations on a Universal Human Need*. Cambridge: Cambridge University Press.

Oushakine, Serguei A. 2009. *The Patriotism of Despair: Nation, War, and Loss in Russia*. Ithaca, NY: Cornell University Press.

Panizo, Laura Marina. 2012. Exhumación e identificación de cuerpos: el caso de desaparecidos de la última dictadura militar en Argentina. *Sociotam* 22(1): 225–250.

Park, Rebekah. 2014. *The Reappeared: Argentine Former Political Prisoners*. New Brunswick, NJ: Rutgers University Press.

Parry, Jonathan. 1986. *The Gift*, the Indian Gift and the "Indian Gift." *Man* 21: 453–473.

Payne, Leigh. A. 2008. *Unsettling Accounts: Neither Truth nor Reconciliation in Confessions of State Violence*. Durham, NC: Duke University Press.

PEN (Poder Ejecutivo Nacional). 1975. Decretos 2770/2771/2772. 6 October. Copy in author's possession.

Perdía, Roberto Cirilo. 1997. *La otra historia: Testimonio de un jefe montonero*. Fuente General Roca: Grupo Agora.

Perón, Juan Domingo. 1973 [1956]. Instrucciones generales para los dirigentes. In *Perón-Cooke Correspondencia* 2: 388–398. Buenos Aires: Granica Editor.

Perón, Juan Domingo. 1985a [1952]. Conducción Política. *Obras Completas*, ed. Fermín Chávez, vol. 14. Buenos Aires: Editorial Docencia.

Perón, Juan Domingo. 1985b [1957]. Los Vendepatria: Las Pruebas de una Traición. *Obras Completas*, ed. Fermín Chávez, vol. 22. Buenos Aires: Editorial Docencia.

Petraglia, Ricardo. 2008. *Estela: La muerte de la hija parió una abuela*. La Plata: EDULP.

Phelps, Teresa Godwin. 2004. *Shattered Voices: Language, Violence, and the Work of Truth Commissions*. Philadelphia: University of Pennsylvania Press.

Pillen, Alex. 2016. Language, Translation, Trauma. *Annual Review of Anthropology* 45: 95–111.

Plotkin, Mariano Ben. 2001. *Freud in the Pampas: The Emergence and Development of a Psychoanalytic Culture in Argentina*. Stanford, CA: Stanford University Press.

Portnoy, Alicia. 1986. *The Little School: Tales of Disappearance and Survival in Argentina*. Pittsburgh, PA: Cleis Press.

Portugheis, Rosa Elsa, ed. 2015. *Bombardeo del 16 de junio de 1955*. Buenos Aires: Ministerio de Justicia y Derechos Humanos de la Nación.

Potash, Robert A. 1980. *The Army and Politics in Argentina, 1945–1962: Perón to Frondizi*. London: Athlone Press.

Potash, Robert A. 1996. *The Army and Politics in Argentina, 1962–1973: From Frondizi's Fall to the Peronist Restoration*. Stanford, CA: Stanford University Press.

Poviña, Fernando Luis. 2012. Procesamiento de Carlos Pedro Tadeo Blaquier y Alberto Enrique Lemos, 15 November, Federal Court 4, Jujuy. http://www.cij.gov.ar/adj/pdfs/ADJ-0.180555001353018079.pdf. Accessed on 3 March 2016.

Presos Políticos de la Argentina. 2010. Los terroristas entre nosotros. 26 July. http://presospoliticosargentina-archivo.blogspot.com/2010_07_01_archive.html; accessed on 23 August 2010. Defunct website; hard copy in author's possession.

Procuraduría de Crímenes contra la Humanidad. 2016a. *El estado de las causas por delitos de lesa humanidad en Argentina. Balance y desafíos*. Buenos Aires: Ministerio Público Fiscal.

Procuraduría de Crímenes contra la Humanidad. 2016b. *El estado de las causas por delitos de lesa humanidad en Argentina. Diagnóstico del primer semestre de 2016*. Buenos Aires: Ministerio Público Fiscal.

Punzi, Orlando Mario. 1979. Las campañas del desierto. *Todo Es Historia* 144: 9–23.

Quinn, Naomi and Jeannette Marie Mageo, eds. 2013. *Attachment Reconsidered: Cultural Perspectives on a Western Theory*. Houndmills: Palgrave Macmillan.

Rafecas, Daniel Eduardo. 2011. Le reapertura de los procesos judiciales por crímenes contra la humanidad en Argentina. In *Juicios por crímenes de lesa humanidad en Argentina*, ed. Gabriele Andreozzi, 155–176. Buenos Aires: Editorial Atuel.

Raggio, Sandra. 2010. La construcción de un relato emblemático de la represión: La "noche de los lápices." In *Los desaparecidos en la Argentina: Memorias, representaciones e ideas (1983–2008)*, ed. Emilio Crenzel, 137–160. Buenos Aires: Editorial Biblos.

Ramos Padilla, Juan Martín. 2006. *Chicha: La fundadora de Abuelas de Plaza de Mayo*. Buenos Aires: Editorial Dunken.

Ramus, Susana Jorgelina. 2000. *Sueños sobrevivientes de una Montonera: A pesar de la ESMA*. Buenos Aires: Ediciones Colihue.

Ranalletti, Mario. 2010. Denial of the Reality of State Terrorism in Argentina as Narrative of the Recent Past: A New Case of "Negationism"? *Genocide and Prevention Studies* 5(2): 160–173.

Ranalletti, Mario. 2014. When Death Is Not the End: Towards a Typology of the Treatment of Corpses of "Disappeared Detainees" in Argentina from 1975 to 1983. In *Destruction and Human Remains: Disposal and Concealment in Genocide and Mass Violence*, ed. Élisabeth Anstett and Jean-Marc Dreyfus, 146–179. Manchester: Manchester University Press.

Rasmussen, Susan. 2002. The Uses of Memory. *Culture and Psychology* 8(1): 113–129.

Reato, Ceferino. 2012. *Disposición Final: La confesión de Videla sobre los desaparecidos*. Buenos Aires: Editorial Sudamericana.

República Argentina 1987 [1958]. *Libro Negro de la Segunda Tirania*. 4th ed. Buenos Aires: Comisión de Afirmación de la Revolución Libertadora.

Ricoeur, Paul. 2000. *The Just*. Chicago: University of Chicago Press.

Ricoeur, Paul. 2006. *Memory, History, Forgetting*. Chicago: University of Chicago Press.

Robben, Antonius C. G. M. 1995. The Politics of Truth and Emotion Among Victims and Perpetrators of Violence. In *Fieldwork Under Fire: Contemporary Studies of Violence and Survival*, ed. Carolyn Nordstrom and Antonius C. G. M. Robben, 81–103. Berkeley: University of California Press.

Robben, Antonius C. G. M. 1996. Ethnographic Seduction, Transference, and Resistance in Dialogues About Terror and Violence in Argentina. *Ethos* 24(1): 71–106.

Robben, Antonius C. G. M. 2000a. State Terror in the Netherworld: Disappearance and Reburial in Argentina. In *Death Squad: The Anthropology of State Terror*, ed. Jeffrey A. Sluka, 91–113. Philadelphia: University of Pennsylvania Press.

Robben, Antonius C. G. M. 2000b. The Assault on Basic Trust: Disappearance, Protest, and Reburial in Argentina. In *Cultures Under Siege: Collective Violence and Trauma*, ed. Antonius C. G. M. Robben and Marcelo M. Suárez-Orozco, 70–101. Cambridge: Cambridge University Press.

Robben, Antonius C. G. M. 2005a. *Political Violence and Trauma in Argentina*. Philadelphia: University of Pennsylvania Press.

Robben, Antonius C. G. M. 2005b. How Traumatized Societies Remember: The Aftermath of Argentina's Dirty War. *Cultural Critique* 59: 120–164.

Robben, Antonius C. G. M. 2010a. Testimonies, Truths, and Transitions of Justice in Argentina and Chile. In *Transitional Justice: Global Mechanisms and Local Realities in the Aftermath of Genocide and Mass Violence*, ed. Alexander Laban Hinton, 179–205. New Brunswick, NJ: Rutgers University Press.

Robben, Antonius C. G. M. 2010b. Memory Politics Among Perpetrators and Bereaved Relatives About Spain's Mass Graves. In *Unearthing Franco's Legacy: Mass Graves and the Recovery of Historical Memory in Spain*, ed. Carlos Jerez-Farrán and Samuel Amago, 264–278. Notre Dame, IN: University of Notre Dame Press.

Robben, Antonius C. G. M. 2011. Silence, Denial and Confession About State Terror by the Argentine Military. In *Violence Expressed: An Anthropological Approach*, ed. Maria Six-Hohenbalken and Nerina Weiss, 169–186. Farnham: Ashgate.

Robben, Antonius C. G. M. 2014. Massive Violent Death and Contested National Mourning in Post-Authoritarian Chile and Argentina: A Sociocultural Application of the Dual Process Model. *Death Studies* 38(5): 335–345.

Robben, Antonius C. G. M. 2015. Exhumations, Territoriality, and Necropolitics in Chile and Argentina. In *Necropolitics: Mass Graves and Exhumations in the Age of Human Rights*, ed. Francisco Ferrándiz and Antonius C. G. M. Robben, 53–75. Philadelphia: University of Pennsylvania Press.

Robben, Antonius C. G. M. and Marcelo M. Suárez-Orozco, eds. 2000. *Cultures Under Siege: Collective Violence and Trauma*. Cambridge: Cambridge University Press.

Robin, Marie-Monique. 2005. *Escuadrones de la muerte: La escuela francesa*. Buenos Aires: Editorial Sudamericana.

Rock, David. 1987. *Argentina, 1516–1987: From Spanish Colonization to Alfonsín*. Berkeley: University of California Press.

Roht-Arriaza, Naomi. 2005. *The Pinochet Effect: Transnational Justice in the Age of Human Rights*. Philadelphia: University of Pennsylvania Press.

Rothberg, Michael. 2009. *Multidirectional Memory: Remembering the Holocaust in the Age of Decolonization*. Stanford, CA: Stanford University Press.

Rozanski, Carlos Alberto, Horacio Alfredo Isaurralde, and Norberto Lorenzo. 2006. *Fallo Etchecolatz, Miguel Osvaldo*. Tribunal Oral en lo Criminal Federal n. 1 de La Plata, 26 September, p. 101. http://www.derechos.org/nizkor/arg/ley/etche.html. Accessed on 28 April 2015.

Rugg, Julie. 2000. Defining the Place of Burial: What Makes a Cemetery a Cemetery? *Mortality* 5(3): 259–275.

Ruggie, John Gerard. 2013. *Just Business: Multinational Corporations and Human Rights*. New York: W. W. Norton and Company.

Sahlins, Marshall. 1979. *Stone Age Economics*. Hawthorne: Aldine.

San Martino de Dromi, María Laura. 1988. *Historia política Argentina (1955–1988)*. 2 vols. Buenos Aires: Editorial Astrea.

Sánchez, Matilde. 1985. *Historias de vida: Hebe de Bonafini*. Buenos Aires: Fraterna/del Nuevo Extremo.

Sanford, Victoria. 2003. *Buried Secrets: Truth and Human Rights in Guatemala*. New York: Palgrave Macmillan.

Sant Cassia, Paul. 2007. *Bodies of Evidence: Burial, Memory and the Recovery of Missing Persons in Cyprus*. New York: Berghahn.

Santner, Eric L. 1990. *Stranded Objects: Mourning, Memory, and Film in Postwar Germany*. Ithaca, NY: Cornell University Press.

Santucho, Julio. 1988. *Los últimos Guevaristas: Surgimiento y eclipse del Ejército Revolucionario del Pueblo*. Buenos Aires: Puntosur.

Santucho, Mario Roberto. 1988 [1974]. *Poder burgués y poder revolucionario*. Buenos Aires: Editorial 19 de Julio.

Saporta, José A. and Bessel A. van der Kolk. 1992. Psychobiological Consequences of Severe Trauma. In *Torture and Its Consequences: Current Treatment Approaches*, ed. Metin Başoğlu, 151–181. Cambridge: Cambridge University Press.

Sarlo, Beatriz. 2009. Vocación de memoria: Ciudad y museo. In *El estado y la memoria: Gobiernos y ciudadanos frente a los traumas de la historia*, ed. Ricard Vinyes, 499–521. Barcelona: RBA Libros.

Scarry, Elaine. 1985. *The Body in Pain: The Making and Unmaking of the World*. New York: Oxford University Press.

Schabas, William A. 2009. *Genocide in International Law: The Crime of Crimes*. Cambridge: Cambridge University Press.

Schacter, Daniel L. 2001. *The Seven Sins of Memory: How the Mind Forgets and Remembers*. Boston: Houghton Mifflin.

Schell, Jr., Orville H. 1979. Report of the Mission of Lawyers to Argentina, April 1–7, 1979. *Record of the Association of the Bar of the City of New York* 34(7): 473–503.

Scheper-Hughes, Nancy. 1992. *Death Without Weeping: The Violence of Everday Life in Brazil*. Berkeley: University of California Press.

Scheper-Hughes, Nancy. 2014. Family Life as *Bricolage*—Reflections on Intimacy and Attachment in *Death Without Weeping*. In *Different Faces of Attachment: Cultural Variations on a Universal Human Need*, ed. Hiltrud Otto and Heidi Keller, 230–260. Cambridge: Cambridge University Press.

Schwenkel, Christina. 2009. *The American War in Contemporary Vietnam: Transnational Remembrance and Representation*. Bloomington: Indiana University Press.

Scilingo, Adolfo Francisco. 2000. *¡Por siempre, nunca más!* Buenos Aires: Editorial del Plata. http://www.derechos.org/nizkor/espana/juicioral/doc/librosciling.html. Accessed on 20 March 2015.

Secretaría de Derechos Humanos. 2015. *Registro unificado de víctimas del terrorismo de Estado*. Anexo 4: *Cuadros estadísticas*. Buenos Aires: Ministerio de Justicia y Derechos Humanos de la Nación. http://www.jus.gob.ar/media/3122380/5._anexo_iv___cuadros_estad_sticos.pdf. Accessed on 28 April 2016.

Segev, Tom. 2000 [1991]. *The Seventh Million: The Israelis and the Holocaust*. New York: Henry Holt and Company.

Seidel, Katja E. 2014. The Power of Absence: An Ethnography of Justice, Memories of Genocide, and Political Activism of a New Generation in Post-Transitional Argentina. Ph.D. thesis, National University of Ireland.

Seoane, María. 1991. *Todo o Nada*. Buenos Aires: Planeta.

Seoane, María and Hector Ruiz Núñez. 1986. *La Noche de los Lápices*. Buenos Aires: Editorial Contrapunto.

Shay, Jonathan. 1995. *Achilles in Vietnam: Combat Trauma and the Undoing of Character*. New York: Simon & Schuster.

Shayne, Julie, ed. 2014. *Taking Risks: Feminist Activism and Research in the Americas*. Albany: State University of New York Press.

Shipton, Parker. 2007. *The Nature of Entrustment: Intimacy, Exchange, and the Sacred in Africa*. New Haven, CT: Yale University Press.

Sikkink, Kathryn. 2011. *The Justice Cascade: How Human Rights Prosecutions Are Changing World Politics*. New York: W. W. Norton and Company.

Simmel, Georg. 1906. The Sociology of Secrecy and of Secret Societies. *American Journal of Sociology* 11(4): 441–498.

Simmel, Georg. 1950. *The Sociology of Georg Simmel*. New York: Free Press.

Simpson, John and Jana Bennett. 1985. *The Disappeared and the Mothers of the Plaza*. New York: St. Martin's Press.

Skaar, Elin, Siri Gloppen, and Astri Suhrke, eds. 2005. *Roads to Reconciliation*. Lanham, MD: Lexington Books.

Skidmore, Monique. 2004. *Karaoke Fascism: Burma and the Politics of Fear*. Philadelphia: University of Pennsylvania Press.

Slyomovics, Susan. 1998. *The Object of Memory: Arab and Jew Narrate the Palestinian Village*. Philadelphia: University of Pennsylvania Press.

Smelser, Neil J. 2004. Toward a Theory of Cultural Trauma. In *Cultural Trauma and Collective Identity*, by Jeffrey C. Alexander, Ron Eyerman, Bernhard Giessen, Neil J. Smelser, and Piotr Sztompka, 31–59. Berkeley: University of California Press.

Smith, William C. 1991. *Authoritarianism and the Crisis of the Argentine Political Economy*. Stanford: Stanford University Press.

Somasundaram, Daya. 2014. Addressing Collective Trauma: Conceptualizations and Interventions. *Intervention* 12(supplement 1): 43–60.

Somigiliana, Maco and Darío Olmo. 2002. La huella del genocidio. *Encrucijadas* 2(January): 22–35.

Sontag, Susan. 1990. *Illness as Metaphor and AIDS and Its Metaphors*. New York: Doubleday.

Stephen, Lynn, ed. 1997. *Women and Social Movements in Latin America: Power from Below*. Austin: University of Texas Press.

Stewart, James G. 2012. Overdetermined Atrocities. *New York University School of Law, Public Law and Legal Theory Research Paper Series* Working Paper 12–53(October): 1–37.

Stoll, David. 2008. *Rigoberta Menchú and the Story of All Poor Guatemalans*. 2nd ed. Boulder, CO: Westview Press.

Strathern, Marilyn. 1988. *The Gender of the Gift: Problems with Women and Problems with Society in Melanesia*. Berkeley: University of California Press.

Strathern, Marilyn, ed. 2000. *Audit Cultures: Anthropological Studies in Accountability, Ethics and the Academy*. London: Routledge.

Stroebe, Margaret and Henk Schut. 1999. The Dual Process Model of Coping with Bereavement: Rationale and Description. *Death Studies* 23: 197–224.

Stroebe, Margaret and Henk Schut. 2001. Meaning Making in the Dual Process Model of Coping with Bereavement. In *Meaning Reconstruction and the Experience of Loss*, ed. Robert A. Neimeyer, 55–73. Washington, DC: American Psychological Association.

Summerfield, Derek. 1995. Addressing Human Response to War and Atrocity: Major Challenges in Research and Practices and the Limitations of Western Psychiatric Models. In *Beyond Trauma: Cultural and Societal Dynamics*, ed. Rolf J. Kleber, Charles R. Figley, and Berthold P. R. Gersons, 17–29. New York: Plenum Press.

Summerfield, Derek. 1999. A Critique of Seven Assumptions Behind Psychological Trauma Programmes in War-Affected Countries. *Social Science and Medicine* 48: 1449–1462.

Sztompka, Piotr. 1999. *Trust: A Sociological Theory*. Cambridge: Cambridge University Press.

Sztompka, Piotr. 2000. Cultural Trauma: The Other Face of Social Change. *European Journal of Social Theory* 3(4): 449–466.

Tamburini, Claudio M. 2002. *Pase Libre: La fuga de la Mansión Seré*. Buenos Aires: Ediciones Continente.

Tappatá de Valdez, Patricia. 2003. El Parque de la Memoria en Buenos Aires. In *Monumentos, memoriales y marcas territoriales*, ed. Elizabeth Jelin and Victoria Langland, 97–111. Madrid: Siglo Veintiuno.

Taussig, Michael. 1987. *Shamanism, Colonialism, and the Wild Man: A Study in Terror and Healing*. Chicago: University of Chicago Press.

Taylor, Diana. 1997. *Disappearing Acts: Spectacles of Gender and Nationalism in Argentina's "Dirty War."* Durham, NC: Duke University Press.

Teitel, Ruti G. 2000. *Transitional Justice.* New York: Oxford University Press.

Theidon, Kimberly. 2013. *Intimate Enemies: Violence and Reconciliation in Peru.* Philadelphia: University of Pennsylvania Press.

Thiranagama, Sharika and Tobias Kelly, eds. 2010. *Traitors: Suspicion, Intimacy, and the Ethics of State-Building.* Philadelphia: University of Pennsylvania Press.

Timerman, Jacobo. 1981. *Prisoner Without a Name, Cell Without a Number.* New York: Alfred A. Knopf.

Todorov, Tzvetan. 1996. *Facing the Extreme: Moral Life in the Concentration Camps.* New York: Henry Holt and Company.

Torre, Juan Carlos, ed. 1995. *El 17 de Octubre de 1945.* Buenos Aires: Ariel.

Torre, Juan Carlos and Liliana de Riz. 1993. Argentina Since 1946. In *Argentina Since Independence,* ed. Leslie Bethell, 243–363. Cambridge: Cambridge University Press.

Tumini, María Carina, Lucía Soledad Garay, and Carla María Banchieri. 2007. Procesos de exhumaciones: Un espacio posible. In *Resistencias contra el olvido: Trabajo psicosocial en procesos de exhumaciones en América Latina,* ed. Pau Pérez-Sales and Susana Navarro García, 153–185. Barcelona: Gedisa Editorial.

Ulla, Noemí and Hugo Echave. 1986. *Después de la noche: Diálogo con Graciela Fernández Meijide.* Buenos Aires: Editorial Contrapunto.

Unamuno, Miguel. 1988. La primera gran represión. *Todo Es Historia* 248: 6–33.

Urondo, Francisco. 1988 [1973]. *Trelew: La patria fusilada.* Buenos Aires: Editorial Contrapunto.

Van Creveld, Martin. 1991. *The Transformation of War.* New York: Free Press.

Van der Kolk, Bessel A., Alexander C. McFarlane, and Lars Weisaeth, eds. 1996. *Traumatic Stress: The Effects of Overwhelming Experience on Mind, Body, and Society.* New York: Guilford Press.

Van Gennep, Arnold. 1960 [1909]. *The Rites of Passage.* Chicago: University of Chicago Press.

Van Roekel, Eva. 2016. *Phenomenal Justice: State Violence, Emotion, and the Law in Argentina.* 's Hertogenbosch: ADC.

Valentine, Christine. 2006. Academic Constructions of Bereavement. *Mortality* 11: 57–78.

Vázquez, Arturo. 1988. *Polvo enamorado.* Buenos Aires: Editorial Contrapunto.

Vázquez, Arturo and Inés Vázquez. 1984. *Con vida los llevaron: 12 historias del tiempo de violencia.* Buenos Aires: Ediciones La Campana.

Vecchioli, Virginia. 2000. "Os trabalhos pela memória." Um esboço de campo dos direitos humanos na Argentina através da construção social da categoria de vítima do terrorismo de estado. M.A. thesis, Museu Nacional da Universidade Federal do Rio de Janeiro.

Vecchioli, Virginia. 2001. Políticas de la memoria y formas de classificación social. ¿Quiénes son las "Víctimas del Terrorismo de Estado" en la Argentina? In *La imposibilidad del olvido: Recorridos de la memoria en Argentina, Chile y Uruguay,* ed. Bruno Groppo and Patricia Flier, 83–102. La Plata: Ediciones Al Margen.

Verbitsky, Horacio. 1986. *Ezeiza.* Buenos Aires: Editorial Contrapunto.

Verbitsky, Horacio. 1988. *Medio siglo de proclamas militares.* Buenos Aires: Editora/12.

Verbitsky, Horacio. 1995. *El Vuelo.* Buenos Aires: Planeta.

Verbitsky, Horacio. 2005. *El Silencio.* Buenos Aires: Editorial Sudamericana.

Verbitsky, Horacio. 2006. *Doble Juego: La Argentina Católica y Militar.* Buenos Aires: Editorial Sudamericana.

Verbitsky, Horacio and Juan Pablo Bohoslavsky. 2013. Introducción. Terrorismo de Estado y economía: de Nüremberg a Buenos Aires. In *Cuentas pendientes: Los cómplices económicos de la dictadura*, ed. Horacio Verbitsky and Juan Pablo Bohoslavsky, 11–27. Buenos Aires: Siglo Ventiuno.

Verdery, Katherine. 1999. *The Political Lives of Dead Bodies: Reburial and Postsocialist Change.* New York: Columbia University Press.

Vezzetti, Hugo. 2003. *Pasado y Presente*: *Guerra, dictadura y sociedad en la Argentina*. Buenos Aires: Siglo Veintiuno Editores.

Vezzetti, Hugo. 2009. *Sobre la violencia revolucionaria: memorias y olvidos*. Buenos Aires: Siglo Veintiuno Editores.

Vilas, Acdel Edgardo. 1976. Reflexiones sobre la guerra subversiva. *Revista de la Escuela Superior de Guerra* 54(427): 7–14.

Villarruel, Victoria. 2009. *Los llaman "jóvenes idealistas."* Buenos Aires: CELTYV.

Villegas, Osiris Guillermo. 1976. *No Acuso, Reflexiono*. Buenos Aires: Editorial Pleamar.

Villegas, Osiris Guillermo. 1987. La estrategia integral de la guerra subversiva. *Revista Militar* 716: 11–19.

Villegas, Osiris G. 1990. *Testimonio de un alegato*. Buenos Aires: Author's edition.

Viñas, David. 1982. *Indios, ejército y frontera*. Buenos Aires: Siglo Veintiuno Editores.

Viotto Romano, Leandro. 2005. *Silencio de Mudos. La subversión en Argentina: De las armas al poder institucional y político*. Buenos Aires: Author's edition.

Waisbord, Silvio. 1991. Politics and Identity in the Argentine Army: Cleavages and the Generational Factor. *Latin American Research Review* 26(2): 157–170.

Walsh, Rodolfo. 1988 [1957]. *Operación Massacre*. Buenos Aires: Ediciones de la Flor.

Walsh, Rodolfo. 1995. *El violento oficio de escribir. Obra periodística (1953–1977)*. Buenos Aires: Planeta.

Walter, Tony. 1996. A New Model of Grief: Bereavement and Biography. *Mortality* 1: 7–25.

Walter, Tony. 1999. *On Bereavement: The Culture of Grief*. Buckingham: Open University Press.

Walther, Juan Carlos. 1980. *La conquista del desierto*. Buenos Aires: EUDEBA.

Walzer, Michael. 1977. *Just and Unjust Wars: A Moral Argument with Historical Illustrations*. New York: Basic Books.

Watson, Gary. 2004. *Agency and Answerability: Selected Essays*. Oxford: Oxford University Press.

Watson, Rubie S., ed. 1994. *Memory, History, and Opposition Under State Socialism*. Santa Fe: School of American Research Press.

Weathers, Frank W. and Terence M. Keane. 2007. The Criterion A Problem Revisited: Controversies and Challenges in Defining and Measuring Psychological Trauma. *Journal of Traumatic Stress* 20(2): 107–121.

Weisner, Thomas S. 2014. The Socialization of Trust: Plural Caregiving and Diverse Pathways in Human Development Across Cultures. In *Different Faces of Attachment: Cultural Variations on a Universal Human Need*, ed. Hiltrud Otto and Heidi Keller, 263–277. Cambridge: Cambridge University Press.

Williams, Paul. 2007. *Memorial Museums: The Global Rush to Commemorate Atrocities*. Oxford: Berg.

Wilson, Richard A. 2001. *The Politics of Truth and Reconciliation in South Africa: Legitimizing the Post-Apartheid State*. Cambridge: Cambridge University Press.

Wilson, Richard A. 2003. Anthropological Studies of National Reconciliation Processes. *Anthropological Theory* 3(3): 367–387.

Wohl, Michael J. A. and Nyla R. Branscombe. 2004. Importance of Social Categorization for Forgiveness and Collective Guilt Assignment for the Holocaust. In *Collective Guilt: International Perspectives*, ed. Nyla R. Branscombe and Bertjan Doosje, 284–305. Cambridge: Cambridge University Press.

Young, Allan. 1995. *The Harmony of Illusions: Inventing Post-Traumatic Stress Disorder.* Princeton, NJ: Princeton University Press.

Young, James E. 1993. *The Texture of Memory: Holocaust Memorials and Meaning.* New Haven, CT: Yale University Press.

Ystanes, Margit. 2011. Precarious Trust: Problems of Managing Self and Sociality in Guatemala. Ph.D. diss., University of Bergen.

Ystanes, Margit. 2016. Unfixed Trust: Intimacy, Blood Symbolism and Porous Boundaries in Guatemala. In *Trusting and Its Tribulations: Interdisciplinary Engagements with Intimacy, Sociality and Trust*, ed. Vigdis Broch-Due and Margit Ystanes, 37–59. New York: Berghahn.

Zemon Davis, Natalie and Randolph Starn. 1989. Introduction. *Representations* 26(Spring): 1–6.

Magazines

Boletín Público Ejercito Argentino
El Combatiente
El Diario del Juicio
Esquiú
Evita Montonera
Madres
Somos

INDEX

accountability in Argentina, 27–28, 149–75; Alfonsín and the military, 27, 148, 156–57; attributability and, 151–53; CONADEP truth commission report, 153–56, 230; derogation of the amnesty laws, 27–28, 167–68; the human rights trials, 28, 149–50, 168–74; impunity and the amnesty laws/pardons, 4, 27–28, 69–70, 163, 167–68; the junta commanders' criminal trial, 27, 53–54, 66–67, 99–101, 105, 150, 153, 156–63; and the military's atrocity-producing structure, 162, 165, 168; moral responsibility, 151–52, 162, 167, 174–75; and network of children of the disappeared (HIJOS), 164–65, 167, 217; popular justice, 162–68; post-transitional justice (second wave of trials), 151, 168; street happenings (escraches) to mobilize neighborhoods, 164–65, 166, 167, 217, 223; tension between law and justice, 174–75; transitional justice, 151; the truth trials at La Plata, 150, 165–66

Acosta, Captain Jorge, 171

Agamben, Giorgio, 131, 133, 148

Agosti, Brigadier-General Orlando Ramón, 70, 161, 231

Aizenberg, Roberto, 92–93

Akhavan, Payam, 198

Akselman, Leticia, 229–31

Akselman, Poema, 229–31

Alexander, Jeffrey C., 35

Alfonsín, Raúl: amnesty laws, 27, 54, 69, 167, 212–13; Decree 158/83 (1983), 157; inauguration as president, 1, 12; installation of CONADEP commission, 64; and junta commanders' criminal trial, 27, 66, 148, 156–57; on Menem's pardons, 70; and military accountability, 27, 148, 156–57;

national recovery and reconciliation goals, 1, 27, 68–69, 163, 206–8, 212–13, 221; rejection of term *dirty war*, 65; social peace plan, 207; two-demons theory, 65–66, 76

Alianza Anticomunista Argentina (Argentine Anti-Communist Alliance) (AAA), 42–43

American Convention of Human Rights, 167

American Declaration of the Rights and Duties of Man, 90

Améry, Jean, 20, 47

Amnesty International, 88, 116

amnesty laws and presidential pardons, 4, 27–28, 54, 69–70, 123, 163, 167–68, 212–13, 217–18; and the Catholic episcopacy, 177–78; derogation of, 27–28, 72, 76, 82, 123, 127, 167–68, 217–18; Due Obedience Law, 69, 123, 149–50, 152, 163, 167, 212–13; Full Stop Law, 69, 163, 167, 212–13; Law of National Pacification, 206, 207. *See also* human rights trials

Anahí, Clara, 104–5, 125–26

Anaya, Admiral Jorge, 161

Anguita, Eduardo, 102

anonymous graves and mass graves: cemeteries and burials in Judeo-Christian culture, 137–39; contested exhumations, 145–46, 208–12; and contested sovereignty, 26–27, 129–48; forensic exhumations and forensic identifications, 83, 137, 140–47, 148, 208–12; four ways bodies were disappeared, 141–42; Grand Bourg cemetery, 134–39; graves marked *NN* (Nomen Nescio), 121, 134, 138, 141; meaning for bereaved relatives and human rights organizations, 136–39; meaning for military perpetrators, 135–39; as military monuments, 138; reburials, 143–47, 148, 206–12; San Vicente Cemetery in

ACKNOWLEDGMENTS

This book is the sediment of thirty years of scholarly involvement with Argentina and represents the development of my thinking since the publication of *Political Violence and Trauma in Argentina* (2005). My first acquaintance with Argentina dates from 1975, when I made a one-day visit to Iguazu Falls and was struck by the large military presence at the border with Brazil because of the political turmoil in Argentina. More trips were made during the dictatorship while I was conducting long-term fieldwork in northeast Brazil. My main research period in Buenos Aires was between April 1989 and July 1991, thanks to generous grants from the National Science Foundation and the Harry Frank Guggenheim Foundation. These research funds proved to be good investments because I have been drawing on the abundance of ethnographic data gathered then ever since. In addition, I have made periodic field visits to Argentina with grants from Utrecht University and the Netherlands Foundation for Scientific Research.

The chapters in this book have been written specifically for the present study but many ideas find their origins in my book from 2005 and the articles and essays written in the last twenty-three years. These ideas have matured since they first appeared in print, but I have nevertheless provided many in-text references to acknowledge their bibliographic sources. I have not duplicated any published work here but have reformulated the narrations and interpretations according to my current understanding of Argentina.

This research project was conceived in 2004 during my stay as a visiting scholar at the David Rockefeller Center for Latin American Studies at Harvard University. I want to thank John Coatsworth, Tom Cummins, June Erlick, Evelyn Boria-Rivera, Irene Gándara, and Edwin Ortiz for creating a stimulating intellectual environment and making my stay as pleasant and productive as possible. I also benefited greatly from the Department of

Anthropology's weekly Medical Anthropology and Cultural Psychiatry Research Seminar, organized by Christopher Dole and Erica James, and the astute interventions made by Michael Fischer, Byron Good, Mary-Jo DelVecchio Good, and Arthur Kleinman. I want to express my gratitude to Michael Herzfeld and Richard McNally for welcoming me to Harvard and for the inspiring conversations over lunches and beers. Many thanks go to my long-time friends Marcelo and Carola Suárez-Orozco, now in Los Angeles, who lent me and my family their wonderful house on the Harvard campus, right behind William James Hall.

Thanks to the Department of Cultural Anthropology and the Netherlands Institute of Human Rights (SIM), both at Utrecht University, for the stimulating seminars and conferences. My knowledge about legal evidence, human rights law, and genocide was shaped considerably at SIM. I also benefited much from the workshops and conferences organized by the interdisciplinary programs Conflicts and Human Rights (2007–2013), Cultures, Citizenship, and Human Rights (2014–2018), and the Utrecht Forum for Memory Studies. As a member of their executive boards, I learned much about the latest intellectual developments in fields outside anthropology through long discussions with the other board members, respectively Jenny Goldschmidt and Marcus Düwell, Rosemarie Buikema and Antoine Buyse, and Susanne Knittel and Ann Rigney. I thank the Institute for Economic and Social Development (IDES) in Argentina for its standing invitation to present my work there whenever I am in Buenos Aires. The rich discussions with researchers and students at IDES were always insightful and have somehow found their way into my work. A continued source of intellectual inspiration has been the annual workshop of the research project Policies of Historical Memory (Las políticas de la memoria) that has been organized since 2010 at the Spanish National Research Council (CSIC) in Madrid under the unfailing leadership of Francisco Ferrándiz. The research team of cultural and forensic anthropologists, historians, psychologists, political scientists, and forensic pathologists has been crucial to my understanding of the complexities of mass graves, forensic identifications, and the afterlives of executions and disappearances: not only those of Spain's Civil War and General Franco's authoritarian regime but also elsewhere in the world.

This book's argument was sharpened by the following friends and colleagues who asked critical questions and provided precious insights: Paco Ferrándiz, Willem de Haan, Alex Hinton, Ivan Komproe, Hans de Kruijf,

Brianne McGonicle, Dirk Moses, Sherry Ortner, Ann Rigney, Nancy Scheper-Hughes, Jeff Sluka, and Margit Ystanes. For their inspirational thoughts and suggestions over the years of writing, I am grateful to Chrisje Brants, Luis Fondebrider, Alex Hinton, Martín Lozada, Tania Luhrmann, Richard McNally, Carolyn Nordstrom, Alexandra Pillen, Nancy Scheper-Hughes, Jeff Sluka, and Margaret Stroebe. Long, sometimes heated, discussions with former graduate students Sabina Frederic, Katrien Klep, Lisa Krieg, Sonja Leferink, Eva van Roekel, Sergio Visacovsky, and Nikki Wiegink about their dissertations helped to advance our related research projects. Finally, two anonymous reviewers deserve considerable credit for their perceptive observations on the book manuscript and the detection of empirical lacunae.

This book would not have been possible without the generosity, patience, and time of my Argentine interlocutors. I will not mention them all by name because the number exceeds a hundred people, but my gratitude is boundless. Even though I disagreed with them sometimes privately and at occasion openly about the rendition and interpretation of Argentina's political violence, I have given much attention to their discourse in this book because this study sits at the intersection of history and anthropology. Its approach to historical events is ethnographic, in the sense that the documents, books, newspapers, trial records, and testimonies that I have analyzed here were in part seen through the eyes of the historical protagonists I interviewed. Crucial texts, of which they were ever so often the authors, were discussed with the benefit but also the bias of hindsight.

Unwavering support for my research has been given over the decades by my friends Lucas Assunção, Célia and the late Enrique Gorostiaga, Juan Astica, Liliana Fleurquin, Sabina Frederic, Rosana Guber, and Sergio Visacovsky. The help of Patricia Bernardi, Luis Fondebrider, Darío Olmo, and Maco Somigliana from the Argentine Forensic Anthropology Team has been crucial in forming my thoughts about exhumations in Argentina. They made themselves freely available for lengthy conversations despite their busy schedules.

I have a standing debt to the University of Pennsylvania Press's editor-in-chief, Peter Agree, for his openhandedness, wise counsel, and listening ear. I couldn't wish for a better editor. Peter's professionalism and good nature have created a superb Acquisitions Department at the University of Pennsylvania Press. I want to thank Erica Ginsburg for efficiently managing the publishing process, and Karen Verde for copyediting the manuscript.

My gratitude also goes to the tireless Bert Lockwood, who accepted this book in his monumental Pennsylvania Studies in Human Rights series.

My greatest personal debt is owed to my wife, Ellen, and our children, Oscar and Sofia. They have always supported my work with love and understanding and are the finest companions in life imaginable.